A Foreign and Wicked Institution?

Also by Rene Kollar

Westminster Cathedral: From Dream to Reality

The Return of the Benedictines to London:
The History of Ealing Abbey from 1896 to Independence

Abbot Aelred Carlyle, Caldey Island,
and the Anglo-Catholic Revival in England

A Universal Appeal:
Aspects of the Revival of Monasticism in the West
in the 19th and Early 20th Centuries

Searching for Raymond:
Anglicanism, Spiritualism, and Bereavement
between the Two World Wars

A Foreign and Wicked Institution?

The Campaign against Convents in Victorian England

Rene Kollar

☙PICKWICK *Publications* • Eugene, Oregon

A FOREIGN AND WICKED INSTITUTION?
The Campaign against Convents in Victorian England

Copyright © 2011 Rene Kollar. All rights reserved. Except for brief quotations in critical publications or reviews, no part of this book may be reproduced in any manner without prior written permission from the publisher. Write: Permissions, Wipf & Stock, 199 W. 8th Ave., Suite 3, Eugene, OR 97401.

Pickwick Publications
A Division of Wipf and Stock Publishers
199 W. 8th Ave., Suite 3
Eugene, OR 97401

www.wipfandstock.com

ISBN 13: 978-1-60608-336-9

Cataloging-in-Publication data:

Kollar, Rene Matthew, 1947–.

A foreign and wicked institution? : the campaign against convents in Victorian England / Rene Kollar.

p. ; 23 cm. Includes bibliographical references.

ISBN 13: 978-1-60608-336-9

1. Monasticism and religious order—History—19th century. 2. Women—Religious life. 3. Convents & nuns. 4. Anti-Catholicism—Great Britain—History—19th century. 5. Great Britain—Church history—19th century. 6. Monasticism and religious orders. Anglican. I. Title.

BX1766 K65 2011

Manufactured in the U.S.A.

*To the women students
who pioneered coeducation
at Saint Vincent College*

Contents

Acknowledgments • ix
Introduction • xi

1. Bishop William Ullathorne and His Defense of Convents: The 1851 Bill for Parliamentary Inspection of Convents • 1

2. They Walled Up Nuns, Didn't They? H. Rider Haggard's *Montezuma's Daughter* and Anti-Catholicism in Victorian England • 19

3. Two Lectures at Bath: The Rev. M. Hobart Seymour and Cardinal Nicholas Wiseman and the Nunnery Question • 39

4. The Myth and Reality of Sr. Barbara Ubryk, the Imprisoned Nun of Cracow: English Interpretations of a Victorian Religious Controversy • 57

5. An American "Escaped Nun" on Tour in England: Edith O'Gorman's Critique of Convent Life • 88

6. Those Horrible Iron Cages: The Sisters of the Church and the Care of Orphans in Late Victorian England • 105

7. Flowers, Pictures, and Crosses: Criticisms of Priscilla Lydia Sellon's Care of Young Girls • 126

8. Magdalenes and Nuns: Convent Laundries in Late Victorian England • 147

9. Foreign and Catholic: A Plea to Protestant Parents on the Dangers of Convent Education in Victorian England • 170

10   A Death in the Family: Bishop Archibald Campbell Tait, the
     Rights of Parents, and Anglican Sisterhoods
     in the Diocese of London • 193

11   The Priest, the Nun, and Confession: An Anti-Catholic Stereotype
     and Anglican Sisterhoods in Victorian England • 215

12   Power and Control over Women in Victorian England:
     Male Opposition to Sacramental Confession in the
     Anglican Church • 235

13   An Anglican Sisterhood and Auricular Confession:
     A Popish Practice in a Devonport Sisterhood • 259

14   Giacinto Achilli versus the Roman Catholic Church:
     Morality, Religion, and the Court of Public Opinion
     in Victorian England • 283

Acknowledgments

THIS BOOK GREW OUT of a series of lectures I gave on English anti-Catholicism when I taught Church History at Saint Vincent Seminary, Latrobe, Pennsylvania. The story of Maria Monk fascinated me, and as my work in English religious history introduced me to the widespread anti-Catholicism of Victorian England, I was surprised to discover that nuns, both Anglican and Roman Catholic, were the subjects of hostility and suspicion. In England, the Bodleian Library, the British Library, Lambeth Palace Library, and Pusey House Library provided me with the necessary resources to understand this prejudice. In America, the interlibrary services at Saint Vincent College Library and numerous used book dealers advertising on the web and eBay made it possible for me to consult and purchase important books and pamphlets.

Many people have been instrumental in the project. Archabbot Douglas Nowicki, OSB, and the monks of Saint Vincent Archabbey have always supported and encouraged me in my research. The monks of Ealing Abbey in London, and especially Abbot Francis Rossiter, OSB, welcomed me as a guest on my numerous research trips. It was at Saint Vincent Seminary where I began to develop an interest in English anti-Catholicism, and the faculty was always quick to answer any questions dealing with theology. My colleagues in the School of Humanities and Fine Arts, Ms Marsha Kush, Assistant to the Dean of the School of Humanities and Fine Arts, and Archabbot Paul Maher, OSB, former Archabbot of Saint Vincent Archabbey, have offered me advice as the work progressed. The students of Saint Vincent College, especially the first graduating classes of women, continue to impress me with their enthusiasm, and they have helped to keep me young in spirit.

I would like to acknowledge the journals in which these articles originally appeared and for permission to reprint copyrighted material: "Bishop William Ullathorne and His Defence of Convents: The 1851

Bill for Parliamentary Inspection of Convents," *Tjurunga* 55 (November 1998) 75–90; "They Walled Up Nuns, Didn't They? *Montezuma's Daughter* and Anti-Catholicism in Victorian England," *Downside Review* 119 (July 2001) 157–76; "Two Lectures at Bath: The Rev. M. Hobart Seymour and Cardinal Nicholas Wiseman and the Nunnery Question," *Revue d'Histoire Ecclesiastique* 96 (2001) 372–90; "Foreign and Catholic: A Plea to Protestant Parents on the Dangers of Convent Education in Victorian England," *History of Education* 31 (July 2002) 335–50 (for the journal's web site, see http://www.informaworld.com); "Those Horrible Iron Cages: The Kilburn Sisters and the Management or Mismanagement of Orphanages in Late Victorian England," *American Benedictine Review* 53 (September 2002) 264–84; "A Death in the Family: Bishop Archibald Campbell Tait, The Rights of Parents, and Anglican Sisterhoods in the Diocese of London" *Journal of Religious History* 27 (June 2003) 198–214; "Giacinto Achilli versus the Roman Catholic Church: Morality, Religion and the Court of Public Opinion in Victorian England," *Fides Quaerens Intellectum: A Journal of Theology, Philosophy & History* 3 (Autumn 2003) 87–110; "An Anglican Sisterhood and Auricular Confession: A Popish Practice in a Devonport Sisterhood," *Sewanee Theological Review* 47 (Christmas 2003) 33–52 (*Sewanee Theological Review* is published by the School of Theology of the University of the South in Sewanee, Tennessee); "Flowers, Pictures, and Crosses: Criticisms of Priscilla Lydia Sellon's Care of Young Girls," *Anglican Theological Review* 86 (Summer 2004) 451–71; "Magdalenes and Nuns: Convent Laundries in Late Victorian England," *Anglican and Episcopal History* 73 (September 2004) 309–34 (reprinted with the permission of the Historical Society of the Episcopal Church); "The Priest, the Nun, and Confession: An Anti-Catholic Stereotype and Anglican Sisterhoods in Victorian England," *Faith and Reason* 29 (Summer-Winter 2004) 183–205; "Power and Control over Women in Victorian England: Male Opposition to Sacramental Confession in the Anglican Church," *Journal of Anglican Studies* 3 (June 2005) 11–32; "The Myth and the Reality of Sister Barbara Ubryk, the Imprisoned Nun of Cracow: English Interpretations of a Victorian Religious Controversy," In *Victorian Churches and Churchmen: Essays Presented to Vincent Alan McClelland*, edited by Sheridan Gilley (Woodbridge, Suffolk: Boydell Press, 2005) 139–62; "An American 'Escaped Nun' on Tour in England: Edith O'Gorman's Critique of Convent Life," *Feminist Theology* 14 (January 2006) 205–20.

Introduction

THIS BOOK IS A collection of fourteen articles that explore the hostility toward the establishment of convent life, both Anglican and Roman Catholic, in Victorian England. The majority of the articles deal with Anglican religious life for women. Anglican sisterhoods began to gain popularity in the early part of the nineteenth century, partly due to the influence of the Oxford Movement and the growth of Anglo-Catholicism within the Church of England. This way of life offered women an opportunity to perform valuable work in their church, but it also offended the sensibilities of the Victorian culture that could only conceive of a woman's proper vocation as a wife and mother. Opponents to sisterhoods used traditional anti-Catholic stereotypes, which emphasized the alleged evils of convent life, for example, physical and spiritual abuse associated with convents, the unnatural character of celibacy and sisterhoods, and believed that other questionable practices associated with Roman Catholicism, such as vows, auricular confession, liturgy, and allegiance to the See of Rome, might be introduced into Protestant England. The year 1850 saw the re-establishment of the Roman Catholic Hierarchy in England, and this heightened the fears and suspicions of Catholicism, and the criticism of religious life for woman, both Catholic and Anglican, increased. Chapter 1 describes an early attempt to have Parliament legislate for state inspection of convents to ensure that the nuns did not suffer any abuse or lose of English liberties. Chapters 2, 3, 4, and 5 discuss "some traditional anti-Catholic critiques and alleged abuses associated with convent life. If sisterhoods were allowed to flourish in England free from state inspection, similar occurrences would certainly take place. Anglican sisterhoods, however, did perform valuable services, especially the establishment of orphanages, but even this praiseworthy service faced opposition. Chapters 6 and 7 explore the critiques of two Anglican sisterhoods that worked with orphans. Convents also performed valuable services for the poor and outcast women of society. Chapter 8 deals specifically with the institution of "convent laundries," that is, attempts by Anglican sisterhoods to rehabilitate "fallen women," and the opposition by an Anglican organization, the Convent Enquiry Society.

The education of young girls was another area in which convents, especially Roman Catholic, excelled, and an increasing number of Protestant families wanted to take advantage of this opportunity. Chapter 9 describes how some concerned Britons feared that these convent schools would destroy the English character of Protestant girls. Conversion to Roman Catholicism could become a strong temptation, and consequently parents were admonished to avoid convent schools. In general, the Victorians venerated the patriarchal family structure, and the place of daughters in the family structure was well defined. Chapter 10 points out that convent life, by its nature, tended to destroy this bond and could interfere with the rights of the parents. Chapters 11, 12, 13, and 14 discuss the alleged control of priests over the lives of nuns, and this power, some argued, could lead to abuse. Three of these chapters explore the Roman Catholic practice of auricular confession, which was popular in Anglican sisterhoods, and the reasons why some saw it as a threatening and dangerous practice that could harm naive women. Chapter XIV details the scandalous activities of the ex-Roman Catholic priest, Giacinto Achilli, and the manner in which he corrupted women, including nuns. The court case, which grew out of John Henry Newman's attack against Achilli, illustrated the power that some unscrupulous men might exert over women.

These articles have been published in America and abroad, and this book brings together these studies of anti-convent polemics. In addition to looking at anti-Catholicism and the fear of both Anglican and Catholic sisterhoods being established in England, this book also explores the prejudice which existed against women in Victorian England who sought their independence by joining sisterhoods and working in areas such as orphanages, rescue work, and education. This drew a hostile response from the nineteenth-century masculine ethos. Women, according to this view, should remain passive in matters of religion. This book, consequently, also highlights the significant achievements of sisterhoods in the spiritual, social, and educational areas of Victorian

England. Nuns did play an important role in many areas of life in nineteenth-century England and faced opposition from men who saw their dominance threatened by female religious. Although the open hostility they encountered has subsided to an extent in the twenty-first century, some suspicion of women who speak out and challenge their churches and a patriarchal society has not disappeared. The accomplishments of the nineteenth-century nuns and the opposition they endured should serve as both an example and encouragement to all men and women committed to the Gospel.

My home institution, Saint Vincent College, Latrobe, Pennsylvania, celebrated the twenty-fifth anniversary of co-education during the 2008–2009 academic year. After more than a century, this all-male, Catholic, Benedictine, liberal arts college welcomed its first group of women in August 1983 at a campus-wide celebration. The president of the college, Fr. Augustine Flood, OSB, challenged these women, who correctly saw themselves as pioneers, to take charge of the college. Within a few years, this had taken place. The early classes of women graced the campus with their enthusiasm, scholarship, and determination to make this college, to quote Benedict's Rule, "a school of the Lord's service." This book is dedicated to these first women students at Saint Vincent College and their lasting contributions to higher education in the Benedictine tradition.

—Rene Kollar

Bishop William Ullathorne and His Defense of Convents

The 1851 Bill for Parliamentary Inspection of Convents

IN ANTHONY TROLLOPE'S BOOK, *The Warden*, the reader encounters Sir Abraham Haphazard, who "was deeply engaged in preparing a bill for the mortification of papists, to be called the 'Convent Custody Bill', the purport of which was to enable any Protestant clergyman over fifty years of age to search any nun whom he suspected of being in possession of treasonable papers or Jesuitical symbols . . ."[1] In this account of fiction, Sir Abraham's bill met strong opposition and never became law. In the real world of Victorian England, Bishop William Bernard Ullathorne (1806–1889)[2] vigorously opposed an early piece of legislation designed to inspect convents. As a Benedictine monk, missionary to Australia, and later as Bishop of Birmingham, Ullathorne recognized the valuable contributions that sisterhoods made to the Roman Catholic Church, encouraged the growth of sisterhoods, and never failed to defend the in-

---

1. Trollope, *The Warden*, 94. This passage is "a satire on the Recovery of Personal Liberty in Certain Cases Bill, debated in June 1853, which sought to appoint commissioners to inspect 'premises' (meaning convents) in order to liberate 'any Female . . . detained . . . against her Will,'" 287.

2. For biographies of Bishop Ullathorne, see Butler, *The Life and Times of Bishop Ullathorne 1806–1889*, 2 vols.; *The Dictionary of National Biography*; Ullathorne, *From Cabin-Boy to Archbishop*. See also, Drane, ed., *Letters of Archbishop Ullathorne*.

dependence and integrity of conventual life against hostile critics, such as Henry Charles Lacy, Henry Drummond, and Charles Newdigate. Newdegate, who characterised the convents as prisons and campaigned for parliamentary inspection of these institutions.[3] Ullathorne's defence of nuns in his published letters and pamphlets not only reveals his personal love and deep appreciation for conventual life, but also gives us an insight into the hostile religious climate of mid-Victorian England.

Some Victorians suspected the designs of English Roman Catholicism. The Restoration of the Hierarchy in 1850, ritualism in the Church of England, which appeared to mirror Roman liturgical devotions, and an increasing number of converts from the Oxford Movement to Rome all contributed to a dislike of practices and institutions associated with Roman Catholicism. Some antagonists naturally looked at convents with suspicious eyes.[4] Were sisterhoods seedbeds of disloyalty and sources of subversion against the Protestant constitution? Did they imprison young English women in violation of their legal rights? Were convents really dens of torture, sin and licentiousness? Would not the inspection of convents by the government protect those naive and trusting individuals who became nuns and also safeguard the realm against a papist plot to conquer England? Convents did attract suspicion. Members of sisterhoods had become "the most unpopular single group in Victorian England. Nuns, though less numerous than prostitutes, have at least as good a claim as prostitutes to be considered Victorian 'outcasts', even if unlike the prostitutes they were predominantly women of good family."[5] English nuns, however, found a champion in the Bishop of Birmingham, who attacked the religious bigotry associated with some zealous members of the House of Commons and their attempts in 1851 to legislate for the inspection of Roman Catholic convents.

Ullathorne entered the Benedictine order at Downside, Somerset, in 1824, and was ordained a priest in 1831. He was stationed at Sydney,

---

3. For an analysis of the period and the motives behind Newdegate's crusade to investigate and inspect nunneries, see Arnstein, *Protestant versus Catholic in Mid-Victorian England*. See also Wolffe, *Protestant Crusade*. Both books contain extensive bibliographies.

4. The amount of anti-convent literature published during the nineteenth century in England is enormous. Works of fiction, memoirs and pamphlets described the alleged depravity and sinfulness of convent life. Moreover, anti-convent literature from North America was also published for the English audience.

5. Swift and Gilley, eds. *Irish in the Victorian City*, 8.

Australia, from 1833–36 and again from 1838–40. During this time Ullathorne wrote against the evils of the transportation system, and he also became acquainted with the praiseworthy work done by the nuns. Consequently, five Irish Sisters of Charity accompanied Ullathorne when he returned to Australia in 1838. They "were established at Parramatta, fifteen miles from Sydney, where was the great 'Factory', or house of correction for female convicts, and Dr Ullathorne was placed there."[6] Violence and immorality characterised the atmosphere of the "Factory," which accommodated as many as one thousand women. This became the vineyard where the Sisters laboured, and their work impressed Ullathorne. "The influence of the Sisters upon the women in prison soon told upon the entire colony," he wrote in his autobiography.[7] "And the magistrates repeatedly bore testimony to their services from the bench." Church officials also recognised the importance of the presence of the nuns in Australia within months of their arrival. On 5 March 1838, Fr John Polding described the accomplishments of the Sisters of Charity to Daniel Murray, Archbishop of Dublin. "Their success has gone beyond my most sanguine expectations" and "A change which appears almost miraculous has taken place."[8] "Where, heretofore, all was noise and ribaldry and obscene conversation, you may now see the quiet of a well-ordered family. Not an oath nor curse nor brawling word is heard; and a general desire to frequent the Sacraments prevails." Ullathorne, the resident clergyman who was in charge of the convent, naturally witnessed the valuable labour and efforts of these Irish Sisters. He eventually left Australia for England on 16 November 1840, and his experiences of the Sisters of Charity greatly influenced his appreciation for sisterhoods.

After several years in Coventry, Ullathorne was appointed Vicar for the Western District of England in 1846, and two years later he was transferred to the Central District. In September 1850 when Pope Pius IX restored the hierarchy in England and Wales, William Bernard Ullathorne was named Bishop of Birmingham. And his support of sisterhoods soon became apparent. At Coventry, he had the opportunity to work with Margaret Mary Hallahan, a Dominican secular tertiary, who desired to become a nun and enter a Dominican convent. But Ullathorne

---

6. Butler, *Life and Times of Bishop Ullathorne 1806–1889*, vol. 1, 66.
7. Ullathorne, *From Cabin Boy to Archbishop*, 146.
8. Polding to Murray, 5 March 1838, printed in Butler, *Life and Times of Bishop Ullathorne 1806–1889*. vol. 1, 67.

had other ideas; he wanted to found a "New congregation of Dominican Conventual Tertiary nuns at Coventry"[9] with Margaret Mary Hallahan as foundress. "All this was successfully carried through; Ullathorne was made Vicar of the Master General of the Dominicans in respect of the new foundation; in June 1844 Sister Margaret and three other postulants were clothed by him and on December 6, 1845, they were professed." Almost immediately after his appointment to Birmingham, Ullathorne made plans to bring Mother Margaret's Dominican nuns into his diocese. In 1851, "he was appointed by the Holy See, with the consent of the Master General of the Dominicans, ecclesiastical superior for life of the Congregation of Dominican nuns of the Third Order, of which he had been the Founder."[10] Because the mother house of this congregation should be within his diocese, a large convent, located in Stone, Staffordshire, was opened in 1853 with Mother Margaret Mary as the Mother Provincial of the Institute. This new order joined several other sisterhoods that had already been established in the Birmingham Diocese. Bishop Ullathorne's backing and patronage of convents, however, soon brought him into a public debate concerning the possibility of parliamentary inspection of England's convents.

Suspicion and hatred of Roman Catholicism had peaked following the Restoration of the Hierarchy. The exuberant personality of Nicholas Wiseman, the first Archbishop of Westminster, the strong tone of his pastoral, *Out of the Flaminian Gate*, and the rhetoric of Lord John Russell all made the threat of "papal aggression" very real in the minds of some people. Consequently, "In the early 1850s, as a by-product of the widespread excitement over 'papal aggression', there had been several parliamentary attempts to check into, if not to check altogether, the establishment of Roman convents."[11] Some enthusiasts even argued for the suppression of England's convents, but this approach did not attract much popular support. Parliamentary inspection of the country's institutions, however, had already become an accepted part of Victorian life. The first of these efforts at state inspection occurred on 11 March 1851, when Henry Charles Lacy MP for Bodmin, an opponent to the Poor Law, game laws, taxation on the poor, and endowment of Roman

---

9. Ibid., 128.

10. Ibid., 174–75.

11. Arnstein, *Protestant versus Catholic*, 62.

Catholic priests,¹² introduced a bill into the House of Commons, similar to one enacted several years earlier to supervise lunatic asylums, which would have authorised government inspection of convents.

According to the preamble, this proposed legislation would "make Provision for preventing the forcible Detention of Females in Houses wherein Persons bound by religious or Monastic Vows are resident or associated."¹³ This bill, naturally, would severely infringe upon the freedom and independence of conventual life. It required that a religious house of women must be registered with the Clerk of the Peace of the county where it was located; six or more justices of the Peace, acting as Visitors, would inspect the convent twice each year; if necessary, the Visitors could remove any woman who asked or petitioned to leave the convent; and this person, once removed, would be placed under the care and supervision of "the Matron of the Workhouse of the Union or Parish within which such House shall be situate . . ." Failing to register a convent, obstructing the work of a Visitor, concealing parts of a convent or persons from the Visitors, or refusing to produce or falsifying a list of the membership of the convent would be classified as a misdemeanour. Assault upon a Visitor was a felony, and if convicted, the individual would "be liable to be transported as such for Ten years, or to be imprisoned either with or without hard Labour, and for any Time the Court may direct, not exceeding Two Years."

In reply to this attack against this parliamentary attempt to legislate for the inspection of Roman Catholic convents, Bishop Ullathorne quickly came to the defence of sisterhoods and wrote a pamphlet, *A Plea for the Rights and Liberties of Religious Women with Reference to the Bill Proposed by Mr Lacy*.¹⁴ According to Ullathorne's biographer, Cuthbert Butler, "It is a clear popular exposition of the principles and nature of conventual life, and a protest against the proposed invasion of that inviolability of the domicile so dear to the English heart, and greatly resented by the nuns themselves."¹⁵ After quoting from the preamble of Lacy's bill, Ullathorne stated his objection to Lacy's measure: "If made law, this

---

12. M. Stenton, *Who's Who of British Members of Parliament*, vol. 1.

13. *A Bill to Prevent the Forcible Detention of Females in Religious Houses*, vol. 5, (11 March 1851).

14. Ullathorne, *A Plea for the Rights and Liberties of Religious Women with Reference to the Bill Proposed by Mr. Lacy*.

15. Butler, *Life and Times of Bishop Ullathorne 1806–1889*, vol. 1, 169.

Bill would inflict upon considerable number of ladies amongst the most refined, high minded, and accomplish in the country, a degradation beyond what they would be subject to in workhouses, and approaching the treatment of convicts, whilst it would rank them with presumed criminals. Its provisions are calculated to inflict on the exquisite delicacy of their minds a martyrdom, not of a day, but of a life."[16] Moreover, this bill would "make those ladies who have consecrated themselves to God, appear ignominious before the eyes of the country."[17] Misconceptions, wicked gossip, ignorance on the part of some Protestants, and popular works of fiction had all created a myth of convent tyranny. Ullathorne, therefore, set out to correct these false stories, and he reminded the reader of his vast experience as superior of numerous convents.

Convents, Ullathorne began, were places where liberty and individual freedom flourishes, and checks and balances guarantee these rights. "So far from a convent being under despotic power, I dare boldly affirm, and every one acquainted with the subject will bear me out in the assertion, that the British Constitution has not half the elements of security from abuse of power . . ."[18] Obedience to the elected superiors was not "unlimited," he pointed out to critics and scoffers, but a convent's rules and regulations clearly defined and limited the extent of obedience. Before a sister made a permanent commitment, she enjoyed the time and freedom to make a mature decision to join the sisterhood. Ullathorne then made a comparison, although rather weak, with marriage, and argued that if "Parliament can step into a convent, examine dispositions, and separate the sister from the community, it can equally step into other dwellings, examine dispositions there, and separate wife from husband."[19]

Bishop Ullathorne, hoping to correct the false and malicious stories of prison conditions and deprivation of basic human freedoms, then demonstrated the manner in which the Roman Catholic Church protected the liberty and personal freedoms of those who choose to enter religious life. Most importantly, he began, the bishop of the diocese must make frequent visitations of convents, and each sister must meet with the bishop for an interview. The sisters also enjoyed the right to appeal

16. Ullathorne, *A Plea for the Rights and Liberties of Religious Women*, 3.
17. Ibid., 4.
18. Ibid., 5
19. Ibid., 10.

to the bishop at all times. Hostile critics of conventual life loved to emphasise how the chaplain or confessor might control or manipulate the lives of the sisters, but Ullathorne pointed out that this priest possessed no power in the internal governance of the convent and his tenure or appointment was limited to three years. Finally, Bishop Ullathorne reminded those who supported convent inspection that the relatives and friends of the sisters "have constant access to them."[20]

Bishop Ullathorne next dismissed a series of nasty rumours and scurrilous stories dealing with sisterhoods, such as imprisonment and torture, and told his readers that all convent rules have provisions for dismissing incorrigible members. Consequently, there was no need to imprison or to confine a rebellious or difficult sister. "Of all the stories bruited abroad through the world against our convents, we know nothing except their revolting falsehood."[21] The sanctity of the enclosure, enforced by strict ecclesiastical law, mocks the slanderous notion "that the clergy have much intimacy with religious communities of women."[22]

After this dismissal of false notions or conceptions concerning sisterhoods, Bishop Ullathorne returned to Lacy's bill. Lacy's proposal for visitation of sisterhoods disgusted Ullathorne. "For unknown men, or for any man to enter a Convent, and that at all hours, and even into its most retired recesses, to say nothing of its unmanliness and indecency, approaches so near a sacrilege, and would be so gross an insult, that how even persons the most ultra-Protestant could entertain the idea, seems incredible."[23] The registration and visitation of convents sanctioned by Parliament constituted practices that were "un-English" and would violate the sanctity of one's home and domestic life. And where would this practice stop? Boarding schools and other houses that accommodated groups of people would soon appear on the schedule for possible state inspection. The false allegations that English women were being detained against their will in these religious houses appeared to be the chief motive to inspect or supervise convents. "Now there is no such detention," Ullathorne argued, "The existence of crime must surely be made out before a suit is made for its prevention at great costs to the liberty

20. Ibid., 13.
21. Ibid., 16.
22. Ibid., 17.
23. Ibid., 20.

of the subject."²⁴ Lacy's bill, however, represented more than religious bigotry. It contradicted basic English rights: ". . . the sole effect of legislation would be to occasion many almost sacrilegious acts against private rights and liberties, which in their turn would cause deep suffering and much degradation to many innocent and most exemplary persons."²⁵

Bishop Ullathorne ended his critique of Lacy's bill and his defence of sisterhoods by making reference to some rude and nasty remarks which Henry Drummond, an inveterate enemy of popery and the Romanising tendencies of the Oxford Movement, had made on 20 March 1851, during the second reading of the Ecclesiastical Titles Bill. Ullathorne felt ashamed that a "member of the honourable house thought fit to throw ribaldry of a description with which God forbid I should soil these pages, on Christ's most pure virgins."²⁶ But the remarks by Drummond in the House of Commons do reveal that the subject of convent inspection had become an emotional issue in some parliamentary circles, and consequently several MPs demanded government action to curb alleged abuses in nunneries.

Henry Drummond (1786–1860) MP for West Surrey,²⁷ who would shortly follow up his hostile remarks in the House of Commons against convents with a written attack on Bishop Ullathorne's critique of Lacy's bill, had earlier experienced disillusionment with the frivolities and attractions of the world and embraced religion early in his life. Drummond became a founder and supporter of the Irvingnite Church (the Catholic Apostolic Church),²⁸ and it "was at Drummond's house at Albury, Surrey, that at Advent 1826 the 'little prophetic parliament' of Irving, Wolff, and others met for six days' discussion of the Scriptures, when the catholic apostolic church was practically originated."²⁹ As a politician, he

---

24. Ibid., 22.
25. Ibid., 23.
26. Ibid.
27. *Dictionary of National Biography*; *Oxford Dictionary of the Christian Church*; and Stenton, *Who's Who of British Members of Parliament*.
28. Members of the Catholic Apostolic Church believed that the second coming of Christ was imminent, and "in preparation for which they resolved to reestablish the primitive offices of the Church, namely those of Apostles, prophets, evangelists, pastors, and teachers, to which others, e.g. 'angels' (bishops) and deacons were added later," *Oxford Dictionary of the Christian Church*, s.v. "Catholic Apostolic Church." Drummond was eventually ordained an angel for Scotland in 1834.
29. *Dictionary of National Biography*.

"was a frequent speaker and a remarkable figure in the house, perfectly independent, scarcely pretending to consistency, attacking all parties in turn in speeches delivered in an immovable manner, and with an almost inaudible voice, full of sarcasm and learning, but also of not a little absurdity." Not surprisingly, Drummond spoke frequently on ecclesiastical issues: he supported the Ecclesiastical Titles Bill; opposed the admission of Jews to Parliament; and argued for the inspection of convents. In remarks during the debate on the Ecclesiastical Titles bill on 20 March 1851, two members of Parliament, Charles Newdigate Newdegate and Henry Drummond, directed their invectives not only against the recently established Roman Catholic hierarchy, but also singled out convents for scorn.[30]

This legislation, an attempt to counteract Pius IX's apparent interference in the political and religious life of England and Wales, sought to prohibit the assumption of territorial titles by the recently named bishops by means of fines, and it also attempted to nullify all bequests or donations made to these Roman Catholic prelates. The debates centered around the temporal power of the papacy, the principles of British liberty and freedom, and centuries of mistrust and suspicion of Roman Catholicism. But the question of convents and the need for their inspection also crept into the discussions. On 20 March, Newdegate made a speech in favor of the legislation against the alleged growth of papal power. After a sweeping condemnation of religious orders, which he described as "the police for enforcing synodical decrees—the tools, the instruments which the Romish Church knew so well how to employ," Newdegate turned his attention to convents?[31] The number of sisterhoods in England had recently increased, and the freedom and liberty of those who took vows had to be guaranteed by "some law for the regular inspection of religious houses." English women, Newdegate argued, became captives in "those prisons," and he drew attention to several recent cases where inhabitants of convents had been allegedly held against their will. In conclusion to his plea for parliamentary inspection of nunneries, Newdegate played to the emotions and sense of fair play of his listeners: "The people who were immured in these places mouldered and died.

---

30. *Hansard*, 3rd ser., vol. 115 (1851), cols. 261–80. Henry Drummond's speech was also published with a preface and notes dealing with convent abuse. See Drummond, *Mr. Drummond's Speech*.

31. *Hansard*, 3rd ser., vol. 115 (1851), cols. 248–53.

No account was given of their illness or death. No coroner's inquest was even known to have taken place with respect to any person who had died in a convent." Henry Drummond then continued the criticism against "papal aggression," and worked a condemnation of sisterhoods into his speech. These comments caught Bishop Ullathorne's attention and infuriated him.

Drummond began his attack by stressing the incompatibility of Roman Catholicism with loyalty to the English constitution and to Queen Victoria.[32] Moreover, Cardinal Wiseman's words and actions represented examples "of arrogant aggression." Up to this point, Drummond's rhetoric did not incite much response or reaction, but his hostile description of conventual life soon occasioned fierce and violent reactions from some members of the House of Commons. Referring to the responsibility of the government to protect the weak, such as the insane or the children who worked in factories, Drummond queried, "How can a poor young lady who is locked up, where she may be either starved or whipped to death, that the priests may clutch her money, ask for protection?" This sensational assertion brought cries of protest from some members, but Drummond continued in his critique of sisterhoods. "I assert that nunneries are prisons, and I have seen them so used," he argued. "They have ever been either prisons or brothels."

Immediately following these inflammatory words, the House erupted in "violent cries" of protest against Henry Drummond. The Earl of Arundel and Surrey (Henry Granville), who had just recently arrived, questioned Drummond's scandalous accusations against convents: "I hope I am mistaken in my impression, that nunneries were either prisons or brothels." The Earl described nuns as ladies who devote themselves to the service of God, and endeavour to attain to the perfection of all human virtues . . ." He then asked, "whether it is proper, in this House, to use base terms so disgraceful of those institutions as to have fallen from the hon. Member?" In response, the Speaker, C. S. Lefevre, ruled "that nothing has fallen from the hon. Member for Surrey inconsistent with the freedom of debate." After this brief interruption, Henry Drummond continued his speech and attacked the alleged power of the Roman Catholic bishops and priests, emphasised the traditional English virtues of truth and honour, ridiculed certain Roman Catholic devotions ("What! do you think that you can bring over here with impunity

32. Ibid., cols. 261–80.

a cargo of blinking statues, of bleeding pictures of liquefying blood, and of the Virgin Mary's milk?"), and described the monastic system as "an unmitigated evil."

These indecorous and inflammatory remarks again drew some protests from some members of the House, a caution to Drummond from the Speaker, and a response from Sir James Graham, MP for Ripon. Graham, highly insulted by Drummond's choice of words, argued that these comments had violated the spirit of the rules and order of the House of Commons and insulted those Roman Catholic members present. Drummond's caustic remarks about convents especially offended him. "I will not sully my lips by repeating the words that fell from him," Graham continued, "in reference to their veracity, and still less shall I think of repeating an allusion . . . grossly offensive to the female relatives of those Gentlemen" in the House of Commons. He then described the inhabitants of convents in the most laudatory and praiseworthy terms: "ladies who have devoted themselves to the service of their God, according to their consciences, in lives of seclusion and chastity." The session for 20 March ended without any additional outbursts against sisterhoods, but the convent issue arose again on the following day.

The debate on Henry Drummond's speech continued on Friday, March 21. Mr George Henry Moore, MP for Mayo, drew attention to his "indignation," which he had expressed in the debate of the preceding day, and he apologised if his words had "trespassed in the slightest degree upon the rules and regulations of the House.[33] "My opinion was," he continued, "that the hon. Member for West Surrey [Henry Drummond] had spoken not only with irreverence, but with a levity which almost amounted to indecency." According to Moore, Drummond's language was improper and an insult to the beliefs and practices of the Roman Catholic members. He then addressed the attack against the character and integrity of sisterhoods. "I will say that to apply these terms to Christian ladies who have dedicated their lives to charity and to God, ought not to be permitted in any assembly of English Gentlemen; and I appeal not only to the accomplished and cultivated minds of English gentlemen, but to the instinctive feelings of men, to prevent the repetition of these obscenities of senility, and to repeal these dastardly insinuations." At the conclusion of Moore's speech, and the Speaker of the House forced him to retract the word "dastardly." In compliance,

33. Ibid., cols. 334–40.

he substituted "unmanly" in its place. The Prime Minister, Lord John Russell, then briefly remarked that he regretted if anything during the recent debates had offended the feelings of any member of the House of Commons.

Several other speakers then commented on aspects of Drummond's speech, but it was Mr James H. Reynolds, MP for Dublin, who addressed the anti-convent statements. The scurrilous charges and insinuations insulted Reynolds, who expressed his indignation: "I read the phrase used in describing those convents. I am glad I was not present, because of the rule, and it is a wise one, that no man shall be called to order unless he uses language personally offensive—or at least the offence may be enlarged from one to at least fifty Members, who profess and believe sincerely in the truth of the Catholic religion, and I am one of them." Reynolds pointed out that he had visited many convents, had relatives who were nuns, and had even sent two daughters to a convent to receive an education. "The establishments," he maintained, "have been imagined—brutally and beastly imagined." Contrary to Drummond's contentions, nuns were not treated as inmates of prisons who had forfeited all freedom and liberty. What surprised Reynolds, moreover, was the absence of any censure or any words of disapproval from the Prime Minister, Lord Russell, in his comments on Drummond's speech. Russell's silence on the matter caused him offence. Consequently, the Prime Minister responded, and his remarks on the subject ended the discussion of Henry Drummond's speech and his critique of conventual life. "The fact is, I was not in the house when the hon. Member for West Surrey made his observation," Russell pointed out, "and not having been here, I thought it better for me to refrain altogether from alluding to it."

The House, which eventually passed the Ecclesiastical Titles legislation in 1851, did not, however, approve Lacy's measure.[34] But the passions generated in the political arena by Henry Charles Lacy's bill surfaced outside the House of Commons. Bishop Ullathorne's attack on this piece of legislation, *A Plea for the Rights and Liberties of Religious Women with Reference to the Bill Proposed by Mr. Lacy*, had gone through two edi-

---

34. See *Hansard* 3rd ser., vol. 116 (1851), cols. 961–98. The opponents of Lacy's measure emphasized that he had failed to make a case for the bill, and consequently urged him to withdraw the proposed legislation. They argued that no evidence existed which demonstrated that convents infringed upon and robbed women of their freedom and liberty. Some, however, maintained that the state did have a right to regulate institutions such as convents, but also pointed out some apparent weaknesses of Lacy's bill.

tions in 1851, and the no-popery side did not remain silent. During the same year, Henry Drummond, who had been prominent in his defence of Lacy's bill and who had vilified sisterhoods during the debate on the Ecclesiastical Titles Bill, published a sixty-five-page response, *A Plea for the Rights and Liberties of Women Imprisoned for Life under the Power of Priests. In Answer to Bishop Ullathorne*,[35] directed against Ullathorne's arguments. Drummond's work, sarcastic at times, began by stating that the "rights of women are invaded by being locked up, yet Bishop Ullathorne pretends to be favourable to their rights . . ."[36] "Young women are locked up for life in houses the doors and windows of which are barred with iron; nothing is known by their parents and friend of what goes on within the walls; and the key of the prison is given to a priest."

Drummond used excerpts, taken out of context, from the Council of Trent and from the writings of Alphonsus Liguori to demonstrate the apparent harshness of the life and inhuman discipline that existed within convent walls. To refute Ullathorne's contention that happiness and contentment characterised sisterhoods, the author presented lengthy testimonies of individuals who described the cruel and despotic nature of convent life, for example, the young nun who was "removed from her room to a small damp closet near that of the abbess, and there she lay immured for months, until she was so ill that it became necessary to send for a doctor."[37] Her screams could be heard frequently coming from the convent. Moreover, he argued, rather than being places of peace and contentment, convents tended to produce madness. Alleged stories of torture, starvation, the immorality of priests, and the seduction of nuns by their confessors had been available to the English-speaking public since Maria Monk's *Awful Disclosures of the Hotel Dieu Nunnery of Montreal* appeared in 1836, and to support his allegations Drummond quoted verbatim from a journal, which purported to describe accurately life in a nineteenth-century convent, given to him by a priest.

According to this account, use of the discipline, floggings and severe fasts and punishments, such as eating bread sprinkled with palm ashes, formed part of the inhumane punishment endured by the nuns, whom Ullathorne had recently portrayed as living a peaceful and happy existence. At times, death, moreover, resulted from these penances. Bibles,

35. Drummond, *A Plea for the Rights and Liberties of Women*.
36. Ibid., 3.
37. Ibid., 13.

which would have revealed the hypocrisy of the conventual system, were forbidden. "The undeniable fact is proved," Drummond seemed to taunt the Bishop of Birmingham, "that these locked-up, imprisoned, helpless women, are wholly at the mercy, fanaticism, caprice, cruelty, and every other bad passion of their director."[38] Consequently, the full force of English law must destroy this cruel and inhuman system. Sexual immorality also pervaded the convents. It was not the nuns, however, who led profligate lives, "but the priests, who have used and do use these institutions for gratifying their cruelty or their lusts."[39] The anonymous author of this journal then backed up his accusations by quoting numerous commentaries or histories, sometimes in Latin, which blackened the character of the Roman clergy with charges of gross immorality. For centuries, he pointed out, these unscrupulous clerics possessed the keys to convents and held the inhabitants at their mercy. Not content from gleanings from this journal, Drummond also produced the testimony of a Roman Catholic layman, who described convents as places where the "vilest tyranny" dominates the life, and he boldly challenged Ullathorne's pleasant and idyllic picture of nunnery life: "Why, Bishop Ullathorne, what becomes of your assertion of there being nothing in the British Constitution so free from the despotic power as convents?"[40]

English women, consequently, had to be protected from numerous other evils associated with the conventual system. According to Drummond, the Roman Catholic Church, under the guise of poverty, controlled the wealth and property of the nuns, and thus the riches of the higher clergy increased while the condition of the lower clerics remained poor and destitute. Convent education had traditionally received high marks from Catholics, but he challenged this viewpoint. "As places of education . . . the convents are everything they ought not to be, and in every respect the very opposite in principle and practice of all that is encouraged by the worse education in any other sect."[41] Practices of cruel punishment and the encouragement of telling lies and spreading gossip, all alien to the English character, could best describe convent education.

Drummond concluded his critiques against sisterhoods, and Roman Catholicism in general, by returning to the merits of Lacy's bill.

38. Ibid., 26.
39. Ibid., 32.
40. Ibid., 54.
41. Ibid., 59.

Convents were "incompatible with British liberties and with the rights of Englishmen."[42] "English women must be delivered out of the hands of their tyrants, whether clerical or parental," Drummond told the House, but the "bill introduced by Mr Lacy was quite inadequate to grapple with such a system." He then made an argument for convent inspection, which would later be championed by Charles Newdegate. Inspections or inquiries should not be in the hands of county magistrates, as Lacy's bill stipulated, but "let it be done by parliamentary committees, or by a commission composed of sharp common-law barristers, accustomed to dealing with prevaricating, systematic, and intentional deceivers . . ."

Only parliamentary inspection of convents, Drummond argued, could protect the country from "papal aggression," guarantee the liberty and freedom of the English people, and preserve the Protestant character of the country. In conclusion, he again emphasised the evil or insidious nature of the Roman clergy and urged loyal English Protestants to "insist upon the Government adopting some efficient means of contracting the power of these Popish priests, and rendering them harmless against the peace and property of the people of England."[43] Moreover, Roman Catholic priests tended to subjugate and control women, but this "oppression of women is not owing to the priests being Papists, but owing partly to their being unmarried, and partly to all their doings being carried on in secret."[44] Vice thrived in secrecy; publicity or public knowledge tended to destroy evil. Drummond ended his attack by quoting from a report that had appeared in a newspaper concerning an event in Piedmont where a young girl was allegedly kidnapped from her father and held captive. The article emphasised that this story "gives additional evidence to the assertion recently made in the British Parliament, viz., that these female religious houses are, in point of fact, either prisons or brothels; indeed, with greater truth, one might say they are both."[45]

In spite of the failure of Lacy's bill, others followed his and Drummond's examples and pressed state inspection of convents. "Dr. Thomas Chambers's attempt in 1853 to institute a system of convent inspection won one test vote but was ultimately defeated," Walter Arnstein points out, "as were separate attempts in 1853 and 1854 to establish

---

42. Ibid., 62.
43. Ibid., 63.
44. Ibid., 64.
45. Ibid., 65.

a parliamentary select committee to consider whether the inmates of such institutions and their property required additional legislative protection."[46] Bishop Ullathorne also remained active in his defence of sisterhoods against state inspection after the failure of Lacy's bill. In 1854, he wrote "another pamphlet in the shape of a public Letter to Lord Edward Howard, MP" against a motion in Parliament for a committee of inquiry.[47] But the battle for parliamentary supervision of convents continued during the next two decades, and Charles Newdigate Newdegate, MP for North Warwickshire, led the campaign. In 1865, Newdegate moved in the House of Commons that a select committee be appointed to investigate English sisterhoods. The motion lost, but in his speech Newdegate mentioned that Bishop Ullathorne had been responsible for escorting an "escaped nun" back to her convent at Colwich. A correspondence, which was eventually published, developed between Newdegate and Ullathorne and contained rhetoric and arguments similar to the 1851 debates.[48] Again in 1867, Ullathorne came to the defence of sisterhoods and defended the conventual system against the accusations of a hostile speaker in Birmingham with letters later published in a short pamphlet, *The Alleged Nunnery Scandal*,[49] complied by an interested layman. The accusations and assertions of the lecturer were eventually dismissed as false. In response to this incident, Bishop Ullathorne took the opportunity to give a series of lectures in 1868 that attempted to explain convent life to non-Roman Catholics.[50]

Newdegate, however, refused to surrender. Finally in 1870, "in the period of anti-Catholic hostility attendant upon the Vatican Council,"[51] his motion for parliamentary inspection of convents was carried in the House of Commons, and the pamphlet containing Newdegate's 1865 speech and the correspondence with Bishop Ullathorne was reprinted. This edition, however, contained a letter that declared that the story of

46. Arnstein, *Protestant versus Catholic*, 63.

47. Butler, *Life and Times of Bishop Ullathorne 1806–1889*, vol. 1, 179.

48. *Monastic and Conventual Institutions*. In addition to Newdegate's 1865 speech, this short book contains the correspondence between Newdegate and Bishop Ullathorne, C. Langdale, Charles Clifford, and J. Akeroyd.

49. Gutterson, *The Alleged 'Nunnery Scandal' at Birmingham: Correspondence Relating Thereto and Refutation of the Slander*.

50. Ullathorne, *On the Conventual Life*.

51. Norman, *English Catholic Church*, 187.

the nun who "escaped" from the Colwich convent, which Ullathorne had earlier refuted, was true. Bishop Ullathorne responded quickly to these false accusations and denounced the allegations with a letter to *The Times*.[52] Newdegate's committee, however, proved to be ineffective, and clamour for investigations and inspections of Roman Catholic convents became more and more muted. Special credit for this failure to impose government control over Victorian sisterhoods must be given to William Ullathorne, who stood out as one of the defenders of conventual life against its detractors. Ullathorne had always appreciated the special vocation of nuns and the good works of sisterhoods. His vigorous defence of convents during the 1850s succeeded and spared them from intrusive government oversight. Ullathorne's continued support of sisterhoods during the next two decades against criticism eventually helped to frustrate and weaken Newdegate's campaign for parliamentary inspection of sisterhoods.

---

52. *The Times* 23 April 1870.

A Foreign and Wicked Institution?

Bibliography

Arnstein, William L. *Protestant versus Catholic in Mid-Victorian England: Mr. Newdegate and the Nuns*. Columbia: University of Missouri Press, 1982.

A Bill to Prevent the Forcible Detention of Females in Religious Houses. Vol. 5. 11 March 1851.

Butler, Cuthbert. *The Life and Times of Bishop Ullathorne 1806–1889*. 2 vols. New York: Benziger, 1926.

Cross, F. L., and E. A. Livingstone, editors. *The Oxford Dictionary of the Christian Church*. 3rd ed. Oxford: Oxford University Press, 1997.

Drane, Augusta (Mother Francis Raphael), editor. *Letters of Archbishop Ullathorne*. London: Burns & Oates, 1892.

Drummond, Henry. *Mr. Drummond's Speech on the Second Reading of the Ecclesiastical Titles Bill*. London: Bosworth, 1851.

———. *A Plea for the Rights and Liberties of Women Imprisoned for Life under the Power of Priests*. London: Bosworth, 1851.

Gutterson, Thomas. *The Alleged 'Nunnery Scandal' at Birmingham: Correspondence Relating Thereto and Refutation of the Slander*. Birmingham, UK: Maher & Sons, 1868.

Monastic and Conventual Institutions: Their Legal Position, Property and Disabilities. London: Scottish Reformation Society, 1870.

Norman, E. *The English Catholic Church in the Nineteenth Century*. Oxford: Oxford University Press, 1984.

Stenton, M. *Who's Who of British Members of Parliament*. Vol. 1. Hassocks, UK: Harvester, 1976.

Swift, Roger, and Sheridan Gilley, editors. *The Irish in the Victorian City*. London: Croom Helm, 1985.

Trollope, Anthony. *The Warden*. Introduction and notes by David Skilton and illustrations by Edward Ardizzone. Oxford: Oxford University Press, 1981.

Ullathorne, W. B. *From Cabin-Boy to Archbishop: The Autobiography of Archbishop Ullathorne*. New York: Benziger, 1941.

———. *On the Conventual Life: Three Lectures*. London: Burns & Oates, 1868.

———. *A Plea for the Rights and Liberties of Religious Women with Reference to the Bill Proposed by Mr. Lacy*. London: Richardson, 1851.

Wolffe, John. *The Protestant Crusade in Great Britain 1829–1860*. Oxford: Oxford University Press, 1991.

2

They Walled Up Nuns, Didn't They?

H. Rider Haggard's Montezuma's Daughter *and Anti-Catholicism in Victorian England*

B<small>Y THE LAST DECADE</small> of the nineteenth century, the figure of the Roman Catholic nun had clearly emerged as an important and often misrepresented figure in Victorian fiction. This literature did not deal with nuns, especially those who were Roman Catholic, in a favorable light. But even the Anglican sisterhoods did not escape hostile criticism.[1] In addition to the numerous campaigns throughout the nineteenth century to bring all convents under state control and inspection, some English authors tried to alert their countrymen to the dangers of all sisterhoods by illustrating the evils traditionally associated with Roman Catholic conventual life; for example, loss of traditional English freedoms, sexual abuse at the hands of wicked priests and monks, and the baleful influence of celibacy on Victorian family values. Some writers cautioned Anglican parents about sending their daughters abroad to receive an education at convent schools under the supervision of Catholic nuns. Emma Leslie's *Caught in the Toils* is an outstanding example of this fear. In this novel, horrified fathers and mothers read about the alleged Roman Catholic dislike of the Bible, cruel punishments that the students endured and the attempts of the nuns to convert impressionable young school girls to their religion. Another allegation, more horrific and

---

1. A revival of sisterhoods had taken place in the Anglican Church during the nineteenth century. Peter Anson estimated that over sixty sisterhoods had been founded during that time. See Anson, *Call of the Cloister*.

inhumane, also blackened the history of conventual life during the nineteenth century, namely, that during the Middle Ages and the Inquisition rebellious or sinful nuns were frequently put to death for their transgressions by immuring them within the walls of convents, where they would die a hideous death. Roman Catholics naturally tried to discredit these hateful assertions. When Henry Rider Haggard, the popular Victorian novelist, mentioned in *Montezuma's Daughter* that he had personally seen the remains of an immured or walled-up nun and her child in a Mexico City museum, he started a brief but vigorous controversy with defenders of Roman Catholicism.

The Reformation era saw an outpouring of works that critiqued the monastic life and pointed out a series of abuses that justified the dissolution of religious houses during the reign of Henry VIII. But the criticisms of the inhumane conditions of monasteries and convents continued after England declared her independence from Rome. Incarceration or confinement within the cloister became a recognized abuse. In 1776, Edward Gibbon published the first volume of *The Decline and Fall of the Roman Empire*, and had some harsh words to say about the cruel practices of religious houses, including imprisonment. After enumerating the usual catalogue of abuses and strange acts of Roman Catholic mortification, Gibbon talked about the punishment of recalcitrant monks at the hands of "capricious" superiors: "the slightest offences were corrected by disgrace or confinement, extraordinary fasts, or bloody flagellation."[2] Other authors, however, focused their attacks against convents and emphasized the cruel abuses allegedly committed against the sisters. The story of the imprisoned or walled-up nun entered English literary life in the late eighteenth century.

Matthew "Monk" Lewis introduced the evils of a Spanish convent to the English public in 1796 with the publication of *The Monk*. In addition to the sins of the profligate monk, Ambrosio, Lewis described for the reader numerous evils of convent life, including murder, torture, and the imprisonment of Sr. Agnes, a nun who had become pregnant. In a vivid and emotional scene, the superior of the convent explained the punishment this nun must endure:

> Listen then to the sentence of St Clare. Beneath these Vaults there exist Prisons, intended to receive such criminals as yourself . . . Artfully is their entrance concealed, and She who enters

2. Gibbon, *Decline and Fall*, 596.

them, must resign all hopes of liberty, . . . Food shall be supplied to you, but not sufficient for the indulgence of appetite . . . Chained down in one of these secret dungeons, shut out from the world and light for ever . . . thus must you groan away the remainder of your days.[3]

After the death of her child in the dungeon, Sr. Agnes was eventually rescued. Lewis talked about a nun who was placed in confinement to live out her days separated from the other nuns. Nineteenth-century England was acquainted with other stories of alleged imprisonment within convent walls that were not taken from the pages of fiction.

A well-publicized incident from Europe, namely, the incarceration in Cracow of a Carmelite nun, Sr. Barbara Ubryk, and several stories of confinement and imprisonment in nunneries on English soil, and a number of examples of so-called "escaped nuns" eventually added fuel to the belief that heartless superiors occasionally imprisoned disobedient nuns.[4] But none of these nineteenth century stories of confinement suggested that the victims were literally walled up or immured. Immurement meant loss of freedom and personal liberty, not a punishment or penalty where nuns were placed within the walls of a convent and left to suffer a horrible death. But another interpretation of immurement also became popular during this time. A number of writers and scholars told their readers that throughout the past sinful and unchaste nuns had suffered death by immurement. These individuals never hinted that this wicked practice had continued into the modern era, but nonetheless the image of the walled-up or entombed nun became a powerful image in Victorian anti-Catholicism.

The Romantic Movement of the nineteenth century glorified things medieval, and in a way contributed to the revival of the monastic life for both men and women. One of its leading and most popular writers, Sir Walter Scott, published *Marmion* in 1868, a poem dealing with convent life, and some remarks he made in footnotes helped to perpetuate the myth of the nuns who were sentenced to death by immurement in the

---

3. Lewis, *Monk*, 408.

4. Numerous publications and hostile preachers accused Roman Catholic convents of stripping nuns of their freedom and liberty. In some instances, the superior did restrain the recalcitrant nun within the convent. If a nun happened to run away from her convent, critics painted this incident as an escape from a situation similar to a prison. In the case of Sr. Barbara, the superior claimed that she was restrained because she was mentally ill. See Smith, *Calumnies against Convents*.

walls of a convent. Commenting on "penitential vaults," Scott noted that these vaults "were the *Geissel-gewolbe* [sic] of German convents."[5] Later in the poem, Scott described a frightening scene: "And now that blind old Abbot rose, To speak the Chapter's doom, On those the wall was to enclose, Alive within the tomb."[6] And the author made a startling accusation in a footnote to explain these words. "It is well known," Scott pointed out, "that the religious, who broke their vows of chastity, were subjected to the same penalty as the Roman vestals in a similar case."[7] He described how a small niche was carved out in the wall of a convent to receive the sinful nun. She received some food and water, and then her grave, marked with the words *vade in pace*,[8] was sealed. Convent officials, according to this footnote, did not resort to this punishment frequently "in latter times," but then Scott made a startling statement that some anti-Catholic writers would later repeat: "among the ruins of the abbey of Coldingham were some years ago discovered the remains of a female skeleton, which, from the shape of the niche and the position of the figure, seemed to be that of an immured nun."[9] The legend that the Roman Catholic Church killed disobedient or profligate religious by the punishment of immurement existed outside the world of fiction. In 1851, for example, John Henry Newman gave a series of lectures to the members of the Oratory in Birmingham dealing with the status of Catholicism in England and touched briefly on the myth of ecclesiastical imprisonment. Newman reminded his audience that some people still believed that convents and monasteries, including the Oratory, maintained cells where murders and immurings took place.[10]

Rumors of the imprisonment and immuring of helpless Roman Catholic nuns titillated and delighted some opponents of Roman Catholicism, but were these stories of torture and death credible? Some dismissed the allegations as examples of pure fantasy and vile religious

---

5. Scott, *Marmion*, 84.

6. Ibid., 2.25.1–4.

7. Ibid., 91.

8. Scott accepted the following translations for *vade in pace*: "part in peace," or "go into peace."

9. Scott, *Marmion*, 91. Coldingham was an Anglo-Saxon "double monastery," which included both monks and nuns, located in the northern part of the Kingdom of Bernicia. See Bede, *Ecclesiastical History*, and Eckstein, *Women under Monasticism*.

10. Newman, "Fable," 121–22.

prejudice. On the other hand, some trusted the verdict of Sir Walter Scott. Those who believed that the Catholic Church literally walled up monks and nuns to silence and murder them turned to recent studies of the Inquisition for ammunition. Published in 1871, William Rule's *History of the Inquisition* painted a picture of Fra Tommaso Fabiano di Mileto, who was immured in 1564: "So within four walls built up around him, but with sufficient space to kneel down before a crucifix and an image of the Virgin, this poor man was to be confined . . ."[11] Rule also quoted the testimony of an individual who had seen the bones of people immured in the walls of the Inquisition in Seville.

In 1891, H. Grattan Guinness, evangelical preacher, supporter of foreign missions, and Secretary of the Protestant Alliance, published a poem, "The City of the Seven Hills" complete with illustrations. In the appendix, he stated that during "my recent visit to Mexico, *I saw myself the remains of the victims who had been walled up alive by the Inquisition.*"[12] Guinness quoted a significant passage from Rule's book on the subject, but the most dramatic section was inclusion of two photographs of the skeletal remains of victims who had allegedly been walled up by the Inquisition. Other evidence also came from Mexico. William Butler published *Mexico in Transition* in 1892. This book described the discoveries of bodies that the Inquisition authorities apparently sealed within the convent walls. From the evidence, Butler re-enacted the process of immurement: "He or she (for women were among the number) was placed in the cell, a "brother" of the order who was handy with the trowel was ready to build up the entrance before their face and leave them to a horrible death, while a coat of plaster and whitewash made all invisible, and these fiends in human form may have supposed that they had sealed up their crimes forever and buried their secret beyond discovery."[13] Butler's book also contained photographs of some of these victims and he announced that two bodies had been placed in a museum in Mexico City. Moreover, he noted that "a number of human skeletons

---

11. Rule, *History of the Inquisition*, 2:197.

12. Guinness, *City of the Seven Hills*, 300. The photographs of the victims appear on the following two pages. Chapter 3 of that book, "Rome's Convents," critiqued the alleged abuses of religious life.

13. Butler, *Mexico in Transition*, 294. See also an address that Butler, a "foe of priest-craft," gave in 1888, published as *Roman Catholicism and the Reformation in Mexico*. In the section titled "Secrets of the Prison House," he described the process of immurement carried out by the Inquisition and the discovery of the skeletons in Mexico.

packed together in rows" had also been unearthed.[14] These accounts of the Inquisition's use of immurement as a punishment certainly supplied some solid evidence for the hatred and suspicion of Roman Catholicism that existed in England; they also provided the historical background for a work of fiction by a popular author.

By the l890s, H. Rider Haggard (1856–1925) could draw on many elements to construct a novel dealing with life in sixteenth-century Spain and Mexico: a tradition of anti-Catholicism that stressed abuses in convents, including the incarceration of rebellious or sinful nuns; the well-publicized case of Sr. Barbara, the imprisoned nun of Cracow; stories of nuns who had "escaped" from English convents; recent books dealing with the Inquisition that documented incidents of immuring; and finally, the photographs and testimony of witnesses who saw the remains of victims at a Mexico museum. Haggard's fame and reputation as a writer of fiction were due chiefly to *King Solomon's Mines* (1885) and *She: A History of Adventure* (1887), both set in Africa.[15] Mexico, however, provided the setting for *Montezuma's Daughter*. This romance appeared first in serial form in a London paper, *The Graphic*, during 1893 before it was published as a book in the same year by Longmans, Green and Company. *Montezuma's Daughter* might not have attracted much attention were it not for chapter 10, "The Passing of Isabella de Siguenza," and an explanatory footnote that appeared in the July 29th edition of *The Graphic*. This section of the story described the immuring of a young nun, previously named Isabella, and her illegitimate baby in the presence of monks and nuns. The condemned had broken her religious vows and thus deserved to die for her sins. The author painted the scene of her death in a vivid and chilling manner.

After boasting that England had not engaged in such inhuman punishment as practiced by the Roman Catholic Church, Haggard described the tomb that would soon receive Isabella and her baby. Near the workmen "were squares of dressed stone ranged neatly against the end of the vault, and before them [mother and child] was a niche cut in the thickness of the wall itself, shaped like a large coffin set upon its smaller

---

14. Ibid., 296.

15. For a biography of H. Rider Haggard, see entries in: *Dictionary of Literary Biography. British Short-Fiction Writers, 1880–1914: The Romantic Tradition*; and *The Dictionary of National Biography*.

end."[16] The narrator keenly drew attention to the other coffin-niches already placed within the wall. Eventually the pair were entombed. Haggard's personal comment about the immuring of nuns, which many believed came from the imagination of the novelist, guaranteed that this emotional tale of torture and murder in a convent would not be forgotten soon. After the Dominican priest read the sentence of death by immuring, the reader was directed to a footnote where Haggard stated:

> Lest such cruelty should seem impossible and unprecedented, the writer may mention that in the museum of the city of Mexico he has seen the desiccated body of a young woman which was found immured in the walls of a religious building. With it is the body of an infant. Although the exact cause of her execution remains a matter of conjecture, there can be no doubt as to the manner of her death, for, in addition to other evidences the marks of the rope with which her limbs were bound in life are still distinctly visible. Such in those days were the mercies of religion.

The fame of Rider Haggard and the publication of the story in a book ignited a controversy which would be fought in pamphlets and in the columns of a London paper. Some Roman Catholics, not surprisingly, viewed Haggard's remarks as a slanderous attack against their religion.

Fr Herbert Thurston, SJ (1856–1939) was no stranger to controversy.[17] His books, pamphlets, and articles frequently defended the integrity of Roman Catholicism against prejudiced attacks. In 1892, one year before Haggard's hostile comments about nuns appeared in print, Thurston wrote an article, "Walled-up Alive," for the Jesuit publication, *The Month*. The Catholic Truth Society reprinted the article, with some additional material, in the same year. Fr Thurston's work not only surveyed the recent anti-convent literature, but set the tone or the course that discussion of Haggard's work would take. The Revd W. L. Holland's anti-Catholic lecture, "Convents Romish and Anglican," during which he showed a slide of a skeleton of an immured nun, forced Thurston to take up his pen.[18] He began by recognizing the Protestant stereotype that

---

16. *The Graphic* (London), 29 July 1893.

17. See Crehan, *Father Thurston*. The bibliography shows the extent of this cleric's writings. In addition to Thurston's articles and pamphlets combating prejudice against convents, see also, Thurston, *No Popery*.

18. Holland's lecture was published under the same title by the Church Association and the National Protestant League. In 1895, Holland wrote a book on the subject of walled-up or immured nuns: *Walled Up Nuns and Nuns Walled In*. The twenty illustra-

convents were prisons, and then announced his purpose: "This is what I have tried to do in the pages which follow, with the result that in not one of the alleged instances is there even a fair presumption, much less conclusive proof, that any religious was walled up or starved to death."[19] Thurston admitted that the church had been guilty of "many terrible things" committed in the name of religion in the past, but an appeal to the testimony of people who claimed they saw alleged evidence of immurement in distant countries, such as Mexico, should not be accepted as solid proof.

Thurston began by attacking W. H. Rule's *History of the Inquisition*, and argued that Rule's evidence did not necessarily prove that the Inquisition had actually walled up heretics. Rule had misinterpreted the historical facts. They might have been "confined within four walls" as any other prisoner for punishment. Fr Thurston also dismissed Sir Walter Scott's testimony in *Marmion*. The words *in pace*, he argued, "in no instance have the slightest reference to walling-up alive in the sense of Sir Walter Scott."[20] So-called "prison cells" did exist to restrain "refractory religious," but, Thurston continued, "These cells were in no sense niches in the wall such as Sir Walter Scott has in mind, neither were they walled up, but they were closed with doors like other cells, barred no doubt from the outside by those in charge of the prisoner." Thurston also attacked the findings of the American, H. C. Lea, regarding the torture and punishment associated with the Inquisition. The Jesuit acknowledged Lea's scholarly credentials, but he again repeated his belief that prisoners were not literally walled up and left to die. The authorities incarcerated them, but they were supplied with food. Fr Thurston did not minimize the existence of medieval punishment, but also pointed out that the recent growth of an anti-Catholic tradition had distorted the evidence.

After dismissing the main arguments of these authorities, Fr Thurston returned to Sir Walter Scott. His reputation and popularity counted more than the scholarship of the others, and Scott's reference to the famous nunnery at Coldingham struck closer to home than unknown convents in Spain and Mexico. Thurston mentioned several au-

---

tions of victims served as an additional condemnation of convent life.

19. Thurston, "Walled-up Alive," 174. The Catholic Truth Society published this article, with some additions, in the same year (1892). See "The Immuring of Nuns."

20. Ibid., 178.

thorities that discussed the history of Coldingham, and noted that these and other reputable accounts made no mention of an immured nun discovered in the convent's ruins. Other sources, which Thurston calls "guide books," did make reference to the remains of an immured skeleton found at the nunnery. But he quickly dismissed these antiquarians; historical or archaeological evidence could not support the charges of a nun put to death by immurement at this Anglo-Saxon convent. After discrediting other apparent instances of immurement, for example the legends concerning the burial cell at the Temple Church, Fr Thurston concluded his article by returning to the Revd W. L. Holland's lecture. In it, Holland had made reference to H. Grattan Guinness's eyewitness accounts of seeing the remains of walled-up nuns on a recent trip to Mexico. Thurston, however, told his readers that in southern climates the Capuchins customarily buried their dead "still clothed in the habit . . . fixed upright in a sort of niche, where it is carefully bricked up."[21] Guinness, he argued, probably saw a cemetery similar to where the Capuchins interred their deceased members. Even if an over-zealous religious superior had immured a nun, an isolated even should not discredit the entire Catholic Church. Finally, Thurston expressed surprise at the lack of cases or examples of immured nuns or monks. If it were such a common practice, why the silence? Where was the evidence?

It is not known if H. Rider Haggard had read Fr Thurston's article before the offensive part of *Montezuma's Daughter* appeared in the July 28th edition of *The Graphic*. The response to his short footnote probably shocked him. On August 4th, James Britten, the Honorary Secretary of the Catholic Truth Society, wrote to the editor of *The Graphic* and complained of Haggard's "extremely offensive and untrue assertions with regard to the immuring of nuns and the general management of convents."[22] Britten also expressed regret and disappointment that "a paper which receives considerable support from Catholics should publish so misleading an account of Catholic life and practice." The editor forwarded the complaint to Haggard, who responded to Britten's concerns.

H. Rider Haggard replied and stated that he did not want to engage in a religious controversy, but the tone of Britten's letter demanded an answer. He acknowledged that he was a Protestant, but he had no inten-

---

21. Ibid., 193.
22. Britten to Editor of *The Graphic*, 4 August 1893; printed in *The Pall Mall Gazette*, 17 January 1894.

tion "to give pain to yourself or to any member of the Roman Catholic faith."[23] In fact, Haggard admitted that he had "the greatest veneration for that faith . . ." The author expressed surprise, however, that an incident in a story set in the sixteenth century could "possibly have given offence to the members of a serious society." He did not intend the immurement scene to be interpreted as a commentary on contemporary Catholicism, but he did believe that nuns who had broken their vows of chastity in the Middle Ages often suffered the penalty of death by immurement. Haggard then repeated his contention, which he had stated earlier in the offensive footnote, that he had seen the skeleton of a young woman and a baby who had been immured alive. He reminded James Britten of Sir Walter Scott's poem and suggested that Britten personally investigate the human remains found recently at an old religious house at Waltham Cross, Essex. Haggard concluded his reply by deploring the past horrors committed in the name of religion, but could not understand Britten's objections namely, the "offensive and untrue" assertion of the immurement of nuns. Moreover, he noted, historical scholarship provided "sufficient evidence to justify the use of a similar incident in a romance."

Britten responded immediately to Haggard's letter. He assured the novelist that 'I did not imagine that you had any intention of attacking Catholics."[24] Four days later, he sent Haggard a copy of Fr Thurston's *Immuring of Nuns*, published by The Catholic Truth Society, which refuted Sir Walter Scott and others who believed that nuns in the past had been walled up to punish them by death. But Haggard, as he admitted earlier in the correspondence, did not want to become involved in a debate about religion, and chose not to respond to these letters from Britten. After a third communication asking for a reply the author finally acknowledged Britten's correspondence and told him that he believed cases of immuring of nuns "were rarer than is supposed."[25]

Fr Herbert Thurston jumped into the fray and published an article in *The Month* titled, "Mr Rider Haggard and the Immuring of Nuns."[26] Thurston began by immediately assaulting Haggard: "Seeing that the writer commands a large public, and that it is his pleasant conceit to pose as a man of erudition and a serious student of history his attack may

23. Haggard to Britten, *The Graphic*, 9 August 1893; ibid.
24. Britten to Haggard, 9 August 1893; ibid.
25. Quoted in Britten to Haggard, 6 September 1893; ibid.
26. Thurston, "Mr Rider Haggard and the Immuring of Nuns."

be considered of sufficient importance to our returning to the subject."[27] Prejudice died hard, he argued, and Catholics should not take abuse or calumny passively, especially when a popular newspaper such as *The Graphic* spread the offensive rumors. Thurston again strayed from the path of an objective spokesman for Catholicism and attacked Haggard's literary skills in general, and pointed out that his works, although widely read, had decreased in popularity. He finally discussed the offending scene of immurement in *Montezuma's Daughter* and the offensive footnote. Fr Thurston acknowledged that cells were constructed to house refractory monks and nuns, but no evidence existed to support the walling up or the immurement of religious men and women as a death penalty. Thurston then turned his attention to Haggard's inflammatory contention that he had seen the remains of a woman and her infant while in Mexico City.

Thurston simply stated that Haggard lacked any evidence or proof for his words. In fact, he even questioned if the novelist's "memory or imagination is not playing him tricks."[28] Fr Thurston suggested that the bodies that Haggard saw might be members of an ancient institution similar to the Roman Vestal Virgins who sentenced their members who violated their vows of chastity to death by immuring them. Even if a wicked or evil superior did punish a nun for sins against chastity, Thurston argued, no reason could justify the murder of the innocent baby! Therefore, according to this logic, this alleged case of immurement never took place. Moreover, the Inquisition could not carry out a death sentence; the secular authorities put the victim to death. Fr Thurston believed that the discovery of human remains in Mexico could not be trustworthy evidence. Consequently, "nothing short, in fact, of the testimony of eyewitnesses can justify us in accepting any cases of immuring."[29] No solid or reliable evidence, however, supported the alleged cases of immurement in Europe, at Coldingham, or at Waltham Cross. In fact, it appeared that Haggard had consulted an article on monasticism written by R. F. Littledale for the *Encyclopaedia Britannica*, which was critical of the religious life and contained historical inaccuracies.[30] "But great is the

---

27. Ibid., 14.
28. Ibid., 21.
29. Ibid., 22–23.
30. See Littledale, "Monachism." In addition to Thurston's charges of inaccuracies, the author did exhibit a generally hostile and critical view of monasticism. Littledale even drew attention to Sir Walter Scott's belief in the existence of a skeleton of an

power of the imagination, especially the trained imagination of an historical novelist."[31] Fr Thurston ended his article with another personal attack on Haggard. "Enough has been said," he pointed out, "to show the utter worthlessness of the evidence on which it has been sought to justify a gross and offensive libel."[32] Thurston even quoted an unlikely ally, Oscar Wilde, who had earlier described Haggard and his literary style in *The Decay of Lying*: "who really has, or had once, the makings of a perfectly magnificent liar, he is now so afraid of being suspected of genius that when he does tell us anything marvellous, he feels bound to invent a personal reminiscence, and to put it into a footnote as a land of cowardly corporation."[33]

H. Rider Haggard responded quickly to Fr Thurston's attack. He wrote to the editor of *The Pall Mall Gazette* and enclosed a copy of the correspondence which had taken place between himself and James Britten during the previous August, which the newspaper printed along with Haggard's response to Thurston. Thus began a heated exchange of letters in the columns of this paper. Haggard also acknowledged that he had read Thurston's recent article, and he accepted "the onslaught" of the Jesuit and The Catholic Truth Society with "Christian resignation."[34] The author then talked about the contents of his footnote and stated that he could not provide the proof that his critics demanded. However, Haggard maintained, Thurston "should learn to discriminate between the fibre of a romance and positive allegations such as I have made in this footnote." After repeating his recollection of his visit to the Mexico City museum, Haggard sarcastically replied to the remark that his memory had deceived or played tricks on him and stated that he had also seen the remains of another immured woman. He did admit that he "may have been misinformed as to the origin of these relics; but here I may add that in no country does religious discipline seem to have been more rigorous in past generations than in Mexico." Haggard reminded his readers that the Inquisition did commit horrible deeds and put people to death.

Haggard then talked about the skeletal remains he saw in a dungeon near Waltham Cross. Thurston, in his mind, had failed to disprove alle-

---

immured nun at the Coldingham nunnery.
31. Thurston, "Mr Rider Haggard and the Immuring of Nuns," 28.
32. Ibid., 29.
33. Wilde, *The Decay of Lying*, 973.
34. *The Pall Mall Gazette*, 17 March 1894.

gations of immurement there. Again, Haggard conceded he might have been given false information. Workmen had supposedly discovered the remains, "but it may be that the tale is false, and no such skeletons were found." Consequently, he called upon "the local antiquaries" to investigate the story and even challenged Thurston to visit the house in question. Haggard chose to write to *The Pall Mall Gazette* not to answer his critics' "discourtesies" or to respond to Fr Thurston's article, but rather

> to ask some of the many antiquaries, whom you must number among your readers, to favour those who are interested in the matter with their views as to the alleged walling up of nuns who had broken their vows of chastity, and with arguments deduced from the available facts less impassioned and one-sided than those that emanate from the Catholic Truth Society.

Did immurement of sinful nuns take place in the past? Haggard admitted that his interest in the matter, "formerly impersonal and artistic, has grown quick under the lash of the Rev. Herbert Thurston's wrath . . ." and he eagerly awaited the verdict of experts. Moreover, he believed the reaction of some Roman Catholics to a romance which took place three centuries ago was "nothing short of ridiculous." "It is fortunately impossible to imagine any society representative of the Anglican branch of the Christian Church," Haggard concluded, "opening its heavy guns upon a novelist who wrote in an adverse spirit, say, of the persecution of the Jesuits in the eighteenth century, or the plundering of the religious houses by Henry VIII."

People took up this challenge and began to send their opinions to *The Pall Mall Gazette*. A Roman Catholic layman, not an antiquary or expert in history or archeology, responded first. Haggard, who had no solid evidence for his assertion that unchaste nuns suffered death by immurement in Mexico, at Waltham Cross, or at Coldingham, upset English Roman Catholics, this correspondent maintained, because a number of his countrymen still continued to identify nineteenth-century Catholicism with the practices of the Inquisition.[35] The writer noted that some people believed that a skeleton of a woman could be found beneath the Middle Temple Hall, but did this suggest that "the benchers of that honourable society made a practice of immuring their

---

35. Ibid., 18 January 1894.

wives who proved faithless, or barristers who violated the rules of professional etiquette"? On the following day, another author defended Haggard by pointing out that examples of immurement could be found in works dealing with the Inquisition, especially H. C. Lea's *History of the Inquisition in the Middle Ages*.[36] A Roman Catholic writer hesitated to condemn Haggard by suggesting that he did not consciously intend to deceive or malign Catholics. "We do not accuse you of falsehood, but we think you might correct the errors pointed out to you, and not be so positive as to points on which you may have been misled."[37] Even a Frenchman entered the debate and presented evidence to show that immuring under certain conditions, that is a voluntary, devotional practice by which a person withdrew from the world or a judicial sentence handed down by a secular court, had existed in medieval France.[38] But this letter failed to address charges that the Church had condemned immoral nuns to death by immurement.

The controversy began to heat up when James Britten and Fr Thurston joined in the correspondence. In *The Pall Mall Gazette* of 20 January 1894, James Britten, the Honorary Secretary of the Catholic Truth Society, protested vehemently against the publication of his earlier correspondence with H. Rider Haggard. He also pointed out that Thurston did not belong to the Catholic Truth Society, and again repeated his main objection to Haggard's footnote, which "Catholics regard as an offensive calumny."[39] Britten emphasized Haggard's faulty evidence and lack of proof in regard to Sir Walter Scott's poem, alleged European examples of immurement, the remains associated with Waltham Cross, and the absence of solid documentation to substantiate his experiences in Mexico City.

Herbert Thurston wrote to the paper two days later, and began by apologizing for his remark about Haggard's "imagination or his memory . . . playing him tricks."[40] He also restated his main criticism of the

36. Ibid., 19 January 1894.

37. Ibid., 20 January 1894.

38. Ibid., 22 January 1894. In respect to the judicial sentence, the author gave the example of a woman convicted of killing her husband. "The Parliament [sic] of Paris sentenced her to be "imprisoned and immured for ever in the cemetery of the Holy Innocents in a little house which, at her own expense, and with the first money derived from her estate, shall be built *against the church, as was the ancient custom*."

39. Ibid., 20 January 1894.

40. Ibid., 22 January 1894.

novelist's scene where the nun was sent to her death by immurement. "This he represents not merely as an isolated instance of cruelty, but as a common practice in the sixteenth century sanctioned by the highest ecclesiastical authority." Moreover, Haggard still had not produced any proof to back up his claims of immurement. "But where is the evidence even for a single instance of the sort?"

H. Grattan Guinness quickly answered the challenge of these two Roman Catholic writers and their cries for evidence, and stated that he had seen "these remains in the city of Mexico."[41] Moreover, Guinness had observed the remains of an additional victim he examined in another Mexican city. For proof, he directed the skeptical reader to consult his book, *The City of the Seven Hills*, which contained photographs of walled-up victims.

For the next week, people could read letters that either defended or supported H. Rider Haggard and the belief that the Inquisition had sentenced erring nuns to death by immurement. The latter group quoted passages from history books, such as Rule's study on the Inquisition and Gibbon's *The Decline and Fall of the Roman Empire*, which described the horrors and tortures of the Inquisition, or from travelers who had recently seen the remains of immured nuns. With few exceptions, these writers repeated the opinions contained in the earlier letters on the subject, namely, that the walling up of nuns did happen. One writer noted that the public could view the mummies of immured victims on exhibition in America.[42] Another correspondent deviated from the subject somewhat and argued that tales of incarcerated nuns who had escaped from their convents had recently become a familiar item in anti-Catholic rhetoric in England and should also be treated as a fanciful myth. In addition to the constant refrain that no solid evidence of immurement could be found, one writer did offer a believable explanation for the skeletons or mummies found in Mexico. "Until quite recently (namely, till about 1870) every one who died in Mexico was buried or walled up in a masonry tomb."[43] Because of the wet soil of the area surrounding Mexico City, bodies were placed within walls. Surprisingly, no critic of H. Rider Haggard addressed the photographic evidence offered by H. Grattan Guinness.

41. Ibid., 23 January 1894.
42. Ibid., 23.
43. Ibid., 29 January 1894.

This debate came to a climax in the last two days of January with letters by Fr Thurston and Haggard. Again, Thurston simply dismissed those who supported Haggard; they relied on false or fabricated evidence for their belief in the immurement of nuns. Even some scholars, such as Henry Charles Lea who condemned the Inquisition and its use of torture, never accused the "Inquisition, or the religious orders, of putting offenders to death by walling them up in niches."[44] Details in W. H. Rule's *History of the Inquisition*, a main source for the belief in walled-up nuns, were "inconsistent and demonstrably inaccurate." But Fr Thurston offered no new information or defense of his position. In the same edition, *The Pall Mall Gazette* announced that correspondence on the subject of the immuring of nuns would end on the following day. The paper, it appears, recognized that the debate had run its course and nothing original could be added to the discussion. In fact, the arguments had become repetitive and redundant. It was fitting that Haggard, who sparked the controversy with a footnote in a novel, should also have the final word.

Haggard's long letter began with a defense of his integrity against accusations made by Fr Herbert Thurston: the novelist did not tell "a most deliberate and flagrant falsehood..."[45] Haggard promised to return to this charge of dishonesty later, but then turned his attention to the question of immurement. He admitted: "I was in error when I stated in my letter to Mr Britten on August 9th that I believed the evidence of history to prove that nuns who had broken their vows had been immured in the wails of convents."

> This opinion I arrived at too hastily after consulting such authorities as I had at hand; but further research, and communications that I have received from gentlemen learned in ecclesiastical history, show me that whether or not the taking of "the life of a nun for a grave moral transgression might be conceivably be defended as an act of judicial authority," as Father Thurston suggests in his article, there is no proof that so barbarous a punishment was ever enforced, at any rate in this country.

Haggard, however, refused to absolve the Catholic Church and the Inquisition for their involvement in torture, inhumane activities and death. "The immurement in 'Montezuma's Daughter,'" he pointed out,

---

44. Ibid., 30 January 1894.
45. Ibid., 31 January 1894.

"is supposed to have occurred in Spain, where, as I presume, the most ardent defenders of the Inquisition will admit, cruelties as great or greater, were in those days commonly practiced in the name of religion."

More serious in Haggard's mind than this error or interpretation of fact was "Father Thurston's insinuation against my veracity." Did the skeletal remains at Waltham Cross spring from the imagination of a novelist? Did any evidence exist? In his defense, Haggard stated that two correspondents had written to him and confirmed his descriptions of these bodies. But Thurston's hostile words about the footnote in *Montezuma's Daughter* posed more difficult problems for Haggard, and he reproduced the footnote for the readers of *The Pall Mall Gazette* to examine. Fr Thurston's constant demands for proof and the need for other witnesses to corroborate what he saw in Mexico City irked the author. Haggard drew the attention of the public to H. Grattan Guinness's book and photographs and the personal testimony of the Revd William Butler and his pictures, which W. H. Rule reproduced in woodcut for his book on the Inquisition The imagination of a novelist, he stated, certainly did not create these horrible images. "The remains are to be see in the museum of Mexico and unless Dr Guinness, Dr Rule, and Dr Butler have entered into a conspiracy to deceive their readers it appears certain that they were found immured in the 'walls of a religious building,' namely, in one of the palaces of the Inquisition." Haggard might have admitted his mistake in respect to immurement in nunneries, but he still believed that the victims had been walled up as a death penalty in the walls of an Inquisition building. The skeletons did not come from a common cemetery as Fr Thurston argued. On the other hand, Haggard did not want to offend or insult Roman Catholics. "But had I known that it would prove a stumbling-block and a cause of offence to certain members of the Roman Catholic faith," Haggard pointed out, "I should have been inclined to leave it out, since I have no wish to give pain to them, or indeed to the followers of any creed, and I only send you this further evidence for publication in order to vindicate myself against the attacks and insinuations of Fr Thurston."

The announcement by *The Pall Mall Gazette* that the editor had decided to terminate the discussion of the topic of *Montezuma's Daughter* and the alleged immurement of nuns did not stop all discussion by the main participants. Haggard, who had admitted his mistake and had apologized to Roman Catholics for any hurt, tried to end the controversy by including a retraction in later editions of this novel. Beginning in the 1895 edition, Haggard first reprinted the original and questionable footnote and then acknowledged that the "statements herein contained have been made the subject of much public dispute."[46] "Those who question their accuracy allege, amongst other things, that the bodies spoken of were taken from graves and exhibited in the museum at Mexico, not as a testimony to the terrors of the Inquisition, but to exemplify the preservative effects of soil and climate upon the human tissues. The Author therefore withdraws the note, and expresses regret that, in all good faith, he should have set down as fact that which has been proved to be a matter of controversy." In spite of the animosity he held against Fr Thurston, Haggard did not address the issue again. Thurston, however, could not remain quiet.

Thurston did not graciously accept Haggard's retraction and expression of regret. In an article written for *The Month* shortly after Haggard's final letter to the newspaper, Thurston noted that the author of *Montezuma's Daughter* "has found himself obliged by their [historians and antiquaries] representations to withdraw from an untenable position."[47] The Jesuit certainly savored the victory: "Of course the retreat is effected in accordance with the immemorial custom of strategists, under cover of a good deal of smoke and amid the noise of a seemingly vigorous cannonade, but the evacuation is none the less complete." His sarcasm rose to the surface when he belittled Haggard's sources, which be believed were flawed. According to Thurston, it surprised him that H. Rider Haggard, "a very superior person," should pin "his faith to the lucubrations of the Reverend Doctors Rule, Butler, and Guinness, and joining hands in one of their 'blameless dances' over the prostrate form of the Roman Inquisition."[48] If people did not believe him, Fr Thurston challenged his critics to search the records of the Inquisition which had been preserved in libraries in the British Isles, in Latin America, and on the Continent. Fr Thurston's last word on *Montezuma's Daughter* also appeared in the Jesuit publication, *The Month*. This short article contained an English translation of a Mexican newspaper which printed the correspondence of two Mexicans. One, the Librarian of the National Museum in Mexico City, commented on

---

46. Haggard, "Prefatory Notes," in *Montezuma's Daughter*.
47. Thurston, "Another Mexican Mare's-Nest," 323.
48. Ibid., 324.

the "mummies" in the museum. They were not the remains of nuns, and moreover, the Inquisition and religious superiors never used immurement as a punishment. They constructed prisons for that purpose.[49] Fr Thurston believed that he had successfully trumped H. Rider Haggard.

Eventually the emotions over the question of immured nuns subsided. After the public retraction, the ghost of Haggard's now celebrated scene of convent death and torture lingered on for a few years in the minds of some anti-Catholics,[50] but it never achieved the notoriety and acrimony which characterized the response it drew from Roman Catholic writers, especially Fr Herbert Thurston and James Britten. No rational person believed that convents had in recent years put sinful or disobedient members to death by cementing them up in walls. Immurement or the act of walling up, for the foe of convents and Catholicism, meant the loss of traditional English freedoms, and thus nunneries should come under state control or inspection. Roman Catholics viewed H. Rider Haggard's scene of immurement and his personal testimony as an insult, and they demanded an apology. His supporters argued that Roman Catholics had indeed killed people by immurement. Consequently, the Catholic Church, and not the novelist, should express regret for its sins of the past. The debate started by *Montezuma's Daughter* testifies to the extent of religious prejudice that existed beneath the surface of Victorian society. Even an innocuous comment in a romantic novel could stir up ancient religious feuds or suspicions.

49. Thurston, "Note to the Article on 'Mr Rider Haggard and the Immuring of Nuns.'"

50. Fr. Herbert Thurston continued to write against the belief in the immurement or walling up of sinful nuns, and The Catholic Truth Society published two of his later pamphlets. The first, "The Myth of the Walled-up Nun" (1902), contained the same material, with some minor additions, as his January 1894 article in *The Month*. "A Tale of Mexican Horrors" (1904) devoted the first few pages to the debate surrounding *Montezuma's Daughter*. The rest of the pamphlet discussed other allegations of torture and immurement in Mexico. In 1895, W. Lancelot Holland wrote *Walled Up Nuns and Nuns Walled In*. This book reprinted large sections of Haggard's description of the immurement scene in *Montezuma's Daughter* and also printed some of the correspondence that appeared in *The Pall Mall Gazette*. Holland's book contains the photographs of the alleged victims of clerical immurement that Haggard and others were referred to in the recent debate. The author also included some historical background and evidence dealing with Sir Walter Scott's poem and other stories dealing with immurement. The myth of Maria Monk occupies a prominent place in this anti-Catholic book. Holland probably did not believe that nuns were literally immured in late nineteenth-century convents. However, ". . . in our CLOISTERED Convents more especially, refractory Nuns are to-day undergoing severities to both body and mind, even more awful, because more lasting, than being actually WALLED UP ALIVE."

Bibliography

Britten, James. Letter to Haggard. 11 August 1893.

———. "Letter to the Editor." *The Graphic.* 4 August 1893. Reprinted in *The Pall Mall Gazette.* 17 January 1894.

Butler, William. *Mexico in Transition: From the Power of Political Romanism to Civil and Religious Liberty.* New York: Hunt & Eaton, 1892.

———. *Roman Catholicism and the Reformation in Mexico, with Details of the Inquisition and the Expulsion of the Jesuits.* Belfast: University Printing and Publishing House, 1888.

Crehan, Joseph. *Father Thurston: A Memoir with a Bibliography of His Writings.* London: Sheed & Ward, 1952.

Eckstein, L. *Women under Monasticism.* Cambridge: Cambridge University Press, 1896.

Gibbon, Edward. *The Decline and Fall of the Roman Empire.* Chicago: Encyclopedia Britannica, 1990.

Guinness, H. Grattan. *The City of the Seven Hills: An Illustrated Poem.* Boston: Advent Christian Publication Society, 1891.

Haggard, H. Rider. *Montezuma's Daughter.* London: Longmans, Green, 1895.

Holland, W. Lancelot. *Walled Up Nuns and Nuns Walled In.* London: Kensit, 1895.

Lea, H. C. *History of the Inquisition in the Middle Ages.* New York: Harper, 1887.

Lewis, Matthew. *The Monk.* New York: Oxford University Press, 1980.

Littledale, R. F. "Monachism." In *Encyclopaedia Britannica.* 9th ed.

Newman, John Henry. "Fable the Basis of the Protestant View." In *Lectures on the Present Position of Catholics in England*, 83–126. London: Longmans, Green, 1918.

Rule, William Harris. *History of the Inquisition: From Its Establishment in the Twelfth Century to Its Extinction in the Nineteenth.* 2 vols. London: Hamilton, Adams, 1874.

Scott, Walter Sir. *Marmion: A Poem in Six Cantos.* New York: Crowell, 1844.

Smith, S. *Calumnies against Convents.* London: The Catholic Truth Society, 1894.

Thurston, Herbert. "Another Mexican Mare's-Nest." *The Month* (Mar 1894) 323–24.

———. "The Immuring of Nuns." London: The Catholic Truth Society, 1892.

———. "Mr Rider Haggard and the Immuring of Nuns." *The Month* (Jan 1894) 14–23.

———. "The Myth of the Walled-up Nun." London: The Catholic Truth Society, 1904.

———. *No Popery: Chapters on Anti-Papal Prejudice.* London: Longmans, Green, 1930.

———. "Note to the Article on 'Mr Rider Haggard and the Immuring of Nuns.'" *The Month* (Apr 1894) 574–78.

———. "A Tale of Mexican Horrors." London: The Catholic Truth Society, 1904.

———. "Walled-up Alive." *The Month*, June 1892, 174–93.

Wilde, Oscar. *The Decay of Lying.* In *Complete Works of Oscar Wilde.* Edited by J. B. Foreman. London: Collins, 1971.

3

Two Lectures at Bath

*The Rev. M. Hobart Seymour and
Cardinal Nicholas Wiseman and the Nunnery Question*

IN 1829, GEORGE IV gave royal assent to Catholic Emancipation. By this act, promoted by Wellington's Tory government, Roman Catholics were admitted to Parliament. It appeared that the country had finally welcomed Catholics as loyal citizens after centuries of suspicion and mistrust, and some historians interpret this legislation as an example of liberty and political maturity in England. John Wolffe, however, sounds a note of caution. "Such judgements on Emancipation must not obscure the fact that its effect was, if anything, to strengthen active anti-Catholicism."[1] Prejudice against Catholicism, always present since the Reformation, became more public. "Early in 1831 a Catholic writer complained of the polemical onslaught which was being waged against the faith, on platforms and in the press, associated with the gross misrepresentations of Catholic practices and principles."[2] But the Catholic Church continued to grow and expand, and Rome recognized this spiritual maturity. On September 29, 1850, Pope Pius IX restored the Roman Catholic hierarchy in England and Wales. This act of "papal aggression" insulted and enraged many non-Catholics, who expressed their angry feelings in public demonstrations and secured a piece of legislation, the Ecclesiastical Titles Act. The words and actions of the newly appointed

---

1. Wolffe, *Protestant Crusade*, 1.
2. Ibid.

Cardinal Archbishop of Westminster, Nicholas Wiseman (1802–65), did nothing to ease the growing hostility against Catholicism. One Roman Catholic institution, convents, attracted scrutiny. *The Awful Disclosures of Maria Monk*, published in 1836, had started a tradition of books, pamphlets, and personal testimonies that critiqued the conventual life and exposed alleged evils. State inspection of English convents soon became one remedy against these abuses, and people encouraged this remedy in public lectures. In May 1852, the Rev. Michael Hobart Seymour (1800–1874), a supporter of state inspection of convents, gave a speech at Bath critical of nunneries. Shortly afterwards, Cardinal Wiseman arrived in the same city and defended sisterhoods against the accusations expressed in Seymour's antagonistic talk.

Throughout his clerical career, Michael Hobart Seymour had demonstrated his hostility toward Roman Catholicism. He received his B. A. (1823) and M. A. (1832) from Trinity College, Dublin, and was ordained a deacon in 1823 and a priest in the following year. Seymour ministered as a cleric in Ireland and also served as secretary to the Irish Protestant Reformation Society until 1834, when he moved to London, which was home to several anti-Catholic organizations. His attacks against that religion continued in the capital, where he lectured in defense of Protestant principles and attacked Roman Catholic practices and beliefs at St. George the Martyr, Southwark, and at St. Anne's, Blackfriars. Seymour also served as traveling secretary to the Reformation Society, founded in 1827 to promote and strengthen Protestantism through education, conversions, and publications. The Rev. M. Hobart Seymour soon made his mark as a writer. In 1834, he published a two-volume abridgment of *Foxe's Book of Martyrs*, the classic exposition of the wickedness of Roman Catholicism. "Seymour's edition, frequently reprinted as one of the most popular versions of the *Acts and Monuments*, is notable for the apocalyptic rhetoric with which the editor describes the Catholic menace, held back only by a few great works such as Foxe's and the vigilance of English Protestants . . ."[3] Seymour's choice of words and phrases in the introduction were intended to alert loyal English Protestants to the dangers of the Roman religion. "This state of things is pregnant with the most disastrous consequences to the Protestantism of England . . ."[4]

3. Wooden, *John Foxe*, 103. For biographical information on the Rev. Michael Hobart Seymour, see Boase, *Modern English Biography*, 3:507; and Crockford's *Clerical Directory*, 1874.

4. Quoted in Wooden, *John Foxe*, 103.

And he asked his readers, "Shall it be, that the souls of our children, and our children's children, shall become the merchandize of Friars, and their morals become contaminated by the Priests of the Confessional?" Death, destruction, and desolation were preferable to the triumph of popery in England. Seymour's fame and reputation as an anti-Catholic writer and speaker, however, grew after he left London.

The Rev. Michael Hobart Seymour moved to Bath in 1844, and he would live and write in this Georgian city until his death in 1874. Soon after his arrival, Seymour continued his attack against the Church of Rome in lectures and by publishing a number of books that emphasized the serious threat posed by the Catholics to the English way of life.[5] Accompanied by his wife, he even journeyed into the enemy's capital, Rome, and traveled throughout Italy to obtain information for his books and public presentations. In addition to identifying the doctrinal errors of Roman Catholicism, such as, papal infallibility, intercession of saints, relics, indulgences, mariology, and transubstantiation, he also discussed some of the abuses that existed within Roman Catholic institutions. Seymour mentioned convents as one of these modern scandals, and warned his audience against the insidious nature of sisterhoods.

On April 21, 1852, the Rev. M. Hobart Seymour gave a lecture on nunneries at the Assembly Rooms, Bath. The audience, composed of clergymen and gentlemen but no women, numbered over fifty. W. T. Blair was in the chair and told the listeners that he would offer no apology for a lecture dealing with convents in England.[6] Nunneries, he pointed out, claimed exemption from inspection by the state. By their very nature, convents infringed on the freedom and liberty of their inhabitants. Blair did not argue that sisterhoods had no right to exist, "but looking to the immature age at which females were induced to devote themselves to that kind of life, and to the abuses to which . . . their inmates might be subject, he thought those establishments should be placed under reasonable legal supervision." After a few introductory remarks about the competency and the authority of Seymour to speak about convents, he took his seat, and the Rev. M. Hobart Seymour began his long critique of

5. Seymour, *A Pilgrimage to Rome*; *Mornings among the Jesuits in Rome*; *Certainty Unattainable in the Church of Rome*; *Evenings with the Romanists*; and *The Causes of the Reformation*.

6. *The Bath and Cheltenham Gazette* (Bath), 28 April 1852. This edition printed lengthy excerpts of Seymour's speech and indicated when the crowd interrupted with loud cheers or applause.

convents in England. Seymour commenced by questioning the Roman assumption that the celibate state was superior to marriage, and then started his talk by discussing the two varieties of sisterhoods, namely, the cloistered and the active. The woman who lived a cloistered existence had eliminated from her life all "sympathies, and the ties of human life"[7] and had renounced all family relationships. He again used the image of a prison to describe the inhuman existence that the nun endured. "Like a bird within a cage, she must learn to live for the rest of her existence within the narrow limits of her nunnery." Seymour attacked the Roman Catholic myth of conventual happiness and the contentment of the nuns, and told his listeners that convents resembled more the "bridewells" and penitentiaries of England. He described the sorrow, hopelessness, and despair of the nuns. Seymour also emphasized the prevalence of insanity and related the following testimony of an unnamed informant to his audience: "He [the informant] stated that this was the melancholy destiny of the larger portion of the nuns of Rome, the majority of whom ... died, before twenty-five years of age of madness!"[8]

After this scathing portrayal of cloistered sisterhoods, Seymour outlined a brief history of convents. Quite early in their development, he argued, sisterhoods had become identified with places where females could flee to avoid marriage or were associated with "ecclesiastical prisons" where politically dangerous women could be confined. In other words, religion per se had little to do with the growth of nunneries. "It was the system of the age—a system by which the ambitious, the powerful, and the intriguing, when they found persons inconveniently in their way, removed them out of the way, by placing the man in a convent [that is, a monastery], and enclosing the woman in a nunnery."[9] Moreover, the conventual life soon developed into an acceptable a place where families provided for their unmarried, younger daughters. Seymour must have shocked his audience of Protestant gentlemen by relating the sad story of a young girl who stabbed herself rather than spend her life in a sisterhood. This scandalous system, he continued, grew and flourished throughout Europe until the advent of Napoleon. Nunneries had disappeared from England since the sixteenth century, but they had recently returned to the island.

7. Seymour, *Nunneries*, 4.
8. Ibid., 7.
9. Ibid., 10.

Seymour warned that convents in England, both Roman Catholic and Anglican,[10] posed a danger to the traditional virtues of freedom and liberty, and consequently they must be placed under the supervision of the state. "The truth is, there is a veil spread over all the inner life of the conventual system; and secrecy, and mystery, and concealment, are essentials of its nature."[11] He then listed some of the abuses: the family or parental name of a nun was replaced by a religious name; nuns were never allowed to speak to members of their families in private; and loving embraces or demonstrations of affection with relatives were prohibited. Seymour told the audience of one sisterhood where the nuns had to wait until the yearly visit of their parents to find out if a mother or father had died since the superior only announced that a death had occurred and did not supply the name. This oppressive and demeaning life even drove an abbess in Rome to commit suicide by plunging into the Tiber. Not only did this secrecy harm the nuns psychologically and spiritually, but it also effectively destroyed family ties. In a graphic manner, Seymour described the horrors of a convent:

> prisons in which there is an impenetrable veil thrown over everything—where none but cowled and hooded monks can enter, and where every crime on earth, and every vice of hell may be rife within the walls—where there may be the groans of the persecuted victim, or the shriek of outraged purity; and all is suppressed and stifled within the walls, and never can reach our outer world . . .[12]

More freedom for the nuns, however, could be found in the second class of convents, namely, those who pursued an active apostolate.

These convents conducted schools for young ladies or children of the poor and assisted the local clergy in preparing the youth for the sacraments. But he also pointed out examples of the cruel treatment some of these children received at the hands of the nuns. Seymour horrified his listeners with the tale of young girl who had died as a result of some harsh, ascetic treatments, such as prolonged kneeling before the altar and crucifix, which she endured as preparation for Confirmation. Some convents also provided room and board for young women whose parents

---

10. See Allchin, *Silent Rebellion*; Anson, *Call of the Cloister*; and Mumm, *Stolen Daughters*.

11. Seymour, *Nunneries*, 15.

12. Ibid., 17.

were traveling abroad. While the life of these "active" convents might appeal to the romantic imagination of some English parents, Seymour exhibited a bit of snobbery when he pointed out that these nuns belonged to the inferior class. Some were "so deformed that they are unwilling to appear in society; others who are suffering from incurable ailments . . . others are those unhappy persons—perhaps more sinned against than sinning . . ."[13] He did appreciate the good work done by these sisters, but asked why should one have to enter a convent to perform acts of charity.

Seymour used the example of the women of Bath to prove his point. These holy Protestant women visited prisons, taught in asylums, instructed children in their religion, ministered to the sick, and comforted the poor in their hovels in a humble and self-effacing manner. They did not draw attention to themselves by their dress. Making reference to members of Priscilla Lydia Sellon's Anglican sisterhood, he sarcastically asked, "Why may not all this active charity be exhibited without such frippery as crucifixes and rosaries dangling at their girdles?"[14] Moreover, these pious Bath women were not bound by those awful practices that had corrupted Roman Catholic sisterhoods. Evil priests did not victimize them, and a dowry was not a prerequisite for them to pursue a life of charitable service based on a religious conviction. Seymour then spent some time on the question of the dowry, and told the audience that a small percentage of the money did provide for the upkeep of the nun, but the bulk of the funds eventually went to support the activities of the Roman Catholic Church.

After another brief tirade against the Sellon's Anglican nuns, during which he attacked her dictatorial leadership as mother superior, the absence of freedom within the sisterhood, and her wicked encouragement of the Romish practice of confession, Seymour returned again to the issue of Roman Catholic convents. He spoke about another alleged abuse, namely, the deportation or the removal of the nuns to an affiliated convent on the Continent. While in England, nuns did enjoy the basic rights guaranteed by law, and the legal system would protect the woman who left or escaped from the convent. Sisterhoods, however, resorted to deportation to silence or to punish rebellious or recalcitrant nuns. "The result is," Seymour pointed out, "that she is removed from the protection of our free laws and free institutions, and transferred to some land where

13. Ibid., 22.
14. Ibid., 24.

the ecclesiastical laws justify any, and every, restraint, and where she is destined to become a victim, or a prisoner for life."[15] He then told a story, designed to appeal to the fathers in the audience, of a Roman Catholic nun who was removed from the free soil of England to Europe without informing the family of her new address. Her father "knew not where she was secreted, and had now no hope of seeing his child again!"[16] Moreover, if a nun was apprehended escaping from a foreign convent where she had been moved, she would be treated like a criminal: "she would be hunted down as a murderess by the military, or the police."[17] When caught, this unfortunate nun might have to perform menial tasks in the convent such as working in the laundry or cleaning the kitchen, but the punishment could be worse. She might be "placed in one of those awful nunneries where every crime of earth or hell are, and where the sigh of her breaking heart, or the groan of her tortured frame, or the shriek of her outraged purity, can never be heard or heeded in the outer world, and where she breathes her last . . ."

As Seymour approached the end of this long harangue against Roman Catholic sisterhoods, he offered a solution to the evils fostered by nunneries. He believed that the English Parliament had a duty and responsibility to outlaw convents in England. This action would not violate the rights of Catholics or their church, he argued, and to back up this statement he appealed to the actions of Roman Catholic Italy, which had recently sanctioned the abolition of sisterhoods in Milan. Only two elderly nuns remained in the city. If some of his countrymen, however, might be offended by this policy, Seymour proposed another approach recently debated in Parliament: "I would suggest that every nunnery in the land should be subjected to official visitation."[18] This could easily be carried out by the Justices of the Peace or by a commission appointed for that purpose. Even a Roman Catholic country such as Mexico had a policy of convent visitation. According to Seymour's plan, an official would have the opportunity to meet with the nuns in private and inquire if they wanted to leave or if they were content to remain in the sisterhood. The official would have the power to escort any nun who wanted to depart from the convent and return to her family. This system, more-

15. Ibid., 41.
16. Ibid.
17. Ibid., 43.
18. Ibid., 44.

over, would protect the convents from suspicions or nasty gossip about their life. Seymour did not exclude economics from his program of convent inspection. If a member desired to leave, the convent would have to provide enough money for her to exist "by requiring the nunnery to give such maintenance or support to the nun as may be proportionate to the amount of dowry she originally brought to the institution."[19] This provision, consequently, would not make the dissatisfied nun feel imprisoned or tied to a convent for lack of financial means. Finally, he proposed that a nun in England should not be permitted to take her final or life vows until she reached the age of twenty-four years and argued that laws should be enacted that would protect the wealth or property of the nun for her legal heir, and not the Roman Catholic Church. With these two suggestions, the Rev. M. Hobart Seymour ended his long speech.

The Bath and Cheltenham Gazette reported that before the meeting broke up it adopted a petition that called upon the English government to pursue measures that would provide for the inspection of all convents in the country.[20] The assembly also heard and adopted an address from the ladies of the city of Bath to the Queen that contained the same sentiments. The newspaper reported the comment of one of the members of the audience, E. T. Caufield, who remarked on the character of the Rev. M. Hobart Seymour and emphasized the "impartiality of the talented Lecturer." In particular, Caufield meant Seymour's hostile comments about Anglican sisterhoods: "if there were any Roman Catholics present whose feelings were wounded by what had been said of the system within their Church, they would at least bear witness that the Rev. speaker had not spared his own . . . that in proposing to take from the moat in our brother's eye, we as Churchmen had not forgotten the beam in our own eye." Seymour's Bath lecture and the press coverage of his remarks elicited a response from the recently-created Cardinal of Westminster, Nicholas Wiseman.

Nicholas Wiseman, a bright and combative apologist for the Roman Catholic religion, was made Cardinal Archbishop of Westminster in September 1850, the same month that Pope Pius IX restored the hierarchy in England and Wales.[21] Riots and anti-Catholic demonstrations

---

19. Ibid., 45–46.
20. *The Bath and Cheltenham Gazette*, 28 April 1852.
21. For biographies of Wiseman, see Fothergill, *Nicholas Wiseman*; Reynolds, *Three Cardinals*; Schiefen, *Nicholas Wiseman and the Transformation of English Catholicism*;

greeted the arrival of Cardinal Wiseman in England. No one could doubt Wiseman's commitment to the defense of Catholicism and his courage to challenge the false remarks of opponents. A good example of this pugnacity occurred in May 1852. In that month, Cardinal Nicholas Wiseman journeyed to Bath to answer charges recently made in that city against Roman Catholic convents by the Rev. M. Hobart Seymour. Moreover, the press reports of this talk also give an insight into Wiseman's style and the manner in which he handled the enemies of Catholicism. *The Bath and Cheltenham Gazette*, the same paper that printed selections of Seymour's lecture against convents, also published lengthy extracts from the Cardinal's response.[22] Wiseman gave his talk at the Catholic chapel, Pierrepoint Street, in Bath on Sunday night, May 23. Rumors had circulated that his subject would be a rebuttal of the Rev. M. H. Seymour's recent assault on nunneries, which had already appeared in a pamphlet. A ticket, which cost half a crown, would admit the curious and the interested, and "the pressure to obtain admission was inconveniently great."[23] Cardinal Wiseman entered the chapel and took his seat in front of the altar. The paper gave a rather friendly description of this Roman Catholic prelate. "He is a portly and 'comfortable'-looking man, with little of the appearance or the expression conventionally attributed to the priesthood of his Church; he is thoroughly English in feature and in accent, with a good deal of curling brown hair descending from his head. He was dressed in the scarlet robes of his office, including a small skull-cap of that colour on the crown of his cornered hat."

After a brief prayer, Wiseman introduced the subject of his lecture, and then he took his seat and proceeded for over two hours to attack Seymour's false statements against convent life. According to *The Bulwark*, the organ of the Scottish Reformation Society, the Rev. M. Hobart Seymour was in the audience.[24]

Certain themes surfaced throughout Wiseman's talk: Seymour's lack of objectivity, Seymour's insufficient evidence, and Seymour's reliance on hearsay and rumor. Cardinal Wiseman began by reminding the audience of the current anti-Catholic sentiment in England, prompted

and Ward, *The Life and Times of Cardinal Wiseman*.

22. The Cardinal later published a small pamphlet that contained parts of his first speech at Bath. See Wiseman, *Convents*.

23. *The Bath and Cheltenham Gazette*, 26 May 1852.

24. "Nunneries—Cardinal Wiseman at Bath," *The Bulwark* (Edinburgh), July 1852.

by the "Catholic aggression" that had grown out of the restoration of the hierarchy and his appointment as Archbishop of Westminster. But Seymour's lecture was the chief reason for the Cardinal's address. Wiseman immediately dismissed the veracity of his opponent's lecture. According to Cardinal Wiseman, "it contained some empty, baseless, and groundless declamation, distorted facts and sinful fictions . . . statements without authority, or statements for which the authority had been sought in vain." In short, Seymour could not verify or back up any of his harsh and critical statements about nunneries. If one were to believe these falsehoods, convent life did create an atmosphere of unhappiness and did allow cruel superiors to dictate a life of misery for the poor, naive nuns. Wiseman drew the attention of his listeners to Seymour's remarks about the recent European revolutions that closed convents, "liberated" the nuns from their "prisons," and scattered them throughout the country. And he pointed out that in numerous cases these religious exiles had freely returned to their nunneries once the persecution by the state had ceased. Wiseman queried, "Surely there was something strange and contradictory in this: did they [Seymour's audience] ever hear of prisoners who had been released returning to the scene of their captivity, and by striving to reconstruct their cells and restore themselves to their ancient fetters?"

The Cardinal continued with an attack on Seymour's use of prison images to describe the life of a Roman Catholic nun. These allegations were absurd. High walls, barred gates, and windows with grates protected the nuns from intruders and gave these defenseless creatures a sense of security. For what reason, Wiseman asked, would a priest or bishop force a group of nuns to live a life of sadness incarcerated in a convent? Wiseman could find no good answer. Moreover, he pointed out, the Council of Trent had imposed a penalty of excommunication of any individual who forced a woman to enter a convent against her free will. Part of the misunderstanding of non-Catholics on the admission policy of candidates into the conventual life, however, was based on their ignorance of the correct and canonical procedures, which in fact protected one's freedom. Before a nun's solemn or final vows she enjoyed complete liberty to leave the sisterhood. For example, the bishop who received the vows would inquire of the nun if she was acting freely and without duress.

Seymour claimed that he had proof that young girls were forced into Roman Catholic convents, but the Cardinal demanded that he supply the sources for these accusations. Who was the anonymous informer in Rome Seymour had made reference to in his lecture? Wiseman even promised to protect Seymour's source if his identity were made public. Consequently, the stories of the novice who stabbed herself in desperation at the feet of her father and the unstable abbess who threw herself into the Tiber had no basis in fact. Seymour's allegations that nuns were regularly deported to foreign convents against their will also lacked proof. Wiseman told his audience that some Roman Catholic sisterhoods had convents on the Continent, and when a young girl joined one of these sisterhoods she understood that she could be transferred or assigned to one of these European convents. This did not amount to forcible deportation or kidnapping. Seymour even made references to Anglican young women being coerced into convents by their parents, but again, the Cardinal pointed out, he had failed to supply names and details. Without concrete proof of these incidents, one should treat them as malicious fables.

Cardinal Wiseman also took issue with the "extreme inconsistency and looseness" of Seymour's other statements attacking Catholicism. His portrait of the "Grand Inquisitor at Rome," which did create a powerful picture, was false. The person whom he described turned out to be the Master of the Sacred Palace. Seymour's allegations that the Office of the Inquisition, after being ransacked by a mob, contained numerous devices of torture and evidence of crimes against people amounted to gross deception. When people initially entered the Office of the Inquisition, Wiseman pointed out, they found no instruments of torture. But then the office was locked, and three days later when people were again admitted the torture devices and the remains of the victims had appeared! The Cardinal argued his case: "Why nobody in Rome believed now but the whole thing was prepared; and as for the dead bodies, it was proved, by the most convincing antiquarian and other evidence, that the bones found belonged to a cemetery which had occupied the spot before the Inquisition existed."

In addition to a marked anti-Catholic sentiment, the chief motive behind the Rev. M. Hobart Seymour's lecture was to whip up support for the campaign to impose government inspection on convents. According to the report in *The Bath and Cheltenham Gazette*, Cardinal Wiseman argued that this action would violate English principles of privacy and freedom. "As to the right demanded to enter these establishments at any time, he [Wiseman] put it to the feelings of English gentlemen and ladies whether they would suffer such a thing in their own houses? Why, then, should the feelings of respectable ladies, living in places they themselves had purchased, be outraged by the prying intrusions of country magistrates and hunting squires?"

Those who supported parliamentary inspection of convents maintained that the power of the state would guard against the loss of personal liberty which some believed the cloister destroyed. Seymour, for example, had stated that the family names of the nuns had been kept a secret so that relatives and friends could not trace them to a specific convent. Wiseman labeled this charge absurd; all the nuns in a convent knew the identity of the other sisters.

Cardinal Wiseman's first hand knowledge of the secular climate in Italy gave him the background to refute Seymour's remarks about the suppression of nunneries and the anti-convent legislation in Milan. More controversial, however, was Seymour's suggestion that officials of the local Catholic Church had supported this policy. In response, Cardinal Wiseman stated that seventeen convents currently existed in the city and neighborhood of Milan. Moreover, Seymour got his facts wrong: Napoleon suppressed the religious houses in Milan in 1810, and not the church or the government of that city. Napoleon had provided a home for those sisters who had no place to go. The Cardinal maintained that "two old nuns" were probably the last survivors of that 1810 dissolution, and not the total number of sisters in a city where the conventual life had grown since the suppression.

As Wiseman approached the end of his long talk, he could not avoid mentioning three other points. Seymour's insinuations about the financial improprieties of Roman Catholic convents, his hostile remarks about Anglican nunneries, and the suppression of the Italian nunneries, especially in Tuscany. He quickly dismissed each charge. According to the Cardinal, the "portion alleged to be contributed by each nun was too high." Moreover, instead of becoming affluent on the money of young women who entered their sisterhood, many convents were impoverished and had to resort to public alms to exist. On the subject of the conventual life in the Church of England and its similarities to Catholic sisterhoods, Wiseman emphatically pointed out that "there was not the slightest resemblance between the two." The Roman Catholic Church, he argued, possessed numerous canonical safeguards to prevent the supposed evils and abuses of power by the mother superior that Seymour associated with Anglican nunneries, especially Sellon's sisterhood. Cardinal Wiseman, however, expressed some sympathy for the Anglican sisters. They did not deserve the "obloquy, reproach, or scorn" which came from the mouth of the Rev. M. Hobart Seymour. Finally, the suppression of the convents in Tuscany, Wiseman noted, took place during the last century. The evidence about the life in these nunneries did shock and scandalize some people and contributed to the closure of many convents in the area, but Wiseman questioned the objectivity of the official reports. He maintained that the "inquiry had been instituted by a man who, although holding the position of a Catholic bishop, was almost a greater enemy to the Church than even a declared Protestant would have been. Moreover, witnesses were bullied and intimidated to give false evidence."

Cardinal Nicholas Wiseman finally came to his concluding remarks. He made a direct appeal to "the better feelings of the country upon this subject" of Roman Catholic convents in England. Wiseman urged "those who heard him not to be carried away by empty declarations and groundless assertions in regard to a system that did so vast an amount of good." The Cardinal finally pronounced the customary benediction that ended the evening's event. This newspaper account concluded its report of the Cardinal's lecture with two announcements. The proceeds from the ticket sales would go toward the upkeep of the charity schools attached to the Catholic chapel where he gave the talk. The second, printed as a separate notice next to the Wiseman article, gave notice that the debate over nunneries ignited by Seymour would continue: a second public lecture by "The Rev. M. Hobart Seymour, in reply to the lecture which had been delivered by Cardinal Wiseman on that subject, is in contemplation, and that particulars will shortly be announced."

The Bath and Cheltenham Gazette reported Cardinal Wiseman's speech in the same impartial manner as it did Seymour's earlier attack on convents. Another local newspaper, *The Bath Chronicle*, strayed from the path of neutrality. The first sentence of its report on Wiseman's talk revealed a hostility to both the Cardinal and the Roman Catholic Church. "The manner in which Cardinal Wiseman has forced himself upon the notice of the Protestant inhabitants of this city is strikingly characteristic of the Roman Church."[25] The paper characterized the attitude of Catholicism as "arrogance," its manner of doing things as "mischievous rule," and the Cardinal as deceptive. "No one would have dreamt that so soft-spoken, well mannered, and insinuating a gentleman was the audacious violator not merely of the law, but, what is more, of the political and religious feeling of this realm." *The Bath Chronicle* also reminded its readers of the fires of Smithfield, the St. Bartholomew's Day massacre, and the unspeakable horrors of the Inquisition.

This attack on Catholicism and its chief spokesman in England was not meant as a vindication of Seymour or his views, but attempted to portray "him [Cardinal Wiseman] to the world affecting a contempt while his actions and words betoken fear." The paper even criticized Seymour for accepting "what Roman Catholics themselves accept as facts." *The Bath Chronicle* was more interested in mocking Roman Catholicism and Wiseman's defense of the conventual life. It accused Cardinal Wiseman of ignoring the realities of history which had chronicled and described the evils of Catholicism and its institutions. However, this "off handed way of dealing with ugly facts will not... satisfy hard-headed Englishmen."

> They suspect its zeal for liberty in England, when they see the right of private judgment denounced as a pestilent heresy at Rome. They will not believe that Romanism is void of offence and guile, when they know that its priests conceal conspiracy, have instigated murder, and have created rebellion in our sister island. They see the hard shifts to which Cardinal Wiseman is reduced in asking them to judge from one brick of the soundness to the whole edifice of Romanism...

This newspaper, however, did not forget the issue of nunneries and the message of Seymour's lecture. Intelligent Englishmen, it stated, "regard the idea that these barred doors, and grated windows, are intended to keep people out, not in, [of] the nunneries as simple balderdash... [and] that many a heart has beat against them from within." Cardinal Wiseman's rhetoric had demonstrated his deceitfulness. "To paint a picture of weak and defenceless women charged with ill for doing good — the rude invasion of their homes by men—the violation of the privacy due to modesty—was a sure card in the game which the crafty Cardinal was playing." The paper obviously used the convent topic as an excuse to vilify Roman Catholicism, and ended its report by stating "that there

25. *The Bath Chronicle*, 27 May 1852.

is grafted on the Roman Catholic faith a despotic, unfeeling, political system of which it is to speak mildly to say that it has been the constant oppressor, and is now the open enemy, of civilization and freedom throughout the world."

The Bulwark also commented on Cardinal Wiseman's speech at Bath. Surprisingly, this account of Wiseman's defense of nunneries and his critique of Seymour's presentation was less venomous and hostile than the description that had appeared in *The Bath Chronicle*. The article began by noting that the Rev. M. Hobart Seymour had previously given a lecture in the same city. According to this report, he did not expose "the actual character of conventual life," but rather intimated that evils existed in convents.[26] Consequently, Seymour "attached but little importance to the lecture ... [but] no less a champion than Cardinal Wiseman himself was called to the rescue." The Cardinal denied the so-called facts produced by Seymour, attacked "that gentleman's veracity," and urged the Anglicans in the audience to exercise "their common sense" instead of relying on Seymour's "false statements ... and erroneous and one-sided arguments." *The Bulwark*, in an attempt to highlight Roman Catholic duplicity, pointed out that the public notices announcing the talk stated that it would be free of charge, but an entrance fee was demanded to hear Wiseman defend Catholicism. Wiseman's health and apparent lack of stamina also received attention: "He was much excited, and obliged repeatedly to rest himself in a gilded chair placed by an attendant acolyte in front of the altar." This account ended by drawing attention to the fact that Seymour had taken up the challenge and would shortly defend himself against the Cardinal. The controversy over nunneries and the issue of convent inspection would not disappear, and both speakers would again address the topic, but they offered little or nothing new to their original presentations.

The Rev. M. Hobart Seymour responded to Cardinal Wiseman's talk on June 7 at the Assembly Rooms, Bath. According to the printed version of Seymour's lecture, he spoke for over four hours to an audience of fifteen hundred people.[27] Seymour did not retract or modify any of his earlier accusations. He repeated his criticisms of the conventual system, such as, loss of freedom and the prison atmosphere of the convents, the deportation of nuns to foreign countries, and the large dowries required

26. "Nunneries."
27. Seymour, *Convents or Nunneries*.

of the candidates, which contributed to the wealth of the Roman Catholic Church. The suicide of the abbess who threw herself into the Tiber, he pointed out, was based on accounts printed in Roman newspapers. At this lecture, Seymour did emphasize stories of immorality in nunneries, especially those in Tuscany, and the evils of confession, but he based these allegations on questionable printed sources, including some medieval texts, writings from the eighteenth century, and contemporary anti-clerical tracts. But where was the irrefutable proof to back up his accusations of abuses in the nunneries?

He was forced to rely heavily on the biased and highly prejudiced works of the ex-priest, William Hogan, the facts of the Achilli libel case, and the eyewitness testimony of the Rev. Pierce Connelly. Seymour interpreted a passage from St. Alphonsus Liguori's treatise, *The True Spouse of Jesus Christ*, which he claimed demonstrated that women were forced against their will into convents, and he also quoted decrees from the Council of Trent which he believed gave approval to young and immature girls entering into sisterhoods. Seymour did not waver from his campaign to secure parliamentary inspection of convents, and the assembly did pass a resolution backing this proposal. Toward the end of his address, it appeared that Seymour had softened his tone. He conceded that English sisterhoods did not suffer from the same abuses and evils as their continental counterparts, but state inspection would safeguard and protect them from any misconduct. Seymour, however, refused to listen to one of Cardinal Wiseman's chief demands: he would never reveal the identity of the person who supplied him with the information concerning life in the Italian convents. He feared that the informant might suffer punishment or retribution at the hands of ecclesiastical officials. The Rev. M. Hobart Seymour did not confront Cardinal Wiseman again on the question of convents, although later he did return to topic of nunneries in a public forum.[28]

Cardinal Wiseman ventured into the arena to answer the Rev. M. Hobart Seymour one more time. Wiseman published a short booklet, which also contained extracts from his first appearance at Bath, in response to Seymour's second talk. Wiseman's publication contained little new information. In essence, the Cardinal again refuted Seymour's now familiar arguments against nunneries, such as, deportation, the early death-rate of nuns, and prison-like conditions, which he had addressed

28. See Seymour, *On Convents*.

in his lecture at Bath; and he continued to demand that Seymour supply the names of his informants. Wiseman also pointed out that in Seymour's second talk his opponent had misinterpreted the decrees of Trent and the writings of Alphonsus Liguori. Consequently, the Cardinal gave a lengthy explanation to demonstrate that Seymour had not understood the meaning of either. Finally, he pointed out, if reform of convents was ever needed, the Catholic Church would not hesitate to act. It appeared from this booklet that Wiseman had grown quite weary of this debate, and he concluded his pamphlet by quoting the words which he had used to end his speech at Bath: "I shall be satisfied if I have succeeded, by these remarks, in removing some of those prejudices which have been attempted to be excited amongst you. I shall be satisfied with having given up this portion of my time, and I shall not regret having tried your patience so long, if you bear away with you a spirit of justice, and a determination that none shall be oppressed."[29]

The debate over the character of convent life and the question of state inspection did not cease after the exchange of views at Bath. The opponents of nunneries, such as the Rev. M. Hobart Seymour, continued to argue that inspection of these Roman Catholic institutions was needed to safeguard the freedom and liberty of the nuns. A "secular" visitation of convents might also identify other abuses that could be corrected. English Roman Catholics, on the other hand, protested against parliamentary-sponsored inspections of nunneries as a violation of English rights of privacy. Nunneries were not prisons; women entered freely and could depart without restraint and without fear of reprisal. Moreover, Catholics argued, the stories of mistreatment within the cloister, such as those that Seymour pointed out, were false and merely fabrications of individuals and groups who despised Roman Catholicism. The lectures given by the Rev. M. Hobart Seymour and Cardinal Nicholas Wiseman at Bath, however, demonstrate that the issue of Roman Catholic nunneries had become an important and emotional issue in the political and religious life of mid-Victorian England. Throughout the rest of the nineteenth century, the enemies of nunneries continued to critique this institution and demanded state inspection. And loyal Roman Catholics always responded vigorously in defense of their beloved convents.

---

29. Wiseman, *Convents*, 63.

Bibliography

Allchin, A. M. *The Silent Rebellion: Anglican Religious Communities 1845–1900*. London: SCM, 1958.

Anson, Peter F. *The Call of the Cloister: Religious Communities and Kindred Bodies in the Anglican Communion*. Revised and edited by A. W. Campbell. London: SPCK, 1964.

Boase, Frederic. *Modern English Biography*. Vol. 3. London: Cass, 1965.

Crockford's Clerical Directory: A Directory of the Serving and Retired Clergy of the Church of England, the Church of Wales and the Scottish Episcopal Church. London: Church House Publishing. 1874.

Fothergill, Brian. *Nicholas Wiseman*. London: Faber & Faber, 1963.

Mumm, Susan. *Stolen Daughters, Virgin Mothers: Anglican Sisterhoods in Victorian Britain*. London: Leicester University Press, 1999.

"Nunneries—Cardinal Wiseman at Bath." *The Bulwark, or Reformation Journal* (July 1852)

Reynolds, E. E. *Three Cardinals: Newman, Wiseman, Manning*. London: Burns & Oates, 1958.

Schiefen, Richard J. *Nicholas Wiseman and the Transformation of English Catholicism*. Shepherdstown, WV: Patmos, 1984.

Seymour, M. Hobart. *The Causes of the Reformation*. London: Hatchards, 1869.

———. *Certainty Unattainable in the Church of Rome: A Consideration Bearing upon Secession to Rome*. London: Seeleys, 1852.

———. *Convents or Nunneries: A Lecture in Reply to Cardinal Wiseman, Delivered at the Assembly Rooms, Bath, on Monday, June 7, 1852*. London: Seeleys, 1852.

———. *Evenings with the Romanists*. London: Seeleys, 1854.

———. *Mornings among the Jesuits in Rome*. 3rd ed. London: Seeleys, 1850.

———. *Nunneries: A Lecture Delivered at the Assembly Rooms, Bath, on Wednesday, April 21, 1852*. London: Seeleys, 1852.

———. *On Convents: The Speech of the Rev. M. Hobart Seymour, at the Meeting of the Protestant Alliance, Held in St. James's Hall, Picadilly, on February 24th, 1865*. London: Protestant Alliance, 1865.

———. *A Pilgrimage to Rome: Containing Some Account of the High Ceremonies, the Monastic Institutions, the Religious Services, the Sacred Relics, the Miraculous Pictures, and the General State of Religion in That City*. 4th ed. London: Seeleys, 1851.

Ward, Wilfred Philip. *The Life and Times of Cardinal Wiseman*. 2 vols. 3rd ed. London: Longmans, 1898.

Wiseman, Nicholas. *Convents: A Review of Two Lectures on This Subject, by the Rev. M. Hobart Seymour*. London: Richardson, 1853.

Wolffe, John. *The Protestant Crusade in Great Britain 1829–1860*. Oxford: Clarendon, 1991.

Wooden, W. W. *John Foxe*. Twayne's English Author Series 345. Boston: Twayne, 1983.

The Myth and Reality of Sr. Barbara Ubryk, the Imprisoned Nun of Cracow

English Interpretations of a Victorian Religious Controversy

A RECENT AMERICAN TELEVISION PROGRAM began with scenes of a building where someone had painted Botticelli's The Birth of Venus. The unknown artist sarcastically painted the following phrase, "All History Is Myth," coming from her mouth. This statement might seem true, especially when one studies the rancor and hostile emotions that frequently colored religious controversies in nineteenth century England, where fantasy, falsehood, and hyperbole frequently replaced reality. Stories about nuns and convents were no exception and often supplied the material for a number of hateful legends. In William Makepeace Thackeray's *The Irish Sketch Book*, for example, the narrator visited an Ursuline convent at Blackrock, near Cork, and admitted "this is a great privilege for a heretic."[1] He encountered a nun, and acknowledged that he had never been in the presence of one before this meeting. The reader quickly learns, however, that the narrator harbored some anti-Catholic prejudices. After some caustic comments about Roman Catholicism, the narrator wondered out loud, "has she any of her sisterhood immured in

---

1. Thackeray, "Irish Sketch Book," 328.

oubliettes down below... is her poor little weak delicate body scarred all over with scourgings, iron collars, hair-shirts?"[2]

In some circles of Victorian England a number of educated people also held this impression of nuns and conventual life. Many reasons gave rise to this hostile and critical view of convents. In addition to a general anti-Catholic prejudice which saw all practices associated with that religion as either immoral or idolatrous, a stereotype of the inhuman existence which nuns allegedly endured might have developed out of specific happenings or events which people had either exaggerated or misinterpreted. A Benedictine monk in London understood this possibility. Writing in 1899, this cleric described an event at a local convent. A nun, obviously suffering from mental problems, threatened to harm herself and to set fire to the buildings. The other sisters, consequently, kept a close watch on her, but she managed to escape. The nun "got out of the window, and halfdressed [sic] as she was making for the garden, through the hedge across a field and into one of the new roads close by."[3] A kindly man eventually rescued the fleeing nun and took her home, where his wife cared for her until authorities from the convent arrived. The monk understood the possibilities for trouble, which, however, did not materialize: "we are likely to have the 'escaped nun' cry for a time."

By the 1860s the figure of the poor, imprisoned nun, languishing in a dank convent cell on the orders of a diabolical mother superior or churchman, had become a symbol of the baseness of Roman Catholicism. *The Monk*, written by the nineteen-year-old Matthew Lewis in 1794, had already told the sad and horrific story of Agnes, a young Spanish girl who suffered imprisonment within the vaults of the convent. In 1836 the fabricated story of Maria Monk shocked and titillated readers on both sides of the Atlantic with tales of a Montreal convent where seduction, murder, infanticide, and, of course, imprisonment, formed part of the daily routine of the nuns. The quantity of literature and publications that attacked conventual life and emphasized its abuses was phenomenal, and those Victorians who read the memoirs of Henrietta Caracciolo and Sister Lucy became well acquainted with themes of imprisonment and loss of personal freedom[4] from north of the border, *The Bulwark*, a pub-

2. Ibid., 331.

3. G. Dolan to H. E. Ford, 10 October 1899, Dolan Papers, Ealing Abbey Archives, London.

4. Caracciolo, *Memoirs of Henrietta Caracciolo*; and *Marvellous Escape of 'Sister Lucy.'*

lication of the Scottish Reformation Society, reported several escapes from convents,[5] and *Priests and Their Victims; or, Scenes in a Convent*, published in 1852, illustrated another theme that would play an important role in the case of Sr. Barbara, namely, the immoral actions of those priests associated with convents.[6]

Criticisms of sisterhoods were not confined to print. Beginning in 1851 with a bill introduced by Henry Charles Lacy, several attempts, especially those associated with Charles Newdigate Newdegate, were made to require parliamentary or government inspection of sisterhoods. Naturally, those who argued for inspection made references to the alleged imprisonment or the incarceration of nuns, and the supporters of state supervision tried to educate the British public to the evils of convent life by means of lectures and pamphlets.[7] In 1869 an event occurred in Cracow, then part of the Habsburg Empire, which concerned a Carmelite nun, Barbara Ubryk, who had been imprisoned within the walls of her convent. The incident quickly caught the attention of individuals in England who had already watched with interest the developments of the Hull convent case[8] and who saw this foreign incident as another example of the cruelty practiced by Roman Catholic sisterhoods.

The news of Sr. Barbara's incarceration first reached England in July 1869, when *The Times* reported some disturbances that occurred on 21 July when a mob broke a door and several windows at the convent of Carmelite nuns in Cracow. According to the paper, "The cause of the demonstration was that a nun had been in close confinement in the Convent for 20 Years, and was only liberated . . . by the interference of a judicial Commission."[9] The rabble returned to the convent four days later and attempted to break into the convent where the nun had been held captive. Driven back, the mob continued to cause havoc within the

---

5. See, for example, *The Bulwark*, August 1852; 2 February 1857; 1 April 1859; 1 May 1865; and 1 June 1866.

6. Viner, *Priests and Their Victims*.

7. See Arnstein, *Protestant versus Catholic*, for Newdegate's campaign to legislate for government inspection of England's convents. Several groups opposed to Anglo-Catholicism and what they believed was the growing influence of Roman Catholicism in the British Isles supported Newdegate's program with an outpouring of pamphlets, for example, *A Plea for the Inspection or Suppression of Convents* (London, 1870).

8. For accounts of the "Great Convent Case," see, Arnstein, *Protestant versus Catholic*; and McClelland, "The First Hull Mercy Nuns."

9. *The Times* (London), 26 July 1869.

city and threatened other Catholic establishments. The paper noted that a number of arrests had been made and that government officials had already initiated an investigation into the case of Sr. Barbara. Several days later *The Times* again devoted more space to these religious riots in Poland, and the British public soon became acquainted with the life and trials of Barbara Ubryk.

The 31 July edition of *The Times* printed a hostile article dealing with the imprisoned nun. It contained reports from two Austrian correspondents who sketched the background and the events surrounding her discovery. This story most certainly repulsed and shocked British readers. One correspondent noted that "an anonymous letter stating that a nun had been immured in a neighbouring cloister since 1848, and begging that justice might be done to her"[10] had led to the discovery of Sr. Barbara. The article pointed out that Sr. Barbara had been born in 1817 and entered the Carmelite convent in 1841. After informing the Bishop of Cracow, Antonio Galecki, of a possible abuse at the convent, a representative of the city's magistracy, along with a delegate of the bishop, went to the convent, where they met with some resistance from a sister, who refused to receive them. The investigators, however, made their way to the cell of the nun "with its strongly fastened double door," and the sights and sounds that the rescue party encountered nauseated them.

According to the prejudiced language of *The Times*, on "entering the cell, a spectacle met them scarcely to be described, and yet it ought to be told, for it shows what fearful wrongs may be perpetrated if individuals are handed over to the tender mercy of Concordats, and to arbitrary, irresponsible rule."[11] The tiny room, it noted, measured seven feet by six

---

10. *The Times*, 31 July 1869. A second article in the same edition, written by another correspondent, followed the outline of the first report, and also quoted at length from a Vienna newspaper that described the horrific conditions in which Sr. Barbara was found.

11. In 1855 a concordat was signed between the Holy See and Austria. "Among other concessions to Rome were the freedom of communication between the bishops and the Vatican, the control of the elementary schools, the education of the clergy by the Jesuits, the surrender by the state of all share in the administration of ecclesiastical property, and the increase of clerical authority in questions connected with marriage." Latourette, *History of Christianity*, 2:1108–9. In spite of an edict of toleration (1861) that eased restrictions on those who were not Catholic, elements within the empire resented concessions given to the Roman Catholic Church and agitated for the abrogation of the concordat. In 1870, however, the concordat with the papacy was suspended in response to the dogma of papal infallibility promulgated by Pope Pius IX in that year.

feet, its window was walled up allowing only a sliver of light, and no furniture could be found. The appearance of Sr. Barbara sickened the investigators.

> In a corner, lying on rotten, stinking straw, lay the poor crouching creature, "*halb Mensch, halb Thier*," half human, half a brute, half savage, half mad, utterly naked," her body filthy, for she had not been washed for years. Her lean bones hanging loose, her cheeks sunken, her hair dishevelled and dirty—a fearful being, whom even Dante, with his amazing imaginative force could not have portrayed. This poor skeleton of a woman at the sight of her visitors shook herself up, and folding her hands and bitterly weeping said, "I am hungry, have pity on me, give me food (*Fleisch*) and I will be obedient."[12]

Immediately after this discovery, Bishop Galecki arrived at the convent and reprimanded both the mother superior and the confessor "with the utmost severity." The latter claimed that the ecclesiastical authorities had known about "the immuring of the nun," but the bishop denied this accusation. When asked why she had been imprisoned, Sr. Barbara answered that she had broken her vow of chastity, but she immediately told the bishop that "These nuns also are not pure; they are no angels." Before he left, Bishop Galecki suspended both the mother superior and the priest from their duties at the convent. Sr. Barbara's mental and physical health quickly became a concern. According to the opinion of the medical authorities who examined her on the day following her release, "she is rather 'verwilder' . . . wild and savage." They did not diagnose her as "deranged," and held out hope for her recovery. As to her testimony—especially the breaking of her vows—*The Times* pointed out, "it still remains to be seen whether this be not a delusion of the brain." Sr. Barbara was then immediately taken to a nearby asylum for the insane. The correspondent ended his report by hoping that justice would be carried out, but he also expressed concern that the local ecclesiastical authorities might try to obstruct any investigation, especially in respect to the testimony of the other nuns.

The Times printed another article concerning Sr. Barbara on 2 August. This report, written by the paper's correspondent in Vienna, also described the hostile mood of the Cracow crowd after Sr. Barbara's liberation from her confinement and the violence directed against the

12. *The Times*, 31 July 1869.

convent and a nearby Jesuit residence. The civil authorities cautioned the crowd against any more unlawful actions and urged the people to wait for the outcome of an investigation. A petition, however, had already been circulated demanding the removal of the Jesuits from the city. The correspondent also introduced some intrigue and mystery into the Sr. Barbara incident. Citing a Cracow 2 August 1869 newspaper, he revealed that "the proprietor of an intelligence office" admitted writing the anonymous letter which had first led the civil and religious authorities to the Carmelite convent.[13] Moreover, the Carmelite confessor to the convent, whom the paper incorrectly identified as Fr. Lavkowick, had left the city before the discovery of Sr. Barbara, and "in a state of intoxication discovered [that is, revealed] the mystery to the parish priest, who in his turn told it to his cousin, the above-mentioned proprietor of the intelligence office." (In the different versions of the Sr. Barbara story, the confessor to the Carmelite convent would be known by different names.) But stranger and more suspicious things also allegedly happened.

The first was the sudden death of the confessor. This Carmelite priest died unexpectedly on 25 July, and according to the judgment of the Vienna correspondent, "the chief witness is removed just at the most inopportune moment." *The Times* also quoted a special edition of a Cracow newspaper, which added another element to the riddle. Early one morning in April 1848, a patrol of the National Guard had noticed a carriage before the gate of the convent. Two members of the guard peered into the carriage and saw two men, "one of whom held on his knees a woman in a nun's dress, and having a nightcap on her head." During some questioning, the woman fled and ran into the convent's courtyard and apparently yelled, "I am lost." No one knew what became of her. The guard arrested the men, but the members of the patrol became convinced that the incident was nothing more than a "love adventure," and released them. The Cracow paper now believed that some connection existed between this 1848 incident and the recent discovery of the imprisoned nun at the same convent, and it began a search to identify the members of the National Guard on duty that night.

By August 1869, therefore, all the elements for a gothic suspense story were in place to excite or to repulse the British public: the ambience of a foreign city, tales of the torture and imprisonment of a Roman Catholic nun at the hands of her community, stories of insanity and

13. *The Times*, 2 August 1869.

broken religious vows, mysterious letters, the sudden and suspicious death of one of the main participants in the drama, an array of shadowy characters, and the strange incident of that early morning in April 1848. Moreover, *The Times* continued to contribute to the controversy by attacking sisterhoods in general; this soon became an important ingredient in the unfolding mythology of Sr. Barbara. Writing in the 31 July edition, the correspondent quickly vented his indignation and disgust at a religion that could allow so cruel an imprisonment to occur in a convent. "Any one who, in tale or drama, should have represented such an event as happening in a civilized city in this age of humanity would have been accused of imagining impossible horrors to discredit a creed against which he had a fanatical antipathy."[14] The article drew attention to the suspicions of some English concerning the morality "engendered by the so-called religious life," and described the Sr. Barbara incident as a "perversion of human instincts." Nuns and convents did not naturally produce "scenes of crime," it argued, and a program of state inspection would protect innocent young women against such crimes and misdeeds happening in England as had come to light in Cracow.

But was Sr. Barbara mad? Was her incarceration necessary to protect herself and the other sisters? *The Times* reported that Sr. Barbara claimed that she had been placed in solitary confinement because she had broken her vow of chastity, but her "coarsest language" on her release and the lack of any evidence concerning sexual misconduct suggested that she had gone insane. Because of the nun's mental condition, some apologists might excuse the misguided but understandable actions of the nuns. The only other explanation, which could be taken from the pages of works inspired by Matthew Lewis, was unthinkable to the Victorian mind. According to *The Times*, "To assume that the nuns shut up an erring Sister in a den and kept her there for twenty-one years in darkness, cold, and nakedness till she fell a victim to madness which they at first falsely imputed to her would be not unnatural if we could admit that the practices charged against the religious bodies of Western Europe three or four centuries since still linger among the Catholics of Poland." But even the more charitable explanation of the imprisonment of a mad nun for twenty-one years could not be defended. Even a violently insane person deserved better treatment. The article then recounted the events surrounding the discovery and release of Sr. Barbara, and asked

14. *The Times*, 31 July 1869.

about the authorship of the letter that revealed her plight. Who wrote the anonymous letter that led to her freedom: a nun, a vindictive or hateful servant at the convent, or the intelligence officer? More importantly, however, who should bear the responsibility for the imprisonment and persecution of Sr. Barbara?

The Roman Catholic officials must be held accountable. Taking into account all the circumstances of the case and all the possible explanations behind her long confinement, the London paper refused to accept any excuses for Sr. Barbara's mistreatment. "The ignorance of the Church authorities," *The Times* declared, "is the most extraordinary part of the business." The newspaper dismissed the contention, which it had printed earlier, that influential churchmen in the city had known of Sr. Barbara's situation for at least a decade. The surprised reaction of the bishop and his indignation suggested that he had no previous knowledge of the happenings at the convent. But ecclesiastical ignorance would not remove culpability: "It is evident that, even if it was known that a Sister of unsound mind remained in the convent, there was no suspicion in any one's mind that she was being treated with such atrocious cruelty." Moreover, nothing could excuse the actions of the other nuns. "To shut up a woman, still young, in a dungeon a few feet wide, to leave her there year after year without clothing or fire, wallowing in filth, and, with her wailings . . . in their ears, to go daily through the long routine of religious service, has in it something diabolical!" The newspaper characterized the nuns as having "seared consciences" and possessing "perverted minds." And what about the convent's confessor? Did he attempt to tell the nuns that the imprisonment of a member of their community constituted a crime that threatened her mental and physical health? Or did the nuns refuse to listen to their confessor's pleadings? Other accounts of Sr. Barbara's sufferings, however, would later argue that this cleric was responsible for her incarceration.

With a sense of indignation and a helping of pious wrath against the nuns and Roman Catholicism in general, the rhetoric of *The Times* supplied the reading public with the circumstances surrounding the case of Sr. Barbara. The article also predicted the possible consequences of the case. In the first place, it would inflame the passion of anti-Catholicism. According to the paper, "The incident will tend to confirm the repulsion with which Protestants regard these institutions [convents]." Second, the privileged position of religious communities, particularly within the

Austrian Empire, would be questioned and even altered. The advance of liberal ideas throughout Europe would eventually challenge and then destroy the domination of the Roman Catholic Church over the lives and minds of citizens. And last, the revelations of the Cracow convent would increase the demand for state inspection of all convents. "If religious orders are to be maintained," *The Times* demanded, "their dwellings must be open to public inspection, and their customs and bylaws accommodated to those of the State."

By August 1869, therefore, men and women in Great Britain who had read *The Times* had become acquainted with the saga and rescue of Sr. Barbara. The 7 August edition of the paper reported that the inquiry into the nunnery case continued to hear evidence, Sr. Barbara was making a good recovery in an asylum and no longer acted as a savage, the confessor to the convent had in fact died from natural causes, and the animosity against the Carmelite nuns for their supposed lack of compassion had subsided.[15] Regardless of its rhetoric, which clearly displayed its prejudice, the paper accurately supplied its readers with the facts of the case, but also raised many questions and introduced several mysterious incidents and persons into Sr. Barbara's story. Like a playwright or director who writes a number of final scenes for a play or movie, reports of the events at the Polish Carmelite convent produced different interpretations of the incident. Religious prejudices and personal motives played a large part in the different versions, and the conflicting results shed some light on the human element in historical interpretation and the strength of religious passions in fashioning an historical narrative. This helped to create the myth of Sr. Barbara Ubryk.

An anti-Catholic element quickly made use of Sr. Barbara. *The Rock*, that inveterate opponent of the High Church party and practices associated with Roman Catholicism such as sisterhoods, printed a short piece dealing with Sr. Barbara in its 6 August 1869 edition. The article paraphrased the reports from the Vienna press found in *The Times*. It did not, however, address the Cracow case per se, but rather used the example of Sr. Barbara to attack all sisterhoods, both Roman Catholic and especially those in the Anglican Church. *The Rock* described the reports from Poland as "a touching story of mingled suffering and horror . . ."[16] Instead of emphasizing the alleged cruelty and barbarism which

15. *The Times*, 7 August 1869.
16. *The Rock* (London), 6 August 1869.

Sr. Barbara had to endure, this paper took up another of the positions of those who loathed and feared the conventual life: the harsh existence which a nun vowed to live constituted an unhealthy, unusual, and unscriptural life. "It is not without cause," the paper pointed out, "that the Popish priests draw the veil, and keep it drawn very close, over the scenes enacted within convent walls." If the facade disappeared, one would catch a glimpse of "that strange and unnatural life—to which women devote themselves in the supposed interest of religion . . ."

As more and more information about the misdeeds occurring behind the convent walls became public knowledge, *The Rock* argued, people would no longer regard sisterhoods as "nurseries of heaven," or "estimate their inmates as anything rather than angels." "Can we commit the greatest outrage on the social aptitudes of womanhood, and do the grossest wrong to her tenderest and most characteristic sympathies, as a woman, and then expect to find her as perfect as when her nature was left to its proper perfection and to its natural development? Can we take away the heart of woman and expect to find its emotions still beating in her bosom, still overflowing with the milk of human kindness?"

Women committed acts of folly when they fled from the world and entered convents. Marriage and the family were the proper state for Victorian women; God had preordained this state of life as the ideal. According to this article, the Roman Church had sinned against the divine plan by its promotion and approval of sisterhoods. Moreover, the conventual life encouraged abnormal and inhuman activities, for example, "by withholding a sister's sympathy, and intercourse, and affections from those who need it most, even to their own sister . . ." The events at the Carmelite convent in Cracow did not surprise *The Rock*. "It is this hard and heartless want of sympathy to their own suffering sisters that is the crowning folly of convent life, and which will we trust," the newspaper predicted, "prove to be its ruin, if only allowed to develop its unnatural tendencies and tortures . . ." Naturally, the defenders of sisterhoods did not remain silent.

The Sr. Barbara case also found its way into the columns of the English Roman Catholic press. In the summer of 1869 *The Tablet*, a London weekly, reported on the incident. The length of the articles and the emphasis of the reports differed greatly from those of *The Times*. On 14 August the paper commented on the campaign, currently being waged in England, that advocated government inspection of convents, and thanked "the liberals in general for their consistent refusal to be startled by wild tales from Cracow . . . into the smallest of small tyrannies."[17] In the same edition, a short article noted that the case of Sr. Barbara had become the topic of numerous Protestant sermons which urged the state to inspect convents, and after sarcastically asking if "lunatics have never been and never are illtreated [sic] in Protestant England," it went on to describe the shocking case of an elderly man in Leicestershire. On 21 August, *The Tablet* tried to dispel wild talk of convent cruelty and consequently described the preliminary results of the investigation in Cracow. This Catholic paper pointed out that Sr. Barbara had suffered from mental illness, and then praised the charity offered by the sisters. The account differed greatly from the reports and interpretations of *The Times*. "There is no doubt," the paper stated, "that poor Barbara Ubryk has long been afflicted with the most distressing kind of madness; there is no doubt that she has been treated by the Carmelite Sisters with the most devoted and self-denying care and attention; there is no doubt that she was constantly well fed, and that her body health is excellent."[18] The precautions taken by the Carmelites to restrain Sr. Barbara, moreover, "were nothing more than the simple measures required for the sake, as well of her own safety as of natural decency."

According to *The Tablet*, a sacristan, who had worked at the convent for thirty years, knew of Sr. Barbara's madness and had walled up the lower part of the window in the room where she was confined in order to protect her. This person, contradicting other accounts, testified that her confinement was no secret. A doctor had paid her frequent visits, the former superior general of the Carmelites, Fr. Natalis Hanzet, had ordered that she should be kept in the convent, and on numerous occasions several of the sisters had unsuccessfully applied to diocesan officials to have her removed to an asylum because of her "fearful language." Ecclesiastical officials had known of Sr. Barbara's existence and her confinement: the diocese refused the request because "the duty of the nuns was to take care of a mad sister, and not to send her to a lunatic asylum." *The Tablet* also told its readers that the mother superior and her assistants were still in prison, "although the minute researches made in all the convent papers and in every part of the building, have not produced the slightest scrap of evidence in support of the slanderous

17. *The Tablet* (London), 14 August 1869.
18. *The Tablet*, 21 August 1869.

charges of cruelty." The article concluded by noting that the uproar and shock among the people of Cracow had subsided, and warned that other individuals would use this case as an example in their crusade to suppress religious orders and convents.[19] Roman Catholic opinion believed that the results of the public inquiry would eventually clear the Carmelites of any barbarous actions. Initial reports from Cracow seemed to justify this view.

The Tablet also printed a communication from Austria concerning the preliminary proceedings against the mother superior and other nuns accused of cruelty against Sr. Barbara. These nuns were "declared guilty of the objective, but not subjective, offence of overtly violating the right of personal freedom, and are adjudged to stand a special trial accordingly."[20] They had already appealed this decision. The report, however, emphasized the changed public attitude toward the actions of the Carmelite nuns and also supplied new information about Sr. Barbara. Before arriving in Cracow, it reported, Barbara Ubryk had formerly been a nun at a convent in Warsaw where "she showed symptoms of insanity, and a change of scene was recommended." The Carmelites received her, but the superior did not know about her history of mental health problems. If Sr. Barbara's past had been known, the Cracow nuns would probably not have welcomed her. For seven years, the article continued, Sr. Barbara exhibited no symptoms of insanity, and even wrote to her friends in Warsaw and described her contentment and happiness. Conditions at the convent then changed.

> In a short time her madness seized her more violently than ever, [and] it took the shape of "Erotomania." She seemed possessed of the devil of impurity, and believed herself to be the Holy Trinity. She tore off her clothes, destroyed her bed, her furniture, littered the floor with the straw of her mattress. Her clothes were renewed, her bed, her furniture restored, her cell cleaned out, continually. It was of no use. She wrecked everything again immediately. She

---

19. The same edition of *The Tablet* also reported that the Home Minister had recently withdrawn the annual state allowance to the Carmelite convent in Cracow because of the Sr. Barbara incident. After appealing unsuccessfully to the Austrian Chancellor, the papal nuncio went directly to Emperor Francis Joseph. The emperor refused to interfere in the case officially, but promised to give the convent the annual allowance from his personal funds. The paper took this story as a sign that the furor over Sr. Barbara was decreasing. "Whether literally correct or not, this story is believed in Vienna, and is, in itself, a fresh sign that the original calumny is dying away."

20. *The Tablet*, 21 August 1869.

showed herself at her window naked, and shouted the most horrible obscenities and blasphemies outside.

To stop this scandal, the convent officials walled up part of Sr. Barbara's window, but she continued to receive the same food as the other sisters.

According to this Roman Catholic report, her condition remained unchanged after she had been released and removed to an asylum, where the authorities had to secure her with a strait jacket. Were the Carmelite sisters culpable for their treatment of Sr. Barbara? Were they guilty of the cruel and inhumane treatment of another person, or were their actions only imprudent? The Catholic explanation stressed the naiveté of the convent's method of treatment. The sisters, for example, did not physically restrain her, as *The Times* had contended. In fact some noted the imprudence of the sisters for not sending Sr. Barbara to an institution for proper treatment. Those who tried to view the case objectively drew attention to the cloistered state of the sisters' life and the horrible nature of Sr. Barbara's illness. Moreover, they pointed out, several people, including her relatives, knew the seriousness of her mental condition and the manner of her confinement in the convent. This article, originating from Austria, offered an explanation for the curiosity and interest shown in the case of Sr. Barbara: "That the Cracow affair is another case among so many of gross and malignant slander and exaggeration, seems now taken for granted in the Catholic world here, while some non-Catholic journals of a more orderly sort are moderating their tone." The report ended by noting that the Bishop of Cracow had recently withdrawn his "harsh expression against the nuns." Another writer in *The Tablet* pointed out that a doctor had visited Sr. Barbara, who "was suffering from a peculiar and most painful form of madness," and had found no fault with the treatment she received from the nuns. Moreover, the paper concluded, "Negligence and ignorance of the proper treatment may be urged against the nuns, but neither cruelty nor immorality." Nonetheless, people in England, eager to blacken the reputation of Roman Catholicism and those suspicious of life behind convent walls, soon began to exploit Sr. Barbara's trials to their own ends. At times, writers took great liberties with the facts of the case and diverged greatly from the reports in *The Times* and *The Tablet*.

In 1869, the year that the news of Sr. Barbara became public, a small pamphlet, *The Horrors of Roman Catholic Convents and the Sufferings of*

Sister Barbara, appeared in England.[21] The cover presented the reader with a shocking picture depicting the discovery of a sickly, emaciated woman in tattered clothes, chained in a dungeon. Her expression revealed a mixture of suffering and fear; her clerical rescuers displayed shock. The caption beneath this illustration captured the message of the publication: "With an awful Description of her horrible condition when she was first discovered in her dismal, loathsome Den, and the fiendish treatment inflicted upon her by inhuman Priests, Lady Superioress and Nuns, who styled themselves 'Spiritual Wives,' and the 'Brides of Heaven'!" The introduction by the editor called attention to the alleged wickedness of the Roman Catholic Church and the crimes this religion had perpetrated in the British Isles throughout history. The writer singled out wicked priests, the abominations of auricular confession, and the evils of convent life, and then called upon the readers to defend "the Unalloyed Gospel of the Holy Scriptures" and the "Unity of England's National Church, and the Purity of Her Christian Teaching." For those who doubted the evil of the Roman Church, the case of Sr. Barbara would open their eyes.

This version of her story began with a number of anti-papal diatribes that warned the English nation against the wicked designs of the Catholic Church, especially the increasing popularity of sisterhoods within Anglicanism. According to the pamphlet, these Anglo-Catholic convents "have steadily gone on undermining Protestantism within and without the walls of our places of worship, and enticing our daughters into the numerous convents they [Roman Catholics] have everywhere established." This posed a real threat to England's "Civil and religious liberty." The corrupting character of Roman priests and nuns seriously jeopardized "those precious rights, liberties and principles for which the fathers of the Reformation suffered and died." Sisterhoods promoted unnatural practices, and the sufferings of poor Sr. Barbara visibly demonstrated the insidious and cruel nature of Catholicism. The outline of this story did not differ from the facts reported by *The Times* and *The Tablet*, and in many instances the report was based on the information already contained in the former newspaper, but its interpretation strayed from objective reporting.

In this anti-Catholic account of the rescue, Sr. Barbara's cell was located "close to a dung-hole." The graphic description of the nun also

21. *The Horrors of Roman Catholic Convents* (London, 1869).

differed somewhat from other portrayals: "In a dark, infected hole adjoining the sewer, sat, or rather, cowered, on a heap of straw, an entirely naked, totally neglected, half insane woman, who, at the unaccustomed view of light, the outer world, and human beings, folded her hands and pitifully implored: 'I am hungry' . . ." In addition to the disgusting description of the accommodation of Sr. Barbara, the diatribe described the convent and the nuns as, "This den, the inhumane sisters, who call themselves women, spiritual wives, the brides of heaven . . ." Closely following the language of *The Times*, the report described the astonished reaction of the Bishop of Cracow, recounted Sr. Barbara's account that she was imprisoned because she had broken her vow of chastity, and quoted the mother superior, who stated that Sr. Barbara had been kept in close confinement since 1848 "by order of the physician, because of her unsound mind."

Other disturbing and shocking additions also found their way into this narration. The investigators discovered torture devices, and told the readers that these instruments had "been used for torturing other poor nuns immured in the same convent and subjected to the iniquitous doings of their wicked father-confessors, as nuns formerly were . . ." Another example of editorial license to discredit Catholicism and convents can be found in the alleged discoveries made by the government commission when it investigated the convent grounds.

> In passing through the refectory they discovered a secret chamber containing a whole collection of mediaeval instruments of torture. Amongst these are two huge crosses, weighing 80 lb each, which guilty nuns had to wear on their backs as a punishment, two heavy stones of marble to be placed on the chest, and a number of "crowns of thorns" with long and sharp iron nails. There were also several girdles, also fitted with nails pointing in wards [*sic*], which it is said were worn next to the skin by penitents, and a sort of knout for flogging the refractory.

These devices, unique to this rendition of the story but found frequently in numerous other anti-Catholic tracts, formed part of that sacred arsenal which all nuns supposedly used to punish or to mortify the flesh.

The pamphlet also examined the role of the confessor, following other published reports in describing the part played by the convent's confessor, Fr. Lewkowicz, in the rescue of Sr. Barbara and the eventual arrest of the mother superior after her rescue. But in this version the circumstances surrounding the death of the priest took on a new and diabolical character. (A different spelling of the priest's name appeared in the account printed by *The Times*.) According to both *The Times* and *The Tablet*, the confessor died suddenly, and the latter told its readers that the cause was natural. This publication, however, added a sinister element. "The body of the former confessor, Father Lewkowicz, has been exhumed," it claimed, "and the news from Cracow is that traces of poison have been discovered in the body." Additional tests would either confirm or disprove the report, but "it seems certainly strange that the chief witness should have died just at the moment when the discovery [of Sr. Barbara] became public." The pamphlet also claimed that the superior of the nuns, a Carmelite priest, had visited the convent before her release, saw Sr. Barbara "in her horrible state, but had made no complaint." *The Horrors of Roman Catholic Convents*, however, did acknowledge that Sr. Barbara had a history of mental illness, but still described the manner in which the other nuns cared for her as an imprisonment.

The story of Sr. Barbara only formed a part of this anti-Catholic polemic. The other pages contained allegations of cruel and inhumane treatment associated with Roman Catholicism and even mocked some of its doctrines and liturgical practices. The main theme running throughout, however, pertained to the question of freedom. English Protestantism had traditionally championed personal liberty, while Catholicism, on the other hand, sought to make vassals and slaves of its followers. Popery and Catholic institutions, such as convents, would destroy the freedom and independence of Protestant Britain. Like Sr. Barbara, British citizens would become imprisoned and enslaved by Roman Catholicism. In concluding the discussion of Sr. Barbara, the author stated: "Leaving these sickening details to make their own impression, we will fill up the last part of our pamphlet with proofs, from the best sources (some Catholic) of the unchristian and soul-destroying character of Popery." Sr. Barbara, thus, had become a warning to those people who would welcome or embrace Roman Catholicism. State supervision would provide a safeguard against loss of liberty and freedom in convents. In 1870, for example, John Kensit, an anti-Roman Catholic writer and speaker and future secretary of the Protestant Truth Society, published *English Convents, What Are They?*[22] Kensit argued his case for parliamentary inspection of

22. Kensit, *English Convents*. Kensit published another work in the 1890s, *The Inquisition and Confessional of the Present Century*, which made explicit references to

convents, and he used two short newspaper references to Sr. Barbara as examples of convent abuse.

Anti-Catholic writers or those seeking state inspection of convents did not use the case of Sr. Barbara and the circumstances surrounding her confinement and release again until the end of the nineteenth century. During the 1890s anti-convent writings still criticized sisterhoods. Alleged reports of the imprisonment of nuns in England and Europe, charges of mismanagement of orphanages operated by nuns, numerous pamphlets and novels that stereotyped the wickedness of sisterhoods, and the old campaign to force open convent doors to government inspection kept the question of convents before the public.[23] For example, a footnote in H. Rider Haggard's 1893 novel, *Montezuma's Daughter*,[24] claimed that the author had seen in a Mexican museum the remains of a nun who had been "walled up." The Jesuit writer Fr. Herbert Thurston successfully attacked this allegation both in the press and in a pamphlet published by the Catholic Truth Society, and eventually forced the author to retract his misleading statement. And Sr. Barbara was not entirely forgotten. At the end of the century the Rev. W. Lancelot Holland, a vocal opponent and critic of sisterhoods, lectured on numerous cases of imprisoned nuns and wrote articles in Protestant papers attacking convents. He drew attention to the case of Sr. Barbara, who had died in 1891, as an example of convent cruelty, and thus began the last great debate over the facts of the "imprisoned nun of Cracow."

---

imprisoned nuns and their confinement in vaults located within convents. He drew special attention to a case of imprisoned nuns that occurred in Paris in 1871. To shock his readers, Kensit supplied a drawing of the three wooden cages in which were imprisoned three nuns.

23. Examples of anti-convent propaganda during this decade are numerous. Three publications illustrate this type of literature. During the 1890s the Church Association published *The Fashionable Torture Instruments of the Ritualists; or, the Gospel of 'Expiation.'* This short pamphlet printed drawings of torture devices or instruments allegedly used by nuns to impose self-discipline on their bodies. "Convents as Prisons and Lunatic Asylums" appeared in *The Monthly Letter of the Protestant Alliance*. The work described numerous examples of the alleged imprisonment of nuns in England and on the Continent. A short mention of Sr. Barbara was included. H. Grattan Guinness produced a book of poetry, *City of the Seven Hills*. One poem, "Rome's Convents," ridiculed sisterhoods. The author also included a series of notes to back up his arguments and a series of pictures of victims allegedly "walled up" by the Inquisition in Mexico.

24. Haggard, *Montezuma's Daughter*. The author later retracted his statement about immured nuns in Mexico after a lengthy debate with Fr. Herbert Thurston, SJ, which appeared in the English press.

Responding to some of Holland's remarks, the Rev. Sydney Smith, SJ, wrote a pamphlet, *Calumnies against Convents*, which the Catholic Truth Society published in 1894.[25] This apologetic work critiqued some of the recent slanders addressed against convents in England such as "the escape and the recapture of a nun from Colwich," charges of cruelty made against a convent at Norwood, and hostile reports of the activities at an orphanage operated by nuns at Carlisle Place, London. Finally the author addressed the case of Sr. Barbara. Smith began his discussion of the Cracow convent incident by quoting at length a report of the rescue of Sr. Barbara that had appeared in a publication of the Protestant Association, and which closely paralleled the language contained in *The Horrors of Roman Catholic Convents*. Smith pointed out: "This ghastly story was repeated by the journals of nearly every country at the time, and was received on every side with a chorus of indignation."[26] Writers and publications hostile to Roman Catholicism gleefully blamed the institutions and beliefs of that religion for the alleged inhumane treatment of Sr. Barbara. This Jesuit writer believed that another culprit had wickedly encouraged anti-Catholic feelings.

The opponents of Roman Catholicism throughout Europe feared a papal plot to convert the world, and the Catholics became convinced that in self-defense these forces had started a conspiracy against the threatened onslaught from Rome. According to Fr. Smith: "Those, however, who understood the methods by which the Masonic Governments on the Continent were in the habit of arousing a popular feeling in favor of the measures that they were projecting against the Church, asked themselves what sort of Ministry were at the head of affairs in Austria, and what projects they had in contemplation." This sinister Masonic threat, Smith believed, had unduly exaggerated and distorted the case of Sr. Barbara. The Austrian ministry, according to this conspiracy theory, had used the public indignation and outrage against the Cracow convent to further its policy, which was "bent on the suppression of the religious orders and the confiscation of their goods." In fact, Fr. Smith argued, a government official "in a feigned female hand" had written the mysterious and anonymous letter that had exposed the existence of Sr. Barbara. Moreover, the civil authorities had failed to act with dispatch when a mob attacked the convent in Cracow. The Masonic influence

25. Smith, *Calumnies against Convents*.
26. Ibid., 18.

The Myth and Reality of Sr. Barbara Ubryk, the Imprisoned Nun of Cracow 75

in the government, Smith told his readers, had followed a pre-arranged plan and moved quickly to "withhold the annual pension on which the convent depended for its subsistence, and even suppress the convent altogether."[27] Other Polish municipalities followed the lead of Cracow, and all this had transpired before the outcome of the trial and inquest. "Why this indecent haste," Smith reasoned, "save because all had been arranged beforehand, and they were anxious to use the opportunity before it was destroyed by the detection of the fraud?"

Fr. Smith noted that the major English newspapers, in particular *The Times*, had quickly lost interest in the Sr. Barbara case. The curious reader in England did not know the results of the trial of the nuns accused of cruelty against Sr. Barbara, and consequently he set out to inform them. The English Jesuit made no apologies for relying on the reports printed in *The Tablet*.[28] Smith repeated the 21 August 1869 story of that Roman Catholic paper, which stated that the two nuns were found guilty of an objective offence of violating the right of Sr. Barbara to personal freedom and were ordered "to stand a special trial accordingly."[29] In other words, he pointed out, "it was judged that they had unwittingly been guilty of a legal offence in locking the door on a mad woman without having first gone through the legal formalities."[30] Fr. Smith also revealed the outcome and verdict of "the special" trial, information the anti-Catholic sources had failed to include in their histories of Sr. Barbara. Quoting from the edition of 12 February 1870 of the *Civilta Cattolica*, the Jesuit-operated publication located in Rome, Smith proudly announced:

> Hence Giska ["the Masonic" Minister for Home Affairs] and his fellow-conspirators had to put up with the passing of a verdict in good form to the effect that Barbara Ubryk had in no way been shewn to have undergone any cruelty to which her madness could be imputed, and that throughout its course she had been treated as well as possible according to the method consistent with her deplorable state, and had received every attention which the most tender Christian charity could inspire.

---

27. Ibid., 19.
28. Fr. Smith also made use of the reports contained the Catholic newspaper, *Civilta Cattolica*.
29. *The Tablet*, 21 August 1869.
30. Smith, *Calumnies*, 20.

No previous written accounts of the alleged Cracow cruelties had mentioned this verdict. Smith ended his short pamphlet by noting that the citizens of Cracow had started a subscription to replace those funds that the government had succeeded in sequestering. These arguments, however, did not convince the Rev. W. Lancelot Holland.

Holland reacted immediately to the challenge thrown down by Fr. Smith, and wrote a response that attempted to expose the evils and inhumanity of convent life. Its title, *Walled Up Nuns and Nuns Walled In*, captured the purpose of the author.[31] The introduction drew the reader's attention to the increasing power and nefarious influence of the papacy, and pointed out that the Roman Church had "advanced in all the refinements of cruelty, practicing every method or torture that human ingenuity and satanic influence could devise upon those who ventured to dissent from her principles, or attempted in any way to spread the light of truth."[32] This type of punishment also applied to recalcitrant or erring nuns. The British public, Holland argued, must be informed of the true nature of the convent. Defenseless, young, and sentimental women in Britain needed protection from the inherent evils of sisterhoods. According to his reasoning, "if the public would only grasp the real foulness so often underlying the whited sepulchres called Convents, there would not be many of these places left in Great Britain within a month after the discovery." After illustrating the evils of conventual life from other examples of alleged abuses, the author discussed the case of Sr. Barbara.

Holland began by telling his audience that he had earlier written a pamphlet concerning the Cracow incident,[33] and this had caused Fr. Sidney Smith to reply with *Calumnies against Convents*, a defense of sisterhoods and a vindication of the treatment of Sr. Barbara. In respect of the Cracow incident, the author attacked Smith's work and accused him of manufacturing "palpable misrepresentations."[34] Holland sneered at Smith's version of the story and questioned the veracity of the Jesuit: "for unless the facts are well grasped, it would be impossible to withstand

---

31. Holland, *Walled Up Nuns*.

32. Ibid., 11.

33. Holland, *Somebody's Child*. The pamphlet was out of print by 1895. This earlier work by Holland cannot be found, but probably contained the same material as *Walled Up Nuns*.

34. Holland, *Walled Up Nuns*, 163.

The Myth and Reality of Sr. Barbara Ubryk, the Imprisoned Nun of Cracow 77

the varnished lies and subtle arguments of the trained sophists who are put forward by the Church of Rome to discredit the truth."³⁵ Holland's story of the rescue, however, introduced several new elements, and the narration now began to read like a gothic fiction. A new character and savior, Sr. Mary, appeared. This nun had discovered that Sr. Barbara was confined to a "dungeon," and taking pity on her, Sr. Mary had stolen the key from the mother superior and smuggled food into Sr. Barbara. According to this rendition, Sr. Mary found Sr. Barbara sane, heard her story, and consequently vowed to rescue her. Moreover, Holland added another new twist, and claimed that Sr. Mary had written the letter which eventually resulted in the release of Sr. Barbara by the authorities!

Holland's narration of the rescue of Sr. Barbara paralleled other accounts, but it appears that he exaggerated his description of the poor creature: "her body entirely nude, bristling with long jagged hair, filth and vermin; her limbs shrunk and bent like withered sticks, her head and hair squalid and diseased; her thin, hollow cheeks nearly touching each other, and the great wild eyes flashing and glaring out from their deep sockets."³⁶ An extremely disturbing drawing in this book depicted the scared and skeletal figure of a naked person cowering in the corner of a dark cell. As in the other accounts, the Roman Catholic bishop expressed horror at the discovery. Before leaving the convent, Sr. Barbara explained that she had been imprisoned because she had broken her vows. In this version of the story, Holland identified the confessor as Fr. Calenski, another new name for the priest, and he did not suggest poison to account for the confessor's sudden death. Rather, the priest committed suicide, and left a note which stated: "I have resolved to kill myself: farewell to all on earth."³⁷

After some criticism of Fr. Smith and his interpretation of the case, Holland outlined his own interpretation of the results of the commission set up by the Austrian government to investigate the happening at the Cracow convent. He admitted that he had gleaned the information from the Vienna papers. The bishop, who sat on the commission, accepted the explanation of Sr. Mary's authorship of the letter, but this story conflicted with Fr. Smith's allegation that a government official had written it. Sr. Mary testified next and stated that Sr. Barbara had never exhibited

35. Ibid., 165.
36. Ibid., 169.
37. Ibid., 171.

any symptoms of mental illness when she first entered the convent. She also insinuated that Sr. Barbara was "imprisoned" because she resisted the advances of the confessor, and moreover the mother superior played a significant part in this conspiracy. The question of Sr. Barbara's sanity remained a crucial issue. Sr. Mary gave evidence that suggested that Sr. Barbara had previously suffered from mental problems, but immediately before her release, the imprisoned nun "returned sensible, rational replies," though she exhibited an excessive amount of nervousness.[38] Holland then revealed the decision of the commission, which clashed with Fr. Smith's account:

> That the said Barbara Ubryk has been for twenty-one years unlawfully imprisoned in a loathsome, underground dungeon of the Carmelite Convent, and most cruelly and barbarously oppressed and maltreated by Mother Josepha, the Abbess thereof, and Father Calenski, the Confessor thereof. We also find that the said Barbara Ubryk was not of unsound mind, and therefore that it was unnecessary to deprive her of her liberty.

The commission noted that the convent's confessor had already committed suicide, but recommended, again conflicting with Smith's report, that the mother superior should be punished for her misdeeds.

Holland's book next introduced several new pieces of evidence. For the first time, interested people could actually read the testimony of Sr. Barbara, who now appeared to be perfectly lucid and cured of any mental infirmities. The nun related that she had entered the Carmelite convent at Cracow, at the age of sixteen, after a failed romance. Holland presented additional testimony that stated that Sr. Barbara had first joined another convent, and then transferred to Cracow after a bout of mental illness. She described her first years at Cracow in idyllic terms; the mother superior, Sr. Josepha, and the confessor all treated her very well. However, the priest soon began to become more and more interested in her. One night he visited Sr. Barbara's room to console her about some penances she had received from the mother superior. According to Sr. Barbara, this did not "excite her suspicions until he put his arm around her and kissed her full on the lips."[39] She admitted that the actions of this cleric, who had also left some gifts of food, bewildered her.

38. Ibid., 175.
39. Ibid., 178.

Sr. Barbara's account of what happened next introduced the new twist of a sexual element into the already complex story.

Apparently the confessor had laced the cakes and fruit with drugs with the intention of sexually assaulting her, since she immediately fell into a deep slumber after enjoying the gifts. When Sr. Barbara awoke, she discovered Fr. Calenski, the confessor, lurking in her room. She then related the following scene:

> Evidently perceiving by his actions his wicked designs, she sprang away from him, struck him in the face, and screamed out, "Go away from my cell, Father Calenski! Why do you behave so wickedly?" He struck her a heavy blow with his hand, and in a low hissing tone said, "Silence; if you utter another scream I will kill you!"[40]

The frightened nun screamed, and the mother superior arrived. After consulting with the confessor, the mother superior left Sr. Barbara's room, telling her, "Girl, your silly lips have sealed your doom!" After a week's confinement in her convent room, Sr. Barbara was eventually taken to a dungeon in the basement of the convent, where the mother superior told her she would remain until her death. The confessor continued to visit her, but finally exclaimed, "I am tired of you now, why don't you die or go really crazy?"[41] Sr. Barbara admitted becoming insane and she also remembered the cold, the hunger, and the physical torture she had endured as a prisoner, especially at the hands of the priest. After threatening to murder her, the confessor began to attack her physically. According to her testimony, Fr. Calenski, "raising his cane and giving me several heavy blows with it, and causing me such agony that I became nearly crazy . . . [I] could not help screaming out . . ."[42] She suffered for days with a "numbness in my neck and back" and the pain began to affect her mental state. But the abuse did not stop. "On several occasions after this Father Calenski and Mother Josepha beat me, and I became so filled with despair . . ." Sr. Barbara's story ended with a visit from Sr. Mary and her eventual rescue.

If Holland's accusations were true, then cruel and inhumane punishments, similar to those allegedly used by the Inquisitors, had taken place

---

40. Ibid., 179.
41. Ibid., 180.
42. Ibid., 182.

in a Cracow convent. Moreover, nuns throughout England and Europe probably encountered similar punishments on a regular basis. The Roman Catholic newspapers and writers who had sought to explain the Sr. Barbara episode as an example of naive nuns attempting to deal with an insane member of their convent had obviously lied. Consequently, the Rev. Sydney Smith, SJ, whose earlier work on anti-convent literature had already irked the Rev. W. Lancelot Holland, responded with another pamphlet published by the Catholic Truth Society. In this booklet, Smith branded Holland as a bigot and identified him as an important member of the Protestant Alliance, a violent anti-Catholic organization. Smith then returned to his central thesis: strong Masonic influences in the Austrian government had caused the furor and violence in Cracow against Roman Catholicism and its convents. He restated the contentions of his previous article, which contradicted all the main arguments of Holland, and reminded his readers that the accused Carmelite nuns, including the mother superior, had been acquitted. He referred the interested person back to the article in *Civilta Cattolica* that vindicated the conduct of these nuns.[43] Fr. Smith also repeated the evidence printed by *The Tablet*. He then addressed the charges brought by Holland's book dealing with Sr. Barbara.

Smith totally dismissed Holland's evidence. According to his pamphlet, "Mr. Holland's new authorities are not only false, but, it is to be feared, fraudulent."[44] Fr. Smith questioned the veracity of Holland's interpretation of the commission's report, the evidence given, and the testimony of Sr. Barbara. In fact, the Jesuit pointed out, Holland's chapter on Sr. Barbara relied almost exclusively on an American pamphlet that dealt with the Cracow convent and Sr. Barbara.[45] It did not utilize documentation from Poland. This booklet, Smith argued, represented "nothing better than a romance absolutely unsupported by any reference whatever. Yet it is from it, not from any authentic document, in spite of his express declaration to the contrary, that his quotations within

---

43. The article in the 12 February 1870 edition of *Civilta Cattolica* reported a verdict which stated that no evidence proved that Barbara Ubryk had suffered any cruelty at the hands of the Carmelite nuns and that the nuns had treated Sr. Barbara's madness in an appropriate and Christian manner.

44. Smith, *True Story*, 8.

45. See *Convent Horror*. This booklet was also published in England.

inverted commas are extracted."[46] Smith set out to destroy the credibility of this factitious and spurious American pamphlet. As his ammunition, he identified and cited the medical and legal records associated with the case.

The most impressive of Holland's sources remained the testimony of Sr. Barbara herself. Smith, however, named and then quoted four sources that attested that in her poor mental state she could not have given a coherent statement about her life and imprisonment in the convent. "All concur in testifying to facts which prove that Barbara Ubryk could not possibly have made the alleged deposition either on 16 August 1869, or on any other date previous or subsequent."[47] Smith urged cynics and unbelievers to visit the hospital in Cracow where Sr. Barbara resided until her death in 1891. There they could enquire about her mental state after she was freed from the convent. Fr. Smith also pointed out errors of fact in Holland's account of her life prior to becoming a nun and of her mental state before arriving at Cracow. For example, Sr. Barbara had previously suffered from a history of mental health problems. Fr. Smith dismissed the accusation of the alleged attempt at seduction and cruelty at the hands of the confessor, whom Holland had apparently falsely identified as Fr. Calenski. He pointed out that "no person of that name had at any time anything whatever to do with her case . . ."[48] Consequently, Fr. Smith came to the following conclusion:

> In view of all this evidence it is excessive to say that Mr. Holland and his nameless American friend (who for aught we know may be himself under another guise) must share between them the responsibility of having attempted to pass off as genuine a palpably spurious document containing the grossest charges against others, and this with the express object of exciting prejudice and persecution against the peaceful priests, nuns, and other Catholics of English-speaking countries.

Smith next attacked the decision of the commissioners that Holland had presented, and the Jesuit argued that this so-called evidence contained several errors or untrue statements, "a plain proof that it is spurious."[49] The signatures to Holland's questionable document that

46. Smith, *True Story*, 9.
47. Ibid., 11.
48. Ibid., 12.
49. Ibid., 13.

condemned the Carmelite nuns, Fr. Smith contended, were "made-up names." He noted that only one commission had been established in Cracow, and the name of a judge (Gebhardt) that could be found in numerous other documents as a member failed to appear on Holland's list. As he had previously stated, Holland incorrectly identified the confessor as Calenski, and Fr. Smith named the convent's confessor as Fr. Piatkewicz. Smith also contradicted other false stories about this priest by pointing out that the confessor had died a natural death at the age of 75 in 1881. Moreover, Sr. Barbara's place of confinement was not "an underground dungeon," but a room situated on the first floor of the convent at the end of a hall occupied by other nuns. Smith backed up these contentions with numerous references to documentary sources, reports in the press, and witnesses.

Fr. Smith enumerated other errors in Holland's account, delighting in destroying the testimony of the heroine of his story, Sr. Mary. The Jesuit laughed at her ignorance concerning the correct name of the confessor and the location of Sr. Barbara's room, and he found it hard to believe that nuns living on the same corridor would be ignorant of her existence. At least, he reasoned, her cries and shrieks would have alerted others to her presence. The name of the mother superior of the convent came into question: Holland called her Sr. Josepha; but Smith's sources identified this nun as Sr. Maria Wenzyk. Smith then looked at the legal proceedings against the Carmelite superior and her accomplice, and he repeated the findings contained in his earlier work, *Calumnies against Convents*: sufficient evidence did not exist to prosecute the nuns; they had illegally locked Sr. Barbara's door against her will, but had not acted in a cruel or criminal manner; and the charges against the two nuns had been dismissed. Moreover, Fr. Smith again supplied the proper documentation to back up these statements. He also quickly dismissed Holland's other contentions: Sr. Barbara was not sane; there was no attempt to conceal her mental condition or the method of dealing with her problems from ecclesiastical superiors; and the physical condition of her room was not as harsh and severe as some described. Fr. Smith directed the interested reader to a list of sources to corroborate his statements, and he ended his pamphlet by surprisingly agreeing with his adversary, Holland, on one point: "some fresh legislation in reference to convents is imperatively needed."[50] He did not advocate parliamentary measures

50. Ibid., 23.

which would subject convents to inspection by the government, but rather "a remodelling of the law of libel as shall enable the innocent and peaceful inhabitants of English convents to protect themselves against slanderers cowardly enough to attack them under the guise of charges against other convents in distant lands" such as Poland.[51]

With the publication of Fr. Sydney Smith's blistering and well-reasoned attack against Holland and the other critics of sisterhoods whom he mentioned, the literature devoted to mocking convents and describing alleged abuses within the cloister decreased markedly.[52] Anti-convent publications continued to decline as the new century opened in England, and along with other popular stories the figure of Sr. Barbara also began to fade from memory.[53] To the end of the nineteenth century, individuals who interpreted Sr. Barbara's life in a manner to fit their purposes—anti-Roman Catholic writers or defenders of Catholic sisterhoods who tried to justify the actions of the Cracow Carmelites—had distorted the real personality and the life of this woman, who died in 1891. Discrepancies can be seen in the numerous narrations. One interpretation of the case pointed the finger at the influence of the Masons, attempting to dis-

---

51. Ibid., 24.

52. The anti-convent literature did not, however, disappear altogether. See, for example, Walter Walsh's critique of Anglo-Catholicism, which stated some harsh things about Anglican sisterhoods. Walsh, *Secret History*. In 1899 an anonymous author wrote *The Martyrdom of an Empress* (New York, 1899), which attempted to canonize the Austrian Empress Elizabeth, who had been assassinated in 1898. This biography took some liberties with the life of Sr. Barbara, such as her background prior to entering the convent, the important role played by her brother in starting the investigation concerning her well-being, and the significant part played by the Empress Elizabeth, who asked the ecclesiastical authorities in Cracow to intervene. In addition to the graphic descriptions of the incarcerated nun, the account stated that the nuns had imprisoned Sr. Barbara because she had kept up a correspondence with a former admirer and planned to elope with him. The story of the Cracow convent is included in this biography not necessarily to castigate the Roman Catholic Church, but to emphasize the charity of the murdered empress, who frequently sent flowers to Sr. Barbara while she was in an asylum.

53. The case of Sr. Barbara did make another brief appearance. Early in the century S. J. Abbott, Secretary of the Convent Enquiry Society, published *Empress and the Carmelite Nun*. This short pamphlet took its name from the recently-published biography of the *Empress Elizabeth*. It also contained excerpts from various newspapers that had carried the story of Sr. Barbara during the previous century. Abbott used the case to argue for the necessity of government inspection of convents. Fr. Herbert Thurston, SJ, published two pamphlets that attacked the stories that had developed out of Haggard's *Montezuma's Daughter*. Thurston made no mention of Sr. Barbara. See *Myth of the Walled-Up Nun* and *A Tale of Mexican Horrors*.

credit Roman Catholicism, and another argued that cruel and heartless convents routinely tortured recalcitrant members, and consequently they should be suppressed or brought under government supervision. Moreover, disagreements about Sr. Barbara's background, reasons for entering the convent, state of mental health before and after her release, and the reasons for her confinement appeared in the stories about her. Confusion surrounding the name of the confessor and the mode of his death, the author of the letter that prompted officials to visit the convent, and the correct name and the role of the mother superior also added to the mystery. Differing descriptions of Sr. Barbara's sufferings and the condition of the room where she was discovered also appeared in print.

Some common elements, however, surfaced in all the accounts of her life. Sr. Barbara Ubryk, by common agreement, was placed under confinement in a Carmelite convent in Cracow until she was set free in 1869. Cracow did experience some anti-Catholic violence because of rumours about her wretched physical and mental state, and numerous newspapers, some with an obvious prejudice, took delight in reporting the story. An inquiry did take place that eventually exonerated the convent's superior. The confessor to the convent appeared in all the accounts, and Sr. Barbara did die in an asylum in 1891. Beside these accepted facts, the story of Sr. Barbara had merged with fiction and legend by the end of the century. One became acquainted with the myth of Sr. Barbara, and not the person.

Is history, as the figure of Venus painted on the wall announced to all onlookers, merely a collection of myths? The story or legend of Sr. Barbara Ubryk clearly demonstrates the power of history. People can easily manipulate or misuse facts to fit pre-conceived stereotypes or agendas. In matters dealing with religion, people in nineteenth-century England often engaged in polemics or crusades against religious rivals, as the case of Sr. Barbara clearly demonstrates. Most fierce and vitriolic was the suspicion and hatred directed against Roman Catholics in that country.[54] In the minds of some anti-Catholics, moreover, convents represented cruel and inhumane places of mental and physical torture. If one accepts and acknowledges the tendency in Victorian England to attack theological and doctrinal opponents in newspapers, pamphlets,

---

54. For example, see D. G. Paz, *Popular Anti-Catholicism in Mid-Victorian England*; Wallis, *Popular Anti-Catholicism in Mid-Victorian Britain*; and Wolffe, *Protestant Crusade in Great Britain*.

and books, even to the point of creating falsehoods, one may arrive at a better understanding of the dynamics of religious hatred and bigotry. If, on the other hand, people accept uncritically stories that fit a stereotype, such as the wickedness of convent life, then the verdict of Venus about the mythic nature of history has some validity.

Bibliography

Abbott, S. J. *The Empress and the Carmelite Nun: Twenty-One Years in a Convent Dungeon*. London: Convent Enquiry Society, n.d.

Arnstein, Walter L. *Protestant versus Catholic in Mid-Victorian England: Mr. Newdegate and the Nuns*. Columbia: University of Missouri Press, 1982.

Caracciolo, Henrietta. *Memoirs of Henrietta Caracciolo of the Princes of Forino: Ex-Benedictine Nun*. New ed. London: Bentley, 1865.

"Convents as Prisons and Lunatic Asylums." *The Monthly Letter of the Protestant Alliance* (October 1891) 1–24.

The Convent Horror: Story of Barbara Ubryk Twenty-One Years in the Dungeon, Eight Feet Long, Six Feet Wide. from Official Records. Toledo, OH: King, 1896.

The Fashionable Torture Instruments of the Ritualists; or, the Gospel of 'Expiation.' London, 1890.

Guinness, H. Grattan. *The City of the Seven Hills: An Illustrated Poem*. London: Nisbet, 1891.

Haggard, H. Rider. *Montezuma's Daughter*. London: Longmans, Green, 1893.

———. *Somebody's Child: or Sister Barbara, the Carmelite Nun*.

Holland, W. Lancelot. *Walled Up Nuns and Nuns Walled In*. London: J. Kensit, 1895.

The Horrors of Roman Catholic Convents, Exposed in a True Heartrending Account of the Shocking Imprisonment and Sufferings of Sister Barbara, a Polish Carmelite Nun, Who was Walled Up Alive for Twenty-One Years in the Cold Dark Cell of an Infected Underground Dungeon! London, 1869.

Kensit, John. *English Convents, What Are They? Or Is There Any Necessity for Conventual Inspection?* London: Worthing, 1870.

———. *The Inquisition and Confessional of the Present Century*. London, 1893?

Latourette, Kenneth Scott. *A History of Christianity*. Vol. 2. Rev. ed. New York: Harper & Row, 1975.

Lewis, M. G. *The Monk: A Romance*. London: Bell, 1796.

The Martyrdom of an Empress. New York: Harper, 1899.

The Marvellous Escape of 'Sister Lucy,' and Her Awful Disclosures Respecting New Hall Convent, Boreham, Essex. London: Murray, 1868.

McClelland, Maria. "The First Hull Mercy Nuns: A Nineteenth Century Case Study." *Recusant History* 22 (1994) 199–221.

Paz, D. G. *Popular Anti-Catholicism in Mid-Victorian England*. Stanford: Stanford University Press, 1992.

A Plea for the Inspection or Suppression of Convents. London: Protestant Evangelical Mission & Electoral Union, 1870.

Smith, Sydney, SJ. *Calumnies against Convents*. London: Catholic Truth Society, 1894.

———. *The True Story of Barbara Ubryk*. London: Catholic Truth Society, 1897.

Thackeray, William Makepeace. "The Irish Sketch Book." In *The Complete Works of William Makepeace Thackeray*. New York: Harper & Brothers, 1903.

Thurston, Herbert. *The Myth of the Walled-Up Nun*. London: Catholic Truth Society, 1904.

———. *A Tale of Mexican Horrors*. London: Catholic Truth Society, 1904.

Viner, G. M. *Priests and Their Victims; or Scenes in a Convent! In Which the Reader Is Shown the Cause of a Nun's Entry into a Convent, the Manner of Her Education, the Cunning of the Priesthood, Their Midnight Orgies, the Mode of Getting Rid of the Offspring, with a Correct Copy of the Secret Instructions of the Jesuits; and an Account of Their Brutal Treatment of an Italian Lady, Compiled from M. S. "Confessions of a Nun," etc. etc. by Signor—*. London: Elliot, 1852.

Wallis, Frank. *Popular Anti-Catholicism in Mid-Victorian Britain*. Texts and Studies in Religion 60. Lewiston, NY: Mellen, 1993.

Walsh, Walter. *The Secret History of the Oxford Movement*. London: Thynne, 1899.

Wolffe, John. *The Protestant Crusade in Great Britain*. Oxford Historical Monographs. Oxford: Clarendon, 1991.

5

An American "Escaped Nun" on Tour in England

Edith O'Gorman's Critique of Convent Life

RELIGION PLAYED A DOMINANT role in the social and political life of Victorian England, and loyal Anglicans did not hesitate to defend their country and Church against perceived or real threats, especially from Roman Catholicism. The Catholic Emancipation Act of 1829, the government's generous financial policies toward Maynooth College, and finally the Restoration of the Hierarchy in September 1850 frightened many individuals in England. Numerous organizations, pamphlets and works of fiction, petitions to Parliament, and dedicated speakers, usually men, worked to defend the Protestant character of Anglicanism against perceived Roman influences, usually associated with the Anglo-Catholic party in the Anglican Church which encouraged the growth of sisterhoods in England. This frightened the Protestant element, which believed that convents preyed upon naive and romantic English girls and robbed them of basic English liberties. Moreover, the opponents of sisterhoods also believed that they might encourage and hasten conversions to Catholicism. An American, Edith O'Gorman, brought a different perspective to the debate over convents. Here was a woman who could speak about the cruelties in a sisterhood from personal experiences. An immigrant to America from Ireland who converted from Roman Catholicism, her lectures would also reinforce English prejudices against the Irish and their Catholicism. O'Gorman, consequently, became a woman who found acceptance and success in the patriarchal atmosphere of Victorian England because of her critiques of convents.

Anti-Catholicism also played an important part in early American history, and some believed that Roman Catholic sisterhoods imprisoned defenseless women and deprived them of their rights. Some brave souls escaped from sisterhoods, and their stories contributed to the convent escape narrative, a popular form of anti-Catholic literature. Jenny Franchot points out that "these nineteenth-century 'maidens' [escaped nuns] claimed to have met savagery behind the religious guise of priest and nun,"[1] and their tales of religious corruption and oppression appealed to the Yankee spirit, which distrusted popery. The written testimonies of three former nuns, Rebecca Reed's *Six Months in a Convent* (1835), Maria Monk's *Awful Disclosures, by Maria Monk, of the Hotel Dieu Nunnery of Montreal* (1836), and Josephine Bunkley's *Miss Bunkley's Book: The Testimony of an Escaped Novice* (1855) described sisterhoods in shocking terms. When Edith O'Gorman fled from her convent, she not only wrote about her experiences, but—as Maureen McCarthy observed—became the first so-called escaped nun to make a career out of lecturing about the horrors of convent life in America and abroad.[2]

Miss Edith O'Gorman joined the ranks of escaped nuns in 1868, and soon afterwards she put pen to paper and wrote *Trials and Persecutions of Miss Edith O'Gorman*.[3] O'Gorman was born in 1842 in Ireland, and the family emigrated to America eight years later. In 1862, Miss O'Gorman entered the Sisters of Charity in Madison, New Jersey. As a novice, she received her name in religion, Sister Teresa de Chantal, and thus began her period of trials. Two years later, she was sent to an orphanage to work, and within a few months, she took her religious vows. Soon afterwards, O'Gorman and two other nuns journeyed to Hudson City, New Jersey, to establish a new convent. In January 1868, she fled or escaped from this convent after a priest, Fr. Walsh, allegedly tried to seduce her. In addition to the improper actions of this cleric, the penances performed by the sisters shocked readers in America and abroad. A nun working in the garden, for example, screamed at the sight of a worm, and as a punishment it was forced into her mouth. Another sister was beaten, and another had to bite off the head of a mouse. A penance familiar in

---

1. Franchot, *Roads to Rome*, 118.
2. McCarthy, *Rescue of True Womanhood*, 375.
3. O'Gorman, *Trials and Persecutions*.

anti-convent literature, licking the floor with one's tongue, also appeared in her account of nunnery life. O'Gorman, who characterized herself as a martyr, a heroine, and a saint, also related stories about the existence of convent dungeons, priestly sexual impropriety, tyrannical superiors, and abuses of the children under the care of the nuns at the orphanage.

O'Gorman remained a Roman Catholic for a time following her escape from the convent, and she continued to experience what she perceived as Roman Catholic deception, including an alleged attempt to abduct her and then force her into another convent. She even attempted suicide. Miss O'Gorman eventually began to recognize what she believed were the errors and shallowness of the Roman Catholic religion and, in September 1869, she gave her first talk in Jersey City, the place where she had spent a number of years as a Catholic nun, about the wickedness of Catholicism. This lecture was met by loud protests by the Catholics in the audience, and O'Gorman later recalled that when she left the hall "an attempt was made to 'lynch' me, several kitchen girls threatening to 'mash my face' with their umbrellas."[4] She eventually left the Catholic Church in December 1869, and was "re-baptized" in the North Baptist Church in Jersey City. During the next year, O'Gorman married William Auffray, a former Roman Catholic priest.

The subsequent chapters of *Trials and Persecutions* told the story of her marriage, described the attempts of Catholics to silence her or to discredit the truth of her statements, and summarized her attacks against Roman Catholic doctrines, "priestcraft," and the parochial school system in America. Edith O'Gorman championed Bible-based religion and also argued for government inspection of convents. This book also informed the reader of her decision to embark upon a vocation that she would pursue both on American and foreign soil. "One of the signs of a perfect conversion is a great zeal to convert others," O'Gorman wrote, "and with this desire my heart was filled." When asked by a friend what she planned to do, she immediately replied: "I am going to lecture."[5] At first, her missionary zeal took her to Oregon, California, and Canada, but her crusade would not be limited to North America. The religious climate in England would prove receptive to someone who had personally experienced convent atrocities, but she would also encounter hostility and protests from Roman Catholics who would defend their religion against her attacks.

4. Ibid., 184.
5. Ibid., 181.

A culture of anti-Catholicism certainly existed in England. The presence on stage of a survivor of convent life would prove more effective than any pamphlet or book. Those suspicious of convent life would welcome O'Gorman's tale of horror. Works of fiction dealing with the stories of women who had fled from convents had effectively prepared the ground in England for O'Gorman's lectures. *The Nun and Her Daughter; or, Memoirs of the Courville Family: A Novel* (1805), Sarah Wilkinson's *Convent or Grey Penitents; or, the Apostate Nun: A Romance* (1810), H. Thornton's *The Little Nun: A Bit of Scandal* (1850), Edward Massey's *Love's Strife with the Convent; or, the Heiress of Strange Hall* (1864), J. Wimsett Baulding's *The Spanish Nun; and Other Poems* (1870), and E. C. Grenville-Murray's *Imprisoned in a Spanish Convent: An English Girl's Experience* (1886) are several examples of the literature telling English readers about the evils of the convent. To avoid suffering and death, escape had become the only option for the distressed nun. *Priests and Their Victims, or Scenes in a Convent* (1852), for example, appealed to English pride. Set in Roman Catholic Italy, the author, "Maria Nun," described the murder of pregnant nuns and newborn children, orgies, lusty priests, and the sexual misdeeds of the other sisters. The main character eventually fled to England, implying that the freedom of that country would not permit such atrocities committed in the name of religion.

In England, several anti-Catholic societies, such as the Protestant Alliance, the British Society for Promoting the Religious Principles of the Reformation, and the Protestant Truth Society worked to protect the Protestant character of Anglicanism. They published tracts which illustrated the evils of the convent system associated with the Romanizing tendencies of the Anglo-Catholics and told the public about the dramatic escapes by brave nuns who wanted to preserve their physical and spiritual health. In his pamphlet, *English Convents, What Are They?*, John Kensit included newspaper clippings which reported escapes or attempted flights from convents in Dublin, Limerick, Colwich, Staplehill, and Bristol, which allegedly took place between 1865–70.[6] Memoirs, much like those written by Rebecca Reed and Edith O'Gorman, also delighted the enemies of sisterhoods in England. *The Marvellous Escape of "Sister Lucy," and Her Awful Disclosures Respecting New Hall Convent, Boreham, Essex*, for example, used the language and rhetoric of Maria Monk's tale

6. Kensit, *English Convents*, 19–22.

of suffering and deliverance. Using a makeshift rope, Sister Lucy escaped from the convent window in April 1865. Her story used images associated with prisons to describe life in the convent. Sister Lucy (Ann Cullen) told the public about the cruel and inhumane treatment which she and the other sisters endured, and she related stories of wild drinking parties involving priests and nuns, "indelicate" questions about sex asked by the convent's confessor, and flagellation with "a small spike chain" as a penance. Her story ended with a plea that "*Convent Prisons—Sacerdotal Harems*" should be subject to state inspection.[7] These revelations, some of questionable veracity, and the details of dramatic escapes of imprisoned nuns prepared the English public for Edith O'Gorman's arrival and her speaking tours in the 1880s. Moreover, people who feared the growth and influence of Roman Catholicism were well acquainted with several ex-Catholics who lashed out against their former church such as O'Gorman would eventually do. Edith O'Gorman's sex, however, would set her apart.

These male peripatetic speakers highlighted the alleged evils of Roman Catholicism. The hostile reactions from loyal Catholics who defended their faith against these detractors became part of the religious culture of Victorian England. "By the 1860s, there was rioting," Edward Norman points out, "localized, small in scale, and usually produced by the presence of itinerant preachers and lecturers."[8] Like O'Gorman, the most celebrated and provocative were not English: Giacinto Achilli (ex-Dominican), Alessandro Gavazzi (former monk) and William Murphy (convert from Catholicism) from County Limerick. Their rhetoric sometimes caused fights and pitched battles between their Protestant supporters and loyal Roman Catholics, most frequently Irish immigrants.[9] Edith O'Gorman's career as an anti-Catholic speaker in many respects appears similar to Murphy's crusade against the spread of popery in England, which lasted from 1863 to his death following an attack in 1872: hostile reactions from Roman Catholics in their audiences, especially the Irish; incidents of physical violence following their presentations; the pugnacity to take their crusade into largely Catholic areas of the country; and

---

7. *Marvellous Escape of 'Sister Lucy,'* 24.
8. Norman, *English Catholic Church*, 20.
9. Gilley, "Garibaldi Riots."

the audacity to challenge anyone, layman, cleric or prelate, to refute publicly their accusations against the Roman faith.[10]

The English first became aware of Miss O'Gorman's activities through the report of an attempt to assassinate her following an American lecture in 1870. This story appeared in the Irish and English press in May of that year, and it gave a brief outline of her life as a nun, her escape, and the details of the shot fired as she entered a carriage following her talk.[11] Eleven years later, O'Gorman and her husband arrived in England in 1881 after touring North America, and she immediately began her attack against Roman Catholic sisterhoods. One of her first lectures took place in Weymouth, and the Evangelical paper, *The Rock*, recorded the event in its 30 September 1881 edition. This early talk did not dwell on her experiences in the American convent, but emphasized her "conversion experience," which inspired her to flee from the cloister. O'Gorman fancied herself as a modern St. Paul. She told the audience "she was overpowered with God's omnipotence, as St Paul was overpowered."[12] The same divine voice that had called Paul to conversion also spoke to her in the convent and summoned her to leave and preach the Gospel to all people. She obeyed, fled from the sisterhood, and "consecrated herself to the Lord." Shortly after this talk, O'Gorman also published for the English public, a cheap edition of her book about her life as a nun and her escape.[13]

Edith O'Gorman's allies defended her from Roman Catholic criticisms. The *Bulwark*, published by the Scottish Reformation Society, came to O'Gorman's aid by printing her letter which attempted to refute the Catholic attacks against her honesty. O'Gorman drew attention to remarks which recently appeared in the Catholic newspaper, the *Universe*, and she labeled the editor as "blinded by malice, and imbued with the false teaching of his Church."[14] O'Gorman also took this opportunity to tell the readers of the *Bulwark* about some of the unchristian practices which she had witnessed in the Roman Catholic sisterhood: "When nuns prove refractory and disobedient, they [the Roman Catholic hierarchies] find safer means for subjecting them; for instance, shutting them up in

10. Arnstein, "Murphy Riots."
11. *Oxford and Roman Railway*, 24–25.
12. *The Rock* (London), 30 September 1881.
13. O'Gorman, *Convent Life Unveiled*, 5.
14. "Escaped Nun's Reply," 165.

dark cells, feeding them on bread and water, and other cruel treatment which soon brings them to the grave or the insane asylum."[15] She ended her defense by appealing to the English sense of honour to hear her out and then judge her. One year later, in 1883, another edition of her book was printed in England, and the *Bulwark* printed lengthy extracts from it and praised her truthfulness and courage.[16] This article also made mention of Miss O'Gorman's increasing popularity on the lecture circuit, but did not condone this activity. Her gender, and not her message, was the reason. "We have an insuperable objection to female lecturers and preachers," it pointed out, since in "every instance of their lecturing or preaching, they contravene a commandment of God." Moreover "it is contrary to our idea of that womanly modesty which is the very beauty of the female character."[17] This slap on the wrist from a fellow enemy of popery did not deter Miss O'Gorman.

In 1884, she journeyed into the Manchester area where she publicly challenged Herbert Vaughan, the Roman Catholic Bishop of Salford who would later become the Archbishop of Westminster in 1892, to meet with her. Together, this ex-nun suggested, they would both examine the truth and the authenticity of some accusations that English Catholics had recently made to defame her.[18] Vaughan politely refused the invitation. O'Gorman's three lectures in January—her life in the convent, auricular confession (for women only), and her escape—were well received by the Mancunians. Her reception in this largely Roman Catholic area of the country pleased *The Rock*. It remarked that she "must have been encouraged in her Protestant Mission," and moreover, her lectures "are much needed in Manchester and elsewhere." "The diabolical Convent system," it announced, must be investigated and exposed.[19] Miss Edith O'Gorman probably felt satisfied about her reception in England since hostile reactions had not yet materialized. But like her spiritual mentor, St Paul, O'Gorman would soon experience antagonism and expressions of hatred as she spread her anti-convent message. The first instance of opposition and protest, however, appeared outside of England.

---

15. Ibid.
16. "Edith O'Gorman, A Converted Nun," 159–61.
17. Ibid., 158.
18. "Escaped Nun, Edith O'Gorman," 260.
19. *The Rock*, 25 January 1884.

Like any devoted and zealous missionary, Edith O'Gorman labored to spread religious truth and to reveal the secrets of convent life, and in 1885 she and her husband left England and travelled throughout New Zealand and Australia for three years. O'Gorman's presentations dealt with her experiences in the American convent, her conversion and daring escape, and the hidden dangers of sisterhoods. The *Bulwark* carried a story about a public debate in Dunedin, and told its readers of her untiring work to expose the "inequalities of the convent system" and the evils of Romanism. At this particular meeting, O'Gorman answered the challenge of a Mr. Fulton, who claimed that she was "a fraud and a show-woman, obtaining money on false pretenses."[20] The chairman of this meeting called on him to substantiate these serious charges of dishonesty. According to the *Bulwark*, Fulton failed to back up his accusations, and his response lacked logic and sounded more like a personal harangue against O'Gorman. The audience, consequently, did not give him a favorable or kind hearing, but welcomed Edith O'Gorman, who quickly pointed out some inconsistencies in Mr. Fulton's testimony. She then recounted the facts surrounding her religious conversion, and the assembly showed their approval of O'Gorman's presentation by a show of hands. On the following evening, she delivered her usual lecture against the evils of Roman Catholic convents without any incidents.

Miss O'Gorman's tour of New Zealand lasted six months, and then she and her husband went to Australia, where the pair remained for two years before returning to England. The subject of her presentations remained the same, namely, life in the convent, her escape, and her acceptance of Protestantism, but at one venue she was met with violence. At Lismore, the assembly included a large number of Roman Catholics, some of whom "professed to be under the influence of liquor, which turned out to be only a sham," and they instigated a noisy disturbance.[21] As O'Gorman and her husband appeared on the stage, the Catholics began to groan and hiss. The Protestants replied with cheers; the Catholic protestors hurled eggs at her, but missed their target. A fight consequently broke out between the two rival religions. The papists "were immediately confronted by a body of Orangemen, when a hand-to-hand fight took place, chairs, sticks, loaded whips, shillelaghs, etc., being freely used." According to this report, the fracas lasted an hour, ending with "broken

20. "Edith O'Gorman Auffray, the Escaped Nun," 122.
21. "The 'Escaped Nun' in Australia," 27.

heads and bruised limbs." The Catholic rioters apparently won the day. They forced the Orangemen out of the assembly hall, and announced that they had come to disrupt the meeting and had succeeded. O'Gorman, protected by an estimated one hundred Protestants, escaped unharmed. After appeals from the Colonial Secretary to the Roman Catholic authorities and the local magistrates calling for peace and decorum at her future talks, she eventually gave her lecture to a large and supportive crowd two weeks later on her usual themes. "The large audience broke into rapturous applause," a telegram to a Sydney newspaper reported, and "Protestants and all lovers of free speech rejoice at the great success of this grand demonstration."[22] In 1888, O'Gorman and her husband returned to England, but the reception she received at some of these talks was much less friendly and encouraging than the warm welcome she had experienced during her previous speaking tour of the country.

During October of that year, she gave numerous lectures throughout England dealing with her life as a Roman Catholic nun. At first, O'Gorman concentrated her efforts in Sussex, lecturing at Littlehampton, Chichester, Portsmouth, Brighton, Bognor, Hawkhurst, Cranbrook, Lewes, and Worthing about the horrors she had endured in the convent.[23] But her talk at Littlehampton, where "her lectures were interrupted by Romanists from Arundel, where the Duke of Norfolk resides," must have reminded her of the rowdy reception she had received in Australia. The chair at the Littlehampton meeting introduced O'Gorman as a woman who possessed a stellar Christian character and a person whom Catholic enemies had repeatedly slandered. During these short remarks, shouting and hoots from some of the assembly forced him to stop. This angry demonstration did not, however, deter Edith O'Gorman. According to the local newspaper, she courageously confronted these hecklers: "Christian friends, I regretted to find Littlehampton contains some men who are not worthy of that name."[24] This rebuke was met with smirks and derisive laughter, but O'Gorman continued to describe her life at the New Jersey convent. Sustained protests from the audience finally unnerved the speaker.

22. Printed in ibid., 27.

23. *The Protestant Observer* (London), November 1888.

24. *Littlehampton News*, 16 October 1888, printed in *The Protestant Observer*, November 1888.

After being frequently interrupted by unwelcome remarks, O'Gorman asked the chairman to have the Roman Catholic intruders removed. Miss O'Gorman also stated that she would answer any question asked in a gentlemanly manner at the conclusion of her presentation. Moreover, she challenged any person to appear on stage with her the following night to refute any of her statements about Catholicism or its convents. Order prevailed for a short time until a man entered the hall and made for the stage followed by the hooting crowd. After a short exchange with the chairman, a policeman was called to remove this intruder and restore order, and O'Gorman and her party escaped through a door at the back of the platform. Even after her departure, other accusations came from the audience that questioned the truth of O'Gorman's unkind statements about Roman Catholicism. A number of persons mounted the stage to confront the chairman, and in response the police dispersed the crowd and ended the meeting.

Edith O'Gorman gave two other lectures at Littlehampton, one especially for women and the other, an open meeting where she spoke about the details of her conversion to Protestantism, which attracted some noisy demonstrators. These individuals again voiced their opposition to her derogatory remarks about Catholicism, but the presence of the police guaranteed that the meeting did not turn into a circus. She did, however, receive some support and backing from the Sussex area. A letter to *The Protestant Observer*, for example, disagreed with an article written by an American that had appeared in the Roman Catholic publication the *Universe*. It described O'Gorman as an impostor and a bigot speaking humbug to the English. In her defense, the author of this letter encouraged Edith O'Gorman and had strong words for the disreputable and disgusting actions of the Catholics at the Littlehampton lectures: "However, that is only in harmony with the spirit of persecution which always has been one of their chief features. The weapons of the Romish Church are not truth, argument, and reason; but calumny, slander, stones, bludgeons, and others calculated to do bodily injury."[25]

The challenges from angry audiences probably made her more eager to confront the Catholic protestors, an unlikely vocation for a woman in Victorian England. During the spring and summer of 1889, "She has journeyed from Birmingham to Portsmouth, and from Lowestoft to Penzance, visiting nearly fifty places and giving an average of three

25. *The Protestant Observer*, December 1888.

lectures in each place, besides holding many private meetings and delivering various drawing-room addresses" reported *The Protestant Observer*.[26] In Eastbourne, for example, the *Sussex Daily News* reported that O'Gorman stated that "Life in a convent . . . was a hell on earth." She mentioned "the difficulty of escape from them owing to the rigid discipline that prevailed in them, and denounced the Romish school system."[27] During these presentations, she also urged the English government to supervise convents in order to safeguard the liberty and rights of the nuns, and because of her lectures a large number of people signed petitions to be presented to Parliament asking for state inspection of convents.

Speaking to an audience at Birmingham in April 1889, however, O'Gorman strayed from her usual subjects, and entertained a challenge from one of the listeners who did not like her message. Miss O'Gorman began her talk by recalling the rough receptions she had recently received from Roman Catholics who were intent on denying her freedom of speech, and she maintained that the Catholic press, manipulated by Cardinal Henry Edward Manning, had mounted a campaign to discredit her. As she continued with the presentation, a Roman Catholic priest questioned some of her statements in an "ungentlemanly and unchristian behaviour" and characterized her statements as lies and falsehoods. A debate between the two people then erupted concerning the doctrine of the Immaculate Conception (which O'Gorman called a "blasphemous dogma") and the recent pronouncement of papal infallibility (in her words, "the last blasphemous error" of Vatican Council I). According to the report of *The Protestant Observer*, Miss O'Gorman appealed to the authority of Sacred Scripture and bested the zealous and embarrassed priest. Birmingham certainly did not prove to be a friendly city to O'Gorman's crusade. Her other seven lectures there occasioned protests on a greater scale: after each lecture "her carriage was followed by a howling mob[but] her lectures have done great good here."[28]

From the Midlands, she made her way towards the capital, and entertained audiences at Walthamstow and Richmond. By the time Miss O'Gorman arrived in the London area this woman had acquired a reputation for her anti-Catholic diatribes, and she could expect

26. *The Protestant Observer*, July 1889.
27. Quoted in ibid.
28. *The Protestant Observer*, April 1889.

crowds of loyal Roman Catholics to express their outrage and anger at her lectures. O'Gorman gave several presentations in London, and she received substantial press coverage. One engagement, at the Town Hall in Kensington, proved especially riotous. *The Protestant Observer* noted that representatives of several Roman Catholic groups had arrived to disrupt her talk about life in the convent as they had done previously during an engagement at Bromley.[29] According to the *English Churchman*, a publication of the extreme Evangelical wing of the Anglican Church, a large number of Roman Catholics gathered to hear Miss O'Gorman on 20 June, and although attempts were made to keep possible troublemakers outside, about thirty hooligans managed to enter the hall.[30] Several were ejected, including one intoxicated individual who attacked the crowd with obscenities. On the following day, a large group of Roman Catholics had again gathered at the Town Hall to protest at her appearance. This hostile crowd waited outside for her to conclude her unfavorable reminiscences of convent life, and they blocked the exits hoping to heckle the lady as she departed. She escaped, however, through the adjoining buildings. The *Echo* described the threat more vividly: O'Gorman spoke "at the risk of a broken head," and she might have suffered the same fate as an earlier anti-Catholic orator, William Murphy, who was murdered by a mob in 1871 after leaving a meeting.[31] *The Protestant Observer* concluded its coverage of the story by recounting the success of Edith O'Gorman's lectures in London and by reminding its readers that if Rome "had the power, freedom of speech and liberty of conscience would not be permitted."[32] The year 1889 ended with other noisy demonstrations at Tunbridge Wells, where the police had to clear the room after a protestor mounted the stage to express his anger at her words.[33]

Miss O'Gorman returned to America in 1890 to lecture again in her adopted country about the evils of Catholicism and sisterhoods. She spent approximately two years away from England. When O'Gorman

---

29. *The Protestant Observer*, July 1889.

30. *English Churchman*, 20 June 1889, quoted in *The Protestant Observer*, July 1889.

31. *Echo*, 20 June 1889, quoted in *The Protestant Observer*, July 1889.

32. *The Protestant Observer*, July 1889.

33. *Tunbridge Wells Gazette*, 8 November 1889, printed in *The Protestant Observer*, December 1889.

returned to England, she continued her campaign denouncing Roman Catholic sisterhoods and arguing for government inspection of convents. Her public appearances became less frequent, but her presence and her message still generated controversy and opposition. In December 1892, for example, Miss O'Gorman wrote a letter to *The Times* complaining about the opposition she had recently experienced by some Anglo-Catholic priests who claimed that her lectures were "stirring up bad blood" within the Church of England.[34] O'Gorman also became involved in another contentious issue, namely, the career of an English "escaped nun." Was this individual, Ellen Golding, a rival to O'Gorman, or did Golding jeopardize the American ex-nun's reputation or her campaign against sisterhoods by some questionable and unsubstantiated statements about convent life? Golding's escape from a French convent certainly matched Miss O'Gorman's in drama and daring. Whatever the motives, O'Gorman worked to distance herself from Ellen Golding.

The August 1891 edition of *The Times* reported that a member of a London law firm had journeyed to France to rescue Golding, who had written to the solicitor and asked for his help.[35] Upon his arrival at the convent, Miss Golding begged this hero to help her escape from the clutches of the sisterhood. When the other nuns realized what Golding had in mind, they tried to restrain her, but on hearing her screams the solicitor rushed in, grabbed Miss Golding, and took her away to freedom in England. O'Gorman's escape seemed mild in comparison with this story. Golding's description of convent life, however, sounded similar to Miss O'Gorman's recollections: a cruel and tyrannical superior, hard work, harsh punishments and penances, and the early deaths of nuns.[36] But her story contained no hint of sexual impropriety or imprisonment as found in Miss O'Gorman's testimony. The Roman Catholic authorities in England ridiculed and criticized Ellen Golding as they did Edith O'Gorman.

Miss Golding did not remain silent, and like O'Gorman she took to the road and described her imprisonment in a French convent and the heroic rescue by a brave Englishman. With the assistance of a manager, she began attracting large audiences to her lectures. Here was someone whose story might appeal to the English sense of honour and patriotism—she was rescued from a French community of nuns—more

---

34. *The Times*, 17 December 1892.
35. *The Times*, 31 August 1891, printed in *The Protestant Observer*, October 1891.
36. *The Times*, 31 August 1891.

than an American who merely had the good luck to stumble across an unlocked door in the convent. Moreover, Ellen Golding was English! As her popularity grew, it appeared that she began to embellish some of her experiences and even invented some stories of convent horrors. Consequently, Edith O'Gorman began to denounce Golding. Was the motive jealousy, or was Ellen Golding hurting the cause of Protestantism by creating and propagating lies? In the 17 February 1894 edition of the *Surrey Mirror*, O'Gorman revealed that she had unsuccessfully appealed to Miss Golding "not to deviate one iota from the simple truth of her real experiences." O'Gorman now believed that she had a duty to expose Ellen Golding's pronouncements as "grossly exaggerated . . . [and] so discrepant to both Protestants and Papists." She attacked Golding as having "invented deliberate falsehoods about murders, poisonings, and gross immoralities in convents."[37] Two weeks later in the same paper, Miss O'Gorman argued that falsehoods and fabrications hurt the crusade to unmask the evils of Catholicism.

Another ex-nun, M. F. Cusack, also criticized some of Golding's statements in the same manner as O'Gorman. The so-called "Nun of Kenmare," Cusack left the Poor Clares sisterhood at Kenmare, Ireland, in 1888. She did not, however, tolerate any Protestant who attacked Roman Catholic sisterhoods without proof or evidence, and she especially had strong words of disapproval for the actions of Ellen Golding. In 1893, Cusack expressed her feelings in a letter to the Bournemouth Observer: "I must say, after many years experience of convent life, and a far wider experience than any escaped or rescued nun ever had, I never saw anything even approaching the horrible accusations which have been made by Miss Golding."[38] The fame of Golding did not last long, and before the end of the decade, the Catholic Truth Society, a long time opponent of convent bashing, asked, "Where is she now?"[39] Moreover, Miss Edith O'Gorman's speaking tours throughout England also began to decrease, and little was heard of her during the early years of the twentieth century.

In 1919, Miss O'Gorman, at the age of seventy-seven, surfaced again and announced that she planned to give up her mission in England and return to America.[40] She then sketched a brief overview of her recent

---

37. *Surrey Mirror*, 17 February 1894, quoted in Britten, *Truth about Convents*, 9.

38. *Bournemouth Observer*, 8 November 1893, quoted in Britten, *Truth about Convents*, 9.

39. Cf. Britten, *Truth about Convents*, 7.

40. *Norwood Press* (London), 15 November 1919, printed in O'Gorman, *Convent Life Unveiled*, 157.

activities and travels, which included a tour in South Africa two months before the Great War broke out in Europe. from 1915, O'Gorman lived in West Norwood, London, and she told supporters that she had to dismiss a servant because of the high cost of living in the city. The lack of income, which she previously earned from her speaking engagements, probably contributed to her decision to cut expenses. One event, however, brought her out of the shadows and also occasioned a sharp response from concerned Roman Catholics. The first edition of her book, *Convent Life Unveiled*, had appeared in 1871 in America and was reprinted several times in England. This book had been out of print for a long time, and consequently some of her English supporters planned to bring out a new edition. In 1913, the Catholic Truth Society published *Edith O'Gorman and Her Book* to alert the public to the duplicity of this publication. The author, G. Elliot Anstruther, accused O'Gorman of deception. Anstruther, who was the Organizing Secretary of the CTS, pointed out several discrepancies between the original American publication and the later English editions, for example, conflicting versions of life in the convent, her escape, and her dealings with the priest, Fr. Walsh. He also argued that the 1901 English edition, which would be reprinted, contained much more anti-Catholic rhetoric, and was thus suited to the Protestant traditions of England. The CTS pamphlet maintained that this plan to publish Miss O'Gorman's work represented the last gasp of a lecturer whose words had begun to wear thin. Moreover, the author maintained that the "whole book is a mass of suspicion and a monument of inconsistency, and Edith O'Gorman herself gives the lie to the wild charges of the 'Escaped Nun'" legend.[41] Commenting on her waning support, the pamphlet stated: "It is a matter for satisfaction that the class of people who are nowadays found associated with Edith O'Gorman and her campaign represent a dwindling Protestant interest both as to quality and quantity."[42]

The new edition of O'Gorman's book was the first of several which were eventually published in England. Because of her advanced age the printed word had become the only outlet for Miss O'Gorman's diatribes about convent life. Miss Edith O'Gorman's popularity eventually declined, people lost interest in her message, and some began to doubt the truthfulness of her stories. In 1928, nearly eighty-six years old, she

41. Anstruther, *Edith O'Gorman and Her Book*, 22.
42. Ibid., 23.

wrote a preface to another edition of her book. O'Gorman died one year later on 25 May 1929, and was buried in London. The appeal of her message, however, had reached its high point before the turn of the century. Stories of convent cruelties and attacks on sisterhoods, along with prejudices against Roman Catholicism in general, had declined significantly in England. According to Edward Norman, "Toward the end of the nineteenth century, educated opinion began to demonstrate an increasing tolerance toward Roman Catholicism."[43] The decline in bigotry must not be exaggerated, he argues, since some anti-Catholic feeling could still be found following the death of Queen Victoria. Nonetheless, "Roman Catholics were in reality getting an increasing amount of tolerant consideration from a society whose government added legal recognition and sometimes legal benefits."[44]

The success Miss Edith O'Gorman enjoyed as a speaker illustrates the fascination of some non-Catholics with the mysterious inner workings of sisterhoods. What did take place behind convent walls? Were the stories of cruelty, loss of liberty, and sexual impropriety the creations of prejudicial minds, or should the government take the lead and investigate sisterhoods? The drama became much more enticing and entertaining because the public had the opportunity to hear the stories of an ill-treated woman who survived and escaped from the clutches of a convent. Some critics in the male dominated society of Victorian England could find a degree of comfort in the fact that a woman also expressed concern at the existence of sisterhoods where females could enjoy some independence. Moreover, some degree of O'Gorman's appeal was because of her Irish background. Anti-Catholics could delight in the fact that she had converted from Catholicism and then mocked the religion associated with the country of her birth. Maureen McCarthy has correctly described Miss O'Gorman as "the first woman to shape a whole public career out of her identity as an escaped nun."[45] Edith O'Gorman's career and popularity, however, suffered from the growing acceptance and toleration of Roman Catholicism that developed in the early years of the twentieth century.

---

43. Norman, *Anti-Catholicism in Victorian England*, 20.
44. Ibid., 20–21.
45. McCarthy, "Rescue of Womanhood," 375.

Bibliography

Anstruther, G. Elliot. *Edith O'Gorman and Her Book*. London: Catholic Truth Society, 1913.

Arnstein, Walter L. "The Murphy Riots: A Victorian Drama." *Victorian Studies* 19 (1975) 51–71.

Britten, James. *The Truth about Convents*. London: Catholic Truth Society, 1898.

Cullen, Ann. *The Marvellous Escape of Sister Lucy, and Her Awful Disclosures Respecting New Hall Convent, Boreham, Essex*. London: Protestant Evangelical Mission, 1865.

"Edith O'Gorman, A Converted Nun." *Bulwark* 12.6 (1883) 158–61.

"Edith O'Gorman Auffray, the Escaped Nun." *Bulwark* 15.8 (1886) 122.

"The Escaped Nun, Edith O'Gorman, Now Mrs. Auffray." *Bulwark* 16.10 (1887) 260.

"The 'Escaped Nun' in Australia—Fearful Riots." *Bulwark* 16.2 (1887) 25.

"The Escaped Nun's Reply." *Bulwark* 11.6 (1882) 165.

Franchot, Jenny. *Roads to Rome: The Antebellum Protestant Encounter with Catholicism*. Berkeley: University of California Press, 1994.

Gilley, Sheridan. "The Garibaldi Riots of 1862." *The Historical Journal* 16 (1973) 697–732.

Kensit, John. *English Convents, What Are They? Or Is There Any Necessity for Conventual Inspection?* London: Macintosh, 1870.

McCarthy, Maureen A. "The Rescue of True Womanhood: Convents and the Anti-Catholicism in 1830s America." PhD diss., Rutgers University, 1996.

Norman, Edward R. *Anti-Catholicism in Victorian England*. London: Allen & Unwin, 1968.

———. *The English Catholic Church in the Nineteenth Century*. Oxford: Oxford University Press, 1984.

O'Gorman, Edith. *Convent Life Unveiled*. 39th ed. London: Protestant Truth Society, 1923.

———. *Trials and Persecutions of Miss Edith O'Gorman, Otherwise Sister Teresa De Chantal, of St. Joseph's Convent, Hudson City, N.J.*. Hartford, CT: Connecticut Publishing, 1871.

The Oxford and Roman Railway: Of Which the Chief Ministers of the Church and State and Their Ladies Are Directors and Managers. London: Protestant Evangelical Mission and Electoral Union, 1871.

6

Those Horrible Iron Cages

The Sisters of the Church and the Care of Orphans in Late Victorian England

O RPHANAGES HAVE ALWAYS PROVIDED an essential service for those societies that have valued the importance of caring for infants or young children who faced the prospect of survival in a harsh and threatening world without the aid, protection, or care of parents. These institutions offered an alternative to infanticide, abandonment, and the buying or selling of babies on the open market as any other commodity. But orphanages did not always measure up to their high ideals. In Victorian England, tales of mistreatment can be frequently found in the pages of fiction and in the testimony of those children who "survived" the rigorous regime of a nineteenth-century orphanage. The abuses became much more heinous and reprehensible if a church or one of its agencies supervised one of these orphanages. Reports of mistreatment and cruelty have continued throughout the twentieth century. Recent stories, which chronicle the sexual, physical, and mental abuse that took place in several orphanages and industrial schools operated by Roman Catholic brotherhoods and sisterhoods, continue to portray the sinister and demoniac side of life in orphanages.[1] During the 1890s, an Anglican sisterhood, the Sisters of the Church, also known as the Kilburn Sisters, attracted strong criticisms because of the manner in which these sisters operated an orphanage for young girls and the Roman Catholic practices which they allegedly promoted in this institution.

1. See, for example, Coldrey, "A Mixture of Caring and Corruption."

MOTHER EMILY AYCKBOWM

Founded in 1870 by Emily Ayckbowm, the Community of the Sisters of the Church had experienced remarkable growth. In 1894, for example, the Sisters of the Church reported to Edward White Benson, the Archbishop of Canterbury, the following works of the sisterhood: four orphanages for girls and three for boys; twelve day-schools in London, four outside of the capital, and eight schools overseas; a women's teacher training college in Kilburn; and other apostolates such as workshops for youth, night shelters and refuges, mission houses, restaurants, a dispensary, and a rest home.[2] In spite of these accomplishments, the sisters came under attack during the same decade by organizations and individuals who criticized the manner in which they cared for orphan girls.

Emily Ayckbowm (1836–1900)[3] founded her sisterhood rather late in the nineteenth century when compared with other communities of women which had been in existence since the 1840s.[4] This group of religious women owed its rapid expansion and success to the personality and drive of Mother Emily. In addition to her dedication to the philanthropic spirit of the Victorian age, some commentators have also emphasized her holiness, saintly personality, and strong commitment to Christian principles. Susan Mumm describes her as "a woman with an acutely sensitive social conscience and extraordinary charisma."[5] Others, however, characterize Mother Emily as abrasive, pugnacious, and dictatorial. A. M. Allchin in *The Silent Rebellion* gives a good picture of this woman, especially in her relations with Anglican bishops. "The Mother Foundress on her side was naturally unwilling, even if she was somewhat brusque in her actions," he writes, "to defer entirely to the decisions of one who had little practical experience of sisterhood life,"[6] such as Anglican clerics, including bishops and archbishops. But her vision and determination did contribute to the success of the Sisters of the Church.

---

2. Mumm, *Stolen Daughters, Virgin Mothers*, 224–25.

3. For biographies of Emily Ayckbowm, see Anonymous, *Emily H. E. Ackbowm*; and Anonymous, *A Valiant Victorian*. The Sisters of the Church still exist today. The community is involved in education, pastoral work, and retreats.

4. For the history and development of Anglican sisterhoods, see Allchin, *Silent Rebellion*; Anson, *Call of the Cloister*; and Mumm, *Stolen Daughters, Virgin Mothers*.

5. Mumm, *Stolen Daughters, Virgin Mothers*, 9.

6. Allchin, *Silent Rebellion*, 215.

Emily Ayckbowm moved from Chester to London in 1864, and in 1875 the Sisters of the Church opened their first orphanage on Shrove Tuesday in Kilburn. The biography of Ayckbowm, published by the Church Extension Association, described this event in maudlin terms. "For years past our Foundress had thought with tender concern of the workhouse children, and now at last the way seemed clear, and she was able to make a very quiet and unassuming beginning to the Orphanage work that so often haunted her dreams, as well as her waking thoughts."[7] A year later, Mother Emily, the "saintly Mother Superior," launched a public appeal to construct the necessary building, which eventually opened its doors in 1880. Mother Emily, moreover, made it clear that the orphanage operated by the Sisters of the Church would welcome not only those children whose parents had died, but also foundlings, that is, abandoned children of unknown parentage. For Mother Emily, this also meant illegitimate children who were given to the care of the sisters by unwed mothers.

This procedure for the admittance of these children angered some Victorians, who argued that this practice encouraged vice and sin. Mother Emily saw her responsibility in a different light: "The utter helplessness and defenseless misery of these poor babies, thrown upon the world by unnatural parents, or left to the baby-farmers, appealed to her tender heart overwhelmingly."[8] She pointed to recent public revelations of infanticide and the absence of properly operated homes for foundlings to justify her course of action. This indiscriminate acceptance of illegitimate children by the Sisters of the Church introduced a new approach. Generally, "Most sisterhoods followed the example of secular institutions in demanding that children be proved legitimate by the production of marriage and birth certificates."[9]

FOUNDLING HOSPITAL AND THE CHARITY ORGANIZATION SOCIETY

The only national foundling hospital was London's Foundling Hospital, established by Thomas Coram in 1739 to receive both orphaned and

---

7. Anonymous, *Emily H. E. Ackbowm*, 95.
8. Ibid., 103.
9. Mumm, *Stolen Daughters, Virgin Mothers*, 111.

abandoned children.[10] At first, the hospital had no admittance procedure, and people did take advantage of the opportunity to place unwanted newborn children in the care of this hospital. "The riotous scenes staged by mothers who stormed the doors of the Hospital led the governors to introduce a plan of admission by drawing lots, a white ball assuring immediate admission, a black ball meaning rejection, and a red ball giving an alternate's position."[11] Instead of the sixty infants that the hospital expected in the first year, officials admitted nearly twice that number. Problems, financial and administrative, plagued its early years. In 1760, the government suspended funding to the hospital, and consequently the governors refused to accept any new admissions.

When the Foundling Hospital eventually resumed operation a few years later, a drastic change in policy had taken place. "First the number of admissions was reduced, then admission was restricted to war orphans and children of deserted wives; finally, from 1801, only illegitimate children were accepted."[12] Officials now demanded a detailed, and very embarrassing, questionnaire to be completed by the mother before the hospital accepted the baby. According to Professor Barret-Ducrocq's study of love and sexuality in Victorian England, the unmarried mother "had to be able to show that her good faith had been betrayed, that she had given way to carnal passion only after a promise of marriage or against her will; that she therefore had no other children; and that her conduct had always been irreproachable in every other aspect. She must also be without any sort of material aid. Finally, the child had to be under one year old."[13] The mother had to complete a printed form, which revealed the most intimate aspects of her sexual life and the circumstances surrounding the child's birth, and she had to give a statement detailing the events of her life since the sexual encounter with the father of the child. The officials believed that this process would be the most successful way "of ensuring that the children would be brought up under good conditions and of promoting the moral rehabilitation of single women deserted by their seducers."

---

10. For the history and philosophy behind Coram's hospital, see Brownlow, *History and Objects*; Nichols and Wray, *History of the Foundling Hospital*; Owen, *English Philanthropy*; and Porter, *London*.

11. Porter, *London*, 54.

12. Barret-Ducrocq, *Love in the Time of Victoria*, 40.

13. Ibid., 41; see also Brownlow, *History and Objects*, 24–27.

Although the mother was required to supply the name, occupation, and address of the father, this procedure certainly placed the shame and onus on the woman. She had become a "fallen woman" in need of rehabilitation. Moreover, "The system was designed to avoid giving unwitting encouragement to women who were selling their bodies."[14] Barret-Ducrocq effectively argues that these "handwritten, first-person statements thus have the appearance of confessions made to an unchanging, ritual pattern."[15] "Like a priest in the confessional," she points out, "it [the administration of the hospital] was seeking repentance, catharsis." Mother Emily Ayckbowm and the Sisters of the Church, however, completely abandoned this practice. Mother Emily also pointed the finger of shame at the father. "Society, she said, concentrated its ungenerous attitude on the mother, letting the guilty father escape."[16] Consequently, the foundress and the sisterhood came in for bitter criticism from another organization also devoted to charitable works, including the care of orphans and illegitimate children.

Following the spirit of the Poor Law Amendment Act (1834), the Charity Organization Society, founded in 1869, firmly believed that indiscriminate charity demoralized and did not help the country's poor. It also equated poverty with moral weakness.[17] But pauperism still existed. Some maintained that the strict guidelines of the 1834 legislation had fallen into abeyance, and thus poverty continued to flourish. Consequently, a "return to the spirit of 1834 in the administration of the poor law was widely advocated as the answer to the persistence of indigence."[18] The Charity Organization Society (COS) sought "to establish the worthiness of those seeking help so that private charity would not be wasted or duplicated. This would clear the way for the poor law authorities to threaten the unworthy with the full rigours of the 1834 Act."[19] The COS believed that the so-called deserving poor should "be aided by the charities, the undeserving by the Poor Law."[20] This organization pioneered modern social work by its close interaction with indi-

14. Brownlow, *History and Objects*, 24–27.
15. Barret-Ducrocq, *Love in the Time of Victoria*, 41.
16. Anonymous, *Valiant Victorian*, 151.
17. See Mowat, *Charity Organization Society*.
18. Price, *English Society*, 188.
19. Royle, *Modern Britain*, 187.
20. Fraser, "Introduction," 11.

vidual families; however, "it still reflected the traditional idea that the poor were responsible because of their personal failings, and remained largely blind to the underlying social causes."[21]

The COS argued that wholesale charity undermined and weakened the 1834 Poor Law and encouraged laziness.[22] "The COS believed it necessary to investigate the circumstances of the destitute carefully and, wherever possible, to substitute charity for poor relief."[23] If private means could not help to ease one's poverty, then that individual should enter the workhouse. Since the government came to believe that local charities must work closely with the local Poor Law Boards, "the disparate mass of charitable effort would be co-ordinated and assimilated to operate on common principles under the guidance of the Charity Organization Society."[24] According to Charles Loch Mowat, the grandson of Sir Charles Loch, the individual who greatly influenced the development of the COS, it "embodied an idea of charity which claimed to reconcile the divisions in society, to remove poverty and to produce a happy, self-reliant community"[25] And this approach to England's poor certainly appealed to the central government, the Poor Law Boards, and the ratepayer because they thought that this solution "would both improve the moral character of society and reduce relief expenditure."[26]

THE SISTERS OF THE CHURCH AND THE ORPHANAGE WORK

The Sisters of the Church and the principles that animated their philosophy toward orphanages, therefore, conflicted with the approach of two established Victorian institutions: London's Foundling Hospital and the Charity Organization Society The practice of Mother Emily and her sisters came under scrutiny, and a bitter criticism of their methods resulted. In 1892, a prospectus appeared which the sisterhood directed toward working class readers. It informed them that the officials of the orphanages operated by the Sisters of the Church would not, like the

21. Pugh, *State and Society*, 50.
22. Hall, *Social Services*, 130.
23. MacKinnon, "English Poor Law Policy," 606.
24. Thane, "Government and Society," 38.
25. Mowat, *Charity Organization Society*, 1.
26. MacKinnson, "English Poor Law Policy," 607.

London Foundling Hospital, pry into the personal lives of the mothers who wished to place their illegitimate babies with the sisters. "The managers have no desire to inquire into the private affairs of those who desire to place children in the Home," this prospectus read, and "All clue to the identity of such children will in this case . . . be destroyed."[27] The officials did not require the name or address of the mother or the baby for admittance, and to ensure anonymity, a new name would be given to the child by the managers of the orphanage. The requirement of entrance fees, which were related to the type of education the child would receive, also did not correspond with the popular notion of a charitable organization. For £20, the child, "who must be old enough to walk," would be trained to work as a domestic servant. For infants, a fee of £120 would guarantee training in a profession such as teaching. For children over two, the mother would pay £100 for the same training. Moreover, she promised not to communicate with the child and had to sign a form stipulating "that its name should be changed, and all traces of identity be destroyed, should it be thought desirable."[28] If the mother had a change of mind and wanted to reclaim her baby, she had to reimburse the home. She agreed "to pay the managers the sum of £100 (one hundred pounds) and 6s. per week for board and expenses during the time the child has been under care." Advertisements for orphans also appeared in several newspapers, and emphasized the issue of confidentiality and also brought up the question of an entrance fee.

The letter and spirit of these public ads conflicted with the accepted policies of the London Foundling Hospital and the principles of the Charity Organization Society, and Mother Emily offered an explanation. Writing in *Our Work*, the publication of the sisterhood, she argued that "the poor babes who come into the world with no paternal love to welcome them, no good influence to surround them, have a very special claim upon Sisters."[29] She also pointed out that "St. Vincent de Paul, the great founder of the Sisters of Charity, called the first members of his order together for the express purpose of 'mothering' the illegitimate little castaways of Paris." Nonetheless, complaints about the Sisters of the Church found their way to the desk of the Bishop of London, Frederick Temple, and also reached the Archbishop of Canterbury, Edward White Benson.

27. Printed in *Report upon the Orphanages*, 18.
28. Ibid., 19.
29. Quoted in Anonymous, *Valiant Victorian*, 151.

Temple, who served as Bishop of London from 1885 until he became Archbishop of Canterbury in 1896, was familiar with the Sisters of the Church.[30] The nuns had invited him to become their patron in 1892, and having "heard nothing but good of their work, he accepted the position."[31] He even gave them implicit approval to resume the profession of vows, a practice discontinued by Temple's predecessor as Bishop of London, John Jackson. The issue of the offensive prospectus or circular, however, had a different outcome. Bishop Temple must have been shocked when he saw a copy of this prospectus. Temple also wanted to send the Bishop of Marlborough, Alfred Earle, or another bishop to inspect the conditions at the house. Mother Emily and the sisters, however, refused. Eventually in 1895 they removed Bishop Temple, Edward White Benson, the Archbishop of Canterbury, and the Archbishop of York, William Dalrymple Maclagan, from the list of patrons of the sisterhood. According to Temple, "they had determined to dispense with all Patrons (including Abp. of York and me) on the grounds that they did not wish their friends to bear any of the unpopularity which in these days attended their philanthropic efforts."[32] While Archbishop of Canterbury, Temple would not officially recognize the Sisters of the Church until they accepted some sort of episcopal oversight, namely, an episcopal Visitor,[33] and the Evangelical press falsely interpreted this as a critique of the alleged ritualism and Romish spirit of the sisterhood.[34]

The Sisters of the Church also came to the attention of another Anglican prelate, Edward White Benson, Archbishop of Canterbury (1883–96). Commenting on his visit to Kilburn in 1889, Benson noted that "all was dignity, gravity, silence, beauty—most eager work for 600 orphans."[35] He also described the community as "a very formidable body." In the same year, Benson recorded another positive experience concerning the work of the sisterhood when he toured their new school

---

30. For the correspondence between the Sisters of the Church and Bishop Frederick Temple, see Fuhlam Papers, F. Temple, vol. 48, Lambeth Palace Library, Lambeth Palace, London. For Temple's dealings with the sisterhood after he became Archbishop of Canterbury in 1896, see F. Temple Papers, vols. 5, 54, Lambeth Palace Library.

31. Hinchliff, *Frederick Temple*, 228.

32. Quoted in ibid., 229.

33. Allchin, *Silent Rebellion*, 215.

34. *The Church Intelligencer*, July 1895.

35. Quoted in Benson, *Life of Edward White Benson*, 273.

at Croyden. By 1895, however, the Archbishop began to modify his cheery impression of the sisterhood and its superior. A proper constitution and an episcopal Visitor, he now realized, had become imperative. In May 1895, he noted that "The Mother Superior is the most comically audacious Mother in the Universe."[36] Archbishop Benson also "wrote again to her saying that her method of receiving illegitimate children, sum down, no questions asked, entirely taken charge of for life, is facilitating vice." Apparently Mother Emily chose not to respond. This independence of spirit, consequently, contributed to a stereotype that Mother Emily's orphanage was a maverick organization that should be exposed, disciplined, and supervised by churchmen.

A well-publicized and embarrassing secession of several disgruntled sisters also cast doubt on the philosophy of the Sisters of the Church, their relationship to the Anglican Church, and their work with children. Beginning in April 1894, the first of two mass departures, described by one Evangelical newspaper as a "schism," took place.[37] *The Church Intelligencer* printed a letter that Mother Emily sent to several bishops that gave her explanation for the secession. She loudly proclaimed the devotion of the sisterhood to the Anglican Church. "The only reason they [the sisters who left] gave at the time," the Superior told the Bishops, "was a desire for the introduction of Roman services, which in loyalty to our Church, I could not sanction."[38] A brother of one of these "seceders" took exception with the superior's interpretation, and the same paper published his explanation why his sister and the others walked out of the community, especially the advertising for illegitimate children and the alleged tyranny of the Mother Superior.[39] Moreover, this writer contended, none of these former Sisters of the Church had any desire to introduce Roman Catholic practices into the community's liturgy. The questions raised by the departure of these Sisters might have died down if the Charity Organization Society had not criticized the Sisters of the Church and their care of orphan girls.

---

36. Ibid., 640.
37. *The Church Intelligencer*, September 1894.
38. E. Ayckbowm (Mother Emily) to Bishops, July 19, 1894, printed in ibid.
39. Ayckbowm to Bishops.

QUESTIONS OF ABUSE AND THE IRON CAGES

In 1895, the COS published *A Report upon the Orphanages and Other Charitable Institutions Conducted by the Church Extension Association*. It repeated some earlier concerns about admission policies that differed from those of the London Foundling Hospital and supplied extracts from letters to criticize these procedures, especially the payment of an entrance fee. Abuses had resulted from these practices, for example, the failure to notify the family of a child's death because of the custom of changing names to protect the identity of the child. Finally, it accused the managers of the orphanage of shoddy financial recordkeeping. With the exception of the mismanagement of charitable funds, which the Sisters of the Church later admitted was due to a mistake in bookkeeping, these objections dealt with the different approach to charity, but the COS also made other serious accusations.

The report of the COS mentioned an incident and the resulting punishment which took place in 1893. According to this account, "In May or June of that year some of the children [young girls] were detected in habits of indecency, and the managers found it necessary to take steps to check the evil."[40] Most probably caught in the act of mutual masturbation, these girls had to be punished. And the COS condemned the method used. An appropriate response, the report suggested, would have been "quietly separateing the naughty children from the rest and exercising greater watchfulness over them." The older children, fourteen and above, however, were removed to other homes where they were accused of immorality and, according to the report, physically disciplined until they confessed. As a punishment, the orphanage officials shipped some of the girls to the local workhouse at Paddington.

Mother Emily offered a different interpretation of the events. In a circular letter to the Sisters, she pointed out that an "Evil of a peculiarly revolting type has been introduced by some girls whom we imprudently received when above our usual limit of age."[41] She recognized the "irremediable damage" this might have on the younger girls, and believed that she had to send the older girls away: "it was imperatively necessary to remove [them] for the sake of others." For the younger girls who remained, however, the Sisters employed a device which would soon become syn-

---

40. *Report upon the Orphanages*, 21.
41. Anonymous, *Valiant Victorian*, 152.

onymous with the Sisters of the Church and their care of orphans, namely, the iron cages or cubicles: "[the managers] introduced mechanical contrivances—some of them of a very objectionable character—to keep the children apart."[42] The report of the COS refrained from commenting on the religious aspects of the sisterhood, but it strongly urged reform "to secure an honest, open, and efficient administration of charitable institutions supported by the voluntary contributions of the public."[43]

Other critics of the Sisters of the Church, prompted also by a suspicion that all sisterhoods were really secret Romanizing institutions, drew the attention of the public to the cruel and evil iron cages. In August 1895, *The Protestant Observer* printed an article which had appeared earlier in "Monthly Letter" of the Protestant Alliance.[44] The author, Alexander Roger, listed the familiar objections such as the lack of episcopal authority and the now infamous prospectus. This list of grievances also emphasized the "cruel punishments administered to the orphans," specifically pointing out the "use of iron cages in which all the children were fastened at night and occasionally (as a punishment) in the day time." Mr. Roger even noted that advertisements for these cages had actually appeared in the *Church Times*, a paper usually friendly to sisterhoods, and *Our Work*, the chief publication of the Sisters of the Church. The sisterhood, it appears, immediately withdrew the advertisement for the so-called cubicles after the author drew attention to this type of punishment at the annual conference of the Protestant Alliance held earlier at Exeter Hall in May.

But Alexander Roger had to examine one of these iron cages or cubicles for himself, and with a friend he visited the Educational Union, which he described as "one of the aliases of the Sisters of the Church" dedicated to the instruction of the country's youth. At the location, 20 Harrow Road, London, one of the Sisters showed the object to the curious visitors. According to Roger,

> The sides are covered with galvanized wire-work similar to the fencing now sold for garden purposes . . . Top of this fence is covered with very sharp spikes made of brass, which prevent the inmates from placing their hands on the top, and would cruelly

42. *Report upon the Orphanages*, 21–22.

43. Ibid., 32.

44. *The Protestant Observer*, August 1895. The Protestant Alliance, founded in 1851, was a political pressure group that supported the principles of Protestantism against Romanizing tendencies in the Anglican Church.

tear any portion of the body coming into contact with them, if an attempt was made to scale the sides, which in truth is impossible. Entrance is obtained through a door at one of the ends made of the same material as the sides, about two feet wide, and fitted with a brass lock-latch.

Moreover, the door of each cubicle was fitted in such a manner that an "electric communication" would notify the Sister if the occupant attempted to escape.

Mr. Roger and his associate expressed some disbelief that the orphanage actually used these barbarous cubicles, and the Sister led them to a part of the building where several of the cages accommodated a number of young girls. Again the visitors from the Protestant Alliance examined the workings of the iron cages, which they described as prisons, and found that escape was a virtual impossibility due to the design of the padlock and the bolt. from this location, the two investigators went to the orphanage at Kilburn, and they inspected the cages there, "where some had been used with even the tops caged over, as in the earlier patterns, before the cruel spikes were introduced . . ." The final comment effectively expressed their indignation: "we withdrew, pitying the lot of these poor orphans, barred and bolted in these cages, should a fire break out in the orphanage, or any accidental disaster occur, which would be attended with serious loss of life."

The iron cages or cubicles quickly became the main focus of the attack against the Sisters of the Church. *The Church Intelligencer* printed the article written by Alexander Roger which commented on the cages: "all experience goes to shew that a devotee-spinster with the most lofty intentions is capable of almost any conceivable cruelty, partly from ignorance of child nature and lack of true maternal sympathy."[45] The Protestant Alliance did more than describe the now infamous cages. A pamphlet, *Exposure of the Kilburn Sisterhood*, printed an engraving of the iron cage, complete with a detailed explanation of its working parts.[46] The pamphlet pointed out that the illustration did not show the tops to the cages, a later addition occasioned "by the fact that some of the Orphans imprisoned in these cages had escaped from them by placing their pillows upon

---

45. *The Church Intelligencer*, September 1895.

46. *Exposure of the Kilburn Sisterhood*. The engraving appeared on both the cover and the first page. This pamphlet, published by the Protestant Alliance, also printed a copy of the advertisement that had appeared in the *Church Times* and *Our Work*.

the spikes at the top, and climbing over them."[47] The Protestant Alliance also included stories on the secession of several of the Sisters, the lack of proper episcopal supervision, the charges of "immoral" acts among some of the girls and their cruel punishment, and the alleged Roman Catholic teachings, but the graphic description or picture of the cage or cubicle became the chief weapon against the Sisters of the Church.

Mother Emily, not surprisingly, interpreted the iron cubicles in a different and positive manner. Being rather proud of them, she described the cages as "private and hygienic, little thinking that they could by a certain section of the public be transformed into 'cages.'"[48] The November, 1895, edition of *Our Work*, the official publication of the sisterhood, printed a visitor's sympathetic description of the cubicles: "Not long since, a clergyman asked to see the dormitories. He stood looking at the pretty, comfortable beds in stupefied amazement for a few moments, and then exclaimed, 'Why, they are little rooms, and very nice cosy rooms too . . . A little room, containing a spring bed, with hair mattress, bolster, pillow, and the whitest of sheets and blankets, a nice appointed washstand, clothes-basket and shelf.'"[49] The Mother Superior also emphasized that the children took pride in their little space and had no complaints about these accommodations. Moreover, the Sisters always welcomed visitors to the orphanage to inspect the surroundings. In spite of Mother Emily's defense of these methods employed at the orphanages, the issues raised by the COS report did not disappear.

EPISCOPAL SUPERVISION

The Church Times asked some leading questions. On September 27, 1895, the paper published a letter that questioned the alleged freewheeling character of the sisterhood, and asked why it had dismissed the two archbishops as patrons and why it refused to yield to episcopal supervision.[50] It also printed a recent memorandum written by the Archbishop of Canterbury, E. W. Benson. On June 13, Benson composed a lengthy document that outlined his relationship with the Sisters of the Church

47. Ibid., 2.
48. Anonymous, *Valiant Victorian*, 153.
49. Printed in ibid., 153.
50. *The Church Times*, September 27, 1895.

and described his growing frustration with their independence of spirit.[51] Archbishop Benson described how he had become a patron of the sisterhood in October 1892, and had criticized the prospectus that announced the acceptance of illegitimate children for money. He also stated that Mother Emily had told him that the advertisement had been withdrawn, and that enemies of the community had circulated this announcement. Benson had also expressed his disapproval with the admission process, and the Mother Superior had informed him that the sisterhood now followed the practice of the Foundling Hospital.

The Archbishop of Canterbury then talked about the cubicles or iron cages. The Archbishop expressed his concern: "These sets of rumours were injurious to a benevolent society of such widespread activities and I am desirous that, if untrue, they should be authoritatively contradicted, and if true corrected." The Mother Superior, he mentioned, believed that the "cubicles were perfectly safe and girls were not locked in rooms." Benson also "strongly condemned the sending of unruly girls to the work house," and he understood from Mother Emily's response that it would never happen again. Archbishop Benson suggested that a person appointed by him should be allowed to inspect the orphanages to dispel any rumors of cruelty. Mother Emily, however, had vetoed the two candidates proposed by the Archbishop on the grounds that both persons held biased opinions against the sisterhood. The Archbishop also unsuccessfully proposed that an independent inspector should be allowed to look at the financial records. Finally, Benson admitted that he had no power to institute an investigation into these matters on his own.

Archbishop Benson's chief point, consequently, centered around the issue of episcopal authority and the appointment of an episcopal Visitor to supervise the affairs of the Sisters of the Church. "In the strongest way I urged the propriety for so large an establishment and administration of having a regular Constitution with a responsible governing body and a Visitor" with firm principles to guide their lives. In response, Mother Emily "said that a constitution would be framed when time permitted, but that the community would object to having a Visitor." Throughout the spring of 1895, the memorandum continued, Benson had carried on negotiations with the Mother Superior on these points through a series of letters, and a precis of each appeared in his memo,

---

51. *Memorandum—Kilburn Sisters of the Church (Church Extension Society)*, Benson Papers, vol. 159, Lambeth Palace.

but she failed to acknowledge them. In June, he wrote again, mentioning that he had received "no answer to my offers of aid and guidance ... [and] must let matters take their course." Archbishop Benson's final action in regard to the troubles concerning the Sisters of the Church was to submit this memorandum to the Bishops' Meetings in June 1895 for their information.

MORE CRITITQUES OF THE SISTERS OF THE CHURCH

Questions surrounding the orphanages run by the Sisters of the Church continued to appear in the public forum. The *Truth*, a newspaper edited by Henry du Pre Labouchere, which had become famous for exposing fraud, took up the assault on the inhuman iron cages. The December 12, 1895, edition praised the earlier report of the Charity Organization Society which brought to light some questionable practices. It did not neglect to mention the alleged barbarity on the part of the Sisters. "Some account is also given of a deplorable scandal which has lately occurred in the Orphanages," the paper pointed out referring to the cages, "and which has been dealt with by methods incredibly cruel, unjust, and demoralizing."[52] A public debate over the policies of the Sisters of the Church raged throughout the next year.

In early 1896, the publishers of *Church Bells*, a newspaper which favored comprehensiveness and which never advocated the so-called "extreme" party within the Anglican Church, that is, those churchmen who supported ritualism, printed a booklet which defended the sisterhood against the report of the Charity Organization Society and the recent article in the *Truth*.[53] This publication, *The Kilburn Sisters and Their Accusers*, began by refuting the claims of the COS report. The secession of the disgruntled Sisters had created an unfortunate incident, but their departure arose from theological differences within the sisterhood. The COS had raised the serious question of the possible misappropriation of public funds, and the *Church Bells* had a simple answer: a regrettable accounting mistake had been made. Finally, the removal of the names of the Archbishops of Canterbury and York, Benson and Maclagan, from the list of patrons certainly did not indicate that the Sisters of the Church

52. *Truth* (London), December 12, 1895.
53. *The Killburn Sisters and Their Accusers*.

refused to conform to the teachings of the Anglican Church: "that in all ecclesiastical matters the community are [sic] absolutely under episcopal control, both at home and in the colonies."[54]

The *Church Bells* report also addressed the question of the iron cages allegedly used to punish the children. To refute the pictorial presentations of these devices that had appeared earlier in a hostile publication, the cover page of this pamphlet showed the reader a cubicle complete with a door that could be easily opened. The atmosphere reflected serenity and peacefulness, and not one of punishment or incarceration. The face of the child in the cubicle beamed with contentment. A second picture showed a baby's cot, similar to a modern crib, and the child's smile also contradicted the accusations of harsh treatment. Refuting the charges that these devices were fire traps, the authors pointed out that the doors of these cubicles could be easily opened, and concluded: "We object to the terms 'mechanical contrivances of objectionable character for keeping the children apart,' as mysterious, misleading, and absurd when applied to a door, locked or open. We consider that public reports should be couched in plain, straightforward terms, impossible of misinterpretation . . . the charges of cruelty are absolutely unproven, and, in our opinion, should never have been advanced upon such flimsy and untrustworthy evidence."[55] This defense of the Sisters of the Church ended by stating "that the much-described cubicles are inoffensive enough."[56] Finally, a number of letters from former orphans also scorned the description of the cubicles as prisons, praised their safety and health benefits, and emphasized the good treatment they had received at the hands of the Sisters.

The *Church Bells* publication tried to clarify some other unfounded accusations against the Sisters of the Church. The change of the baby's names did cause confusion, and the failure to report the death of a child had been an inexcusable mistake on the part of the managers. The officials now recorded the child's birth name along with the so-called orphanage name. The punishment of the girls who took part in group masturbation caused some concern, but this report alleged that someone critical of the sisterhood had coached the girls to give negative testimonies. Moreover, no ratepayer suffered any financial hardship because of the removal of

---

54. Ibid., 32.
55. Ibid., 19.
56. Ibid., 39.

the girls to the Paddington workhouse. No one had to shoulder the cost of their upkeep during the period before they were sent away. One of the chief complaints of the Charity Organization Society concerned the policy by which the Sisters of the Church accepted the foundlings or illegitimate children. The 1893 prospectus, which protected the identity of the parents and children, had caused an uproar since people argued that this cloak of anonymity actually encouraged vice. The sisterhood, the pages of the *Church Bells* argued, had changed the wording of the prospectus to bring it into line with the policy of the Foundling Hospital. The new prerequisites for entrance required that: the "virtuous" character of the mother must be confirmed; a "concise record of the history of each child . . . [was] kept, after the manner of the Foundling Hospital; names and address of the parents were registered; the birth name of the child was recorded; in normal circumstances," the payment of fee should not be enforced."[57] The *Church Bells* report even printed a copy of the Foundling Hospital Register to illustrate the similarity with the new policy adopted by the Sisters of the Church.[58] This defense of the sisterhood, however, failed to silence the critics of the Sisters of the Church.

The *Truth* took issue with the conclusions of the investigation carried out by *Church Bells* and published a long supplement to its June 18, 1896, edition. After mentioning that the sisterhood had threatened to institute legal proceedings for libel against the paper, the editor of the *Truth* outlined the history of his relationship with the Sisters of the Church and discussed the substance of recent interviews that took place between himself and representatives of the sisterhood concerning the treatment of orphans. The editor mentioned the incident of the "evil" girls being punished and dispatched to the workhouse, and maintained that these serious allegations "constitute a most serious indictment of those responsible for the management of the Kilburn Orphanage."[59] He believed that the Sisters did not act out of malice, but "through want of sense and want of knowledge." The existence of the cubicles or iron cages did not escape the paper's attention. Sister Francis, the spokesperson for the sisterhood, told Labouchere that "the children liked them," and they did not present a danger to the child in the event of a fire. The editor disagreed with this interpretation. After inspecting one of the cubicles,

57. Ibid., 27.
58. Ibid., 29.
59. *Truth*, June 18, 1896.

he described it in derogatory terms, and argued that they did constitute a threat to life in case of an emergency. The design and construction, he believed, lacked "common-sense and forethought."

Labouchere again returned to the question of the girls expelled for acts of "immorality." Sister Francis denied any undue pressure to make these girls confess, and she also disputed other accusations of cruelty against the orphans, for example, corporal punishment and solitary confinement. To counter this, he introduced the testimony of several girls that contradicted the statement of Sister Francis. The *Truth* finally reached a conclusion critical of the Sisters of the Church and the operation of their orphanage. The sisterhood did good and worthwhile work, but the lack of experience and poor organization compromised any positive benefits. The emphasis of the sisterhood on making money, for example, appeals to charity and the alleged "falsehood of some [financial] statements," constituted a more grievous shortcoming. Consequently, the paper suggested, "it would seem to be inevitable that a Sisterhood run on these lines and permeated by this spirit must tend to lose its distinctive character, and 'cease to be a religious community.'"

After the publication of this report by Labouchere, the debate on the Sisters of the Church and the operation of their orphanage at Kilburn came to an end. The reason can be found in the action taken by the Anglican Church. In 1897, the year following the report by the *Truth*, the Lambeth Conference, the meeting of Anglican Bishops that took place every ten years, met in London. One item on their agenda concerned the existence of religious life for men and women within the church. The resolutions of the Lambeth Conference had no binding authority, but they did express the mind of the bishops on critical issues. The relationship between brotherhoods and sisterhoods had became an important item for discussion, and a group of concerned laity brought the questionable position of the Sisters of the Church to the bishops' attention by writing an open letter to them. Entitled "Anglican Sisterhoods," it described the history of the sisterhood, reprinted the original 1893 prospectus for the admission of illegitimate children into the orphanages (which it noted had been withdrawn), described the relationship between the community and Bishop Temple and Archbishop Benson, and noted some of the complaints voiced by the COS and the *Truth*. This letter, consequently, asked for a clarification on the relationship of the sisterhood to the Anglican Church.[60] "Facts like these speak for themselves," this letter concluded, "and surely show plainly the lamentable results of works conducted by a band of utterly irresponsible ladies, and point to the necessity of placing all Anglican Sisterhoods under real, not nominal, authority."

The report of the Lambeth Conference, which studied all religious communities, emphasized the important role of episcopal authority in their lives. Sisterhoods and brotherhoods, in the mind of the committee, must not live a life independently of the local bishop, who should assume the role of episcopal Visitor.[61] The report, which would be submitted to the 1908 Lambeth Conference, acknowledged the good and worthwhile work performed by these communities of men and women, but on the other hand stressed that "there should be on the part of the Communities a distinct recognition of the authority of the Episcopate."[62] The Visitor would guarantee that the community did not stray beyond the wide boundaries of Anglican comprehensiveness. The report then articulated the duties of this bishop. Among other things, he would review and approve the constitution of brotherhood or sisterhood, monitor the profession of solemn vows, and make sure that the community used the Book of Common Prayer in their worship. These guidelines certainly went a long way to satisfy and to silence the critics of the Sisters of the Church.

In April 1901, however, the *Protestant Alliance Official Organ* repeated stories of cruelty associated with the so-called "Kilburn Cages for Children."[63] A resident of Liverpool had received a letter from the sisterhood soliciting money, and replied that he could not contribute to an institution "which used spiked iron cages for the incarceration of children." One of the sisters wrote back and invited this gentleman to visit the orphanage and inspect the surroundings for himself. The Protestant Alliance, therefore, sent a representative to look at the Kilburn establishment. He reported that "the spiked iron cages are still in use ... [and] that

60. "Anglican Sisterhoods. A Letter to the Bishops Assembled in Conference at Lambeth, July 1897," F. Temple Papers, vol. 4, Lambeth Palace Library.

61. Kollar, "1897 Lambeth Conference," 56.

62. "Report of the Committee Appointed in 1897 to Consider the Relation of Religious Communities within the Church to the Episcopate," 1908, Lambeth Palace Library.

63. *Protestant Alliance Official Organ* (London), April 1901.

he was shown several long rows of them by one of the 'Sisters.'" The paper even reprinted an illustration and explanation of the cage which had appeared earlier in other attacks against the Sisters of the Church. The article argued that escape, even with the aid of a pillow, was impossible because of the size of the spikes placed at the top of the cage. The *Protestant Alliance Official Organ* quickly turned the reader's attention from alleged abuses in the orphanage to accusations of Roman Catholic practices: "A large crucifix stood over the 'altar,' with six candles. On the steps was a sacring-bell, while round the walls were numerous images of 'saints' and pictures of Mary, the whole presenting a thoroughly popish appearance."

CONCLUSION

Nonetheless, the attacks against the Sisters of the Church died down. An explanation for this can be found in the attitude adopted by the Anglican Church, which began to exert its control over the life of sisterhoods. Moreover, in 1903, following the deaths of Archbishop Temple and Mother Emily, the Sisters of the Church elected to have an episcopal Visitor, thus answering critics that they had little regard for the official church. The story of the Sisters of the Church offers an insight into the nature of the criticism against sisterhoods during the nineteenth century. Their opponents found questionable areas for concern in addition to Romanizing practices usually associated with Catholic convents. Unfriendly accusations came from the Charity Organization Society, which critiqued the management and the daily running of the Kilburn orphanage. Other critics asked why this sisterhood avoided episcopal oversight for such a long period of time. These concerns began to disappear at the turn of the century. Not surprisingly, however, some opponents continued to see this sisterhood as a bastion of Roman Catholicism, and it was this last fear that survived the longest. Another element of the controversy also remained. The use of the questionable iron cages, it appears, continued into the twentieth century.

Bibliography

Allchin, A. M. *The Silent Rebellion: Anglican Religious Communities 1845-1900*. London: SCM, 1958.
Anonymous. *Emily H. E. Ayckbowm: Mother Foundress of the Community of the Sisters of the Church*. London: Church Extension Association, 1914.
Anonymous. *A Valiant Victorian: The Life and Times of Mother Emily Ayckbowm, 1836-1900, of the Community of the Sisters of the Church*. London: Mowbray, 1964.
Anson, Peter F. *The Call of the Cloister: Religious Communities and Kindred Bodies in the Anglican Communion*. Revised and edited by A. W. Campbell. London: SPCK, 1964.
Barret-Ducrocq, Francoise. *Love in the Time of Victoria. Sexuality and Desire among Working-Class Men and Women in Nineteenth-Century London*. Translated by John Howe. New York: Penguin, 1991.
Benson, Arthur C. *The Life of Edward White Benson, Sometime Archbishop of Canterbury*. Vol. 2. London: MacMillan, 1900.
Brownlow, John. *The History and Objects of the Foundling Hospital, with a Memoir of the Founder*. London: Jaques, 1865.
Coldrey, Barry M. "A Mixture of Caring and Corruption: Church Orphanages and Industrial Schools." *Studies: An Irish Quarterly Review* 89 (Spring 2000) 7-18.
Exposure of the Kilburn Sisterhood. London: Protestant Alliance, 1896.
Fraser, Derek. "Introduction." In *The New Poor Law in the Nineteenth Century*. Edited by Derek Fraser. New York: St. Martin's, 1976.
Hall, M. Penelope. *The Social Services in Modern England*. London: Routledge & Kegan Paul 1960.
Hinchliff, Peter. *Frederick Temple, Archbishop of Canterbury: A Life*. Oxford: Oxford University Press, 1998.
The Killburn Sisters and Their Accusers. London: *Church Bells*.
Kollar, Rene. "The 1897 Lambeth Conference and the Question of Religious Life in the Anglican Communion." *Cistercian Studies* 26 (December 1991) 319-29.
MacKinnon, Mary. "English Poor Law Policy and the Crusade against Outrelief." *Journal of Economic History* 47 (1987) 603-25.
Mowat, C. L. *The Charity Organization Society 1869-1913: Its Ideas and Work*. London: Meuthen, 1961.
Mumm, Susan. *Stolen Daughters, Virgin Mothers*. London: Leicester University Press, 1999.
Nichols, R. H., and F. A. Wray. *The History of the Foundling Hospital*. London: Oxford University Press, 1935.
Owen, David Edward. *English Philanthropy, 1660-1960*. Cambridge: Harvard University Press, 1964.
Porter, Roy. *London: A Social History*. Cambridge: Harvard University Press, 1995.
Price, Richard. *British Society 1680-1880: Dynamism, Containment, and Change*. Cambridge: Cambridge University Press, 1999.
Pugh, Martin. *State and Society: A Social and Political History of Britain 1870-1997*. New York: Arnold, 1999.
A Report upon the Orphanages and Other Charitable Institutions Conducted by the Church Extension Association. London: The Charity Organization Society, 1895.
Royle, Edward. *Modern Britain: A Social History 1750-1997*. New York: Arnold, 1997.
Thane, Pat. "Government and Society in England and Wales, 1750-1914." In *The Cambridge Social History of Britain 1750-1950*, Vol. 3, *Social Agencies and Institutions*, edited by F. M. L. Thompson. Cambridge: Cambridge University Press, 1993.

7

Flowers, Pictures, and Crosses

Criticisms of Priscilla Lydia Sellon's Care of Young Girls

NINETEENTH-CENTURY ENGLAND EXPERIENCED A sudden and dramatic growth in the establishment of Anglican sisterhoods, and with this development also came a sustained campaign against these nuns and their convents. Books, pamphlets, speeches, and articles in the newspapers attacked and criticized the sisterhoods. Some opponents maintained that the sisterhoods might become carbon copies of their Roman Catholic counterparts, and thus harm the religious fabric of the Church of England. Others, however, believed that all convents, Roman Catholic and Anglican, would destroy certain prized English virtues such as individual freedom, the authority of parents, and the sanctity of the family in an attempt to create good and compliant nuns. Roman Catholic convents could certainly never appreciate the English character of these sacred institutions, but many Britons could not understand how the established church could tolerate sisterhoods within its ranks. Still other critics of the conventual life for women laughed at the apparent uselessness of contemplative or cloistered sisterhoods, and expressed a bit more toleration for those who engaged in some sort of so-called active work such as education, nursing, or work among the poor and outcast of Victorian society, including orphans. But a danger still existed. Anglican sisterhoods that ministered to young girls, some feared, might unintentionally turn the eyes of these impressionable and vulnerable females in the direction of Roman Catholicism. Priscilla Lydia Sellon's efforts in Devonport, near Plymouth—especially her work with orphan girls—came under scrutiny by some Evangelicals who wanted to protect the Anglican integrity of those young women. They tried to identify this sisterhood with the disreputable religious practices of Roman Catholicism in an attempt to alert the public of the threat posed by Sellon, but her orphanage survived the attack.

During the early 1850s, a number of zealots, mostly Anglican clergymen, attacked Sellon (1821–1876) and her sisterhood in the Diocese of Exeter. Church of England sisterhoods began to flourish within the Tractarian tradition, and they necessarily looked to the Roman Catholic nuns for constitutions, rules, customs, and even dress. At times, consequently, these Anglican communities of nuns adopted some liturgical practices associated with Roman Catholicism which had been banned by the reformers of the sixteenth century. The first convent in the Anglican Church was the Sisterhood of the Holy Cross, founded in 1845 at Park Village West, London, and it was followed by the Community of St. Mary the Virgin in Berkshire during 1848.[1] In the same year, Lydia Sellon established the Society of the Most Holy Trinity at Devonport. These early pioneering sisterhoods possessed certain common traits. The founders or first superiors had strong and independent personalities, and critics accused them of despotic behavior toward the other sisters. Since convents were novelties in the Anglican Church, the ecclesiastical officials had not yet developed any means to supervise or to incorporate these women within the comprehensiveness of Anglicanism. The sisterhoods developed freely without episcopal oversight, and opponents saw them as mavericks and demanded more control from the bishops. Many saw in the convents the spirit of Roman Catholicism. This was in part due to the influence of Tractarianism and the support that its leading figures, especially Edward Bouverie Pusey, gave to the revival of conventual life. These traits can be seen in the life of Lydia Sellon's Devonport sisterhood. The romanizing tendencies of her sisterhood also accounted for the hostility the opponents leveled against the small orphanage directed by Sellon.

1. For a comprehensive history of Anglican brotherhoods and sisterhoods in the nineteenth century, see Allchin, *Silent Rebellion*; and Anson, *Call of the Cloister*. The following books also contain valuable information on the revival of religious life in the Anglican Church: Campbell-Jones, *In Habit*; Hill, *Religious Order*; and Mumm, *Stolen Daughters, Virgin Mothers*. Reed's *Glorious Battle* discusses the growth of Anglican sisterhoods and the Anglo-Catholic environment which supported them.

Thomas Jay Williams, her biographer, and other commentators on the revival of sisterhoods have identified the influences on Sellon's life.[2] Her mother died early, and she was raised by her father, who would later defend his daughter and her sisterhood from the attacks against her character and the work of the sisterhood. The absence of a mother, it appears, contributed to her sense of adventure, freedom, and single-mindedness. *The Dictionary of National Biography* points out that her father, William Richard Baker Sellon, trained his daughter in a spirit of independence. John Shelton Reed recognizes Sellon's "iron will" in the face of violent opposition to her sisterhood,[3] and Peter Anson describes her as a "bold and determined pioneer."[4] Margaret Goodman, who had spent time as a member of Lydia Sellon's sisterhood, had many critical things to say about her. Goodman wrote about the harshness of the rules that governed the community, Sellon's unchecked authority, spiritual pride, and her aloofness from the other sisters.[5]

Like other women of this nature and outlook, Sellon sought a life outside the domestic setting. When she read an appeal from the bishop of Exeter, Henry Phillpotts, in the January 5, 1848, edition of *The Guardian* for help in Plymouth and Devonport, she quickly gave up her plans to travel to Italy for reasons of health because "the spiritual destitution of thousands of poor people had a strong claim on the nation at large."[6] Sellon's arrival in this area of the country and the establishment of a sisterhood to work among the destitute and the sick would ignite a religious war of words between her supporters and antagonists. The identification of her project with the bishop of Exeter contributed in part to the animosity.

Henry Phillpotts (1778–1869), appointed bishop of Exeter in 1830, became involved in several controversies involving issues of discipline within the Anglican Church. High Church by tradition, he was, however, no friend of the extreme Tractarian theologians. In Exeter, Phillpotts worked to reduce incidents of pluralism and nonresidence, sought to employ only educated and well-trained clergymen who would

   2. Williams, *Priscilla Lydia Sellon*. See also *Dictionary of National Biography*; and Vicinus, *Independent Women*.
   3. Reed, *Glorious Battle*, 13.
   4. Anson, *Call of the Cloister*, 260.
   5. Goodman, *Experiences of an English Sister of Mercy*.
   6. Anson, *Call of the Cloister*, 261.

receive a fair salary, encouraged the development of new parishes and the construction of needed churches to meet the growing number of the faithful, and enforced the letter and spirit of approved rubric of the Church of England.[7] Some of his disputes attracted national attention, such as his opposition to the appointment in 1847 of R. D. Hampden as bishop of Hereford, but it was the so-called Gorham Judgment that caused Phillpotts much heartache and marked him as an enemy of the Evangelical wing of the Anglican Church. G. C. Gorham refused to subscribe to baptismal regeneration, and in 1847, after an examination of nine days, Bishop Phillpotts refused to institute him to the living of Brampford Speke.[8] Gorham then appealed to the Court of Arches, which upheld Phillpotts's decision. A later appeal to the Judicial Committee of the Privy Council, however, found in favor of Gorham.[9] In another case, which some interpreted as tolerance in matters liturgical, the bishop refused to censure strongly a number of questionable liturgical practices of some of his clergy, and his treatment of G. R. Prynne, a ritualist and supporter of Sellons sisterhood, seemed too lenient.[10] In the eyes of some Evangelical clergymen, therefore, Bishop Phillpotts appeared as a champion of Tractarian views, and his strong support and encouragement of Lydia Sellon's sisterhood tended to confirm this suspicion.

In April 1848, Sellon arrived in Devonport and began her work among the poor. Soon afterwards, Bishop Phillpotts extended his episcopal approval to this experiment. "On the 27th October the bishop officially sanctioned the formation of The Church of England Sisterhood in Devonport and Plymouth' and gave Sellon and her companion, Miss Catherine Chambers, his blessing and benediction."[11] The bishop's acceptance of her sisterhood, also known as the Sisters of Mercy because of the work these women undertook, helped to put it in a recognized but shaky position. Commenting in 1852 about Phillpotts's patronage of Sellon, *The Christian Observer*, an Evangelical publication critical of the

---

7. Wolffe, "Bishop Henry Phillpotts."

8. Chadwick, *Victorian Church*, 250–71.

9. See Howell, *Judicial Committee of the Privy Council, 1833–1876* for a history and the work of the Judicial Committee of the Privy Council. Phillpotts refused to acknowledge this court's ruling, and eventually the Archbishop of Canterbury, J. B. Sumner, instituted Gorham.

10. Wolffe, "Bishop Henry Phillpotts," 109.

11. Hill, *Religious Orders*, 216.

bishop and the sisterhood, stated: "from the first, the Bishop gave Miss Sellon the broadest and distinguishing support. He flattered her in public and stimulated her in private."[12] The bishop's High Church sympathies and his support of Sellon's sisterhood, a Romish institution in the eyes of many, helped to increase the suspicions of this small sisterhood and its work.

The influence and support of another prominent Anglican cleric and his close association with the Devonport community also contributed to Sellon's troubles. And, as in the case of Bishop Phillpotts, the Evangelicals in the Devonport area scorned his Tractarian views. Edward Bouverie Pusey, the doyen of the Oxford Movement, played a significant part in Sellon's enterprise. She had an interview with him before her arrival at Devonport, and Pusey sent a letter of introduction to one of the local clerics, W. B. Killpack, who would become one of her strongest supporters.[13] His frequent visits soon after her arrival and the questionable liturgies for the sisters also contributed to the dislike and distrust of Sellon. The nature of the work that Sellon undertook should have eased some anxieties, but her ministry among the orphans in the area actually became the catalyst for the years of criticism.

The life of a cloistered and contemplative nun seemed useless and unnecessary to some Anglicans, but others recognized the value in a more active life outside of convent walls based on the principles and work of the German order of deaconesses. Founded in 1836 at Kaiserswerth by T. Fliedner, these women labored among the sick and orphans. If females felt called to ministry within the church, many Anglicans argued, they should eschew the quiet life and devote their energies to the less fortunate in the manner of the deaconesses. The Evangelicals also saw a danger to their church and to individuals who sought the contemplative life, namely, the possibility that these women might convert to Roman Catholicism. The High Church party certainly did not wholeheartedly endorse the cloistered life either. *The English Churchman*, a publication of this group, warned its readers of the dangers of a "life of solitude" a few years before Sellon left for Devonport. Responding to a letter from a

---

12. *The Christian Observer* (London), 1852; quoted in Williams, *Priscilla Lydia Sellon*, 116.

13. Liddon, *Life of Edward Bouverie Pusey*, vol. 4, 192. For some additional information on Killpack and J. Hatchard, who would become a critic of Sellon, see *The Clergy List for 1859*.

cleric who expressed a desire that such institutions be established in the Anglican Church, the newspaper described this "pining for solitude" as not only morbid "but deeply sinful."[14] But the author of the article would certainly have praised individuals such as Lydia Sellon, "who apprehend that, in our day, when so much ignorance, vice, poverty, misery, and sorrow prevails on all sides Solitude, except in very peculiar cases, is selfish and sinful. Christian men and women must be up and doing." Moreover, this commentary pointed out, "If they have no duties at home, or among their kindred and acquaintance, they have duties abroad, among the ignorant, the poor, and the afflicted." At least in this area of active ministry to the less fortunate, it appeared that Sellon's sisterhood would be accepted and welcomed.

The numerous charitable activities that Sellon and her sisters undertook should have impressed anyone. Her biographer details the manner in which she threw herself into her work, even making personal contact with children on the street and recruiting them as students. Her strong personality proved successful, and a number of projects soon came under her supervision. "By 1851 Sellon's community, as well as having supplied a number of nurses for Florence Nightingale's hospital in the Crimea, was running an orphanage, a training school for sailor boys, a refuge for girls, a home for elderly seamen, a large industrial school, six model lodging houses, a soup kitchen, five ragged schools, a convalescent home and a hospital, with sisters working in Devonport, Bristol and Averstoke in Hampshire."[15]

After visiting Sellon's vineyard, Pusey wrote a glowing report of what he had observed. He emphasized the religious care given to the children in the industrial school and the orphanage, which she established in 1848 for the orphan daughters of poor sailors. Pusey estimated that "there are the poor orphans to be gathered in, and continually tended and taught, and carefully watched too (just as a parent's eye is over a child, though it perceives it not) lest, before they have unlearnt their evil and learnt good, any should teach another evil it may have learnt."[16] In spite of this praiseworthy work, Sellon soon became an object of scorn and hatred in newspaper articles and public denunciations because of her care of orphan girls who lodged with her and Catherine Chambers.

14. *The English Churchman* (London), June 26, 1845.
15. Mumm, *Stolen Daughters, Virgin Mothers*, 7.
16. Pusey to Coleridge, January 1849, in Liddon, *Life of Edward Bouverie Pusey*, 193.

This attack against Sellon and her methods was sparked both by fear that the orphanage would become a recruiting ground for future papists, and by jealousy of Sellon's successes.

Both the secular and religious press became the arena for this controversy. By the end of January 1849, a local clergyman, John Hatchard, vicar of St. Andrews in Plymouth, had expressed some criticism of Sellon's methods and religious practices. Rivalry and envy, and not religious conformity, however, played a major role in this critique. According to Thomas Jay Williams, "The example of the Sisters in providing a shelter for orphans other than the workhouse was copied by a group of Low Church clergy and laity, who, in alarm over the success of the Puseyites' venture, opened a rival establishment, known as The Orphan Asylum."[17] And true to her character, Lydia Sellon responded to his concerns about the spiritual and material well-being of her orphans. Sellon told Hatchard that she had come to Devonport because of the apparent "spiritual destitution" of the area, and her work, especially among the area's youth, had enjoyed some success. "It pleased God to bless my endeavours, especially among the children," she told him, and "in a few months I had gathered together several schools, and the sick and destitute eagerly welcomed my visit."[18] Her small sisterhood wanted to spread the gospel as understood and practiced by the Anglican Church, and she concluded by urging Hatchard to work together with her for a common purpose: "Life is very short—too short for the words of parties, or the strife of tongues." Hatchard mistakenly took Sellon's words as an invitation, and within a few days he visited the small orphanage and had an opportunity to speak with her about the life of the sisterhood and its work. This, however, did not dispel any of his suspicions.

John Hatchard did not waste any time in reaching a conclusion after his interview with Sellon. In some respects, he did not change his views about her work. Hatchard assured her that he did not believe that she was a papist, but rather lived life according to the principles of Tractarianism. This mode of misguided religious enthusiasm, he pointed out, invariably led to Catholicism. Moreover, the Roman Catholic name, "Sisters of Mercy," the attire of the sisters, and Sellon's title as "Superior of the Sisterhood" would not endear the sisterhood or her projects, especially the orphanage, to the public, which could not "fail to look with

---

17. Williams, *Priscilla Lydia Sellon*, 56.
18. Sellon to Hatchard, January 25, 1849, *The Guardian* (London), February 14, 1849.

very great jealousy upon your proceedings, in which too I cannot cease most fully to join."[19] The sisterhood, he concluded, must work to avoid any suspicion of disloyalty to Anglicanism. Sellon's response expressed a sorrow that differences existed between two people who wanted to advance God's kingdom on earth. Prayer might dispel mistrust, and she promised to pray for Hatchard and asked for his prayers in return.[20] But their disagreement could not be resolved, and their differences of opinion could be read in newspaper columns and heard in speeches.

Prior to his interview with Lydia Sellon, Hatchard had attacked her sisterhood in a public address. He emphasized the presence of some questionable practices that he believed were Roman Catholic, especially the wearing of crosses. The publication and dissemination of this hostile speech drew a reaction from a group of friendly clergymen who quickly came to the women's defense. On the day following Hatchard's meeting with Sellon at the orphanage, the mayor of Devonport, three Anglican clergymen, and two dissenting ministers signed a statement which praised her "works of piety and charity" in the area.[21] These individuals maintained that the sisters did not promote or encourage Roman traditions and assured the public that the books used to teach the orphans came from a list approved by the Society for Promoting Christian Knowledge. The operation of Sellon's orphanage also received strong support. The statement also tried to clear up some misleading reports: "We have visited this establishment, and have fully ascertained the principles on which it is conducted," namely, the sisters "who superintend it are sincerely attached to the Church of England."

Hatchard answered this challenge and his reply appeared in the Plymouth area papers on January 30. He pointed out that the sisters had only dropped wearing the cross in public because Bishop Phillpotts had requested it. A cross also adorned the interior of Sellon's house, which he had just recently visited. And this dwelling housed the young orphans. He refused to modify his views on the Tractarian nature of the sisterhood, but the operation of an orphanage under Lydia Sellon's supervision offended his Protestant sensitivities more that the adoption of questionable religious symbols. "You add that a principal object they have in view is the establishment of a female orphan asylum in this

---

19. Hatchard to Sellon, January 26, 1849, *The Guardian*, February 14, 1849.
20. Sellon to Hatchard, January 27, 1849, *The Guardian*, February 14, 1849.
21. Printed in *The English Churchman*, February 22, 1849.

populous neighbourhood," he argued, and "now, if there be a portion of their actions more open to suspicion than another, this seems to be one of the chief."[22] Hatchard then gave the local newspapers his correspondence with Sellon and his recollections of the visit to her orphanage. This information appeared first in the local papers and then in the national religious press, and concerns about Lydia Sellon's orphanage consequently became public.

Lydia Sellon, however, could count on some local clerical support. W. B. Killpack of Stoke Damerel, the area of Devonport where the sisterhood was located, immediately came to her defense. Killpack asked Lydia Sellon to supply him with some information and background on her dealings with Hatchard, and she replied that her interview with him was meant to be private. She had only wanted to clear up some misrepresentations and errors which he had circulated about the sisterhood and the orphanage. According to Sellon, "It seemed to me that perhaps he might through ignorance fall into greater evil."[23] She told Killpack that Hatchard's visit took her by surprise. She then related that he had come prepared with a list of questions, which she thought were of "too trifling a nature for me to attach any importance to them." Sellon told her friend that she had answered Hatchard's queries in an attempt to clear up any misunderstandings he might have, but she never intended that their correspondence or the contents of the interview should become public knowledge. "I considered the letters which passed, and his call as a private matter," she told Killpack. Moreover, Sellon had not given Hatchard permission to publish them, and their appearance in the newspaper had shocked her. Consequently, Killpack asked for and received Sellon's permission to publish her earlier January correspondence with Hatchard, along with her recollections of her dealings with him. Killpack argued that Sellon's critic had violated charity and had invaded the privacy of her sisterhood by making the letters public. This, Killpack admitted, forced him to acquaint the public with Lydia Sellon's side of the story.

By early February 1849, therefore, the dispute about Sellon's orphanage no longer remained behind closed doors. Others soon joined the fray. If one could prove that an unhealthy religious environment of the home, namely the presence of extreme Tractarian or even Roman

---

22. Printed in *The Guardian*, February 14, 1849. Excerpts of this letter also appeared in *The English Churchman*.

23. Sellon to Killpack, February 5, 1849, *The Guardian*, February 14, 1849.

Catholic practices, might adversely influence the young girls and even entice them out of the Anglican Church into the arms of Rome, then a public outcry might force the sisterhood to discontinue its ministry among the orphans. Consequently, the editor of *The Devonport Telegraph*, Mr. Richards, interviewed three former residents of the orphanage, and the resulting picture, published on February 10 in his paper, described the strong Roman Catholic atmosphere that prevailed in the home. The religious press reacted to Richards's conclusions. *The English Churchman* believed that his findings "confirmed the worst report which had been circulated respecting the Sisters of Mercy."[24] *The Guardian* suggested another motive for the investigation by this local newspaper and disagreed with the method employed and the validity of the outcome of the investigation: representatives of the press "under the pretence of being sent by the Queen [Adelaide, wife of William IV], have induced three of those who have eaten the bread of charity to make some statements relative to the private and devotional habits of the Sisters and arrangements of the house, so strung together, as to give a general impression of an institution very different indeed from what we believe to be the truth."[25]

Lydia Sellon's biographer saw another reason behind the interest in the three former orphans, and not primarily the uprooting of Roman Catholic practices, as the chief motive behind the intentions of Hatchard and his newspaper confederates, namely, jealousy over the orphanage operated by the sisterhood. Hatchard and *The Devonport Telegraph*, therefore, hoped to blacken the reputation of the sisterhood by forcing three girls to make damaging statements about the religious environment at Sellon's orphanage. The testimony of Sarah Ann Clarke, Mary Pochetty, and Selina Jones appeared in this newspaper. Their reports related exclusively to the devotional and liturgical routine of the orphans under Sellon's care, and did not reveal any damaging or questionable incidents concerning the treatment of the three girls. They described several practices abhorred by Evangelicals: the presence of the cross throughout the house, on the "altar" in the chapel (the "oratory"), and attached to the sisters' garb; bowing and kneeling before the cross; and the placement of flowers and a picture of the Blessed Virgin Mary on the "altar."[26] One of the girls complained that the time and the names of

---

24. *The English Churchman*, February 22, 1849.
25. *The Guardian*, February 14, 1849.
26. *The English Churchman*, February 22, 1849. The testimony of these three girls

the community prayer copied Roman Catholic practices (for example, Lauds, Prime, Terce, Sext, None, Vespers), and made much of the visits of Pusey to the sisterhood and also accused him of celebrating Holy Communion illegally.[27]

Only one girl's testimony strayed from the area of religious observances and liturgical practices. Sarah Ann Clarke maintained that Sellon enforced a high degree of secrecy throughout the house, paid her no wages for the hard work she did, prohibited visits to friends, and allowed her to leave the orphanage with poor and tattered clothing instead of the nice dress which she wore on her arrival. The publication of the report of the three orphan girls in *The Devonport Telegraph* had two consequences: because of the adverse and harmful comments about Sellon's orphanage, the Dowager Queen Adelaide withdrew her support from the sisterhood; and the bishop of Exeter, Henry Phillpotts, announced that he would conduct a public inquiry into the charges against Lydia Sellon and her orphanage.

The inquiry took place on February 15, 1849, at the Mechanics' Institute at Devonport.[28] Phillpotts, the episcopal visitor of the orphans' home, was in the chair. This stormy meeting lasted seven hours. The plan of Sellon's enemies seemed rather simple: establish the Tractarian or Roman character of the orphanage and the sisterhood; associate the institution with the notorious High Churchman Phillpotts and the Tractarian Pusey; and then destroy Sellon's integrity and credibility. The proceedings of this meeting were published in a report, and extracts appeared in several newspapers. The report introduced the activities of the meeting with the contentious article from *The Devonport Telegraph* that prompted Phillpotts to call for a public and open inquiry. Phillpotts began the inquiry by making an opening statement that pleaded for a peaceful, constructive, and informative meeting. He stated that he would

---

also appeared in a published report of the inquiry conducted by Bishop Henry Phillpotts into the orphanage.

27. Allchin, *Silent Rebellion*, 66.

28. *The Report of the Inquiry Instituted by the Right Reverend Lord Bishop of Exeter, as Visitor of the Orphans' Home, Established by the Sisters of Mercy, at Morice Town, Devonport, into the Truth of Certain Statements Published in the "Devonport Telegraph," February 10, 1849* (Plymouth: Roger Lidstone, 1849). This report was also published in Exeter, Plymouth, and London. Sections of the inquiry appeared in a number of local papers, and *The Guardian* of February 21, 1849, printed extracts collated from several of these newspapers.

first interview the witnesses, and would then allow time for others to ask questions, but the queries had to be directed to the bishop and he would decide if they were appropriate or not. Finally, Bishop Phillpotts revealed the strong sympathies and the admiration he felt for Sellon and the work of the sisterhood. He told the assembly, which included some of her strongest critics, including the editor of *The Devonport Telegraph* and Hatchard, that he called the meeting to "investigate a matter that has been made very public, an accusation of a very grave kind against certain ladies—ladies who profess to come here for the purpose of devoting themselves, their talents of all kinds, whether of mental ability, or money, or health—to devote these and all other their talents [sic] to the cause of God and the assistance of poor people in the most distressed neighbourhood." Phillpotts then called upon the editor of the Devonport newspaper to step forward and give evidence.

Richards told Bishop Phillpotts that he had taken all the notes during the meetings with the three girls, and that other interested gentlemen had witnessed the proceedings also. The editor explained to the audience that he felt he had a duty to the public to investigate rumors concerning life at the orphanage after receiving some anonymous letters that made some serious charges against the sisters. Moreover, he had additional information that the three girls left the orphanage because of offensive religious ceremonies and practices. Phillpotts then inquired as to the objective nature of the questions that Richards had put to the girls. The editor responded that he had tried to be fair, but also admitted that he did edit some of the responses prior to publication. One of the men who had witnessed the meeting with one of the girls asked to be heard, and he told the bishop that the mother had feared that her daughter might become a Roman Catholic, and thus had her daughter removed from Sellon's care. Bishop Phillpotts then began to examine each of the three girls, and asked Sarah Ann Clarke, who was accompanied by her mother, to answer some questions.

Before interrogating Miss Clarke, the bishop asked her mother to leave the room, which she did after voicing strong objections. Phillpotts asked the girl to describe the Roman Catholic ambience at the orphanage, and his choice of words, for example, "the corruptions of the Church of Rome," demonstrated his position. At this point, some members attending the meeting began to disrupt the proceedings with questions about potential witnesses being present during the testimony of the girls. The issue could not be resolved, and in an attempt to bring some order to the meeting, Phillpotts rescinded his earlier decision and permitted Mrs. Clarke to return. The girl then responded to the bishop's queries about Pusey and his dealings with the sisterhood. At this point, a member of the audience began to interrupt constantly with questions, and Bishop Phillpotts threatened to stop the meeting. With order restored, it came to light that Pusey had celebrated Communion for the Sick, because his son, Philip, was recuperating at the house during this time. Thus, according to Phillpotts, Pusey committed no liturgical irregularity in this instance.[29]

Bishop Phillpotts then moved on to some specific instances contained in Miss Clarke's statement in *The Devonport Telegraph*, drawing attention to the crosses, the holy pictures, and the shabby clothing she wore when she left. The girl testified that the newspaper had accurately recorded her testimony In response, Phillpotts announced that Lydia Sellon would appear later in the session. For the time being, however, he read a statement from Sellon which threw some light on the stories of all three girls: the worship and religious customs of the house, she argued, were certainly not popish. With this rebuttal from Lydia Sellon, Miss Clarke's testimony came to an end. At this point, Bishop Phillpotts allowed as evidence several testimonies from the diocesan inspectors of education, which maintained that the sisters promoted Christian principles and fostered high standards of education at the orphans' school.

The questions asked of the second girl, fifteen-year-old Mary Pochetty, sought clarification on the same liturgical and religious aspects of the orphanage. Miss Pochetty began by stating that she left after nearly four months because she could not cope with the work and discipline of the institution. In response to a query about her life immediately after she departed the orphanage, the revealed that she stayed with Mrs. Clarke and her daughter, Sarah Ann. Pochetty did admit that she had made a mistake in her signed statement given to *The Devonport Telegraph*, namely, that she had never seen Lydia Sellon wearing a cross, but that everything else was truthful, including the picture of the Virgin Mary

---

29. Before the public inquiry took place, Bishop Phillpotts was aware that a charge was brought against Pusey for celebrating Holy Communion in an unconsecrated building without a proper license. The bishop wrote to Pusey on February 12 and told him: "This is a most unfortunate case." Phillpotts told him that if "a grave irregularity seems to me to have been committed by you . . . you are the last person to think me wrong in enforcing discipline." Phillpotts to Pusey February 12, 1849, in Williams, *Priscilla Lydia Sellon*, 58.

and the flowers on the altar. Moreover, Miss Pochetty contradicted one of the girls and stated that only the sisters, and not the children, bowed before the cross in the oratory. This witness also admitted that Sellon did not venerate the cross in such a manner, but performed this gesture out of "reverence to the place" of prayer. Phillpotts interjected and stated that he saw no harm in the act of bowing when entering a holy place, but could not justify the use of the term "altar," nor could he approve of the sisters giving this room in a private house the character "of a church by preparing for the celebration of Holy Communion in it." Phillpotts, however, softened his view of Sellon's indiscreet actions by referring to them as "mistaken" and "unfortunate." "But if there be a human being here," he pointed out, "who does not honour these generous Sisters of Charity, I disclaim him." Throughout this testimony, the bishop several times had to call the meeting to order when some in attendance shouted their disapproval of his obvious sympathy toward Sellon. The examination of the final girl, Selina Jones, lasted only minutes, as Lydia Sellon was waiting to give her side of the story.

When Sellon entered the hall, Bishop Phillpotts greeted her affectionately and told the meeting that the chief charge against her orphanage was that "Miss Sellon and the ladies [the sisters] were in the habit of bowing to the Cross, and also taught the orphans to do so." She responded and adamantly denied this charge, and stated that the sisters do bow when entering the oratory or place of prayer out of reverence, and not to venerate the cross. Sellon then clarified the situation: she did not possess a rosary; the sisters did instruct the children in the Bible; she told the assembly that she had no knowledge that Bishop Phillpotts had taken action "against a clergyman in this diocese, for having a Cross and flowers on the Communion Table"; and she did not know that it was contrary to the law of the Church of England to celebrate the Lord's Supper in a private house, except in cases of sickness as with Pusey's son. Sellon, however, did admit that Holy Communion had been celebrated at other times, arguing that it took place in the holy and reverent space of the oratory. The bishop's response to this liturgical irregularity[30] probably shocked Lydia Sellon's enemies: "I do not blame you—but I wish that it had not been done." Concerning the objectionable pictures of the Blessed Virgin Mary, Sellon maintained that the image "pleased" the

---

30. See the preceding note for the position of the Anglican Church and Phillpotts's views on the celebration of the Lord's Supper outside of a consecrated building.

children, and after examining the pictures for himself, Phillpotts "remarked in warm praise of their merits" in spite of some objection to the Roman character of these prints. Sellon then told her detractors in the audience that the designation "Sisters of Mercy" did not mean that she wanted to imitate Roman Catholic convents, and she stated emphatically that she had never intended to turn her sisterhood into a Roman nunnery.

After some questions from the assembly, including Hatchard (her critic) and Killpack (her supporter), Sellon read a prepared statement and began by arguing that the statements of the three former residents of the orphanage "are as false a picture of the Sisterhood, as are the false pretences of which it was extracted." Moreover, Sellon appealed to the English sense of honor and pointed out that "domestic privacy has been outraged." She loudly proclaimed the loyalty of the sisterhood to the Anglican Church and explained the presence of the flowers, the pictures, and the crosses as the indulgence of women in "innocent pleasures." After this defense of the Anglican character of the orphanage and tracing her background and the reasons which brought her to Devonport, namely to work among the poor and the orphans, Lydia Sellon defended her care of orphan girls. She reminded her listeners of the favorable evaluations of the orphanage presented by the diocesan education inspectors. The academic training the girls received, she emphasized, was rooted in the Anglican faith and based on the Bible, and thus contradicted the accusations of her opponents. Sellon's statement concluded with a plea to the audience: "Thousands are at this moment surrounding us, persisting in ignorance, and want, and sin . . . if those who so bitterly criticise and watch our way of life, would but go and labour amongst the poor."

The business of this long and tedious meeting finally came to an end. In his concluding remarks, Bishop Phillpotts again could not conceal his admiration for the work of Lydia Sellon and his displeasure at unfounded accusations against the life at the orphanage. He thanked Sellon for her presence in the Diocese of Exeter and the notable achievements of the sisterhood among the poor, especially the orphan girls. Moreover, Phillpotts acknowledged that some would accuse him of being a papist who wanted to introduce Roman Catholicism into the diocese because of his support of Sellon and her orphanage. The bishop stated that he could not condone all the liturgical and devotional activities of the sisterhood, such as the flowers and the crosses, but remarked,

"If there have been some things which these ladies have adopted in executing their work that I wish had not been adopted, they are absolutely overpowered by the cloud of virtues and graces exemplified in their conduct." He then expressed a hope that the questionable practices would not reappear in the orphanage. Lydia Sellon did unfortunately receive harsh and unwarranted treatment, he told the assembly, but nonetheless "she rises before us, and makes us all feel—the greatest, the proudest, the most self-righteous among us—what poor miserable things we are in the presence of her." Bishop Phillpotts's high praise of Sellon, however, made some cynics laugh and hiss, and he concluded with words of admiration for her character: "I conceive it as an honour to have the reproach of those who can express reprobation on my attempting to do justice to that excellent lady."

It appeared that the campaign to discredit Lydia Sellon's work among the orphans of Devonport by identifying it with Roman Catholic practices had failed. The public inquiry had succeeded in casting doubt on the testimony of the three girls and created misgivings about the motives employed by both Hatchard and *The Devonport Telegraph*. The published report of the meeting, moreover, also vindicated Sellon. In addition to a verbatim account of the proceedings and the testimonies of the three girls, this publication also included the rules and regulations of the orphans' home, which clearly described the disciplined life of the home and the goal of the sisters to educate the youth in the basics of the Christian faith. An appendix, which consisted of two statements that contradicted the evidence of the girls and supplied an insight into their motives, proved more damaging to the cause of Sellon's enemies. Bishop Phillpotts knew the contents of these testimonies, and the parties who supplied the information were present at the inquiry, but the bishop did not call upon them. The first, given by an aunt of an orphan currently under Sellon's care, stated that Sarah Clarke and Mary Pochetty, two of the girls who had supplied adverse comments about life at the orphanage, told her that her niece was "very uncomfortable" at the orphanage, and that the sisters wanted to bring up this girl as a Roman Catholic. They also told the aunt that the two gentlemen who interviewed them claimed that they represented Queen Adelaide and stated that the sisters were papists. Moreover, they informed her that the sisters had hidden the pictures and crosses when the men visited the orphans' home. The aunt, consequently, visited Sellon at the orphanage, and found out that her niece was happy and in no danger of converting to Rome.

A neighbor of Mrs. Clarke supplied the evidence for the second appended document, and thus interjected the element of conspiracy into the story. This person, Mrs. Thomas, related that Clarke had been hired to clean and prepare the house before Lydia Sellon and the orphans arrived, and that afterwards Sellon employed her as a laundress for the orphanage. Mrs. Clarke told the neighbor that Sellon "was a very nice young lady, and what a blessing it was that such a nice young lady should be sent upon earth to do the good which she was now doing for the little children in the schools." This appreciation soon changed. Sellon, according to this statement, had decided to give the job of washing the orphans' clothes to a poor woman, and Mrs. Clarke lost a welcome source of income. According to the neighbor's recollection, "Mrs. Clarke was in a most violent passion, she called Miss Sellon a good-for-nothing b—h for so doing... [and] said that she was a liar, and called her dreadful names." Clarke, therefore, began to hate Sellon and brought her daughter back home. The neighbor also related that up to this point the girl, Sarah, had told her she was "so happy and comfortable" at Sellon's home.

The alleged conspiracy against Sellon's orphanage developed further. Mrs. Thomas's testimony stated that the editor of *The Devonport Telegraph*, Mr. Richards, and another man visited the Clarke family in late January. A neighbor related the conversation which she overheard after the men departed. Apparently, Mrs. Clarke told her daughter to reveal everything about the life at the orphanage, and she "will be well paid for." The father told the girl to demand new clothes before she talked to the gentlemen when they returned again. Eventually, one of the other girls who spoke critical words against Sellon, Mary Pochetty, moved into the household, and also met with the editor to discuss the affairs at the orphanage. This conversation convinced the neighbor that this group planned to fabricate the charges against the sisterhood: "I am sure Mrs. Clarke would do anything to spite Miss Sellon."

In the opinion of her supporters, therefore, the charges against Lydia Sellon's sisterhood grew out of a gigantic conspiracy primarily directed against the operation of the orphanage. According to this theory, if one could make a connection between the orphanage with Roman practices and worship, one might be able to discredit Sellon's work among the children because they lived in an environment that might turn them into Roman Catholics. A number of Sellon's friends, especially Bishop Phillpotts, sought to downplay any liturgical irregularities at the home because of the praiseworthy work undertaken by the sisterhood among the orphaned youth of the area. Any questionable devotions did not necessarily mean that the sisters promoted papist tendencies, but rather came about because of some unfortunate indiscretions on the part of Sellon. Her champions, therefore, believed that the charges brought against the sisterhood were false and libelous and grew out of the jealousy of a rival orphanage.

A more sober and objective evaluation of Sellon's ministry in Devonport tended to separate the religious aspects of her sisterhood from the work among the orphans, and then judged each separately. *The English Churchman*, for example, followed this approach. The newspaper wanted to warn others who might want to embrace apostolic works along the lines adopted by this sisterhood of possible hostility. Any deviation from strict Anglican norms, however minor, would guarantee reprisals, and, the paper noted, "a very high degree of personal piety, and practical charity, is an insufficient shield from popular suspicion and clamour for those who go one step beyond its [the Prayer Books] letter or its spirit."[31] According to the paper, some of the objections, especially the flowers, the cross, and the pictures, had some merit; others, such as the Latin names for the hours of prayer, seemed trivial. In the midst of this uproar against Sellon's sisterhood, her laudable work among the needy children should not be forgotten. *The English Churchman* told its readers that Sellon's example represented a needed response to the outstanding work of Roman Catholics and added something seriously lacking in the Anglican Church: "If there is any single point in which the Church of England is ill-furnished with an answer to Roman assailants, it is with regard to the absence of that entire self-denial, and devotion to the service of GOD, which has so often, in other Churches, been the fruit of an earnest and lively faith." The paper reserved its strongest critique for those who had brought the baseless and hateful charges against Sellon, not primarily because of their loyalty to Anglicanism, but for personal and vindictive reasons. The article expressed a sense of shame "that an assembly of Englishmen could have so disgraced themselves in the presence of their Bishop and his Clergy, as to have met with repeated 'groans,' 'hisses,' and 'laughter.'" The article also suggested that the bad

---

31. *The English Churchman*, February 22, 1849.

publicity that Sellon and her orphanage had suffered would not permanently damage her enterprise.

In addition to support from this High Church paper, Sellon and her orphanage also received encouragement from other newspapers, which may have contributed to the temporary cessation of hostilities. Sellon's biographer notes that the "better class of newspapers were unanimous in their praise of Miss Sellon's achievements, and in condemnation of the petty prejudices and contemptible tactics of her opponents," especially Hatchard.[32] *The Exeter Journal*, *The Morning Chronicle* (London), and *The Morning Post* (London) all supported the work of Sellon's sisterhood. Even the radical publication *The Spectator* (London) praised Sellon's involvement with the poor children and applauded Bishop Phillpotts's resolve, which he demonstrated "with characteristic 'pluck,'" during the public inquiry, and castigated the spineless motives of her accusers. The paper also identified the real cause which ignited the controversy, namely, jealousy, and not concern for the integrity of Anglicanism: "The managers of another orphan asylum [orphanage] at Plymouth became indignant at the usages of the Orphans' Home; Churchmen and Dissenters joined in accusing the young ladies of Popery; and a regular system of social persecution was set on foot."[33] Finally, a lengthy letter to *The Times* of London emphasized the superior quality of education which Lydia Sellon's students received.[34] This correspondent did admit that Lydia Sellon might have sinned against discretion or prudence by placing a cross or flowers on the Communion Table, but on a visit to Devonport, he observed the high teaching standards demanded by Sellon and the affection which the students showed toward her.

Lydia Sellon's work in Devonport continued to prosper and more women joined her, but the sisterhood again became the center of attention in a pamphlet war that commenced in 1852. A number of Anglican clerics and a former member of the sisterhood again attacked Sellon for promoting Roman Catholic practices and exercising an almost tyrannical control over the sisters. These critics probably realized that it was useless to criticize her ministry to the less fortunate, and did not mention the orphan children under her supervision. Supporters of Sellon, including her father, also responded in print in an attempt to discredit these

32. Williams, *Priscilla Lydia Sellon*, 63.
33. *The Guardian*, February 28, 1849.
34. Ibid.

accusations. One casualty on Sellon's side was Bishop Phillpotts, who resigned as the episcopal visitor of the sisterhood in 1852. He believed he had lost control over the internal development of the community and could not agree with some of its practices, such as vows and auricular confession. Phillpotts, however, continued to express his admiration for Sellon's work and he had no desire to force her out of his diocese. This controversy eventually subsided in 1853, probably due to the public's interest in the outbreak of war in the Crimea and the publicity given to a number of Anglican sisters, some from Lydia Sellon's community, who nursed the wounded.

Religious differences within Anglicanism, especially questions dealing with ritualism or the suspicion of Roman Catholic practices attracted the eye of the Protestant or Low Church party in their distrust of the early sisterhoods, and they could count on an audience who would take up the cause against popery. But when a community of women, such as Sellon's sisterhood, did such praiseworthy and universally appreciated work among the poor, the sick, and the children questions about devotional practice could be overlooked or minimized. Sellon might have been guilty of placing flowers, a cross, or a picture of the Blessed Virgin upon the Communion Table, which she unfortunately called an altar, but her ministry to the outcasts of Devonport far outweighed questions of liturgical propriety and effectively silenced the critics of her orphans' home.

Bibliography

Allchin, A. M. *The Silent Rebellion: Anglican Religious Communities, 1845–1900.* London: SCM, 1958.

Anson, Peter F. *The Call of the Cloister: Religious Communities and Kindred Bodies in the Anglican Communion.* Revised and edited by A. W. Campbell. London: SPCK, 1964.

Campbell-Jones, Suzanne. *In Habit: An Anthropological Study of Working Nuns.* London: Faber & Faber, 1979.

Chadwick, Owen. *The Victorian Church.* Part 1. London: Adam & Black, 1971.

The Clergy List for 1859. London: Cox, 1850.

Goodman, Margaret. *Experiences of an English Sister of Mercy.* London: Smith, Elder, 1862.

Hill, Michael. *The Religious Order: A Study of Virtuoso Religion and Its Legitimation in the Nineteenth-Century Church of England.* London: Heinemann Educational Books, 1973.

Howell, P. A. *The Judicial Committee of the Privy Council, 1833–1876: Its Origins, Structure, and Development.* Cambridge: Cambridge University Press, 1979.

Liddon, Henry Parry. *Life of Edward Bouverie Pusey.* Vol. 4. London: Longmans, Green, 1894.

Mumm, Susan. *Stolen Daughters, Virgin Mothers: Anglican Sisterhoods in Victorian Britain.* London: Leicester University Press, 1999.

Reed, John Shelton. *Glorious Battle: The Cultural Politics of Victorian Anglo-Catholicism.* Nashville: Vanderbilt University Press, 1996.

The Report of the Inquiry Instituted by the Right Reverend Lord Bishop of Exeter, as Visitor of the Orphans' Home, Established by the Sisters of Mercy, at Morice Town, Devonport, into the Truth of Certain Statements Published in the "Devonport Telegraph," February 10, 1849. Plymouth: Roger Lidstone, 1849.

Vicinus, Martha. *Independent Women: Work and Community for Single Women, 1850–1920.* Chicago: University of Chicago Press, 1985.

Williams, Thomas Jay. *Priscilla Lydia Sellon: The Restorer after Three Centuries of the Religious Life in the English Church.* London: SPCK, 1950.

Wolffe, John R. "Bishop Henry Phillpotts and the Administration of the Diocese of Exeter, 1830–1869." *Transactions of the Devonshire Association* 114 (1982) 99–113.

Magdalenes and Nuns

Convent Laundries in Late Victorian England

THE LIFE AND EXPLOITS of Mrs. Minnie Morrison, born to Protestant parents on 19 April 1897, in Indianapolis, Indiana, and the privately published story of her alleged sufferings probably did not attract much attention.[1] Product of a broken home, Minnie spent her early years with a foster family and in orphanages until the age of ten, when she was sent to an institution run by a local convent, the Home of Good Shepherd, where the mother superior changed Minnie's name to "Teresa Shepherd." She described her first night in a locked dormitory as a miserable experience. The next day began at 4:30 a.m. when all the girls, including the non-Catholics, were forced to pray Roman Catholic prayers and attend Mass. Following worship the nuns introduced Minnie to her new work, ironing clothes in the laundry. Her young life suddenly became a servitude: her letters were censored, she was humiliated and physically abused by the nuns, and the work in this sweatshop demeaned her. Some time later, the convent placed her with a family, but then for some reason—Minnie was unclear about the circumstances—she was "chloroformed" and forcibly taken back to the Home of Good Shepherd. Again she toiled in the laundry. Alleged atrocities continued. The mother superior, annoyed that Minnie wore some prohibited jewelry, "put the red hot poker against my rings and melted them from my fingers."[2] Because of the

---

1. Morrison, *Life Story*.
2. Ibid., 13.

severity of this wound, she was admitted to a hospital, where a doctor amputated her hand. After returning to the convent, she was forced to work with large sewing machines. The other girls treated her as a pariah, and the nuns continued to punish her for breaches of the severe rules. Minnie claimed, for example, that she had to kneel in the middle of a room for five days as a penance and lived on a starvation diet for three weeks in a so-called dungeon. Finally in 1919 when she was twenty-two years old, Minnie made a dramatic escape from the convent and her laundry prison. She eventually got married, renounced the Roman Catholic Church, and wrote about her experiences. This personal uncorroborated account of one woman's alleged sufferings represents an example of that sensationalism and anti-Catholicism which earlier sought to portray convent life as unnatural, inhumane, and cruel, and therefore a serious threat to American society.

Recently, however, the public was introduced to the existence of convent laundries through news reports and an unsettling movie. These presentations, naturally, captured more attention and elicited more outrage than Minnie Morrison's 1925 exposé. A television documentary, "Sex in a Cold Climate," appeared in England on Channel 4 in March 1998. It detailed the life of young Irish girls sent to laundry asylums run by convents because of alleged sexual sins or inappropriate behavior. Many had become pregnant outside of marriage. Named Magdalene Asylums after the woman who reformed her supposedly dissolute life when Jesus forgave her (Luke 7:36–38; 8:2), these institutions sought to reform the modern day Magdalenes through hard work, prayer, and the discipline associated with Roman Catholic convents. Interviews with survivors detailed examples of physical and mental brutality and the degrading work in the convents' laundries. The last of these asylums closed in 1966; over thirty thousand girls and young women had spent some time there as Magdalenes. More explosive and unflattering, however, was the attention generated by the release of the 2003 film, *The Magdalene Sisters*, which explored the life of four Dublin women and their debasing experiences in a convent laundry. The four "crimes," coquettish behavior, suffering rape during a wedding celebration, and two girls bearing children out of wedlock, sent these Magdalenes to the convent to perform penance for their transgressions through hard labor and rigid discipline. Ill-treatment by the nuns also became a part of the daily routine at the laundry.

The movie portrayed the nuns as cruel, sadistic, and wicked. Inhumane physical punishments and a humiliating routine were intended to "wash away" the sexual sins of the inmates. Most reviews of the film described the historical circumstances that gave rise to these institutions during the nineteenth century and acknowledged the dehumanizing conditions the girls suffered at the hands of overzealous nuns. The power of the cinema did more to expose conditions within these convent laundries and the life the Magdalenes than Minnie Morrison's short pamphlet did. The movie also generated a number of responses. CBS rebroadcast a special report dealing with the convent laundries that originally was aired in 1999. Several interviews with former Magdalenes also appeared on television and in the press. Survivors recounted how their names were changed (this signified a new beginning for these "sinners"), discussed the demanding work in the laundries, and described the enforced schedule of prayer and military discipline. Convent authorities, moreover, strictly regulated contact with the world outside of the convent walls. These poignant testimonies evoked images of a prison. One report even noted the discovery of a number of unmarked graves on the grounds of a convent that operated a laundry for Magdalenes.

The Roman Catholic Church soon reacted to the conditions of convent life that *The Magdalene Sisters* described. A statement from the Vatican questioned the objectivity of the film. Other prominent churchmen, however, acknowledged the wrong doings associated with the convent laundries and the shameful treatment of the Magdalenes. A review in *Commonweal* emphasized the cruel nature of the nuns in *The Magdalene Sisters* and compared the treatment of the girls to the harsh environment of Charles Dickens's workhouse.[3] The author stated, "As a child, I suffered at the hands of two nuns who were just as cruel as Sister Bridget (same order, too: the Sisters of Mercy!)."[4] Roman Catholic convents in Ireland, however, provided assistance to helpless women, and the laundries were an early response to the impoverished conditions of the country.

The late eighteenth and early nineteenth centuries, which Caitriona Clear describes as a period of intense evangelism, saw an increase in Irish sisterhoods due to a relaxation of the penal laws and then politi-

---

3. Alleva, "Heart of Darkness," 21–22.
4. Ibid., 31.

cal independence with the passage of Catholic Emancipation in 1829.[5] Orders of Irish nuns soon extended their ministry beyond the cloister walls and began to care for the country's poor and destitute, and English women recognized and praised the charitable work of these Irish sisterhoods. At the end of the nineteenth century, a paper which discussed the philanthropic contributions of Irish women singled out for praise the work of Catholic nuns in schools, orphanages, training of the blind, and the establishment of hospices for those approaching death. Moreover, the work and inspiration of nuns also strengthened the moral and spiritual character of impressionable young women.[6] The Irish nuns, like their Anglican counterparts, also operated laundries to save women of dubious character from a life of sin.

In these laundry asylums, "the 'purest' women looked after the most 'impure.'"[7] Maria Luddy's study of prostitution and rescue work in nineteenth century Ireland sketches the evolution of these institutions and she points out that convents generally took over the management of private or public institutions which had experienced financial difficulties, and the nuns made the necessary improvements and ran the asylums on a more efficient basis.[8] She maintains that many of these Magdalenes entered freely—the only alternative being the workhouse—and could leave at will. Priests, nuns, or family members could also refer individuals of questionable moral standing, including unmarried pregnant women, to these asylums for rehabilitation. Life was harsh. "The women who ran these refuges played out their maternal role creating homes for the penitent 'child.' They sought to inculcate in the penitent the correct attitudes and behaviour expected of women in that age," stressing one's personal guilt and emphasizing that only stringent discipline could lead to salvation.[9] Hard work in laundries associated with a convent also became a suitable catharsis for the sinful Magdalene.

Frances Finnegan's 2001 book, *Do Penance or Perish: A Study of Magdalene Asylums in Ireland*, paints a critical picture of the laundries and the nuns who ran them. In general, she argues, the laundry system enjoyed support and approval, declining only with the arrival of "washing

5. Clear, "Limits of Female Autonomy," 27.
6. Gilbert, "On Philanthropic Work of Women in Ireland."
7. Luddy, "Prostitution and Rescue Work," 69.
8. Ibid., 71.
9. Ibid., 77.

machines [which] destroyed its financial basis, and dwindling vocations its power to control."[10] Yet the legacy was tragic: "Many of these women's lives were damaged, sometimes destroyed, in an attempt to wipe our female 'sin.' Confinement, forced labor and senseless atonement, obsessively urged was but part of their penance. Often, the separation from a child was an added torment, and some, without hope and resigned to that unnatural existence, remained in the Homes until they died."[11]

The Catholic sisters who operated these asylums must share in the blame for this scandal according to Finnegan. "Their own fanatical commitment, the distasteful relish with which they carried out their activities, their determination to inflict their rule on others and their refusal to change until forced to do so" cannot be justified.[12] Her evaluation of these institutions might appear to be exceedingly harsh, but her argument that Irish society did not question the laundry asylums and the work of the Magdalenes is based on research and evidence. These laundry institutions which Catholic sisterhoods established to save or redeem "fallen women" not only existed in Ireland but also in Protestant England during the nineteenth and early twentieth centuries as well. The development of rescue work among women on the part of Catholic nuns in England and the establishment of laundries to transform the character of Magdalenes generally followed the same lines of development as in Ireland.

Because of a thaw in religious prejudice and the arrival of nuns fleeing the persecutions of Napoleon's policies, Roman Catholic sisterhoods had established themselves in England. The Catholic Emancipation Act of 1829, which gave Catholics the right to sit in Parliament and made them eligible for most public offices, and the Restoration of the Hierarchy by Pope Pius IX in 1850 re-establishing dioceses in England and Wales, testified to the growing strength of Catholics. European sisterhoods, especially French and Belgian, continued to establish foundations on English soil, but an increasing number of English women and girls became nuns. In 1840, for example, less than twenty convents existed, but "By 1880 the Catholic Directory listed more than three hundred convents offering extra-parochial opportunities for worship and devotions

---

10. Finnegan, *Do Penance or Perish*, 2. In an interview, Finnegan stated that some of the scenes in the movie were exaggerated, but in other instances the portrayal of life in the asylums was too gentle.

11. Ibid., 242.

12. Ibid., 243–44.

and administering a well-developed system of Catholic educational and welfare services."[13] Some of these religious orders eventually worked among the poor and outcast of the country, and they established laundries to rehabilitate young women of questionable moral character.

As Roman Catholic, and later Anglican, sisterhoods gained a degree of popularity in England and as more women entered their cloisters, convents came in for hostile criticism based on religious prejudice. Anti-Catholic literature portrayed convents as dens of debauchery where young women surrendered their English liberties to fanatical religious superiors. With the publication in 1836 of *The Awful Disclosures of Maria Monk* and its fictitious stories of murder, infanticide, and sexual immorality in a Montreal convent, critics of the conventual life for women in England became more vocal. Books, pamphlets, and lectures drew attention to numerous stereotypes some associated with sisterhoods: loss of individual freedom, the despotic rule of religious superiors, harsh and demeaning rules and regulations, disruption of family ties and the married state, and the corrupting influence of Roman Catholic practices present in many convents. On a more fictional but titillating level, critics told stories of torture, imprisonment, sexual licentiousness, the murder of nuns and illegitimate children, kidnapping, and secret burial grounds. Some even found fault with the worthwhile activity of nuns in education and orphanages and sought recourse in an accepted English institution—parliamentary inspection—to verify and then to correct alleged evil deeds.

Charles Newdigate Newdegate, the MP for North Warwickshire, worked vigorously for state inspection of convents in the same manner which the government policed the country's insane asylums. "The question of inspecting convents to make sure that no nuns were being entombed alive, exploited for the sake of their money, or otherwise abused, first arose as a response to the Papal Aggression episode [that is, the reestablishment of the Catholic Hierarchy in 1850] and the convent cases of the early 1850s."[14] Beginning in 1851 and 1852 with unsuccessful

13. O'Brien, "Religious Life for Women," 112.

14. Paz, *Popular Anti-Catholicism in Mid-Victorian England*, 17. Several court cases raised serious and embarrassing questions about convent life. According to Paz (12–13), "The most notorious cases, which gained the widest publicity . . . were those of Metaine v. Wiseman and Others, the Talbot Case, Connelly v. Connelly, and Achilli v. Newman; they had to do with sex, money and priestly domination." See also Wolffe, *Protestant Crusade in Great Britain 1829–1860*, for an excellent discussion of anti-Catholicism.

attempts to legislate for parliamentary inspection of convents and then the creation of a select committee in 1870, the drive to open cloister doors to government scrutiny continued throughout the nineteenth and early twentieth centuries.[15] Parliamentary debates, however, proved ineffective in securing legislation for the inspection of convents, but numerous anti-Catholic organizations, such as the Protestant Association, the Evangelical Alliance, the Protestant Alliance, the Protestant Union, and several Scottish organizations, attacked Roman Catholicism through the written word and speeches.

Anglican sisterhoods, which appeared to some as carbon copies of Roman Catholic communities of women, likewise attracted scrutiny. Some operated laundry asylums similar to the Irish convents. Also described as Magdalenes, young Anglican and Protestant women of questionable moral character endured the same disciplined conditions, complete with prayer and physical work, as their Irish counterparts, but did not suffer the same physical and psychological torments often associated with the Catholic laundries. Nonetheless, the alleged shortcomings of convent laundries became an important issue, and inspection would safeguard the rights of these vulnerable women.

As nuns became engaged in mundane responsibilities and Christian duties such as charity and social work, religion, and specifically membership in an Anglican sisterhood, offered women a sense of independence and an opportunity to work within patriarchal English society in non-traditional ways.[16] Religious life for women in the Church of England began in 1841 when Marion Hughes took religious vows in the presence of Edward Bouverie Pusey. Leading members of the Oxford Movement recognized the value of the monastic life, and it was Pusey who encouraged and supported the development of the conventual life for women. The first community, the Sisterhood of the Holy Cross, was established in London in 1845, and at the end of the nineteenth century over sixty convents had been founded, although some were short-lived. These nuns quickly became involved in ministering to the homeless women and girls, orphans, prostitutes, and alcoholics, and several es-

---

15. For Newdegate's campaign to legislate for parliamentary inspection of convents, see Arnstein, *Protestant versus Catholic in Mid-Victorian England*. See chapter 1 above, where I discuss the first attempt to bring Great Britain's convents under the supervision of inspectors.

16. McAdam, "Willing Women." For the important role nuns played in nineteenth century Irish society, see Magray, *Transforming Power of Nuns*.

tablished laundry asylums to save the body and the soul. Bishop Samuel Wilberforce of Oxford recognized the value of the work undertaken by Anglican nuns. In 1861, Wilberforce preached a sermon praising the sisterhoods, and he ended with a prayer: "May our exterior Sisters resolve this day to make greater efforts to bring the ruined of their sex to the ever-hospitable and open gate of this Home of Mercy [St. Mary's Home, Wantage]."[17] In a paper written in 1893 dealing with the philanthropic work undertaken by women in England, Mrs. Boyd Carpenter estimated "that the penitentiaries and refuges alone contain accommodation for upwards of seven thousand women, and that there are worked in connection with them other agencies, such as convalescence homes, training homes, inebriate homes, and so forth, to which special cases are drafted for special assistance."[18] Even Anglicans who feared that these sisterhoods "are hot-beds of out-and-out Romish doctrine" that might adversely effect the religious climate of England recognized "the teaching of members of various Anglican Sisterhoods in hospitals, in our villages, and in the streets and courts of our large towns."[19] Anglican convents, therefore, played an important role in ministering to the "fallen women" of Victorian society as the Catholic nuns did in Ireland.

But should Anglican nuns engage in this type of social work? The philanthropist and author, Frances Power Cobbe, did not think so, and she argued her case in "Female Charity—Lay and Monastic," which appeared in *Fraser's Magazine*. In this 1862 article, she acknowledged the worthwhile services performed by women since the middle of the nineteenth century, but argued that the "fundamental principle of monasticism is not charity, but asceticism."[20] Power Cobbe believed that asceticism and Roman Catholic conventual life, especially for women, have produced an unhealthy environment that effectively depersonalized the nuns, and this destructive spirit had permeated Anglican sisterhoods. Moreover, effective philanthropy encouraged cooperation and the destruction of sectarian hatred, but these orders of women, on the other hand, fostered uniformity. Even the "disagreeable" religious garb of the nuns and their vow of obedience to a superior would throw up a wall between them and the needy, and thus hinder their work. To have any chance of suc-

---

17. Wilberforce, *Secret of the Casting Out of Devils*.
18. Carpenter, "Women's Work," 118.
19. Everard, *"Danger and Duty,"* 11.
20. Cobbe, "Female Charity," 778.

cess, Anglican nuns "must bear in mind that their object is not to earn salvation for themselves by penitential practice and meritorious 'works,' but to do good to others."[21] Monastic asceticism, she believed, prevented this from happening. Others, however, also found fault with the idea of nuns engaging in work among the poor and needy, but this line of attack appealed to the latent anti-Catholicism of nineteenth-century England. Susan Mumm, in her study of Anglican sisterhoods, describes their work in orphanages, schools, hospitals, district visiting, clubs and guilds, and in penitentiary work, that is, in "places of penitence for women who had deviated from conventional sexual morality, or who had offended Victorian decencies in other ways."[22] Laundry institutions or asylums became an accepted way of redeeming these Magdalenes. Caitriona Clear discovers the same trend present in Roman Catholic orders of sisters in Ireland. "In the early 1880s," she argues, "nuns were viewed as agents of religious and moral (or social) reclamation among the Catholic poor."[23] By the end of the century, Irish nuns had also successfully established a presence in schools, hospitals, orphanages, and asylums, such as the laundry institutions.[24] The existence of these laundries associated with both Irish and Anglican convents did not escape criticism in Victorian society. "Both sisters and their penitents were perceived by their society to be violating the norms of proper womanly behaviour, the sisters by repudiating marriage in favour of establishing women-only communities, and the penitents by their violation of sexual or social codes governing respectable female behaviour."[25]

Work in a convent laundry in England represented only one way or method to rehabilitate the penitent woman. Other establishments operated by the Anglican sisterhoods ministered to prostitutes, victims of rape and incest, petty criminals, alcoholics, and women with mental problems. "Penitents of all types were to be reclaimed through hard physical labour, undertaken voluntarily, and directed by the sisters."[26] By the early years of the twentieth century, "there were 238 Anglican penitentiaries,

21. Ibid.
22. Mumm, *Stolen Daughters, Virgin Mothers*, 99.
23. Clear, *Nuns in Nineteenth-Century Ireland*, 101.
24. Ibid., 100.
25. Mumm, "'Not Worse than Other Girls,'" 541–42.
26. Mumm, *Stolen Daughters, Virgin Mothers*, 101.

and more than 200 of these were directed by sisterhoods."²⁷ Unlike the Roman Catholic laundry asylums in Ireland and England, however, other Anglican "female penitentiaries were always open institutions, in that women entered them voluntarily, and could leave at any time during the two-year 'course of penitence' typically undergone therein." Susan Mumm points out that these unfortunate women, unlike the laundry Magdalenes in England and Ireland, freely and eagerly sought assistance. "On the most basic level, penitentiary life offered shelter, food, clothing and care for an extended period, as did the workhouse,"²⁸ where the treatment was at times brutal and harsh. Moreover, these Anglican penitentiaries offered other advantages not available in the Victorian workhouse or present in the laundry establishments: "the opportunity to train for the higher levels of domestic service or for nursing, the maintenance of contact with one's children, a complete outfit upon leaving, good references and assistance in finding positions."²⁹ Others received training as school mistresses, cooks, or nurses. Unlike laundry asylums, the use of physical restraint and harsh punishments were absent; training for a new and worthwhile life and re-introduction back into society became the goals of these institutions. According to Martha Vicinus, a "rigid and strict regimen stripped the women or their former identity and remolded them to a new one."³⁰ In fact, the "ultimate discipline for a disruptive or disobedient inmate was dismissal."³¹

Work in a laundry before the advent of electricity and the advance of technology, however, appeared to some Victorians as a task unfit for any class of woman. "Physical labor had been plainly labeled as demeaning for ladies," Vicinus argues, but the Anglican convents "insisted that no work was unsuitable or degrading, because no lady could lose her innate class status."³² The discipline, the regime, and the manual labor required in the laundry reminded the young girl or woman of the wickedness of her past. Strength and redemption came through suffering. Moreover, people clearly recognized the powerful symbolism associated with cleaning dirty clothes by a Magdalene: "The whitening of

27. Ibid., 99.
28. Ibid., 104.
29. Ibid., 104–5.
30. Vicinus, *Independent Women*, 78.
31. Mumm, *Stolen Daughters, Virgin Mothers*, 106.
32. Vicinus, *Independent Women*, 77.

soiled garments was seen as an external sign of an inner transformation: the cleansing of a tainted soul."[33] Laundry work also had an economic aspect. Anglican convents in England and the Roman Catholic convents in Ireland used the proceeds earned by this commercial enterprise to meet the daily expenses of the sisterhoods and to provide for the upkeep and training of the penitents. But the failure of the sisterhoods to comply with regulations governing Victorian factories, in particular state inspection, incited a campaign to bring convents and their laundries under parliamentary supervision.

The Convent Enquiry Society (CES), an organization associated with Protestant wing of the Anglican church, was established in 1889 to investigate and publish examples of alleged abuses associated with convents. The CES and its secretary, S. J. Abbott, a layman who feared the growth of convents, lobbied for parliamentary inspection of convents during the 1890s and in the opening years of the next century. This organization sought to warn parents about the dangers of convent education and worked to compile a list of all members residing in convents to protect their well-being once they became nuns. In addition to Abbott, the chief spokesman for the organization, T. Myles Sandys, a colonel in the British army who was also a Member of Parliament, served as its president. Other leading supporters included the Deputy Surgeon General, a retired general, and a prolific Scottish clergyman, the Reverend W. Lancelot Holland. Holland's numerous pamphlets against convents and a book, *Walled Up Nuns and Nuns Walled In*, repeated the stereotypical charges of torture, cruelty, murder, and the immuring of erring or disobedient nuns.[34] Throughout the 1890s, however, the CES took up a new crusade and demanded the intervention of parliament to institute a system of state inspectors to correct abuses women endured in convent laundries.

The activities of this organization, in particular its attack against Catholic sisterhoods, quickly caught the attention of the Catholic Truth Society. Founded in 1884, this Roman Catholic group published devotional literature and defended Catholicism from attacks by hostile groups. In response to the words of the CES, James Britten, the secretary of the Catholic Truth Society, published a short history of the CES, which "has from its inception steadily persevered in a course of cowardly

33. Mumm, "'Not Worse than Other Girls,'" 537.
34. Holland, *Walled Up Nuns and Nuns Walled In*.

and libelous attacks upon religious houses."[35] The CES, according to the Catholic Truth Society, wanted "to obtain reliable information respecting the Conventual System from every available source; to assist nuns who wish for their liberty . . . [and] the eventual suppression of these prison houses."[36] In his attempt to secure legislative means to force open the doors of the convents to the eyes of inspectors, S. J. Abbott appealed to the English sense of justice and freedom, but Britten accused him of being highly selective in the use of evidence against convents. Abbott's anti-Catholicism, sounding similar to the accounts of Minnie Morrison and Maria Monk, replaced arguments of reason, Britten judged.

The CES led the fight to bring the country's convents under public scrutiny. Drawing attention to several Reformation statutes, Abbott believed that Catholic convents were illegal institutions and could be suppressed,[37] but since this was unlikely to happen, he argued for inspection of their living quarters and working areas. "Of all systems identified with the name of Christianity," he told the readers of the Scottish publication, *The Bulwark*, "the monastic and conventual have ever been the most unnatural and barbarous."[38] Obedience to a woman superior "who has no reason to fear the interposition of the law, is one of the greatest blots upon the Government of this country." The secrecy and privacy associated with the conventual life not only contradicted the way in which other British institutions such as prisons, factories, and insane asylums operated, but also contributed to arbitrary and at times the cruel treatment of the nuns in the cloister: "Openness and candor form no part of convent life, while deception and distrust are proverbial." Abbott cited examples of despotic superiors, pauper children sent to a convent for care until housing could be found and then kept there against the wishes of their parents, the forcible constraint and imprisonment of nuns, and even the illegal marketing of pigs at a Notting Hill sisterhood. Did sisterhoods exist outside of the jurisdiction of English law? They certainly did not, he argued, but "Unfortunately there is so much deference manifested to the convent authorities that from the police constable to the

---

35. Britten, *Mr. S. J. Abbott and the Convent Enquiry Society*, 4.

36. Quoted in ibid., 8.

37. S. J. Abbott, "Letter to the Editor," *The English Churchman and St. James Chronicle* (London), 28 January 1897, 53.

38. S. J. Abbott, "Is Convent Inspection Necessary?" *The Bulwark* (Edinburgh), October 1897, 118.

member of parliament all seem afraid to do their duty."³⁹ To remedy this evil "prison-house" environment, S. J. Abbott announced that he was soliciting names for a memorial that he would present to the authorities demanding government-supervised inspection.

Earlier attempts to safeguard the rights of nuns against alleged abuses through the use of government inspectors, such as the plans of Newdegate, had failed, and this was probably due to the sensitivity of the state to interfere with religious organizations of women who were involved in charity work. But Abbott and the CES found a Trojan horse that would permit entrance into the cloister walls. If the convent or sisterhood engaged in work similar to that regulated by the numerous Factory Acts, then inspectors could legally seek entrance. The laundries and the unsupervised labor of the Magdalenes, therefore, gave the anti-convent forces an opening. The Benthamite spirit of reform had earlier touched the workplace, and the limited 1833 Act gave inspectors the power to enter and examine places of employment. This legislation applied only to the textile industry and the age and hours of children, but throughout the century, additional acts increased the scope of government supervision. The Factory and Workshops Acts (1878 and 1891) codified the earlier laws and gave the inspectors additional powers to enforce legislation concerning hours and working conditions. Convent laundry work, Abbott argued, had unfortunately escaped the scope of the 1891 Act, and he started a campaign to rectify this omission.

In January 1898, S. J. Abbott sent a petition to the queen signed by 336,250 women. He stressed that "with the growth of feeling in favour of religious toleration the immunity from public control permitted to conventual institutions is unpopular as ever."⁴⁰ After pointing out that the petition contained only the signatures of women who had a concern with the welfare of their sex, it enumerated a number of the traditional complaints against convent life: naive and romantic young women entered a harsh life from which there was no escape; underground cells existed to restrain rebellious nuns; women enjoyed no freedom when they entered a sisterhood; instruments of torture such as the "discipline" were used to deepen one's spiritual life; private and secret burials took place; and nuns had even been transported to convents on the Continent

---

39. Ibid.
40. S. J. Abbott, "To the Queen's Most Excellent Majesty," printed in *The English Churchman*, 3 February 1898, 76.

against their will. Consequently, Abbot believed, the government must take action.

> That the inspection of prisons, lunatic asylums, factories, workshops, &c, has brought comfort and liberty to many thousands of your Majesty's subjects; while convents in Great Britain, unlike those even in Rome, are exempt from any kind of State supervision. And having regard to the well-known fact that unbridled religious fervour has in all ages of the world's existence been productive of gross cruelty, excessive suffering, and even loss of life, your Majesty's memorialists feel that the present state of things in regard to convents is one of the most inexplicable anomalies of British rule.[41]

Abbott's petition drew attention to the abolition of suttee in India by the government, and pointed out that the female petitioners "are therefore absolutely convinced of the necessity for equally stringent laws being passed to prevent practices not less unnatural and cruel, and withal of life-long duration inseparable from convent life." Strengthening of the current Factory Act in regard to convent laundries, therefore, would remedy these evils.

Abbott's short pamphlet, *Slavery in Convent Laundries. Startling Disclosures by Inmates: Why Are These Laundries not Subject to the Factories and Workshop Act?* provided the evidence that he hoped would arouse public indignation and justify the extension of the Act to cover laundries which employed the Magdalenes. A letter that a poor, uneducated woman had to smuggle out of a laundry asylum, because the authorities scrutinized all correspondence with the outside world, told of prison conditions worse than the degrading environment of a workhouse. Abbott argued that a system such as this letter described "ought not to be tolerated for one moment in a land which liberates the slave immediately he sets foot upon its shores."[42] Moreover, he stated, the nuns worked hard to suppress all "natural affection for parents and friends who are not subject to their controlling influence." Abbott then interviewed the girl's mother, who told him: "she had no tidings from her daughter since she was inveigled away by the priest." He eventually located the girl who had left the establishment, and she complained about the long hours—from 6:00 AM to 7:00 PM—even when she was

41. Ibid.
42. Abbott, *Slavery in Convent Laundries*, 3.

seriously ill. Another girl, a Protestant, was sent to a convent laundry because of her involvement in a theft, and she also gave Abbott an interview after she left the convent's laundry asylum, which the author described as "a huge sweating penitentiary, carried on by unpaid labour in competition with other laundries."[43] This person also described a rigid timetable and her demanding work of scrubbing and ironing. The father eventually rescued his daughter after the superior refused to give him any information or even to acknowledge that the girl resided within the convent's precincts. "In short he was prepared for them, and they found in him a Briton who was not to be cajoled by their banishments or tactics at which they are such experts."[44]

Abbott used these examples to appeal to the spirit of fairness and justice which he believed characterized British society. Convent laundries were an insult to the country, "a disgrace to our Victorian civilization." He proposed that existing legislation could easily be amended or enlarged to remedy this sad situation. "No valid reason has ever been given why Convent Laundries should not come within the provisions of the Factories and Workshops Act," Abbott argued, "while on the other hand, there is every reason why they should be subject to the most searching inspection."[45] But economics also played a part in this drive for inspection. Abbott pointed out that convent laundries competed with other commercial laundries for business, but these are "bound to comply with the provisions of the Factories and Workshops Act," thus giving the institutions operated by the nuns an unfair advantage. Defenders of the status quo who believed that state inspectors would violate the privacy of sisterhoods, Abbott pointed out, did not understand the operation of these laundries: they are housed in a building separate from the cloister; and "the work is done by unpaid labour, by women and girls who are virtually prisoners, and not by THE NUNS [author's emphasis]." Moreover, the convent authorities denied the Magdalenes working in their laundries free communication with family and friends, and thus denied rights even enjoyed by convicts or inmates of insane asylums. Abbott ended his arguments for government supervision of the laundries by telling the readers that a bill had been recently introduced in Parliament "to bring the Convent Laundries within the operation of

43. Ibid., 6.
44. Ibid., 10.
45. Ibid., 11.

humane Factory enactments." If unsuccessful, he predicted that this issue might become an important issue in the next general election.

In the following year, 1899, S. J. Abbott increased his campaign against convents with the publication of *Revelations of Modern Convents; or, Life in Convents on British Soil in the Closing Years of the Nineteenth Century, Intended as an Earnest Appeal to the British Public*, a comprehensive attack against sisterhoods that included chapters on the absence of liberty and freedom in convents, cruel and harsh punishments, imprisonment of the nuns, the embezzlement of money and the inheritance of members of sisterhoods, kidnappings, and the evils associated with convent schools and orphanages.[46] The author also included a vivid description of the barbarous conditions of convent laundries. And Abbott used the strong language found in his earlier writings. "The grinding oppression of the poor by the East-end sweaters aroused the righteous indignation of public feeling," he began his dissuasive, "But we believe if the British nation could realise the vast amount of slavery and tyranny carried on in this country in the name of religion and charity such a storm of indignation would be aroused as would sweep away Convent laundries from their midst."[47] Since the sisterhoods effectively concealed the real working conditions of these institutions and the miserable life of the Magdalenes, Abbott argued that these laundries must be governed by the Factories and Workshops Act which legislated for inspectors, and urged public support for an amendment to this effect. He then reprinted the testimonies of the former inmates that appeared in his earlier pamphlet that detailed their sufferings and humiliations at the hands of the nuns and the petition or memorial submitted to the queen. Abbott urged his readers to demand that Parliament act immediately to protect the well-being of the Magdalenes by bring the laundries under the supervision of state inspectors.

Abbott used the anti-Catholic press to keep up the pressure for the inspection of convents and their enterprises. Writing in *The Rock* in December 1898, he repeated his now familiar critiques of sisterhoods and argued that "every conventual institution ought to be subject to Government inspection."[48] His letter to this paper stressed that Roman Catholics "are so mortally afraid of convent inspection, and that

46. Abbott, *Revelations of Modern Convents*.
47. Ibid., 201.
48. S. J. Abbott, "Letter to the Editor," *The Rock* (London), 16 December 1898, 833.

a liberty-loving people are so suspicious of these prisons . . ." Abbott and the CES worked hard to educate the public about the evils of the conventual system in England. Not one Protestant member of the House of Commons, Abbott pointed out, could answer "the most flagrant misstatements and misrepresentations put forward by Roman Catholic members" when a motion to extend inspection to convent laundries was defeated in 1895.[49] The Protestant press also printed reports of appalling working conditions of young European girls in convent industries to show the English the extent of this wicked practice.[50]

Abbott continued to press Parliament for action to deal with the alleged abuses in convent laundries. In August 1901, the CES sent to each member of Parliament a statement concerning the miserable state of conditions which existed in the country's convent laundries. Unfortunately, Abbott pointed out, a move to amend the Factories and Workshops Act which would provide for the inspection of these establishments had recently failed due to the pressure of the "Pope's Irish Brigade in the House of Commons." Nonetheless, he wanted to inform Protestant England of his efforts. After noting the considerable number of convents, a small number of which were Anglican, Abbott stated his case to the MPs: "As a large proportion of the Convents, chiefly of the Congregations, have Laundries and Work-rooms, which are used for trade purposes, it should be clearly understood that the work in these Laundries is done by young women and girls of the poorer class—who, though not under vows, are kept in enforced confinement—and not by the Nuns, who may voluntarily enter Convents and bind themselves by vows to absolute obedience."[51] He then addressed an objection which some raised concerning the inspectors visiting the sisterhoods, namely, the privacy of the nuns. Abbott told the legislators that the workplace and the dormitories of the Magdalenes were not connected to the convent, and thus the "inspection of these institutions under the Factories Act would no more interfere with the religious affairs of the Nuns than the inspection of a Factory or Workshop would interfere with the private or domestic arrangements of the professional Laundress or Manufacturer."

49. S. J. Abbott, "Letter to the Editor," *The English Churchman*, 27 July 1899, 493.

50. See, for example, author unknown, "The Seamy Side of Convents," *Protestant Alliance Official Organ*, February, March 1909, 461.

51. S. J. Abbott, "Inspection of Convent Laundries," *The Protestant Observer* (London), September 1901, 142.

It must be evident, he emphasized, that no other class of women have "greater need of protection from oppression than the imprisoned workers in Convents, and to no institutions in this country is there greater need for the application of the Factories and Workshops Act."[52]

Abbott then argued that "the treatment to which the young girls are compelled is no better, but often worse, than that dealt out to criminals." According to his investigations, they "are absolutely deprived of all liberty . . . They are worked like slaves, and instances have come to our knowledge of poor girls being compelled to work when seriously ill and suffering great pain."[53] These girls received no payment, were badly fed, and could not communicate freely with family or friends. Abbott offered as proof of his allegations several published examples of mistreatment of girls in convent institutions in England, France, and America. Moreover, the convent industries enjoyed an economic advantage: "Then why give these women, who love secrecy, yet compete unfairly in trade, greater privileges and exemption from legal control than is granted to honest traders, who pay the market price for their labour, and do business in the light of day?" This attempt to sway opinion in the House of Commons insisted that questions of humanity and justice need to be addressed, and that "religious susceptibilities" should not "have any weight or influence in excusing or maintaining this cruel wrong in our midst."[54]

In spite of his efforts, Abbott's desire to have Parliament legislate for state inspection of convent laundries to improve the condition of the Magdalenes did not succeed. Protestant newspapers continued to publish articles which demanded action to save these so-called laundry slaves, but this particular campaign steadily lost steam. Attempts to modify the Factories and Workshops Act by parliamentary fiat became a dead issue, but the inspection of convents to root out other perceived evils that might violate the liberties of the nuns remained a goal of the CES. In 1906, another bill designed to open the cloister to the eyes of state inspectors was introduced in the House of Commons failed to gain support, but the CES did not lose heart. One last attempt by Abbott to bring sisterhoods under state supervision was his concern that nuns mistreated children, especially Protestants, under their care in convent homes for orphans and schools, and in 1911 he published *Disclosures*

52. Ibid.
53. Ibid.
54. Ibid.

*by Children Rescued from Convent Homes. Designing Priests and Cruel Sisters.*⁵⁵ But he again failed to secure any parliamentary support that would mandate inspection for sisterhoods, and the campaign to bring convents under state control which began in the 1850s died.

In his determination to secure convent inspection that would investigate alleged cases of abuse and mismanagement, S. J. Abbott and the CES adopted a campaign that pointed out the negative side of convent laundries and failed to recognize some positive aspects of this institution. A more sober or objective approach might have attracted more support. If Abbott would have adopted the viewpoint of an anonymous chaplain to an Anglican convent whose liturgical practices were similar to Roman Catholic sisterhoods, for example, more people might have listened to his concerns. Writing in the 30 August 1901, edition of *Church Bells*, a publication of the high church section of the established church, this anonymous cleric supported state inspection of all convent laundries, Anglican or Roman Catholic. His reasons appeared more rational than those put forth by the CES: "There are all sorts of matters of which the best of Sisters may be very ignorant, and, from ignorance or inexperience, those under their charge may suffer."⁵⁶ The chaplain mentioned the case of a girl who worked in an Anglican laundry for weeks when any doctor would have sent her to bed. The nuns who operated these laundries, he believed, were "good women, who live self-denying lives themselves [and] do not seem to realize what may be bad for the health of others," and inspectors could give valuable assistance on matters such as sanitation, the long work schedule, necessity of exercise, sleeping accommodations, and quality of food.

Inspection, moreover, would put to rest any charges based on "exaggeration and defamation" and would correct any shortcomings in the operation of the laundries, such as existed in some Catholic institutions. "Without, again, imputing any intentional cruelty of any sort to Roman Sisters," he noted that some credible cases of abuse had come to light. And prophetically the author of this letter mentioned the laundries operated by Irish convents and pointed out "their chivalrous resistance to the inspection of laundries managed by their good nuns" as examples of mismanagement which might be corrected by state inspection. In

55. Abbott, *Disclosures by Children Rescued from Convent Homes.*
56. Anonymous, "The Inspection of Convent Laundries: Remarkable Opinion of a Convent Chaplain," printed in *The Protestant Observer*, November 1901, 167.

conclusion, he argued that inspectors should visit both Anglican and Roman Catholic laundry establishments and then make recommendations based on their observations. Unlike the rhetoric of S. J. Abbott and the CES, the chaplain supported government inspection for positive and constructive reasons: "The inspection should not be with the mere object of finding fault, but also for suggestion of improvements, and with the desire, if possible, to praise rather than to condemn, and to encourage the public to have confidence and give more liberal support."[57]

The drive to secure legislation to inspect Anglican and Roman Catholic sisterhoods in order to safeguard the rights and liberties of the nuns began in the nineteenth century when concerned Protestants feared the growing strength of Catholicism. The conventual life, they believed, represented a Roman institution that threatened the integrity of the Protestant country. In addition to the questionable religious aspects of Anglican and Catholic sisterhoods, the conventual life represented cruel prisons that deprived the nuns of their rights as citizens. Institutions operated by sisterhoods such as orphanages and schools also came under attack. Soon convent laundries became objects of scrutiny. These laundries, hidden from the public eye, did not fall under the regulations of the factory acts that mandated for state inspectors, and critics alleged that abuses did exist. Efforts to reform through parliamentary acts failed, but in England the number of Magdalene laundries decreased in the early years of the twentieth century. These institutions could not compete financially with the larger commercial laundries and the state began to expand its range of welfare services the convents had offered to women.

In Ireland, however, the convent laundries existed until the 1960s. They remained competitive with other laundry establishments and received support from the Catholic Church establishment, the faithful, and society in general who believed that these institutions still had a valuable role in reforming and rehabilitating the Magdalenes. The Irish convents stubbornly clung to the past and resisted any form of inspection or supervision. And this contributed to the allegations of abuses and scandals.

Before the development of government agencies or programs which dealt with the plight of poor or marginalized women in industrial England, convent laundries did provide a solution. The only other alternative to a life of crime, poverty, or prostitution for many women or girls

57. Ibid.

was the Victorian workhouse. Critics, however, described workhouses as "bastilles" which robbed the people of their rights and dehumanized them. Shortcomings did exist in the laundry asylums, and state oversight might have identified and corrected these deficiencies. The campaign of S. J. Abbott and the CES, however, tried to capture the anti-Catholic prejudices of some English men and women in the cause of inspection, but this tactic appeared to many as an unjust attack upon the good work and worthwhile contributions of sisterhoods, both Roman Catholic and Anglican. The harshness of Abbott's tactics probably contributed to the lack of popular support for his program and the failure to secure legislation for parliamentary supervision. The balanced and impartial advice of the anonymous convent chaplain who advocated inspection of convent laundries might have been more prudent and constructive. On the other hand, if the Catholic authorities and the sisterhoods in Ireland had appreciated the animosity against convent laundries in England or if they had been acquainted with the benign suggestions of that same Anglican cleric who advocated inspection and then acted upon his recommendations, a movie named *The Magdalene Sisters* might never have been produced.

Bibliography

Abbott, S. J. *Disclosures by Children Rescued from Convent Homes: Designing Priests and Cruel Sisters*. London: n.p., 1911.

———. *Revelations of Modern Convents; or, Life in Convents on British Soil in the Closing Years of the Nineteenth Century: Intended as an Earnest Appeal to the British Public*. London: Wileman, 1899.

———. *Slavery in Convent Laundries. Startling Disclosures by Inmates: Why Are These Laundries not Subject to the Factory and Workshop Act?* London: n.p., 1898.

Alleva, Richard. "Heart of Darkness: 'The Magdalene Sisters.'" *Commonweal* (10 October 2003) 21–22.

Arnstein, Walter. *Protestant versus Catholic in Mid-Victorian England: Mr. Newdegate and the Nuns*. Columbia: University of Missouri Press, 1982.

Carpenter, Mrs. Boyd. "Women's Work in Connection with the Church of England." *Woman's Mission*, edited by The Baroness Burdett-Coutts, 118. London: n.p., 1893.

Clear, Caitriona. "The Limits of Female Autonomy: Nuns in Nineteenth-Century Ireland." In *Women Surviving: Studies in Irish Women's History in the 19th and 20th Centuries*, edited by Maria Luddy and Cliona Murphy, 15-50. Dublin: Poolbet, 1990.

———. *Nuns in Nineteenth-Century Ireland*. Dublin: Gill & Macmillan, 1987.

Cobbe, Frances Power. "Female Charity—Lay and Monastic." *Fraser's Magazine* 65 (December 1862) 778.

Everard, George. *"Danger and Duty": A Few Words to Fellow Protestants*. London: Kensit, 1890.

Finnegan, Frances. *Do Penance or Perish: A Study of Magdalene Asylums in Ireland*. Piltown: Congreve, 2001.

Gilbert, Mrs. John T. "On Philanthropic Work of Women in Ireland." In *Woman's Mission: A Series of Congress Papers on the Philanthropic Work of Women by Eminent Writers*, edited by The Baroness Burdett-Coutts, 228–47. London: n.p., 1893.

Holland, W. Lancelot. *Walled Up Nuns and Nuns Walled In*. London: Kensit, 1895.

Kollar, Rene. "Bishop William Ullathorne and His Defense of Convents: The 1851 Bill for Parliamentary Inspection of Convents." *Tjurunga: An Australasian Benedictine Review* 55 (November 1998) 75–90.

Luddy, Maria. "Prostitution and Rescue Work in Nineteenth-Century Ireland." In *Women Surviving*, edited by Maria Luddy and Cliona Murphy, 51-84, Dublin: Poolbet, 1989.

Magray, Mary Peckham. *The Transforming Power of the Nuns: Women, Religion, and Cultural Change in Ireland, 1750–1900*. New York: Oxford University Press, 1998.

McAdam, Gloria. "Willing Women and the Rise of Convents in Nineteenth-century England." *Women's History Review* 8 (1999) 411–41.

Morrison, *Life Story of Mrs. Minnie Morrison. Awful Revelations of Life in Convent of Good Shepherd, Indianapolis, Ind: A True Story*. Indianapolis: n.p., 1925.

Mumm, Susan. "'Not Worse than Other Girls': The Convent-Based Rehabilitation of Fallen Women in Victorian Britain." *Journal of Social History* 29 (1996) 526–47.

———. *Stolen Daughters, Virgin Mothers: Anglican Sisterhoods in Victorian Britain*. London: Leicester University Press, 1999.

O'Brien, Susan. "Religious Life for Women." In *from Without the Flaminian Gate: 150 Years of Roman Catholicism in England and Wales 1850-2000*, edited by V. Alan McClelland and Michael Hodgetts, 108–41. London: Darton, Longman & Todd, 1999.

Paz, D. G. *Popular Anti-Catholicism in Mid-Victorian England*. Stanford: Stanford University Press, 1992.
Vicinus, Martha. *Independent Women: Work and Community for Single Women 1850–1920*. Women in Culture and Society. Chicago: University of Chicago Press, 1985.
Wilberforce, Samuel. *The Secret of the Casting Out of Devils*. Oxford: Parker, 1861.
Wolffe, John. *The Protestant Crusade in Great Britain 1829–1860*. Oxford: Clarendon, 1991.

9

Foreign and Catholic

A Plea to Protestant Parents on the Dangers of Convent Education in Victorian England

THE RELATIONSHIP BETWEEN RELIGION and education has always been an emotional and contentious issue, and in nineteenth-century England a number of concerned people drew attention to an aspect of this connection, namely, the questionable influence of Roman Catholic nuns on non-Catholic girls attending convent schools. The Catholic population in the country had increased during the century,[1] and education was one area where Catholicism began to exert some influence. English Protestants feared the increased role of Roman Catholic nuns in education, and some believed this involvement might adversely affect the country's young women not only in issues of religious belief but also in matters of patriotism and citizenship. And the stakes were high. With the growth of high-quality secondary schools for girls operated by these nuns in England and on the Continent, non-Catholic parents began to send their daughters to such convent institutions to receive an education similar to one which their sons could receive, and the nuns as a rule promised not to interfere with the religious beliefs of their Protestant students. Some sceptics, however, sensed danger and began to warn parents of the subtle perils which their daughters might encounter in this

---

1. For a history of Roman Catholicism in England during the nineteenth century, see Norman, *English Catholic Church in the Nineteenth Century*; Holmes, *More Roman than Rome*; McClelland and Hodgetts, eds., *From Without the Flaminian Gate*; and Wolffe, *Protestant Crusade in Great Britain 1829–1860*.

Catholic environment: exposure to Roman Catholic teachings; the possible renunciation of the Protestant faith and conversion to Catholicism; and the alleged substandard teachers and poor curriculum at these convent schools. An education at the hands of foreign nuns and the location of some convent schools on the Continent also raised serious questions. This article will discuss these issues. The printed material that described the risks of convent education included both fictional representations or caricatures,[2] often alarmist and anti-Catholic in nature, and more objective and empirical evidence which looked at the shortcomings of convent education. For a number of individuals, therefore, these schools operated by Roman Catholic nuns did present a serious challenge to the spiritual and civic health of England's young women.

Following the return of the religious orders to England because of the hostile policies of the French Revolution, these monks and nuns greatly influenced the history of secondary education in the country. The Benedictines, Jesuits, Dominicans, Rosminians, and De La Salle Brothers established schools for boys, and moreover the "religious orders also predominated in the provision of education for girls."[3] By the time that Pope Pius IX restored the hierarchy in England and Wales in 1850, over 50 religious orders of nuns operated and staffed schools in addition to their other apostolic works. Their educational establishments flourished and increased during the last decades of the century.[4] Part of the reason for the popularity of convent education can be found in the support of Cardinal Nicholas Wiseman, the first Archbishop of Westminster. Wiseman, who believed that education would hasten the conversion of England to Roman Catholicism, strongly encouraged

---

2. These popular works, generally novels, told about the life in convent schools from the viewpoint of the female students. Themes of Protestantism, especially the importance of the Bible, were contrasted favorably with some questionable Roman Catholic practices such as Mariology, cult of the Saints, the Mass, etc., which the students were exposed to at the school. The heroine remained loyal to her Protestant faith by reliance on the Bible. If a student converted to Catholicism, her fascination with the rituals and devotions of the school usually accounted for the change in religion. In addition to these works of fiction, some short satirical poems also poked fun at convent education.

3. Norman, *English Catholic Church in the Nineteenth Century*, 182. See Cruise, "Development of the Religious Orders." See also McAdam, "Willing Women"; and O'Brien, "*Terra Incognita*." For a short history of religious orders of men and women in England, see Anson, *Religious Orders and Congregations*.

4. Norman, *English Catholic Church in the Nineteenth Century*, 182–83.

orders of teaching nuns to come to England from the Continent.[5] "By 1880 the Catholic Directory listed more than three hundred convents offering extraparochial opportunities for worship and devotions and administering a well-developed system of Catholic educational and welfare services."[6]

These schools for girls did certainly teach the basics of the Roman Catholic religion, but other reasons contributed to the appeal of convent schools. The institutions staffed by the Catholic nuns, and the schools operated by other religious groups such as the Quakers and the Unitarians,[7] not only offered an opportunity for young girls to receive a superior education, a service much needed in the patriarchal society of Victorian England, but also were superior. "In terms of education offered to girls," Edward Norman argues, "at all levels, the Catholic schools provided very much better and more extensive facilities than the education available for females generally in nineteenth-century England."[8] In addition to instruction in the Catholic religion, the curriculum at these convent schools might include history, geography, botany, writing, arithmetic and, of course, needlework. The sisters from Europe taught foreign languages, and the English students also had the opportunity to study abroad at one of the order's convents, mainly in Belgium and France.[9] These schools became very popular among the English. According to Adrian Hastings, 'Very probably the [Catholic] Church in England had, in proportion to the number of Catholics, more convent schools than

---

5. Battersby, "Educational Work." Battersby presents a good overview of the growth of the female religious orders and their work in the field of education during the time of Cardinals Wiseman and Manning. He also gives a short description and lists the accomplishments of numerous communities of women in this area of work. See O'Brien, "Religious Life for Women," for a discussion of Battersby's article in light of recent historical methods and research.

6. O'Brien, "Religious Life for Women," 112. In addition to work in England, nuns also contributed to the education of the youth in Ireland: "Throughout the century, 75 to 85 percent of all convents conducted schools," and in 1825, for example, 46 convent schools for girls existed in the country. Magray, *Transforming Power of the Nuns*, 80.

7. The following books discuss the outstanding education offered for women by the Methodists, the Society of Friends, and the Unitarians: Leach and Goodman, "Educating the Women of the Nation"; Smith, *Methodism and Education, 1849–1902*. J. H. Rigg, *Romanism, and Wesleyan Schools*; and Watts, *Gender, Power and the Unitarians*. See also Avery, *The Best Type of Girl*.

8. Norman, *English Catholic Church in the Nineteenth Century*, 183.

9. Battersby, "Educational Work," 342.

the Church in any other part of the world."[10] Moreover, "many of these schools had a considerable number, even a majority, of non-Catholic girls."[11] This caused alarm among some fervent Protestants. Not all the concerns about life in these convent schools, however, dealt with religious matters, the threat to one's Protestant faith or even a possible anti-English bias. In spite of the belief commonly held by some Roman Catholics in the nineteenth and twentieth centuries that these schools offered a superior education, some Victorian critics had other views. In their mind, the education of young girls by the nuns lacked quality in instruction and curriculum. This fact alone, they maintained, should dissuade Protestant parents from enrolling their children at these schools.

The Protestant Alliance, established in 1851 as a political pressure group following the Restoration of the Hierarchy in England and Wales, addressed the alleged poor education offered by the nuns and published a statement to Protestant parents which criticized the lacklustre quality of convent education. The author, A. H. Guinness, acknowledged the popularity of convent schooling throughout the country, but believed that it was important to investigate the alleged superior nature of these schools.[12] He turned his attention to the inadequate education provided by nuns in France, a country where some English sent their children for a convent education, and pointed to recent evidence which "exposed the inefficiency of the teaching given by members of the Religious Orders in France, and the ignorance of their students . . . [and] denounced the immoral character of the instruction given in the schools under the control of these Sisterhoods."[13] He thought that this same sad condition appeared to plague convent schools in England and Ireland, and he noted that a surprisingly high percentage of Protestant children attended these schools operated by Catholic nuns. Why did parents send their children to these institutions, which, he argued, offered inferior education?

10. Hastings, *A History of English Catholicism 1920–1985*, 144.

11. Ibid., 143–44.

12. Guinness, *Education by Nuns*, 1. Guinness was the Secretary of the Protestant Alliance. A contemporary writer, Gillian Avery, also points out some shortcomings in convent schools. She believes that "It is only comparatively recently that they could compete academically with the ordinary girls' public school, or indeed that they concerned themselves with equipping their pupils for professional careers." *Best Type of Girl*, 174. Religion, moreover, took precedence over academic subjects; ibid., 174.

13. Ibid., 2.

Guinness presented a novel answer to this query: "that by the gift of free dinners, gifts of clothes, in addition to free schooling, the Protestant poor are bribed to send their children to R. C. schools."[14] These youth, consequently, received cheap schooling and inefficient teaching. The Protestant Alliance, however, would have been at fault if it did not play upon the fears of proselytism by the Roman Catholic nuns. The sisters, he pointed out, decorated the classrooms with Catholic pictures, crucifixes and statues. These dedicated nuns worked hard to shape impressionable Protestant minds; conversion had become a priority for these teachers. Winning individual souls for Catholicism formed only part of the Catholic master plan. According to the author, "The Church of Rome evidently hopes to win back England to the Pope by means of the educational influences brought to bear on the children who are received in the Roman Catholic schools in this country."[15] A. H. Guinness, consequently, urged parents to give serious consideration to the perils that awaited their children if they attended convent schools in England or on the Continent. Convent schools in Ireland also came in for criticism.

In 1874, *Fraser's Magazine* published a scathing attack on the type of education young girls received at convent schools, especially those institutions in Ireland.[16] This article questioned the teaching qualifications of the nuns and put forward the view that these schools had a weak curriculum and were a poor value for money in comparison with the superior education one received at the national or state schools in Ireland. The magazine then reprinted a lengthy statement from a former student who criticized the harshness of life and the inferior teaching she experienced at a convent school. Her testimony called attention to outdated books, "the total want of any systematic plan of instruction connecting the different classes," and a system of examinations based on "well-prepared pieces chosen months beforehand by the teachers."[17] "As regards that most important study, English grammar," she related, "there was a tacit under-

14. Ibid., 5.

15. Ibid., 8.

16. "Convent Boarding-Schools for Young Ladies," *Fraser's Magazine*, June 1874, 778–85. Excerpts from this article also appeared in the *Bulwark*, September 1874, 240–42. For a critique of convent schools in Ireland, see Cusack, *Life Inside the Church of Rome*. Cusack, a former nun, criticized the poor quality of teaching at convent schools in Ireland.

17. "Convent Boarding-Schools," 780.

standing that any serious attention to it was unnecessary."[18] The total lack of an appreciation of literature also contributed to this deficiency.

Following these reminiscences of the former student, the magazine questioned the qualifications and motives of the nuns, and the author of the article concluded that they were unprepared to enter the classroom. "The whole care of these girls during this all-important period, the forming of their minds, habits, tastes, and characters, is left to the religious, a task which they are eminently unfit to fulfill so far as the interests of society are concerned."[19] On leaving the school, the young graduates did not conform to the Victorian stereotype of a woman. The nuns, according to the magazine, discredited the ideal of marriage and did not teach the necessary "domestic virtues." These teachers exalted virginity and "monastic" virtues. Moreover, a "morbid, ascetic spirit is inculcated." The nuns failed to prepare their students for the traditional role of wife and mother, and consequently the girls would not be able to find employment. This senseless and useless convent education trained them for only one vocation, namely, eventually to enter the convent as nuns. The article concluded by warning the nuns that they must "open their eyes to the need of a sweeping reform which is wanted now to save their institution—long stagnant—from swift decay."[20] But it also issued a caution to Protestant parents. Until the convent schools underwent such a drastic reform, the minds of their pupils would remain "inert and unproductive."[21] If these conditions existed in Irish convent schools, then surely, one could reason, the nuns in England were also unprepared to instruct young girls.

Convent education, however, was not as poor or ineffective as its critics would have liked the public to believe. In her article on French nuns in England during the nineteenth century, Susan O'Brien maintains that these foreign congregations of nuns offered a superior education. "By 1900," claims O'Brien, "these congregations were the providers

18. Ibid., 781.
19. Ibid., 783.
20. Ibid., 786.
21. The October edition of *Fraser's Magazine* contained an article written by "An Old Convent Girl," which refuted point by point the hostile accusations which appeared in June. It did, however, suggest that some reform was needed, but praised the nuns for their outstanding work in the field of education for girls.

of female Catholic and higher education in England."[22] The French background of these nuns did cause concern to some patriotic individuals, and others would question the wisdom of sending impressionable young girls abroad to receive an education. However, some of the French convent schools, especially those staffed by English nuns, offered instruction of a high quality for those who preferred a continental education for their children. "The education provided by these English Catholic schools was on a more proficient level than that provided by similar establishments (of a non-Catholic persuasion) in England."[23] Convent schools in England also received high marks for their education of girls. In 1853, for example, T. W. M. Marshall, Her Majesty's Inspector of Schools, considered Mother Cornelia Connelly's school at St. Leonards to be one of the most perfect institutions of its class in Europe."[24] The same individual reported on the schools operated by the Sisters of Mercy in Birmingham: "All the results which flow from solid and judicious instruction, diligent and affectionate supervision, and the most unstinted liberality, continue to be realised in these admirable schools in which it would not now be easy to detect any defect . . . I have only to report my unqualified admiration of all which is done in these schools, and of the spirit which animates both the managers and teachers."[25] Nathaniel Woodard, founder of the Woodard schools and an advocate for middle-class education, commented in the same positive spirit. When he studied the possibility of schools for girls in the Anglican Church, Woodard mentioned that the Roman Catholic "religious homes and convents are more in harmony with my ideas."[26] Such were the benefits of convent education. But a number of concerned individuals pointed out that these institutions might harm the spiritual life of innocent Protestant girls, who might be tempted to convert to Roman Catholicism. This fear

22. O'Brien, "French Nuns," 158.

23. Bellenger, "France and England," 4.

24. V. Alan McClelland, review of *Girls Growing Up in Late Victorian and Edwardian England*, by Carol Dyhouse, and *Children, School and Society in Nineteenth-Century England*, by Anne Digby and Peter Searby, *Victorian Studies* 27 (Autumn 1983) 107. McClelland criticized both books for ignoring the valuable contributions of both the Quakers and Roman Catholics in the development of education in Victorian England. American by birth, Mother Cornelia Connelly (1809–79) founded the Society of the Holy Child Jesus in 1846.

25. Quoted in W. J. Battersby, "Educational Work," 344.

26. Ibid., 344–45.

caused some to attack and critique Catholicism and its convent system of education.

Following the passage of the Catholic Emancipation Act in 1829, England experienced a wave of anti-Catholicism.[27] The alleged favourable treatment given to Maynooth College, the increase in the Roman Catholic population, especially religious orders, and finally the Restoration of the Hierarchy in England and Wales in 1850 confirmed the suspicion of many who earnestly believed that Catholicism posed a serious threat to the Protestant character of the country. And convents, in the minds of some, represented dens of sin and vice where nuns sacrificed their English freedom and liberty to a despotic superior. Unsuccessful bills in Parliament sought to bring the country's convents, both Roman Catholic and Anglican, under government supervision. The testimonies and public lectures of so-called "escaped nuns" shocked audiences, some gullible individuals believed the fabricated story of Maria Monk and the horrors she experienced at a Montreal convent, and numerous works of fiction hoped to expose the evils of Catholic sisterhoods. In addition to the so-called wicked Romanizing tendencies of the convents and the supposed cruel practices that the sisterhoods carried out against human nature and English freedoms, their schools, which educated young and naive girls, also caused some concern among Protestants. During the nineteenth century, the English did not stand alone in this fear of education at the hands of Roman Catholic nuns.

The dangers to the Protestant religion which some associated with convent schools also surfaced in other English-speaking countries. In Protestant America, the Catholic nuns from Europe had established an educational network for boys and girls, and they faced hostility because of their Catholicism. For example, "A Presbyterian minister in Wisconsin anathematized parents who sent their children to Catholic schools and encouraged boys to throw snowballs when the sisters walked out for mass."[28] Jo Ann Kay McNamara points out that Catharine Beecher challenged Protestant women to embark on a career in teaching "to counter the subversive influence of convent schools on girls."[29] Works of fiction also told American parents of the temptations their daughters would certainly encounter at these schools. Pamela H. Cowan's *The American*

---

27. See Wolffe, *Protestant Crusade*.
28. McNamara, *Sisters in Arms*, 589.
29. Ibid.

Convent as a School for Protestant Children warned mothers and fathers about these dangers to their child's faith. The preface to this 1869 publication maintained that the nuns at these schools "are bound by every consideration of faith and policy to proselyte" the Protestant girls in their care.[30] The evidence in this book, the author stated, was based on fact and the daily occurrences at a specific convent school, and Cowan spoke passionately to the conscience of non-Catholic parents: "Never before has the Roman Church put forth such efforts as it is now making to secure to itself the control of our country; and with its usual consummate strategy, it has seized on education, that great lever for moving nations, by which to effect its object; and shall Protestants prepare their children by such a training, to assist in destroying those free Institutions, civil and religious, which our fathers framed?"[31] In England, the increase in the number of convent schools and their apparent popularity among some non-Catholic families caused the same concern.

An early appeal, published in 1830 following Catholic Emancipation, emphasized to parents the importance of education, but admonished them against taking advantage of the Roman Catholic schools, most probably those operated by nuns. *To Protestant Parents* listed the familiar objections to the spurious and unacceptable Roman doctrines a child would encounter, such as the sacrificial nature of the Mass, Mariology and intercession through the saints. Parents, moreover, had a serious obligation to raise their children according to the traditions of the Reformation, especially by stressing the importance of the Bible as opposed to the "idolatry and blasphemy" that permeated Catholic schools.[32] The anonymous author made no mention of the quality of education or possible attempts by the nuns to convert the children at the "Popish Schools," but instead stressed the subtle consequences of Catholic worship on young and impressionable minds: "If you are [sending your children to Catholic schools] reflect on what you are doing. You may be COMPELLING YOUR CHILDREN to practice that polluted form of worship at which you would yourself shudder. You may be leading them to the very brow of the precipice which overhangs the gulph of hell!"[33]

30. Cowan, *American Convent as a School*, 3.

31. Ibid., 4. This fear of convent schools also surfaced in Canada. See De Mille, *In the Net*.

32. Protestant Parents, *To Protestant Parents*, 2.

33. Ibid., 3.

This pamphlet poked fun at the belief held by many parents that Catholic schools would never teach their "superstitions" to Protestant children and maintained that the education of the country's youth "is, in fact, the greatest power they possess of extending their worship." Publications of this nature, however, probably only reached a limited audience. Popular works of fiction also pointed out the evils of Catholic schools, especially those operated by nuns who educated Catholic and Protestant girls.

Rachel MacCrindell's 1840 book, *The School-Girl in France*, was one of the earliest works that attempted to warn parents about the dangers to the Protestant faith that existed in convent schools.[34] MacCrindell's story contained these, which were to be repeated by other critics throughout the century who feared the influence of such schools on impressionable girls. MacCrindell assured her readers that she based her story on factual occurrences, but had disguised the names, places and dates. In the preface, she emphasized the hidden dangers of these "Romish schools" operated by sisterhoods: "She [the author] has seen the snares spread for the inexperienced, the spells thrown over the warm imagination, the fascination entwined round the youthful heart, by that most dangerous system of false religion, which, appealing with almost irresistible power to the senses, through them prostrates the reasoning faculties, and thus silently, but surely, weaves its fatal net around the unsuspecting victim. She has thus seen the foundation of a Protestant education sapped and undermined."[35] MacCrindell criticized the "deluded" parents who sent their daughters into the snares of popery. Not only did there exist dangers to the Protestant religion, but the convent system might even alienate the young girls from their families. The sisters in charge gave the parents assurances that they would never interfere with the students' religion, but these pledges were meaningless. "The promises thus given," she argued, "are often indirectly, if not directly broken."[36] The saga of two young cousins, Caroline Howard and Emily Mortimer, illustrated the hazards and pitfalls of convent education.

France, long associated with Catholic traditions, provided the setting, and the two cousins at first attended a boarding school operated by

---

34. MacCrindell, *School-Girl in France*. This book went through several editions in England. The first American edition was printed in 1843. References in this essay are taken from this edition: *The School Girl in France* (Philadelphia: Sherman, 1843).

35. Ibid., v.

36. Ibid., vi.

a laywoman, Madame d'Elfort. The ambience, however, was unmistakably Roman Catholic. Emily quickly emerged as the heroine of the story; she remained steadfast in her Protestant faith. To combat the "false allurements" and "temptations of popery," which appealed especially to the senses and emotions of young girls at the school, she continually had recourse to the words of the Bible. Attempts to convert the non-Catholics were subtle. The nuns exposed the students to Roman prayers, rituals, "image worship," questionable doctrines, and the horrible Roman practice of "Sabbath breaking." But other less obvious dangers still lurked in the classrooms and dormitories, as the author reminded the readers: "Yet it is generally about that age that parents send their children to Romish schools—send them into the midst of temptation and peril, without a single friend to watch over their conduct."[37] Despite the absence of any adult Protestant to supervise these students, Emily, the ideal young Christian, persevered in her religion and encouraged the other non-Catholic girls who attended this boarding school by reminding them that the Bible alone contained the truths necessary for salvation. Soon, however, Emily began to fear that her cousin, Caroline, might be attracted to the false teachings and "spells" of Catholicism. The two girls eventually left this school and spent some time at a Protestant school in Paris, but Caroline persuaded her father to enroll her at a French convent school, St Anne's. Emily refused to abandon her cousin, and thus both girls moved to the new school.

The Roman atmosphere was, naturally, more pronounced at this school, and Caroline seemed to become more and more interested in Roman Catholicism. Emily worried that her cousin might even convert! She had reason to be concerned. One of the teachers told Emily that several of the girls had embraced Catholicism in the past because of the subtle influence of the sisters. "The nuns are very skilful in making converts, and the ceremonies well calculated to captivate the minds of young people," the teacher noted, and two or three Protestant girls "are nearly converted."[38] Moreover, Caroline had apparently come under the spell of a young novice, Sophie, and she even began to express an interest in joining the convent. At this point, MacCrindell interrupted the narration to remind the reader of the stereotypical horrors associated with the convent system: "The dungeons might have been filled with miserable captives,

37. Ibid., 267.
38. Ibid., 220.

and the unhappy objects of persecution dragged to the most horrible fate, without one groan of suffering, or one shriek of terror penetrating the solid walls and ponderous doors of this immense building."[39]

Emily, who continued to proclaim the truths of Protestantism to the other like-minded students, became more upset about the influence of the nuns on her cousin. After recounting a terrifying incident when a prospective convert refused to confess her sins to a priest at the school, Rachel MacCrindell again interjected an admonition to the unsuspecting mothers and fathers. "Oh! how little do Protestant parents know, when they so far forget all Christian principle as to send their children to a convent for education," she reminded her readers, and "the evils to which they expose them, or the consequences that may result from their folly!"[40] After one irate father withdrew his daughter because of the Romanizing tendencies at St Anne's, a letter arrived from the local Bishop, which decreed that all the non-Catholics at the school had to convert to Roman Catholicism or leave at once. A crisis quickly developed for the young cousins. Caroline chose to stay, and shocked Emily by telling her that since the Catholic Church was the one, true church, she planned to convert and eventually to become a nun.

This piece of fiction, which appealed to the fears of some Protestants, however, ended in a triumphant and dramatic fashion. While she was seriously ill, Caroline found out that her father had recently died, and his last wish concerned the welfare of his daughter. It was his hope that she should not change her religion without serious thought, should not become a nun until she turned 21, and should live in England for at least three months before she made any important changes in her life. Once back home in her native country, Caroline eventually resolved to remain a Protestant. MacCrindell ended her story by again reminding Protestant parents of their religious heritage, the importance of the Bible in their lives, and the dangers of sending their children to convent schools. Other works of fiction also described the perils of convent schools.

In Emma Leslie's representation of convent education, *Caught in the Toils*, the reader is quickly alerted to the purpose of this work of fiction. The frontispiece portrayed a nun confronting the two main characters and telling these young girls: "The Bible is not needful here." Leslie's description of the convent, moreover, contained themes similar to Rachel

---

39. Ibid., 224.
40. Ibid., 241.

MacCrindell's account. France again provided the setting. Jessie and Maria, like Emily and Caroline in MacCrindell's saga, were cousins, but in *Caught in the Toils* Jessie eventually succumbed to the temptations of the convent school, and converted to Catholicism. Soon afterwards, she entered the convent as a novice. Maria, following the example of faithful Emily, continued to cling steadfastly to her Protestant faith, but unlike Emily she had failed to stop her cousin from slipping into the clutches of Rome. In the first few pages one of the minor characters made a statement, commonly held among Protestant families, that "you can hardly call it a convent school when their religion [non-Catholic students] is never interfered with."[41] Throughout the story, the words and actions of the nuns would contradict this belief. In place of the Word of God found in the Bible, the non-Catholic girls became associated with the Mass, confession and other so-called frivolous practices that the Reformers had abolished in the sixteenth century.

In Leslie's portrayal, the conversion of young girls to Roman Catholicism clearly emerged as the chief danger of convent schools, and Jessie began to give in to the attractions of Catholicism shortly after her arrival: "for unless people have lived in a convent, and seen, and known, and suffered all the nameless things that go on there, they could not understand how silently, secretly, and before a girl knows it for herself, she is taught to despise the Protestant faith, that is called a new religion, that was begun in wickedness, and carried on all through by the devil."[42] The nuns, in spite of promises to parents, did 'tamper with the girls' faith." When Jessie's father visited the school and found out that his daughter had embraced the Catholic religion, he spoke to the conscience of the mothers and fathers who read this book and exclaimed that "the very name of a convent school ought to be enough to deter any Protestant" from sending their daughters there.[43] Mr. Wilton, the father, then introduced a new element into his daughter's fascination with Rome: the destructive power of ritualism or Anglo-Catholicism within the Anglican Church. As an Anglican, she had frequented confession before she arrived at the French school, and "according to her account Jessie was half-way to Rome before she went to this school." The father then expressed this concern to conscientious Protestant parents. The "name

---

41. Leslie, *Caught in the Toils*, 6.
42. Ibid., 157.
43. Ibid., 166.

of Protestant isn't fashionable—isn't polite," he pointed out, "since we've been playing at Romanism and aping the Pope in our churches."

This novel, like MacCrindell's story, also ended in England. After a short stay with her family, Jessie eventually converted to Roman Catholicism and then received the reluctant consent of her father to enter a French convent. Mr. Wilton struggled to understand his daughter's change in religion, and the author again pointed the finger of blame at the Anglo-Catholic tendencies promoted by some Anglicans. Jessie told her father that as an Anglican she had gone to confession before she attended the French convent school and held the same beliefs as a Roman Catholic: "I am not more of a Romanist now than I was before I went to the convent; at least not much more."[44] The nuns at the convent school, however, did foster and encourage her journey to Rome. Her cousin, Maria, continued to remain faithful to Protestantism, and the book concluded by comparing Jessie's romantic and impulsive urge to join the convent with her cousin's dedication to the Gospel. "Maria returned soon afterwards, to India," Emma Leslie proudly proclaimed, "to help her parents spread abroad among the heathen the simple gospel truth, that 'The blood of Jesus Christ cleanseth us from all sin.'"[45]

Another book, *The English Girl in a Convent School*, published in 1874, also emphasized the real dangers to English citizenship which one encountered in convent schools. France again provided the setting for this story. Discipline was tough in this particular convent school on French soil, and "spying and watching," those characteristics the English spirit disliked, governed the life of the students.[46] An anti-English attitude certainly permeated this school. The priest in residence naturally forbade the reading of Protestant books, and in confession he cautioned an English girl against reading Charles Dickens's *David Copperfield* because it touched on the subjects of love and romance. According to his advice, these topics were "very wrong, and dangerous, and sinful."[47] The priest suggested instead books on religious meditation or those dealing with the lives of the saints. Moreover, the school did not tolerate reading the Bible, and ignorance of Sacred Scripture also existed among the nuns who taught at the school. One of the Protestant students, for example,

44. Ibid., 70.
45. Ibid., 71.
46. English Girl, *English Girl in a Convent School*, 24.
47. Ibid., 89.

had to read her copy of the New Testament in secret, and eventually she passed it on to one of the sisters, who was surprised at the truth and wisdom it contained. In addition to reading about the "objectionable" religious practices and Roman Catholic teachings at this convent school, English parents acquainted with this work of fiction realized that their daughters might also return home with a dislike of things English. Patriotism had joined hands with Protestantism. Convent education, consequently, must be strongly resisted not only to protect the spiritual well-being of the individual and the country against Roman Catholicism, but also to ensure that future generations would be brought up as good English subjects.

Patriotism and loyalty to one's country played an important part in anti-convent literature. England, and in the case of Emma Leslie's book the colonies, represented home, while the Continent, especially France, symbolized elements antithetical to the English character. One of these evil foreign elements that emerged in works of fiction and other critiques of the convent schools was French Roman Catholicism and its association with education. Britain, according to Linda Colley, achieved unity as a country because of a long series of conflicts with Catholic France, which reached its climax at Waterloo in 1815.[48] Religion, therefore, had become the glue that bound together the diverse peoples of the island. "Protestantism coloured the way that Britons approached and interpreted their material life. Protestantism determined how most Britons viewed their politics."[49] A large gulf separated loyal Protestants and foreign adherents to Catholicism. The Roman Catholic culture of France continued to raise suspicions throughout the century. Education, consequently, quickly became a vehicle to promote and encourage things British among the country's youth and, in the case of the fictional accounts of convent education, a way to disparage France and Catholicism in order to promote the interests of one's country.[50]

Linda Colley points out, for example, that royal celebrations, such as the birthdays of the monarchs and coronations, were celebrated to foster patriotism at Sunday Schools from the early nineteenth century. These occasions never failed to emphasize the uniqueness of British culture to schoolchildren. Education, Ian Grosvenor argues, contributed

48. Colley, *Britons*.
49. Ibid., 18.
50. Ibid., 226–27.

to the "the making of national identity in nineteenth and twentieth-century Britain."[51] England and its empire became closely associated with the concept of home: "Certainly, in Imperial Britain it was 'home' that was the link between nature and empire."[52] This patriotic concept of home also influenced the way people viewed the education of women. Grosvenor points out that "home" was also the domestic space in which women were called upon to help "create and sustain the nation."[53] Formal education, therefore, emphasized their future role as mothers. "Girls were educated to nourish and nurture and in times of war 'to keep the home fires burning.'" The education of young girls by Roman Catholic nuns was seen as posing a serious threat to the integrity of Britain and its Protestant traditions and was thought to undermine one's patriotism. Moreover, the accepted role of the domesticated British woman might be compromised by periods of residence in France.

The fictional accounts of English girls at French convent schools emphasized these dangers and stressed the difference between the pitfalls of foreign study and the wholesomeness of things British. This fear, however, was not limited to schools that operated on French soil. Susan O'Brien's study of French nuns living and teaching in nineteenth-century England indicates that these nuns did not escape the stereotype of an untrustworthy foreigner. She believes "that 'Frenchness' was both marked and persistent in the life of many congregations in England and, therefore, also in the personal history and experience of women who became sisters in the nineteenth and early twentieth centuries."[54] Non-Catholic England felt uncomfortable with this foreign influence, and her findings sound similar to the conclusions reached by Linda Colley. O'Brien maintains that the hostility directed against Catholic convents came about, in part, because of their "un-Englishness." "Although Popery, unnaturalness and foreignness often merged as categories in the attack on Catholicism," she notes, "it has generally been argued that the continentalism of Roman Catholicism was intrinsic to the hostility it aroused."[55] But on the other hand, the foreign character of these nuns also appealed to a large number of Anglican families: these institutions

51. Grosvenor, "There's No Place Like Home," 235.
52. Ibid., 242.
53. Ibid., 243.
54. O'Brien, "French Nuns," 146.
55. Ibid., 177.

run by French nuns "were clearly seen . . . as the ideal model for feminine formation, particularly when they could offer a French ambience in their schools and parlours."[56] The apparent dangers that threatened English girls studying at convent schools, moreover, were not confined only to the pages of nineteenth-century novels.

In addition to fictional representations that portrayed the dangers of convent schools such as the works of literature already mentioned, some concerned individuals took it upon themselves to appeal directly to the public. Written by a concerned parent from personal experiences, *Do-The-Girls Hall*, for example, was a 16-page booklet published in 1885 that wanted to alert families to the perils of boarding schools for girls located on the Continent. The anonymous author quickly pointed out the subtle attractions of a foreign convent school, such as pretty brochures, spacious surroundings, inexpensive charges for room, board and education, the opportunity to learn a foreign language (French), and the apparent "disinterestedness of the Nuns" in respect of the religious beliefs of non-Catholic students.[57] Recognizing that this particular school, operated by the Ursuline nuns in Belgium, would appeal to many English Protestant parents, the author immediately reminded them of the unfavourable descriptions of another Belgian convent school found in *Villette*, written by Charlotte Brontë in 1853.[58] Lengthy quotations from this novel testified to the "repression of the mind and indulgence of body" of that school.[59] According to *Do-The-Girls Hall*: "The moral atmosphere of false modesty which pervaded it—so utterly different from the fresh, pure air which, we delight to know, English girls habitually breathe in their own land—these objections will probably weigh enough with the majority of conscientious parents to make them dismiss at once the idea of educating their daughters in the country in Europe, wherein Ultramontanism most thoroughly leavens society." The pages of *Villette*, the author argued, effectively dispelled the myth that convent schools did not encourage their students to convert to Roman Catholicism: "the priests and Nuns are making a desperate stand in those kingdoms where they are tolerated, and are endeavouring by every means in their power to make converts to their religion . . . Convents are used as centres or

56. Ibid., 179.
57. A Parent, *Do-The-Girls Hall*, 1–7.
58. Bell (Brontë), *Villette*.
59. A Parent, *Do-The-Girls Hall*, 7.

foci of propagation."⁶⁰ The girls who received an education at schools associated with convents "never leave them until thoroughly imbued with the pernicious tenets of the Roman Catholic Religion." Moreover, the students never read the Bible.

In addition to the pages of fiction and the efforts of worried parents to sound the alarm against convent education, anti-Roman Catholic organizations and their publications also alerted the parents to the dangers which naive young girls were thought to encounter at convent schools, especially the possibility of conversion to Roman Catholicism. This became a constant theme of these organizations throughout the nineteenth century. The *Bulwark*, the publication of the Scottish Reformation Society, which was extremely anti-Catholic, naturally pointed out this hazard to its readers. A May 1878 edition of the paper related the sad story of a girl in Australia. The school officials had promised the parents that they would never interfere with the child's Protestant religion, but this pledge proved hollow. The girl eventually began to question seriously her religion, and the article gave the reason: "How could it be otherwise to an ingenious and unsettled mind? Fifteen months separation from Protestant worship and Christian influence, neglect of the Bible, prayer, and thoughtful devotion, such as only can fix truth in the mind, or bring holiness to the life, and the same period of intercourse with Romish influences . . . [and] all that could cultivate the senses and steal upon the affections . . . were quite enough to shake a faith not firmly fixed on the one foundation."⁶¹ She had fallen victim to the snares of popery. The priest at the convent eventually re-baptized the girl into the Catholic faith, and she made a solemn declaration never to enter a Protestant church again. The article concluded with a word of advice to parents and attacked the pledge given by convent schools that they would never meddle with the religion of their students. "No interference with their religion! When every service has to be attended and direct influence is used there to shake all faith in any form of Protestantism, and to excite a disgust and horror at their teaching?"⁶² Some critics did not distinguish

60. Ibid., 15.
61. *Bulwark* (Edinburgh), May 1878, 123. See also an article in an earlier edition of the same publication written by an American about the dangers present at convent schools in America and the threat they posed to the Protestant faith of their students. *Bulwark*, February 1872.
62. Ibid., 1245.

between the schools operated by Roman Catholic or Anglican nuns, and they maintained that even some Anglo-Catholic convent schools could not be trusted to preserve and foster the tenets of Protestantism.

The Church Association, founded in 1865 by Evangelicals to combat the growth and apparent threat of ritualism within the Anglican Church, informed parents about the nature of religious training children received at schools, and singled out those operated by the Sisters of the Church, also known as the Kilburn Sisterhood. The information contained in this short pamphlet was meant to shock families who entrusted the welfare of their children to Anglican convent schools. The Church Association had studied numerous educational and devotional publications used in the schools operated by this sisterhood, and surprisingly discovered that these students were taught: the infallibility of the church, apostolic succession, the efficacy of "sacramental" grace, invocation of the saints and the necessity of auricular confession.[63] The Church Association also presented other examples to demonstrate that the nuns instructed the boys and girls in the significance of "worship of the wafer," the sacrificial nature of the Mass and the importance of the Virgin Mary in one's religious life. Mention of the Bible seemed to be excluded from the curriculum. It was not only Roman Catholic schools, therefore, which threatened the Protestant faith of the students: the danger also existed in schools associated with the Anglican sisterhoods which patterned their life on their Catholic counterparts. All nuns, some argued, would certainly destroy the allegiance of the children to their Protestant faith, and loyal Anglicans should avoid sending their daughters to schools associated with convents.

Some critics, with little evidence to support their accusations, believed that convent schools, especially ones in France, worked especially hard to weaken the loyalty and patriotism of the Protestant girls from England who attended them. Some probably took delight when a Frenchman, worried about the influence of these schools on the future of his country, sounded the alarm, and his message appeared in an English translation published in 1869. The introduction to this book, written by an Englishman, applauded M. Charles Sauvestre's love for his country and warned that convent education was making disastrous progress in England and Ireland. According to the introduction, Sauvestre feared

---

63. *Religious Education and the Kilburn Sisterhood* (London: Church Association, n.d.).

for the intellectual development of the children and the future of France, and wanted "to see the nation spiritually free and morally great."[64] This must not happen in England. Since priests and nuns, "all . . . celibates, with no prospective social ties or family bonds," controlled the education of young girls, the writer of this introduction asked the readers to consider the following question: "What to them is the future of the nation, its welfare, its elevation, the happiness of its homes, in comparison with the success of the system of ecclesiastical tyranny and thraldom."[65] Sauvestre believed, moreover, that the religious training the students received in convent schools fell short of the mark in qualifying as a truly religious and moral education. No country trained according to these principles "can long escape the evils of socialism, or be fit for freedom."[66] In addition to the snares of popery, the introduction to *On the Knee of the Church* also attacked the idea of a woman's claim to receive an education equal to that of her male counterpart. This strange notion represented an "excess . . . to be deprecated . . . because it leads some to ignore the importance of educating the future wives and mothers of Englishmen for those functions, which they only can fulfil." For the same reasons that Sauvestre pointed out, the serious shortcomings of convent education must be acknowledged and avoided in England.

Anti-Catholicism existed as a strong force in nineteenth-century England because some felt that Roman Catholicism was beginning to threaten the Protestant spirit of the country. The growth of the Roman Catholic population and an increase in self-confidence contributed to this fear. The education of the country's youth, especially girls at convent schools, became another area of concern. Some critics felt that convent schools, even though they did provide a very good education for girls, would harm the spiritual and civic life of generations of women, and they expressed this anxiety in works of fiction and in other poignant appeals to Protestant fathers and mothers. Loving and devoted parents should never send their girls to a Roman Catholic school on the Continent. Authors such as Rachel MacCrindell and Emma Leslie presented fictional images of young girls trapped in French convent schools where the temptation to convert to Roman Catholicism was strong. Only a strong Protestant faith and reliance on the Bible were thought able to

64. Sauvestre, *On the Knee of the Church*, vii.
65. Ibid., viii.
66. Ibid., ix.

protect against the allurements of Catholicism. Several anti-Catholic societies and individual critics of Catholicism also emphasized the danger of conversion to Rome, but they also contradicted the boasts of superior convent education and critiqued the quality of instruction the girls received. Roman Catholics, it appears, chose to offer little defence of convent education and pointed to the number of non-Catholic students who enrolled at these schools as proof of high standards. They could also take comfort in the laudatory words of government inspectors and independent observers.

But the role of convent education for girls and its unique opportunities for English girls began to change, and consequently critiques of this Roman Catholic institution become less frequent. As the twentieth century opened, convent schools no longer appeared to constitute a serious risk to the health of Protestantism because of additional opportunities for the country's youth to receive a good education. State schools became a real challenge to convent education. Balfour's 1902 Education Act, for example, attempted to coordinate and improve the quality of education available at the new fee-charging secondary schools for girls, which offered the gifted student an alternative to convent schools. The nuns, however, "could not remain impervious to changes which seemed to make their services redundant and threatened the financial viability of their congregation," and many convent schools "took on a huge financial burden" in an attempt to retain their Catholic character, and they could not compete with the state schools.[67] Convent education in England also suffered because of other factors. According to Gillian Avery, "up until Vatican Council II it tended to be inflexible, hampered by the deadweight of tradition, by over-zealous obedience to the founder's precepts ... [and] by a timidity."[68] On the Continent, the secularizing policies of the French government severely limited the freedom of convents to train and educate young girls, and consequently parents became more reluctant to send their child abroad when education in their own country was improving. Roman Catholic convent education in England did not disappear, however, but it no longer posed the threat, real or imagined, to the Protestant religion and patriotism that it had done during the reign of Victoria.

---

67. Campbell-Jones, *In Habit*, 116.
68. Avery, *Best Type of Girl*, 8.

Bibliography

Anson, P. *The Religious Orders and Congregations of Great Britain and Ireland.* Worcester: Stanbrook Abbey Press, 1949.
Avery, Gillian. *The Best Type of Girl: A History of Girls' Independent Schools.* London: Deutsch, 1991.
Battersby, "Educational Work of the Religious Orders of Women: 1850–1950." In *The English Catholics 1850–1950: Essays to Commemorate the Centenary of the Restoration of the Hierarchy of England and Wales.* Edited by George A. Beck. London: Burns & Oates, 1950.
Bell, Currer (Charlotte Brontë). *Villette.* 1853. Reprint, London: Penguin, 1979.
Bellenger, A. "France and England: the English Female Religious from Reformation to World War." In *Catholicism in Britain and France since 1789.* Edited by F. Tallet and N. Atkin. London: Hambledon, 1996.
Campbell-Jones, Susan. *In Habit: A Study of Working Nuns.* New York: Pantheon, 1978.
Colley, L. *Britons: Forging the Nation 1707–1837.* New Haven: Yale University Press, 1992.
Cowan, Pamela H. *The American Convent as a School for Protestant Children.* New York: Protestant Episcopal Society for the Promotion of Evangelical Knowledge, 1869.
Cruise, Edward. "Development of the Religious Orders." In *The English Catholics 1850–1950: Essays to Commemorate the Centenary of the Restoration of the Hierarchy of England and Wales.* Edited by George A. Beck. London: Burns & Oates, 1950.
Cusack, M. H. *Life Inside the Church of Rome.* Toronto: Briggs, 1890.
De Mille, A. D. *In the Net: A Warning to Protestants concerning Convent Schools.* London: Morgan & Scott, 1900.
English Girl. *The English Girl in a Convent School: A Record of Experience.* London: Warne, 1874.
Grosvenor, Ian. "'There's No Place Like Home': Education and National Identity." *History of Education* 28 (1999) 235–43.
Guinness, A. H. *Education by Nuns: Its Failures and Injurious Tendencies.* London: Protestant Alliance, 1890.
Hastings, Adrian. *A History of English Catholicism 1920–1985.* London: Fount, 1987.
Holmes, J. Derek. *More Roman than Rome: English Catholicism in the Nineteenth Century.* London: Burns & Oates, 1978.
Leach, Camilla, and Joyce Goodman. "Educating the Women of the Nation: Priscilla Wakefield and the Construction of National Identity, 1798." *Quaker Studies* 5 (2001) 165–82.
Leslie, Emma. *Caught in the Toils: A Story of a Convent School.* London: Sunday School Union, 1880.
MacCrindell, R. *The School-Girl in France: A Narrative.* London: Seeley, 1840.
———. *The School Girl in France.* Philadelphia: Sherman, 1843.
Magray, Mary Peckham. *The Transforming Power of the Nuns: Women, Religion, and Cultural Change in Ireland, 1750–1900.* New York: Oxford University Press, 1998.
McAdam, Gloria. "Willing Women and the Rise of Convents in Nineteenth-century England." *Women's History Review* 8 (1999) 411–41.
McClelland, V. Alan. Review of *Girls Growing Up in Late Victorian and Edwardian England,* by Carol Dyhouse, and *Children, School and Society in Nineteenth-Century England,* by Anne Digby and Peter Searby. *Victorian Studies* 27 (Autumn 1983) 107.

McClelland, V. Alan, and Michael Hodgetts, editors. *From Without the Flaminian Gate: 150 Years of Roman Catholicism in England and Wales 1850–2000*. London: Darton, Longman & Todd, 1999.

McNamara, Jo Ann Kay. *Sisters in Arms: Catholic Nuns through Two Millennia*. Cambridge: Harvard University Press, 1996.

Norman, Edward. *The English Catholic Church in the Nineteenth Century*. Oxford: Oxford University Press, 1984.

O'Brien, Susan. "Religious Life for Women," in *From Without the Flaminian Gate: 150 Years of Roman Catholicism in England and Wales 1850–2000*, edited by V. Alan McClelland and Michael Hodgetts, 108–41. London: Darton, Longman & Todd, 1999.

———. "*Terra Incognita*: The Nun in Nineteenth-century England." *Past & Present* (1988) 110–21.

———. "French Nuns in Nineteenth-Century England." *Past & Present* (1997) 158.

A Parent. *Do-The-Girls Hall, or Convent Life Unveiled: Addressed More Particularly to Parents of Young Girls*. London: Wilson, 1885.

Protestant Parents. *To Protestant Parents*. Loughborough, UK: Cartwright, 1830.

Sauvestre, M. Charles. *On the Knee of the Church: Female Training in Roman Convents and Schools*. London: Macintosh, 1869.

Smith, John T. *Methodism and Education, 1849–1902. J. H. Rigg, Romanism, and Wesleyan Schools*, Oxford: Clarendon, 1998.

Watts, R. *Gender, Power and the Unitarians in England 1760–1860*. London: Addison Wesley Longman, 1998.

Wolffe, John. *The Protestant Crusade in Great Britain 1829–1860*. Oxford: Oxford University Press, 1991.

10

A Death in the Family

Bishop Archibald Campbell Tait, the Rights of Parents, and Anglican Sisterhoods in the Diocese of London

CLERICS HAVE PLAYED AN important role in the history of Anglican sisterhoods. Religious life for women in the Anglican Church began in 1841 when Marion Rebecca Hughes took religious vows and placed herself under the tutelage of Edward Bouverie Pusey. Chaplains, for example, attended to the spiritual and liturgical needs of the nuns and frequently represented the interests of the sisterhoods in dealings with the local bishop. The church did notice the worthwhile pastoral work accomplished by the sisterhoods, but also recognized the need for some sort of episcopal oversight. Some believed women in religious orders could not govern or run their own lives. Convocation saw the need for supervision. In 1891, a resolution stipulated that a candidate for a sisterhood had to be at least "thirty years of age, to undertake life-long engagements to the life and work of the community" and that the statutes of the community "should be sanctioned by the bishop under his hand, and not changed without his approval signified in like manner."[1] This cautious attitude on the part of the Anglican Church to religious communities reached its climax in the Report of the 1897 Lambeth Conference.[2] This document emphasized that religious communities of men and women could not exist independently of the local bishop who,

---

1. Allchin, *Silent Rebellion*, 167.
2. See Kollar, "1897 Lambeth Conference."

as the official ecclesiastical Visitor, would exercise jurisdiction to ensure that they remained loyal to the teachings of the Anglican Church. But it was the sisterhoods, more than the men, that worried the participants of the Lambeth Conference. Some bishops feared that these female communities might develop into carbon copies of Roman Catholic sisterhoods. Archibald Campbell Tait, the bishop of London from 1865 to 1868, had already seen the need to supervise the spiritual life of the sisterhoods in his diocese. Tait also feared that religious life for women could threaten the unity of the Victorian family and weaken the control of parents over their daughters who wanted to become nuns, and consequently he insisted on the necessity of parental permission before they entered a sisterhood.

Conventual life for women began to gain popularity in some sections of the Anglican Church because of the Oxford Movement and the support it received from friendly clerics, but others viewed the growth of sisterhoods with suspicion. Critics associated these religious communities with Roman Catholicism, a religion some still viewed with suspicion in spite of a growing spirit of toleration. John Wolffe believes that the Catholic Emancipation Act of 1829, which some saw as the beginning of a new era of religious acceptance, actually inflamed anti-Catholic sentiments.[3] The Maynooth crisis of 1845, which increased the state grant to this Irish college, and then the Restoration of the Roman Catholic Hierarchy in 1850 also contributed greatly to Protestant prejudices against Catholicism, which was growing in membership and prestige. "The fear and loathing of Roman Catholicism," D. G. Paz argues in *Popular Anti-Catholicism in Mid-Victorian England*, "was a major part of the nineteenth-century cultural context."[4] Consequently, practices and institutions associated with this "foreign religion," such as Roman devotions and liturgies, monasticism, and sisterhoods, must be resisted or else they could easily weaken the state and pollute the Established Church. According to Frank Wallis, "No symbol of Roman Catholicism agitated the ultra-Protestant mind—not even Maynooth—more than convents."[5] The fear and hatred of convents had gathered strength in nineteenth-century England.

---

3. Wolffe, *Protestant Crusade*.
4. Paz, *Popular Anti-Catholicism*, 1.
5. Wallis, *Popular Anti-Catholicism*, 183.

Roman Catholic sisterhoods, according to this stereotype, represented dens of iniquity which caged young women in convents and deprived them of their rights. And the same would happen if the conventual life developed in the Anglican Church. *The Monk*, written by Matthew Lewis in 1794, and Maria Monk's fabricated story, *Awful Disclosures* (1836), described for the readers lurid details of imprisonment, lechery, cruelty, and murder that allegedly took place in Catholic sisterhoods. Moreover, anti-Catholic preachers and publications of numerous Protestant organizations related stories of the same nature that allegedly happened in these English convents. These speakers and the tracts reported that women were forced to flee sisterhoods to avoid inhumane treatment, sexual abuse, and loss of freedom. The "escaped nun" thus became a frequent figure at anti-Catholic rallies. One way to prevent these scandals was to place all sisterhoods under the supervision of Parliament by demanding state inspection. While some individuals wanted to ban convents from English soil altogether, others "aimed rather to secure inspection and regulation of nunneries, and the enactment of safeguards to prevent nuns being detained against their will."[6] Walter L. Arnstein's study of anti-Catholicism in Victorian England describes the attempts to force Parliament, especially the efforts of Charles Newdigate Newdegate, to legislate for the supervision of sisterhoods.[7] This campaign brought stories of shocking and disgraceful behavior before the eye of the public. In spite of this hostile environment, however, sisterhoods continued to attract women to their ranks.

Convents offered numerous opportunities not usually open to Victorian women. Susan Mumm's *Stolen Daughters, Virgin Mothers: Anglican* Sisterhoods *in Victorian Britain*[8] looks at the social and cultural history of these sisterhoods during the nineteenth century, and she believes that women saw religion as an empowering force. Sisterhoods became a way to achieve one's potential independently of a masculine hierarchy. "Religion could be, and sometimes was," she argues, "an avenue for successful revolt against male authority and conventional morality."[9] Moreover, sisterhoods shared common ground with "the feminist tradition, both by their fierce commitment to their woman-created

6. Wolffe, *Protestant Crusade*, 269.
7. Arnstein, *Protestant versus Catholic*.
8. Mumm, *Stolen Daughters, Virgin Mothers*.
9. Ibid., x.

organizations and by their dedication to improving, or at least ameliorating, the lives of working-class women and their children."[10] Anglican sisterhoods operated orphanages, worked with the elderly, cared for "fallen women" such as prostitutes and alcoholics, visited the poor in their homes, and taught at free or cheap urban schools. Roman Catholic sisterhoods also combined teaching with welfare work, but were more cloistered. Moreover, Rome and the English bishops controlled their life and work, while Anglican sisterhoods escaped stringent episcopal oversight until the 1890s. Therefore, the conventual life in the Church of England presented an opportunity to escape the conventions imposed by the dominant masculine culture. "Community life gave Victorian women the freedom to choose to leave the family home without marriage, to participate in the government of a semi-democratic institution, and to undertake demanding and meaningful work at a time when women were believed to seek employment only in response to dire poverty."[11] Not all Anglican clerics could support this broad concept of independence the sisterhoods offered, and some bishops saw the need for episcopal control over these communities.

As bishop of London, Archibald Campbell Tait (1811–1882) certainly recognized the value of sisterhoods in the Church of England, but he also saw the need for some ecclesiastical supervision over their lifestyle. A. M. Allchin believes that Tait was "among the strongest supporters of the works of the sisterhoods, even when . . . [he] did not entirely approve of their manner of life."[12] Even when the bishop severed official episcopal relationships with a sisterhood because of questionable practices, such as confession, he still remained on friendly terms with the community. In spite of this cordiality, Tait did not budge from certain principles concerning doctrine and liturgy that might appear to be Roman Catholic. The rights of parents also concerned him. Consequently, Bishop Tait insisted on parental approval for entrance into a convent. Tait's demand also reflected the view held by members of the Anglican hierarchy that saw women as children who were unable to make decisions without the advice of a father or husband. Sisterhoods represented a challenge, and even an affront, to the patriarchal view of women that pervaded nineteenth-century English society.

10. Ibid., xi.
11. Ibid., xii.
12. Allchin, *Silent Rebellion*, 116.

Nonetheless, some bishops clearly recognized the value of sisterhoods within the Anglican Church, and Church Congresses became an opportunity for these churchmen to voice their support. These unofficial gatherings, which began in 1861, frequently discussed sisterhoods, and their annual reports contained sympathetic words in support of this revival of religious life for women. Tractarian theology greatly influenced the spirit of these meetings, and A. M. Allchin points out that "It is not surprising therefore that the Congresses had something of a High Church reputation, and perhaps something of a High Church bias."[13] The question of Anglican sisterhoods also came before another assembly of churchmen, Convocation. On 14 February 1862 Bishop Tait twice addressed the Upper House of Convocation on the issue of sisterhoods in the Anglican Church. His statements came as a response to a "representation" from the Lower House of Convocation concerning the apostolic and charitable work that women could perform in the country. The Lower House recognized the important contributions that women had made to the spiritual and physical improvement of poor Britons, and noted that "such ministrations on the part of women are to be regarded with great thankfulness, both as a revival of the Scriptural and primitive practice of the Church of Christ."[14] The Lower House, consequently, proposed that a committee be appointed to study sisterhoods and then report its findings to Convocation.

Bishop Tait spoke first and argued in favor of a committee, and he continued by praising the job done by groups of dedicated women in the Diocese of London. Tait acknowledged that some individuals viewed their work with either apprehension or jealousy, but he dismissed this narrow or prejudiced point of view. According to Bishop Tait, "nothing but good can arise from these individuals devoting themselves for Christ's sake, if their labours are judicious."[15] For example, the bishop mentioned the praiseworthy work done by a community of women in the London parish of Saint Pancras among "the destitute poor of the district." He recognized, however, some cause for concern: "it is desirable

---

13. Ibid., 139. Church Congresses met annually until 1913, and then less frequently until the last gathering took place in 1938. The bishop of the diocese where the meeting took place usually presided over the proceedings. For a discussion of the Church Congresses and the question of sisterhoods, see ibid., 139–56.

14. Quoted in *Chronicle of Convocation, Upper House, 1862*, 963.

15. Ibid., 963.

that we should consider what advice can be given and what checks can be put upon any tendency towards a want of that judiciousness which is necessary in such matters." Yet Tait voiced his encouragement of this valuable service and remarked that he had "great reason to be thankful for the amount of self-denial and goodness of every kind which has been evinced by those who have devoted themselves to the work; and I must say that I think we ought not to be too critical in judging of the way in which they perform a work for which we ought to be very thankful."[16]

Following Bishop Tait's remarks, several other bishops also addressed the petition from the Lower House. These speakers also acknowledged the valuable services these women performed for the poor and destitute, and they did not make specific references to the religious or spiritual aspects of the communities, such as vows, internal governance, or their worship. However, the relationship of these women to proper ecclesiastical authority did receive significant attention. The bishop of Oxford, Samuel Wilberforce, argued strongly against Convocation establishing, at the present time, any formal structures for these communities. The local bishop should provide the necessary spiritual guidance. Alfred Ollivant, the bishop of Llandaff, spoke positively about groups of women working in the Anglican Church, and like Wilberforce he did not want to establish a formal committee to oversee their life. Two other Welsh bishops, Thomas Vowler Short (Saint Asaph) and Connop Thirlwall (Saint David's), also questioned the wisdom of any centralized control of these women's life. The latter maintained that if the local bishops already exerted some supervision, then he did not "see the necessity of placing them under any other restraint . . . [and] the matter may be safely left in the hands of the bishop, who ought to have the power to make such regulations as he may think fit."[17]

Bishop Tait responded again. He talked about his experience with communities of women in London and he also emphasized the importance of supervision: "Some of them are directly under my superintendence, the ladies having made it a condition, on forming themselves into a society, that they shall have access to the bishop, and be able to consult him, and look upon him as the Visitor of the institution; and wherever they carried on the work in a manner of which I approved I consented to

---

16. Ibid., 963–64.
17. Ibid., 965–66.

give them my counsel and assistance."[18] Several sisterhoods, he acknowledged, had declined "to place themselves in connection with me—some of them from a love of independence, and others from knowing that my sentiments are not exactly in accordance with their regulations." Tait spoke positively about St John's House of Mercy and its relationship with King's College Hospital. In this regard, he especially praised the efforts of Florence Nightingale and her contributions to improve the training of nurses "carried on in King's College Hospital in connection with St John's House of Mercy." Bishop Tait ended his remarks by again stressing the good work of these communities that placed themselves under his guidance and acted only with the approval of the incumbent of their local parish. As a result of these comments from several bishops, the Upper House adopted a broad resolution dealing with the growing number of women's communities in the Church of England. After acknowledging their valuable contributions and encouraging them to continue, the statement emphasized the importance of ecclesiastical guidance that "should be sought directly from the parochial clergy and the bishops of the districts in which such devoted women labour."[19]

Bishop Tait's next public statement on communities of Anglican women appeared in his 1866 Diocesan Charge. Tait lauded the service of the sisterhoods in his diocese and he pointed out that the conventual life for women was the inheritance of all Christian churches: "Time was, and not long ago, when Roman Catholics were supposed to have a monopoly of Sisters of Mercy: when Protestants all held that women might work as true Sisters of Mercy (and, thank God, they can), one by one, from their own homes, visiting amongst the poor and desolate in their own neighbourhood; but that the system of our Church forbade any organization for a combined effort to use the services of women."[20] However, the courageous and selfless work of Florence Nightingale's nurses in the Crimean War had effectively dispelled this myth. Their valiant spirit during the conflict "told the world that English Churchwomen were ready to combine, where combination was needed, for any great Christian work."

Moreover, he continued, one did not have to search outside of London to find examples of dedicated Christian women, "some acting

18. Ibid., 966.
19. Ibid., 967.
20. Quoted in Davidson and Benham, *Life*, 467.

alone, on the impulse of their own individual generous nature, some living in communities, of which it is the common bond to be ready, for Christ's sake, to tend the poor, at whatever risk." Tait drew attention to their labours in the city's cholera hospitals and the hovels of the East End where the dismal atmosphere was "cheered and blessed by the presence of many true Sisters of the Church of England, without whom it is certain that in those desolate regions the suffering would have been far worse that it was."[21] Bishop Tait acknowledged that groups of Christian women living a community life might unfortunately evoke negative images of Roman Catholic convents. Consequently, the bishop urged that sisterhoods working in the Diocese of London should abandon or "abstain from all practices which make these suspicions reasonable."[22] Tait continued to stress the invaluable contributions "of Christian women living in community" and their work "amongst the sick and poor," but he also pointed out the necessity of encouragement, direction, and supervision from ecclesiastical authority. "God knows we need their help," Tait argued, "if they will give it in the way which our Church approves."

Bishop Tait then described how he dealt with the Anglican sisterhoods in his diocese. His rules or guidelines sought to ensure their loyalty to the principles of the Anglican Church; this would quiet those critics who viewed these communities of women as mere copies of Roman Catholic institutions. Responding to the belief that Catholic sisterhoods destroyed one's personal liberty and thus created a prison environment, Tait stated that the Anglican sisters, on the other hand, enjoyed the freedom to leave the community whenever they wished to depart. Consequently, he forbade the Roman Catholic practice of taking permanent vows: "Hence all vows of continuing in the community, actually taken or mentally implied, are wrong." This would discourage a "self righteous estimate of the life embraced" which might view family life as inferior. He also made his position clear on sisterhoods adopting liturgies and devotional practices associated with the Roman Church. He stated that "Care must be taken also that the worship of the community shall not encourage exaggerated views of doctrine,"[23] and Tait took special care to stress the dangers of auricular confession. He argued that this "tendency must be steadily resisted which women often show

21. Ibid., 468.
22. Ibid.
23. Ibid., 469.

to hang unduly on the guidance of some priestly advisor, to be making confession to him, and to become in fact his slaves."

In his earlier speeches at Convocation in 1862, Bishop Tait had emphasized the important role played by local bishops and the clergy in the life of the sisterhoods, and in this Charge four years later he acknowledged the difficulties in achieving this policy. Some communities had developed customs which Tait did not appreciate, but he hoped that as they matured certain questionable practices would change.

> And I cannot but trust also that, as time goes on, many of these excellent women, who at present adhere somewhat tenaciously to their own peculiarities, will be ready to drop them—learning in their labour of love the infinite value of that simpler and purer Christianity which alone sustains souls on the deathbeds to which they so often minister—becoming willing to sacrifice their own opinions, from a growing truer devotion to our Reformed Church, and prizing as they ought that larger field of usefulness which formal hearty recognition, under proper rules by the clergy and authorities of the Church, would at once open to them.

Sisterhoods, he concluded, formed an essential element in the fight against "the barbarism which, in the overflowing population of a vast people, is apt to spring up side by side with the highest refinements." These female communities worked among all classes of people in London "against worldliness and infidelity and superstition" to advance the cause of "the Christian civilization of the world."

Tait's 1866 Diocesan Charge represented a strong endorsement of Anglican sisterhoods and became his guideline for dealing with them, and he did not compromise these principles. In addition to his negative views on vows and his insistence that the communities remain faithful to the beliefs of the Anglican Church, Bishop Tait also strongly emphasized that sisterhoods must not interfere with or demean the rights and integrity of the family. He knew that the opponents of the conventual life argued that sisterhoods destroyed the sanctity of this valued institution. "Family ties are imposed direct by God," he pointed out, and if "family duties are overlooked, God's blessing can never be expected on any efforts which we make for His Church."[24] Consequently, "Every community . . . of Sisters or Deaconesses ought to consist of persons who have fully satisfied all family obligations." These women must have the freedom to

---

24. Davidson and Benham, *Life*, 468.

depart from the convent at any time. The wishes of parents must not be sacrificed. Tait knew that some supporters of the conventual life believed that it constituted a higher Christian vocation, and he dismissed this contention in his 1866 statement. "There must be no encouragement to a self-righteous estimate of the life embraced," Tait pointed out, "as if it were more perfect than that of the family."

Bishop Tait's views about Anglican sisterhoods, especially concerning parental rights, were put to the test in the Diocese of London. He did not neglect his episcopal responsibilities. During his years as bishop of London, Tait became involved with several sisterhoods,[25] and he knew the criticisms spoken against them. By the middle of the nineteenth century, the opponents of convents had assembled a large catalogue of alleged scandals associated with sisterhoods, both Roman Catholic and Anglican, ranging from sexual abuse by confessors and priests to the adoption of insidious Roman Catholic practices such as vows, auricular confession, and devotions. To prohibit such disgraceful acts and to protect the country's women, some concerned individuals wanted to use the power of Parliament to inspect and supervise all convents in England. Bishop Tait, however, did not need any encouragement from zealots or from Parliament to oversee the convents under his spiritual care. Roman Catholic practices had no place in Anglican sisterhoods. Moreover, Tait wanted to safeguard the right of parents and the sanctity of the family. Some disruptions could not be prevented if one entered the religious life, but Bishop Tait forcefully demanded that a woman must first secure the permission of parents or guardians before she entered an Anglican sisterhood.

Historians have recognized the family as an essential element in the fabric of Victorian society. However, convents did offer attractive alternatives for unmarried women who wanted to escape the oppressive patriarchal family, and some men saw this option as a rebellion against male Victorian values. "Sisterhood life took women out of their homes, gave them important work and sometimes great responsibility, and replaced their ties to fathers, husbands, and brothers by loyalties to Church and sisterhood."[26] Susan Mumm maintains that the masculine view of nineteenth-century women as "domestic creatures" or as an

---

25. In addition to Allchin (*Silent Rebellion*) and Mumm (*Stolen Daughters*), for the history of Anglican sisterhoods in England, see also Anson, *Call of the Cloister*.

26. Reed, *Glorious Battle*, 204.

"angel in the house" created an environment hostile to sisterhoods. In addition to condemning women to domestic service—or servitude—as a wife or mother, this Victorian concept also provided for the welfare of the unmarried woman: "If a woman remained single, she was expected to remain in the family home as long as it continued to exist. It was her duty to live with her parents until their deaths; she was then expected to transfer herself to the household of a sibling or other relative who might require her services. The unspoken half of this bargain was that in return she would be provided with a home for life."[27] In the eyes of many, rejection of these expectations represented an act of defiance and disloyalty. Moreover, the Victorian picture of the family "assumed that women should not act against their parents' lawful wishes, whatever the woman's own desires and ambitions."[28] This line of thought had another implication, namely, "It carried within itself the conviction that unmarried women, in a very real sense, never came of age."

Critics of Anglican sisterhoods recognized the dangers they posed to family values. The Rev. H. Hobart Seymour, for example, argued that once a woman entered a convent, the other nuns effectively worked to crush any connection or relationship with the family. Seymour told the readers of *A Pilgrimage to Rome* (1849) that he knew of an Italian convent that prohibited the nuns from seeing their parents, and the superior even kept the death of a mother or father from them.[29] *Left Home; or, Convent Life*, based on a real story, alerted parents to the dangers of sisterhoods, especially those which placed religion above family ties: "English mothers and fathers, listen to the story I have to tell. English maidens, take heed of my warning. The time has arrived when Protestants should awaken from the lethargy into which they have fallen."[30] Works of fiction such as Catherine Sinclair's *Beatrice: or, the Unknown Relatives* and John Harwood's book, *Miss Jane, the Bishop's Daughter*, both published when Tait was bishop of London, told parents that sisterhoods could easily destroy family relationships.[31] According to Susan Mumm, "Anti-sisterhood literature is full of accusations of disloyalty to the family, and

27. Mumm, *Stolen Daughters*, 174.
28. Ibid., 175.
29. Seymour, *Pilgrimage to Rome*.
30. *Left Home; or, Convent Life*, 5.
31. Sinclair, *Beatrice*, 209; this book was first published in England in 1852. Harwood, *Miss Jane*.

equally replete with dire predictions of what would happen to the women who left homes for communities."[32] Bishop Archibald Campbell Tait certainly understood this critique of sisterhoods, and the tragic deaths of his daughters enforced his belief in the valuable bond between parent and daughter that convent life appeared to jeopardize. Tait's strong belief in the primacy of the family no doubt emanated in part from the tragedy that occurred within his own household.

Tait's relationship with his wife, Catharine, was admittedly affectionate, and by all accounts the Taits were a close-knit family based on mutual love and Christian virtues.[33] After their marriage in 1843, Catharine assisted her husband in his job as Headmaster at Rugby School, and when the family moved to Carlisle after Tait's appointment as dean in that diocese in 1849, she worked among the poor and outcast of the district, duties he would later advocate as appropriate jobs for Anglican sisterhoods in London. But in 1856, disaster struck. During the spring of that year, five daughters died from scarlet fever in less than two months. Pat Jalland's study of death in the Victorian family poignantly records the agony and sorrow which the Taits experienced as they watched their young children suffer.[34] An entry in Dean Tait's diary for 8 May 1856, following the death of his last child, expressed his feelings of grief: "O Lord, for Jesus Christ's sake, comfort our desolate hearts."[35]

The family struggled to recover from this tragedy and accepted these deaths as God's plan. Dean Tait's efforts "to accept God's will were more delayed, more prolonged, and more problematic than in his wife's case."[36] Jalland maintains that "the family was the primary Victorian and Edwardian social institution in which the meaning of individual deaths was constructed and transmitted across the generation."[37] According to his early biographers, he continued to bear the burdens of his daughters' deaths while bishop of London: "Is it wonderful that when the parents came forth from the awful cloud of those spring days their life was lived thenceforward under wholly new conditions, and that through all

32. Mumm, *Stolen Daughters*, 182.

33. For a description of Tait's relationship with his wife, their close-knit family, and the effects of the deaths of the daughter, see Benham, ed., *Catharine and Craufurd Tait*.

34. P. Jalland, *Death in the Victorian Family*, 127-39.

35. Davidson and Benham, *Life*, 190.

36. Jalland, *Death*, 138.

37. Ibid., 2.

the chequered and busy years that followed, whether at Fulham or at Lambeth, they carried consciously upon them the consecration-mark of the holy sorrow they had known?"[38] P. T. Marsh's study of Bishop Tait also mentions the effects of these tragedies. "Commemoration of the anniversaries of his girls' deaths was a . . . recurring feature of his weekly journal for the rest of his life," Marsh points out, and "He would often note how old each would have been and how long she had been with God."[39] Because of these devastating experiences, Tait would certainly understand the feelings of parents who feared losing their daughters to life in a convent. As a man who continued to grieve for his lost daughters, Tait was particularly sensitive to other parents' fears that sisterhoods would cause a similarly devastating destruction of the family.

Bishop Tait supported the growth of sisterhoods, but he also worked to preserve the unity and integrity of the Victorian family. He required parental approval before a woman joined a convent, and several times he was called upon to uphold the rights of parents. In 1858, Tait received a letter from Mrs. Rosamira Lancaster, an early supporter of the revival of sisterhoods, who would later establish the Community of St Peter in 1861. She wrote to him concerning the desire of her "adopted child" to seek admission into the Society of All Saints, Margaret Street, London. Lancaster had no objection to this action, and asked the bishop to continue in his role as Visitor to the community. After commenting on the praiseworthy work done by the All Saints sisterhood, Mrs. Lancaster, who saw the value in Bishop Tait's patronage, addressed the issue of parental permission required before a woman joined the sisterhood and the importance of episcopal approval. "I do not see how parents can possibly give up their daughters to such institutions" if they do not enjoy episcopal sanction, she pointed out, "or feel confident as to the prosperity or continued soundness of such work."[40]

Bishop Tait responded to Mrs. Lancaster's letter and outlined his past experiences as the Visitor to the sisterhood. The bishop reminded her that he had accepted this position because "unless submitted to some such controlling hand as that of the bishop" some "imaginative persons of deep piety might be tempted to follow practices contrary to

38. Davidson and Benham, *Life*, 190.
39. Marsh, *Victorian Church in Decline*, 15.
40. London, Lambeth Palace Library, Tait Papers, vol. 111, Lancaster to Tait, 16 November 1858.

the rules and spirit of our Church."[41] He told Lancaster that he would always investigate any alleged doctrinal abuses brought to his attention and would offer advice to the superior of All Saints, Miss Harriet Brownlow Byron, known as Mother Harriet. The bishop also stressed his opposition to permanent vows, and stated that "every one who joined it [the sisterhood] should be made to feel that she is perfectly free to leave it when she pleases, and also that there would be no sin in her doing so."[42] Moreover, Tait reminded Mrs. Lancaster "that no lady was to join it without the full consent of those who had a right to guide her actions in domestic life." Tait emphasized the sanctity of the family bond and argued that one's parents possessed the wisdom to provide the guidance necessary to take this step. He also told Lancaster that he knew some romantic and naive individuals might "persuade themselves that there is some peculiar sanctity in the life these ladies lead, not to be found in the quite discharge of domestic duties." He quickly cleared up any ambiguity on this point and emphasized that "I have endeavoured to impress upon all who have applied to me respecting this Institution [All Saints] that such is not my view."

In 1860, two years later, a concerned mother wrote to Bishop Tait again concerning the Society of All Saints. This troubled parent, Mrs. Woodgate, told the bishop that she had heard, quite by accident, that her daughter was planning to become a member of this sisterhood. Disapproving of her daughter's decision, she also sent Tait the letter that she had written to the chaplain of the London convent, the Rev. W. Upton Richards. It expressed her surprise and shock upon learning that her daughter wanted to enter the sisterhood within a few days.[43] Mrs. Woodgate stated her opposition to this plan. "You will understand therefore," she informed Richards, "that we view with great pain this further step so contrary to our wishes." The mother acknowledged that her daughter had reached an age which "places her beyond our authority," but she understood that it was policy of the sisterhood, the chaplain, and the episcopal Visitor, in this case Bishop Tait, "not to receive any person who enters it contrary to the wishes of her parents." Mrs. Woodgate told the chaplain that her husband had given permission for their daughter to join the convent, but she claimed that "this was plainly extorted from

41. Davidson and Benham, *Life*, 451.
42. Ibid., 452.
43. Lambeth Palace, Tait Papers, vol. 116, Woodgate to Richards, 16 February 1860.

him—for he has said continually he would never consent to this particular step." "I know" she continued, "the matter is a great grief of heart to him." The distraught mother concluded her plea to the chaplain of All Saints by stating that "I can never accede to our Daughter entering as a Sister the Margaret Street 'Home'—and I trust that you will receive this protest from me and entertain a respect also for her father's feelings." This sisterhood certainly prized the friendly relationship it enjoyed with Tait, and how would the superior explain the situation to the bishop?

Mother Harriet Byron had seen the mother's letter to the chaplain and wrote to Bishop Tait. She expressed surprise and astonishment at the accusations made by Mrs. Woodgate. In respect to the father, the superior told Tait that it "appears that Mr. Woodgate had kept the subject from his wife and she heard of it accidentally."[44] Nonetheless, the superior informed the bishop that under these circumstances her reception into the sisterhood would have to be postponed. She then provided some background about the girl and apologized for any trouble this misunderstanding might have caused Bishop Tait. Byron concluded her letter and stated that the father's "consent was not at all extorted" and that the mother had no objection to her daughter being an associate of the sisterhood or visiting the convent. Bishop Tait's reply to Mother Harriet emphasized the rights of the parents. After reviewing the correspondence on the subject, he stated that the circumstances "make it impossible . . . at the present time to give any consent to Miss Woodgate becoming a Sister of All Saints."[45]

The question of parental permission for admission into the All Saints sisterhood surfaced again three years later in 1863 when a letter arrived on Bishop Tait's desk that expressed a concern that some women working at the convent might be tempted to join the sisterhood. This anonymous writer emphasized the long hours "these young creatures" worked and argued: "their affections become completely alienated from their family circle."[46] To protect these immature girls from a life of misery, the letter maintained that the consent of father and mother should be required before entrance into the All Saints sisterhood: "a rule should be made that young ladies be received only with the written permission of their parents." Tait, who was well acquainted with this sisterhood, sent the

---

44. Ibid., Byron to Tait, 17 February 1860.
45. Ibid., Tait to Byron, 17 February, 1860.
46. Ibid., vol. 133, Anonymous to Tait. 14 August 1863.

letter to the Rev. W. Upton Richards, the chaplain. In reply, Richards told the bishop that parental authorization still remained an essential requirement for entrance into the sisterhood. Moreover, neither he nor Miss Byron knew "of anyone who is working at All Saints Home without the permission of their parents." He understood Tait's policy and concluded: "It is a rule from which I have never deviated." In spite of this strong and forceful statement about the rights of parents from the authorities at All Saints, Bishop Tait never failed to remind the community that parental permission had to be obtained prior to admission into the sisterhood. Writing to the superior three months later, Tait emphasized that "the consent of [the] parents or guardians is always obtained as directed."[47]

In 1867, one year before he became archbishop of Canterbury, Bishop Tait became involved with another London sisterhood over the rights of the family. This case involved a stepfather, an uncle, and an aunt. In 1865, the Rev. Henry Daniel Nihill had moved from Manchester to accept a curacy at St Michael's in the Shoreditch area of London, and he planned to establish a sisterhood there.[48] This cleric immediately invited some interested women to join him in the capital's East End, where he quickly established the Sisters of the Poor. Following the death of the incumbent, Nihill became vicar of the parish in 1867 and the sisters began to minister to the poor and destitute in the slums. Other convents, such as the Sisters of Mercy in Finsbury, soon became associated with the community at St Michael's. In October, a concerned individual wrote to Bishop Tait about "some undue, improper and sinister meanor [which] have been adopted to influence the gentle, yielding and rather weak mind of Miss Westbrook by the authorities of St Michael and All Angels."[49] This sisterhood wanted good relations with Bishop Tait and did not wish to jeopardize his support.

This gentleman, an uncle of Miss Westbrook, enclosed a lengthy memorandum with his letter to Tait which supplied the important background information. It expressed the fears and apprehensions which many Victorians harboured about sisterhoods and the alleged harmful effect on the family. Miss Fanny Emma Westbrook, it began, had been working at the Finsbury convent "connected with Mr Nihill's Church of St Michael and All Angels for a period of two months to aid as it is stated

---

47. Ibid., vol. 134, Tait to Byron, 25 November 1863.

48. See Anson, *Call of the Cloister*, 398-400.

49. Lambeth Palace, Tait Papers, vol. 148, Banting to Tait. 3 October 1867.

in God's work."[50] According to the uncle, Westbrook was 33 years old, but she had undertaken this commitment "in direct opposition to the wishes of her own mother—her step Father [sic] and other friends." The memorandum described her character as "a very mild gentle yielding and pliable for any good Christian work," but also added another element. In addition to her failing health, the woman was the sole heir to some property. This worried Mr. Banting, the uncle, who wanted to alert Tait to his suspicion that the community wanted to take the girl's wealth: "It is firmly believed that the Officials of the Institution to which she has gone will spare no pains to retain her beyond two months by working on her rather weak mind to secure her Property if she should live so long and to detain her by artful schemes beyond that period for which she has mentally bound her self to remain."

The alleged plot to secure her inheritance seemed insidious enough, but the writer quickly returned to the importance of family ties. The stepfather of Miss Westbrook, the writer revealed, had visited the Rev. Henry D. Nihill and obtained "a written release from any promise or engagement" that she might have made as a condition to enter the sisterhood. Yet the woman remained there and continued to work among the poor. Another relative, an aunt, also wanted to prevent Miss Westbrook's "seclusion in this establishment." This woman had also visited her niece, but was only allowed to see her in the presence of the superior of the sisterhood. The aunt immediately recognized the element of pressure and intimidation and noted that the girl "was evidently under the control of the Authorities and would make no promise to return to her distressed relatives." The writer of this long and emotional memo, Mr. Banting, ended with a plea to Bishop Tait. He begged Tait "to lend his powerful aid in preventing the permanent incarceration of his niece in this convent." This memorandum from a concerned uncle contained several issues dealing with sisterhoods in the Anglican Church: lack of freedom, security of inheritance and property, and the rights of the family. Tait would have to act.

By the end of October 1867, Bishop Tait received additional information from a clergyman who had met and talked with the aunt, Mrs. Westbrook, and the stepfather about the woman's association with Nihill's sisterhood. Both acknowledged that it would be difficult to convince her to leave the sisterhood because of her age (33). Miss Fanny Westbrook

50. Ibid., Memorandum, 3 October 1867.

wanted to remain at the convent for the agreed two months period, and she had visited the aunt on two occasions. According to this cleric's report, however, the stepfather maintained that the Rev. Henry Nihill had not treated him in a "straightforward or honourable" manner.[51] He believed that Nihill had "promised to dissuade Miss W but afterwards positively encouraged her" to remain at the sisterhood. Moreover, the stepfather expressed his concerns about the girl's health. She was "naturally most delicate," and the demands of teaching, in addition to other menial jobs such as scrubbing and washing the surplices, had made her ill. The clergyman ended his letter by stating that he did not believe that Miss Westbrook would leave Nihill's sisterhood and even doubted if Tait could resolve the problem. However, he underestimated Bishop Tait's strong resolve to supervise sisterhoods.

In early November, Bishop Tait wrote to the Rev. Henry Nihill about the case of Miss Fanny Emma Westbrook. His words sounded consistent with his past dealings with sisterhoods that involved family issues. Tait began by simply stating the facts: "A complaint has been made to me by the relations of Miss Westbrook who has lately been or still is in a sisterhood under your charge."[52] Tait mentioned the family's concern about the woman's questionable health and stated that the relatives had asked him to use his influence "to induce her to return to and continue in her own home." "I shall be glad to hear from you," Bishop Tait wrote, "that you are doing what you can to prevent any undue influence from being exercised over her by those connected with the sisterhood in question." It appears that Tait's words broke the impasse. The correspondence on this issue suddenly stopped, and Miss Westbrook did not enter the sisterhood.

The example of the 33-year-old Miss Fanny Emma Westbrook demonstrates Bishop Tait's high regard for the sanctity of the family and parental rights. Even at her age, Tait questioned this woman's decision to enter a sisterhood without first securing approval. However, his position contrasted sharply with the age of consent for marriage. Hardwicke's Marriage Act of 1753 defined the Victorian concept of marriage.[53] In an attempt to curb secret or clandestine marriages, this legislation declared that a valid church marriage required banns or the public announcement of the upcoming marriage and a license, and it

51. Ibid., vol. 338, Sponer (?) to Tait, 22 October 1867.
52. Ibid., vol. 148, Tait to Nihill, 11 November 1867.
53. Price, *British Society, 1680–1880*, 203.

had to be performed before witnesses. Moreover, "The act also gave legal backing to the authority of the parents over the marriages of their children under the age of 21." But Bishop Tait, as in the case of Miss Westbrook, used a different standard. His desire to preserve the importance of the family probably played a major role in his arbitrary policy concerning the age of consent for entrance into a convent.

In December 1868, Archibald Campbell Tait succeeded Charles Longley as archbishop of Canterbury. Archbishop Tait's dealings with sisterhoods decreased, but he still maintained his strong views on Anglican conventual life such as his disapproval of auricular confession and perpetual or binding vows, and supported the rights of parents even when their daughter had reached the age of consent required for marriage. Tait continued as the Visitor of the All Saints sisterhood, and in 1874 he became involved in a case involving the wishes of a father who did not want his daughter to become a member of that community. The father, an Anglican cleric, "simply wished to exert his paternal authority in order to prevent his daughter from being professed."[54] Miss Clementine Williams had been a "probationer" at the All Saints community and was "now ready and very desirous to become a full sister," but her father had serious objections.[55]

The chaplain, the Rev. B. Compton, informed Tait of the facts of this case. According to Compton, the Rev. B. Williams had originally consented to his daughter's wish to enter this sisterhood, but he had one reservation: namely, she could leave the community at any time to "render the duties of a daughter to him should it become necessary." However, the father had recently changed his mind; he did not want her to enter the sisterhood. Other factors complicated the story: Clementine was 27 years old; two other daughters lived with the father; and she had not resided at home since leaving school at the age of 17. It was not even clear if the Rev. B. Williams needed help or assistance from Clementine since the other daughters lived with him, but the father certainly did not want her to become an Anglican nun. Compton told Archbishop Tait that he saw no objection to Miss Williams leaving the sisterhood on a temporary basis if the father needed her assistance. The chaplain also informed Tait that "any sister is moreover absolutely at liberty to quit the Home altogether when desired." Consequently, he argued, Miss

54. Mumm, *Stolen Daughters*, 175.
55. Lambeth Palace, Tait Papers, vol. 200, Compton to Tait, 17 January 1874.

Williams should be admitted as a full member of the sisterhood in spite of the father's protests. The father had "previously permitted her to lead an independent life and there is no pretense of requiring her presence at home." How would Archbishop Tait react?

Tait asked the chaplain for a copy of the rules of the sisterhood, which he received within a few days. The archbishop read that the consent of parents or guardian was required of a woman under the age of 21 (Miss Williams was 27) before she could enter the All Saints sisterhood. After this age, "the consent of Relations more distant than a Father or Mother will not be required of necessity, but each case will be judged ... by the Superior and Chaplain, according to the circumstances, who will report to the Visitor and be guided entirely by his decision."[56] A second letter from the chaplain, which accompanied this rule, tended to make the issue more confusing. In his first letter to Archbishop Tait, Compton had stated that a member of the community could "absent herself from the convent for a short or long period" of time. He now corrected this false information, and this probably infuriated Tait because of the high regard that he had always placed on the family. "I think that the confirmed sisters [full members] consider themselves very much more detached from family ties than the probationers do," Compton pointed, and "if Miss Williams becomes a confirmed sister she would regard herself, not as absolved from filial duties altogether, but as having primary calls elsewhere."[57]

Archbishop Tait's response to the chaplain did not deviate from his earlier policies while he was the bishop of London. Tait continued to champion the rights of parents; permission remained an essential requirement before a daughter could enter a sisterhood. According to the archbishop's interpretation, "It appears to me that the Rules distinctly require the consent of Father and Mother before a Lady can be admitted as a confirmed sister."[58] Since Miss Williams's father had refused to give his approval, Tait did not see how she could possibly be admitted into full membership. This case, however, was eventually resolved. Within three months, Miss Williams entered the community as a full member and Archbishop Tait did not object because the Rev. B. Williams had fi-

56. Lambeth Palace, All Saints Home, Rule I, Tait Papers, vol. 200, Compton to Tait, 20 January 1874. The rule was enclosed with a covering letter from the chaplain.

57. Lambeth Palace, Tait Papers, vol. 200, Compton to Tait, 20 January 1874.

58. Ibid., Tait to Compton, 22 January 1874.

nally given his daughter the required permission and blessing to become a member of All Saints sisterhood.[59]

Bishop Archibald Campbell Tait certainly saw great value in the development of sisterhoods in the Anglican Church, and, in particular, those in the Diocese of London. The office of the episcopal Visitor would ensure that these communities would remain loyal to the teachings of the Anglican Church, and he never wavered from this position. Another important element in Bishop Tait's policy was his insistence that parental permission be obtained before a woman joined a sisterhood. This requirement emphasized Bishop Tait's high regard for the family. Tait believed that the clandestine or rebellious action of a woman who joined a convent might bring discord and division into her family, and his correspondence with London sisterhoods stressed the important role of the father or mother in the decision of a daughter to enter a sisterhood. When asked for his views on the matter, Tait told the superior or the chaplain that the permission of parents was a requirement for admission into a community.

The tragic deaths that struck the Tait family in Carlisle contributed to his views on the importance of the family. Disease had taken five daughters from his family, and he had to endure the suffering and grief of their untimely deaths. The loss of a daughter to the religious life also robbed the family of a member, and Bishop Tait wanted to prevent the anguish that this "spiritual" death might inflict on a family. He feared that sisterhoods might weaken this important Victorian institution, and therefore he required parental permission before a daughter entered a convent. This policy might save the family from fragmentation or dissolution. Another important element in Tait's policy was his patronizing view of women. He questioned their judgement and maturity to make a choice as drastic as joining a sisterhood in preference to the acceptable vocation of submissive wife and mother. The requirement of parental permission might mitigate this foolishness.

---

59. Ibid., Byron to Tait, 2 April 1874.

Bibliography

Allchin, A. M. *The Silent Rebellion: Anglican Religious Communities 1845–1900*. London: SCM, 1958.

Anson, Peter F. *The Call of the Cloister: Religious Communities and Kindred Bodies in the Anglican Communion*. Revised and edited by A. W. Campbell. London: SPCK, 1964.

Arnstein, Walter. *Protestant versus Catholic in Mid-Victorian England: Mr. Newdegate and the Nuns*. Columbia: University of Missouri Press, 1982.

Benham, William, editor. *Catharine and Craufurd Tait, Wife and Son of Archibald Campbell, Archbishop of Canterbury: A Memoir*. London: Macmillan, 1879.

The Chronicle of Convocation, Upper House, 1862. London: National Society's Depository, 1862.

Davidson, Randall Thomas, and William Benham. *Life of Archibald Campbell Tait: Archbishop of Canterbury*. Vol. 1. London: Macmillan, 1891.

Harwood, John. *Miss Jane, the Bishop's Daughter*. 3 vols. London: Bentley, 1867.

Jalland, P. *Death in the Victorian Family*. Oxford: Oxford University Press, 1996.

Kollar, Rene. "The 1897 Lambeth Conference and the Question of Religious Life in the Anglican Communion." *Cistercian Studies Quarterly* 26 (1991) 319–29.

Left Home; or, Convent Life. London: Farrah, 1865.

Marsh, P. T. *The Victorian Church in Decline: Archbishop Tait and the Church of England 1868–1882*. London: Routledge & Kegan Paul, 1969.

Mumm, Susan. *Stolen Daughters, Virgin Mothers: Anglican Sisterhoods in Victorian Britain*. London: Leicester University Press, 1999.

Paz, D. G. *Popular Anti-Catholicism in Mid-Victorian England*. Stanford: Stanford University Press, 1992.

Price, Richard. *British Society, 1680–1880: Dynamism, Containment and Change*. Cambridge: Cambridge University Press, 1999.

Reed, John Shelton. *Glorious Battle: The Cultural Polities of Victorian Anglo-Catholicism*. Nashville: Vanderbilt University Press, 1996.

Seymour, M. Hobart. *A Pilgrimage to Rome*. London: Seeleys, 1849.

Sinclair, Catherine. *Beatrice; or, the Unknown Relatives*. 4th ed. New York: DeWitt & Davenport, n.d.

Wallis, Frank H. *Popular Anti-Catholicism in Mid-Victorian Britain*. Texts and Studies in Religion 60. Lewistown, NY: Mellen, 1993.

Wolffe, John. *The Protestant Crusade in Great Britain 1829–1860*. Oxford: Oxford University Press, 1991.

11

The Priest, the Nun, and Confession

An Anti-Catholic Stereotype and Anglican Sisterhoods in Victorian England

WHEN THE FORMER ROMAN Catholic priest, Fr. Chiniquy, wrote *The Priest, the Woman, and the Confessional* in 1874, his words touched a sensitive religious nerve in countries such as England, which treasured its Protestant heritage. In his book, Chiniquy attacked the practice of auricular confession in the Catholic Church and claimed that the confessional represented an evil institution that could harm the integrity of all women, including nuns. Anti-Catholic rhetoric such as this proved to be an essential element in the formation and creation of the modern English state, where Roman Catholicism was seen as an alien and foreign element.[1] The religion of the Reformation created a distrust of the Roman Catholic Church, and a number of traditional institutions of Roman Catholicism also ran contrary to the religious and secular spirit of Victorian England. The English Reformation, using theological and scriptural arguments, condemned both auricular confession and the conventual life for men and women. The nineteenth-century opponents of these Roman practices argued that the secrecy associated with both the confessional and convent life not only offended the traditions of English openness and freedom, but could give rise to numerous abuses. Some Anglicans, however, also actively encouraged confession and sisterhoods.

1. See Colley, *Britons*.

Critics within the Anglican Church, therefore, worked to expose the perceived abuses associated with nuns confessing to celibate priests. One way to attack this perceived danger would be to use traditional anti-Catholic rhetoric that exposed the stereotypical dangers of convents and the confessional. This strategy not only tried to expose the alleged shortcomings of these institutions and their harm to the Church of England, but also became an occasion to keep up the attack against Roman Catholicism. But to what extent did the opponents of convents and the confessional consciously fabricate the evidence to discredit both?

Auricular confession, that is, the secret and spoken acknowledgement of one's sins and the seeking of absolution from a priest, started to replace the earlier practice of public confession by the fifth century.[2] The Celtic monks of the next century emphasized private confession to a priest, and this system eventually supplanted the public or open acknowledgement of a person's sins. By the eighth century, auricular confession became synonymous with the sacrament of Penance. The Fourth Lateran Council (1215) legislated that all believers had to confess their sins to a priest at least once a year. Maintaining that confession was necessary for salvation, theologians drew attention to the "Keys Passage" in the New Testament (Matt 16:18–21) to make their point. The Reformers of the sixteenth century, however, expunged Penance from the list of sacraments and argued that this questionable practice greatly diminished the importance of Christ. They argued that one should approach the Son of God directly and intimately instead of asking a priest for forgiveness. Consequently, the Council of Trent in 1551 considered it necessary to reaffirm the divine origin and the sacramental nature of auricular confession and the necessity of confession to save one's soul.

In England during the nineteenth century, theological views on confession remained polarized. Trent told Catholics that confession was necessary for salvation, but the Protestant theologians continued to speak of the shallowness and worthlessness of auricular confession. The practice of confession, however, began to gain some acceptance within Anglicanism. Writing in 1896, the American Henry Charles Lea argued that in the early church "there was nothing to correspond with the modern conception of absolution—the pardon or remission of sin by one

---

2. See the numerous articles dealing with confession in the *New Catholic Encyclopedia*.

human being to another."³ But commenting on the history of confession in the Anglican Church, Lea admitted that the English Reformation avoided the extremes of its continental counterparts in regard to confession. He pointed out that confession no longer enjoyed the status of a sacrament of the Church of England, but the 1552 Prayer Book still gave the penitent an option to approach the priest for confession and absolution. Anglo-Catholics began to encourage the use of devotions and practices associated with Roman Catholicism, and auricular confession became an option for these Anglicans. These so-called ritualists, consequently, encouraged confession as spiritually beneficial and important.⁴ But anti-Catholicism remained a powerful and emotional force in nineteenth-century England, and any association with Roman practices would naturally stir up latent suspicions and hatred.

During the eighteenth century, legislation against English Roman Catholics slowly began to disappear. Nonetheless, Catholics remained second class citizens who were still not accepted into the country's political and social life. Roman Catholics could not sit in Parliament even though they had demonstrated their loyalty during the Napoleonic era, and the campaign for Catholic Emancipation, which would give Roman Catholics this political right, became the goal for Catholics. The passing of Catholic Emancipation in 1829 represented a landmark in religious toleration in England, but it also ushered in a renewal of religious bigotry. According to John Wolffe, the effect of Emancipation "was, if anything, to strengthen anti-Catholicism."⁵ In 1831, for example, "a Catholic writer complained of the polemical onslaught which was being waged against the faith, on platforms and in the press, associated with the gross misrepresentation of Catholic practices and principles." Other events of the nineteenth century that appeared to favor Catholics—for example, Robert Peel's generous financial policy toward Maynooth College and finally the Restoration of the Hierarchy in 1850—tended to turn the mistrust of Roman Catholicism into a public crusade. More troubling, a section of Anglicanism, the Anglo-Catholics, seemed to be endorsing Catholicism by adopting practices banished at the Reformation. One in particular, auricular confession, especially angered loyal Protestants,

---

3. Lea, *History of Auricular Confession and Indulgences in the Latin Church*, vol. 1, 460.
4. Bentley, *Ritualism and Politics in Victorian Britain*, 30–35.
5. Wolffe, *Protestant Crusade in Great Britain 1829–1860*, 1.

and in addition to theological arguments they also campaigned against the confessional with a more emotional weapon.

Auricular confession, they argued, could seriously harm naive and impressionable women. "What especially affronted the Victorian middle classes, however, were the secrecy of the practice and the fact that women went to confession on their own, without the sanction of their fathers, brothers, or husbands."[6] Some maintained that the priest could easily learn the most intimate secrets of domestic life and even try to control the finances, including the transfer of property and funds to the confessor or his church. The Sacrament of Penance administered to a penitent on the death bed might also give some unscrupulous clerics the opportunity to suggest changes in the last will and testament, thus stealing the inheritance from the family members. Confession also created other potential problems. The priest's questions could deal with the most personal details of married life. Consequently, the opponents of Roman Catholicism believed that the confessional might easily become the occasion of temptation and sin. The atmosphere of religious prejudice in England would welcome examples of scandal, but in fact stories of impropriety existed more in the mind of anti-Catholic writers that in reality. Fabricated stories of the seduction of women in the confessional by wicked priests did appear in some works of fiction, but actual cases of scandalous activities were extremely rare. Commenting on the campaign against confession in the Anglican Church and the amount of literature that emphasized possible dangers, John Shelton Reed notes that "it may be surprising how little seduction there actually was, beyond rumor and conjecture."[7]

The questions allegedly asked by some confessors, however, disturbed many, and when the public became acquainted with the nature of these queries they expressed disbelief and rage. The Rev. M. Hobart Seymour, a critic of the confession, sisterhoods, and Roman Catholicism in general, told the English that the "preparation for the Confession forms a large portion of clerical education."[8] This training for the Roman Catholic priesthood necessarily introduced the future confessor to "every kind of sin, every form of vice, every phase of impurity, and every way in which the vilest passions of our fallen nature can be indulged" Consequently, according to Seymour, teachers at seminaries allegedly instructed future priests

---

6. Paz, *Popular Anti-Catholicism in Mid-Victorian England*, 276.

7. Reed, *Glorious Battle*, 198.

8. Seymour, *The Confessional*, 178.

on the techniques they should use in the confessional on "how to search and ascertain every phase and form of sin in the penitent kneeling before him . . . and every willful indulgence of thought or feeling which might aggravate its guilt." Lewis H. J. Tonna also criticized the subject matter of the questions that the Roman Catholic priests asked, especially when hearing the confessions of nuns. In *Nuns and Nunneries*, he found fault with the preparation clerics received to hear confessions of women in convents, itself "a most unnatural system,"[9] and he discussed the sensitive nature of the dialogue between a priest and the nun who entered the confessional. With no formal preparation for the duties of the confessional, Anglican confessors could acquire the necessary training from Roman Catholic books of moral theology. One written by Pierre Dens (1690–1775) became popular, and opponents of auricular confession translated relevant sections from Latin to English to alert the public of the possible perils associated with the secrecy of the confessional.[10]

One translation of Dens's book pointed out that the author openly acknowledged that actions of a sexual nature might take place during confession, and he set out the procedure by which the woman could denounce the sinful priest to the bishop in writing, and an episcopal investigation would follow.[11] Some opponents maintained that the sexual orientation of the questions contained in Dens's book contributed to "the licentiousness of the clergy"; others believed that the priest's questions led to abuses.[12] The sensitive nature of this interrogation most probably scandalized Victorian society. Kissing, "other greater alternative liberties," and improper thoughts were all appropriate subjects a confessor could discuss with an engaged woman.[13] Another Catholic manual written by Louis Bailly, also translated into English, contained a list of questions that a priest could ask a female, including: "Has she

---

9. Tonna, *Nuns and Nunneries*, 50; see 50–58 for his critique of confession in general and its questionable place in a sisterhood.

10. See P. Dens, *Tractatus Theologicus de Sacramento Poenitentiae*. Sections of Dens's book dealing with confession were published in Dublin in 1836. By the middle of the nineteenth century, several English translations dealing with the questions the priest asked women had appeared. See, for example, Sparry, trans., *Translations (with the Original Latin) from Dens' System of Moral*; and C. B. (David Bryce), trans., *Confessional Unmasked*.

11. Sparry, trans., *Translations*, 21–22.

12. *Confessional: An Exposure of Its Mysteries and Iniquities*, 11.

13. Ibid., 30.

ornamented herself in dress so as to please the male sex . . . or bared her arms, her shoulders, or her bosom . . . [whether] she has allowed him to kiss her?"[14] This book of moral theology, moreover, discussed situations dealing with intimacies between a husband and wife. The general spirit of these two manuals, therefore, could anger Victorian men and could embarrass a woman. But why then did some Anglican wives and daughters frequent the confessional?

Confession for Anglicans remained a voluntary action, and it could be interpreted as a sign of defiance for women who sought freedom or independence. Confessing one's innermost thoughts and transgressions to a cleric, and not the husband, also represented an act of defiance, and this presented a challenge to a society dominated by men. Lucy Snowe in Charlotte Brontë's *Villette*, for example, personified this free spirit of self-expression and empowerment when she boldly entered the confessional box. Some nineteenth-century critics believed, therefore, that it was the "duty of Victorian males to restore patriarchal authority in the family" by attacking the subversive practice of auricular confession in the Anglican Church.[15]

Women seeking out a cleric for confession became associated in the minds of certain critics with an attempt to break the bonds of superficial Victorian mores, and the growth of Anglican sisterhoods in the nineteenth century also represented something more than an idealized desire to recreate the pre-Reformation world of English nunneries. The conventual life in the Anglican Church, like confession, became popular among the Anglo-Catholics, and Roman Catholic nuns arriving from Europe also began to establish convents throughout the country with some success. Detractors of the conventual life for women emphasized what they perceived to be the unnatural nature of the celibate life, drew attention to alleged abuses in convents throughout the centuries, and argued that the strict regime and the secret nature of sisterhoods could deprive pious women of their English liberties. Life within a convent indeed offered women an opportunity to break free from the strictures of Victorian convention. The cloister walls ironically gave them freedom. Entering a convent, much like the act of confession, became a sign of independence. In her study of Anglican convents in Victorian England,

---

14. Bailly, *Theologia Dogmatica et Moralis*, quoted in Bryce, trans. *Confessional Unmasked*, 39.

15. Paz, *Popular Anti-Catholicism in Mid-Victorian England*, 276.

Susan Mumm argues that these nuns "saw religion as an empowering and enabling force, not as a restrictive or crippling limitation on their human potential."[16]

One of the first in-depth studies of religious communities in the Anglican Church, A. M. Allchin's *The Silent Rebellion: Anglican Religious Communities 1845–1900*, views the establishment of the convents as a reaction against the "worldly values and standards" of a prosperous and industrialized country.[17] John Shelton Reed believes that Anglican sisterhoods offered a new path for unmarried women in the fields of education, nursing, and work among "fallen women" such as prostitutes or alcoholics which the individualistic and competitive culture of the Victorians had neglected. The appeal of the conventual life for women, therefore, occasioned some serious concern on the part of Victorian men. Sisterhood life took women out of their homes, gave them important work and sometimes great responsibility, and replaced their ties to fathers, husbands, and brothers by loyalties to Church and sisterhood. It demonstrated that there were callings for women of the upper and middle classes in addition to, or—in they eyes of threatened members of the Protestant establishment—other than those of wife, daughter, and "charitable spinster." And it at least suggested that the religious life was the higher calling.[18]

Sisterhoods appeared as a threat not only to the integrity of the Protestant character of Anglicanism, but also to the status quo of Victorian society. Auricular confession fit the same view, and books of devotion, which influenced both Roman Catholic and Anglican sisterhoods, encouraged nuns to frequent the confessional. St. Alphonsus de Liguori (1696–1787) wrote *The True Spouse of Jesus Christ* in 1760 as a guide for Catholic nuns, and some Anglican sisterhoods eventually adopted his ideas. St. Alphonsus argued that "nothing was more injurious or displeasing to . . . [the devil] than frequent confession."[19] Moreover, he also stressed that nuns must obey their confessors and told them to "fear

---

16. Allchin, *Silent Rebellion*. For a history of Anglican brotherhoods and sisterhoods, see Anson, *Call of the Cloister*. Anson sees the revival of monastic life as a movement to rediscover and then revive this important aspect of Christianity that the English Reformation destroyed.

17. Reed, *Glorious Battle*, 203.

18. Ibid., 204.

19. De Liguori, *True Spouse of Jesus Christ*, 525.

not that in obeying him you may be led astray."[20] Because of the apparent dangers that auricular confession and Anglican sisterhoods posed to the state religion and the Victorian family, they had to be denounced, and critics in nineteenth-century England labored to paint a picture of corruption and wickedness that resulted when a nun went to confession. Stories of alleged abuses of the confessional in Roman Catholic sisterhoods had a long tradition of English anti-Catholicism and dislike of the monastic life, but the re-establishment of these convents in England also attracted some support. Catholic bashing, therefore, might be an important weapon against the growth of Anglo-Catholic sisterhoods.

After the nationalization of the church during the reign of Henry VIII, Roman Catholic monasticism disappeared from the country, but the conventual life, especially for women, began to flourish again in the early nineteenth century. Monks and nuns fleeing the horrors of the French Revolution found a refuge on English soil, and the number of convents grew. Monasticism had contributed to the development of English life and culture, and John Henry Newman stressed the significance of Roman Catholic monasticism throughout history. Prior to his conversion to Roman Catholicism in 1845, Newman made no secret of his admiration of monasticism and its spiritual and educational contributions, and unfortunately these had disappeared from the fabric of English civilization.[21] His writings reveal an appreciation of religious vows, especially celibacy, communal life, and common prayer. Monasticism humanized society; it offered alternative values to the growth of secularism that was occurring in industrialized England. The monastic life, Newman believed, preserved the truths and essentials of the Christian message and also offered a protection against indifference, and he pointed to the past when the monasteries contributed to order and education in Europe. "They were intended as the refuge of piety and holiness, when the increasing spread of religion made Christians more sacred."[22] Newman, however, did not limit his high regard for monasticism to communities of men, but he also recognized the value of the religious life for women.

---

20. Ibid., 550.

21. For Newman's views on monasticism see Kollar, "The Oxford Movement and the Heritage of Benedictine Monasticism."

22. Newman, *Historical Sketches*, vol. 2, 165.

Another leading member of the Oxford Movement, Edward Bouverie Pusey, actively supported the establishment of Anglican sisterhoods, but he also noted that Newman recognized the value of convents. Writing to John Keble in 1839, Pusey pointed out that "Newman and I have separately come to think it necessary to have some Soeurs de Charite in the Anglo-Catholic Church."[23] Newman recognized the importance of women monastics in *The Church of Our Fathers, Historical Sketches*, where he argued that "[t]here is another reason for such establishments, which applies particularly to women; convents are as much demanded, in the model of a perfect Church, by Christian charity, as monastic bodies can be by Christian zeal."[24] He criticized the "cruel temper of Protestantism . . . [and] the determined, bitter, and scoffing spirit in which it has set itself against institutions which give dignity and independence to the position of women in society." The example of Roman Catholic sisterhoods offered an option for women who desired "a maiden life, that holy estate." Newman believed that "foundations for single women, under proper precautions, at once hold out protection to those who avail themselves of them, and give dignity to the single state itself." Newman's commitment to monastic principles was so strong that on April 25, 1842, he and a group of friends moved to Littlemore, outside of Oxford, to live the conventual life. Shortly before his conversion, he disbanded the brotherhood, and this Anglican monastic experiment ceased to exist. John Henry Newman clearly championed the establishment of Anglican sisterhoods modeled on their Roman Catholic counterparts. The positive contributions of Catholic nuns to contemporary English society could not be ignored.

Roman Catholic convents offered valuable services that were absent from government programs. "In 1840 the English Catholic community could lay claim to fewer than twenty convents and an even smaller number of convent schools and welfare institutions," Susan O'Brien points out, but "by 1880 the *Catholic Directory* listed more than three hundred convents . . . administering a well-developed system of Catholic educational and welfare services."[25] Most significant, and an issue that infuriated many anti-Catholics, were the praiseworthy contributions of these

---

23. Pusey, *Letter to the Right Reverend Richard*, 142.
24. Newman, *Historical Sketches*, vol. 2, 165.
25. O'Brien, "Religious Life for Women," 112.

sisterhoods in the area of education to all segments of English society.[26] According to Edward Norman, the convent schools made available an education superior to other institutions: "In terms of education offered to girls . . . at all levels, the Catholic schools provided very much better and more extensive facilities than the education available for females generally in nineteenth-century England."[27] The curriculum at these schools included foreign languages, science, mathematics, geography, and needlework, and moreover, "many of these schools had a considerable number, even a majority, of non-Catholic girls."[28] But Catholic nuns contributed to the well-being of society in other areas:

> crèches [that is, day nurseries for young children], industrial schools and teacher education; retreat work, catechetics and religious instruction; hospital, prison and parish visiting and welfare support in working-class districts; homes for orphans or children unable to be supported by their families, the physically handicapped and the elderly; women's refuges, reformatories and hostels for working-class young women; and, to a lesser extent, dispensaries, home nursing, convalescent homes and hospitals.[29]

A sense of rivalry, embarrassment at their own shortcomings, and fear of conversion to Roman Catholicism (especially in the schools) contributed to the traditional hostility against these sisterhoods, but criticisms could also come from unlikely sources.

A shocking revelation came from Scipio de Ricci (1741–1806), the reforming Bishop of Pistoia and Prato. In 1829 his remarks appeared in England under the title, *Female Convents. Secrets of Nunneries Disclosed*, the same year Catholic Emancipation received royal assent. According to this account, the confessor of a certain Italian convent enjoyed free run of this cloistered institution, and this practice resulted in immoral behaviors.[30] The Bishop's use of an isolated example probably did more harm than good in the cause of convent reform, and the anti-Catholic

26. See Kollar, "Foreign and Catholic." Chapter 9 above.
27. Norman, *English Catholic Church in the Nineteenth Century*, 183.
28. Hastings, *History of English Catholicism 1920–1985*, 143–44.
29. O'Brien, "Religious Life for Women," 120.

30. Roscoe, ed., *Female Convents*, 84. The book was first published in London in 1829. References are from this American edition. The introductory essay to this edition warned the American readers that the same scandal and abuses would take place in their country if Roman Catholicism and its institutions, such as religious orders for men and women, flourished.

mind was quick to generalize. Roman Catholic Italy also provided the scene for another unflattering look at life within sisterhoods. In 1864, an ex-Benedictine nun, Henrietta Caracciolo, published her reminiscences, and writers in England frequently quoted her words throughout the nineteenth century. Caracciolo's purpose was not an exposé, but she wanted to provide a justification for the recent anti-Catholic policy adopted by the Italian government in suppressing sisterhoods.[31] Her descriptions of conventual life, not surprisingly, lacked objectivity. In this account, the religious superior encouraged daily confession, and some of the sisters became fascinated with the priest. The danger centered around the nature of the questions the priest asked the penitent nun: the suggestive language of the confessor could easily result in occasional trysts between the confessor and the sister.[32] These Italian examples contained exaggerated and questionable stories of impropriety, and both authors had an agenda of progressive reform to champion. A book from America reinforced these exaggerated views for readers in England.

A testimony written by the former Roman Catholic priest, William Hogan, tried to give some credibility to the charges of wicked confessors and their corrupting power over naive nuns. His motives, however, appeared to be based on hatred and anti-Catholicism rather than an objective study of alleged abuses. Hogan's training at the Irish seminary at Maynooth touched an English nerve at a time when the public had become agitated because of the government's perceived favorable policy to this Roman Catholic institution. Hogan's book, originally published in America in 1845, appeared in England the following year. Hogan successfully combined his own experiences as a former confessor and the revelations he heard with the traditional critiques, most unsubstantiated, against convent life. He talked about seductions, murders, illegitimate children, infanticide, the immorality of nuns and clergy, and the hidden and seditious dangers of convent education. Hogan began his discussion of confession by reminding the reader that he wanted to demonstrate that it represented "the source and fountain of many, if not all, those treasons, debaucheries, and other evils, which are now flooding" America.[33] Hogan then explored the secret world of the confessional in convents. Bringing his creditability and motives into question, Hogan

---

31. Caracciolo, *Memoirs of Henrietta Caracciolo*, v.

32. Ibid., 102–5.

33. Hogan, *Popery!*, 233.

broke the bond of confidentiality and revealed the subjects of some confessions he heard as a Catholic priest. He boldly claimed that "there is scarcely one of them [nuns] who has not *been herself debauched by her confessor.*"[34] The suggestive and obscene questions that the priest asked were degrading and indecent, and could easily result in the manipulation of females, and members of a sisterhood were the most vulnerable. Hogan stated that he personally knew two nuns in Boston who became pregnant after they had been seduced by the convent's confessor.[35] The English, however, could read the accounts of nuns, Anglican and Roman Catholic, and their stories of sisterhoods in England. Their testimonies seemed tame and mild, and conflicted with the evil stereotype nurtured by anti-Catholic propaganda.

Eliza Richardson published *Personal Experience of Roman Catholicism. With Incidents of Convent Life in 1864*.[36] The so-called "indelicate" questions asked by some father confessors not only embarrassed her, but also enkindled a sense of outrage and shame. Richardson did not single out issues of sexuality, but claimed that one of her confessors cajoled her and pressured her to reveal more information in order to obtain priestly absolution. She felt suffocated, and "a kind of fallen and crushed feeling seemed to paralyze me, both physically and mentally."[37] Richardson characterized auricular confession as a bondage and "an engine of foul spiritual tyranny."[38] Another former nun, Sister Lucy (Ann Cullen) "escaped" from a Roman Catholic convent in 1865, and soon afterwards wrote a small pamphlet that described her life in the sisterhood. She described her Essex convent as a prison and pointed out that the conduct of the nuns at times became frivolous. Sister Lucy attended confession weekly "until the last five or six weeks, when I told the nuns that it was mocking God, and that I would not go again."[39] The probing nature of the confessor's questions offended her and "sometimes caused me to suspect the priest's motives were none of the purest."[40]

34. Ibid., 247.
35. Ibid., 473.
36. Richardson, *Personal Experience of Roman Catholicism*.
37. Ibid., 66.
38. Ibid., 70.
39. Cullen, *Marvelous Escape of "Sister Lucy,"* 16.
40. Ibid.

Nevertheless, no allegation of abuse associated with the confessional appears in her account of her stay in the convent.

Former nuns also wrote about their experiences in Anglican sisterhoods. They complained about several aspects of the conventual life, but none contained the scathing condemnation of the confessional one might expect. Priscilla Lydia Sellon, who established an Anglican sisterhood in Devonport near Plymouth in 1848, attracted a number of critics. Some former members disliked her support of Roman Catholic devotions and her alleged tyrannical manner of supervising the convent, but the criticisms did not reveal anything scandalous or abusive as a result of her encouragement of the confessional. Margaret Goodman's two books about the Devonport convent, for example, skimmed over Sellon's support of confession.[41] Mary Frances Cusack also attacked Sellon's despotic rule and argued that episcopal supervision was needed to ensure a healthy religious life for the nuns, but she actually saw benefit in auricular confession: it could console a troubled soul. "It was to us merely a 'comfort' and nothing more. Indeed, had it been acknowledged to be a sacrament by our spiritual guides, they would have placed themselves in a position of extreme perplexity."[42] In *The Anglican Sister of Mercy*, the author resisted the pressure of other nuns in Sellon's sisterhood to frequent confession, and she backed up her opposition by arguing that since "priestcraft" and the confessional were intimately connected a priest could control and dominate family life in England.[43]

The topic of auricular confession and its place in convents also appeared in other stories by ex-nuns, but the subject did not attract much attention in their descriptions of life in a sisterhood. Sister Mary Agnes, O.S.B., an associate of the Anglican Benedictine, Fr. Ignatius of Llanthony, expressed a sense of disillusionment with convent life and remembered the cruel treatment she endured at the hand of the superior, but she gave the subject of confession only a few passing words.[44] In 1874, Charlotte Myhall published a short pamphlet about her stay in an Anglican sisterhood, complete with illustrations of instruments of torture she claimed convents used, but Myhall did not even mention the confessional as a

---

41. Goodman, *Experiences of an English Sister of Mercy*; and Goodman, *Sisterhoods in the Church of England*.

42. Cusack, *Five Years in a Protestant Sisterhood*, 98.

43. Dill, *The Anglican Sister of Mercy*, 5.

44. Sister Mary Agnes, *Nunnery Life in the Church of England*, 50.

possible source of abuse.[45] A Roman Catholic former nun, Sister Mary Elizabeth, criticized Irish convent life in 1892, but the subject of auricular confession within the cloister was absent.[46] The testimony of Julia Gordon at first sight appeared to be a gold mine for critics of convent confessions. These so-called memoirs, in reality fictional creations of an anti-Catholic mind, rehashed the usual fabrications of infanticide, seduction, torture and murder usually associated with Gothic prose, but Julia Gordon seemed restrained in her comments on the confessional: "I was assigned a Father Confessor, who used, when I was closeted with him at confession, to urge me to confess crimes I never conceived, and interlarded with religious homilies pictured to my mind scenes of licentiousness I could never suppose were enacted."[47] But the testimony of another young woman, Miss A. F. B., who left both the convent and the Roman Catholic Church, took offense at anti-Catholic diatribes against sisterhoods, and wrote in 1875 that she "can nevertheless look back with pleasure upon Convent days and Convent friends."[48] As for Catholic priests, "she still holds [them] in affectionate remembrance." Although accounts of both Anglican and Roman Catholic conventual life could be critical, their negative assessments did not include alleged abuses associated with the confessional.

Writers of fiction, however, enjoyed the option to take more liberty with aspects of convent life, and they could easily portray the confessional in harsher and more threatening terms. *Lorette* was written by an American minister and published in Edinburgh in 1836. The pages of the Rev. George Bourne's book contained the usual litany of anti-Catholic and anti-convent stereotypes, and he did not neglect the apparent dangers of auricular confession. Early in the book one of the main characters announced, "I will never go to the confessional unless I am dragged there. The ceremony is a farce and delusion, and it is connected with wickedness."[49] The book dramatically exposed the alleged evils of the Roman Catholic Church and sisterhoods, but surprisingly did not

45. For the modern edition, see Myhill, *Three Years as a Nun*. The book originally appeared in London in 1874 under the title, *How Perversions Are Effected; or Three Years' Experience as a Nun*.
46. Slattery (Sister Mary Elizabeth), *Convent Life Exposed*.
47. *Awful Disclosures of Miss Julia Gordon*, 6–7.
48. Miss A. F. B. (Adela F. Barlow), *Convent Experiences*, 6.
49. Bourne, *Lorette*, 25.

target the convent's confessional as an occasion of sin. Another work of fiction, however, became the standard work that condemned convent life in stark and pornographic terms, and one might expect vivid descriptions of unethical confessors.

The Awful Disclosures of Maria Monk, published in 1836, quickly became a best seller and soon appeared in England. Marketed as a memoir of Maria Monk, an ex-nun who chronicled her dreadful experiences in a Montreal convent, the scandalous happenings and immoral activities of priests and nuns in the book were quickly exposed as false. Maria Monk, who probably suffered from mental problems, really existed, and a group of anti-Catholic Americans worked with her to compose the book and conjured up the fictional activities within the convent. They used vivid and detailed language to illustrate the unsavory actions of the sisterhood: infanticide of the nuns' children and the crude burial of their young bodies in lime pits, a murder of a nun, the torture and the walling up of disobedient sisters, and the not-to-be-neglected liaisons with predatory priests. In a book of such graphic detail, one might expect that the secrecy associated with auricular confession might also find a prominent place in this attack against sisterhoods, but the confessional was not the object of harsh criticism. Early in the book, however, the subject of confession did appear. A friend of Maria Monk told her about the conduct of a priest in the confessional, which Monk thought was shameful. This nun did not mention the nature of the inappropriate conduct, but it did not appear to be sexual. The only instance of abusive priestly actions in reference to the confessional occurred when Maria Monk related how the questions became detailed and "that the priests became more and more bold, and were at length indecent in their questions and even in their conduct when I confessed to them in the Sacristie."[50] Yet even this reference to improper and questionable actions is mild compared to the other examples of brutality and abuse in this book.

Other works of fiction also described Roman Catholic sisterhoods in unflattering terms, but the indictment against auricular confession was also gentle. Julia McNair Wright's *Secrets of the Convent and the Confessional* and *Priest and Nun* warned America of the dangers to their liberty posed by the Roman Catholic Church, and these books soon appeared in England, where the same fear existed. In the former novel, Wright alerted the country about the evil designs of the Jesuits

---

50. Monk, *Awful Disclosures of the Hotel Dieu of Montreal*, 21.

and the dangers of convent education. The growth of Roman Catholic sisterhoods had to be resisted, and she described the alleged cruelty of convent life, the abusive power of the mother superior, and the unnatural atmosphere, but confession only received a passing comment: "The Confessional is Rome's electric telegraph. Every Confessional is an office, every priest an operator; from parish to parish, from town to town, from diocese to diocese, from State to State, and from land to land, Rome flashes her secret intelligence, until what was spoken in the ear, is proclaimed upon the house-tops, and what was whispered in darkness blazes into the light of action."[51]

In her second book, *Priest and Nun*, Wright briefly mentioned confession as being unscriptural, but she did not discuss the role of this Catholic sacrament in sisterhoods. Another work of fiction also critical of convents, *St. Mary's Convent; or, Chapters in the Life of a Nun*, singled out the lack of freedom in a sisterhood and described the convent as a prison, but in this story, the priest-confessor surprisingly appeared in a positive light. He actually encouraged "ideas of a state of more freedom and enjoyment into the minds of some six or seven of the sisterhood" in a plot to replace the harsh superior with one more "good-natured" and "good humoured."[52] *Love's Strife with the Convent*, another novel, critiqued both sisterhoods and the confessional, but the author did find a redeeming act by the convent's confessor. It noted that Fr. Francis "reproached the abbess in private for having used the vault of penitence without first consulting him, and more particularly for having immured" one of her charges.[53]

Nonetheless, stories of wicked confessors taking advantage of over scrupulous nuns did exist. In 1850, when the Roman Catholic Hierarchy was restored, *Priests and Their Victims; Or Scenes in a Convent* was published. This collection of anti-Catholic and anti-Jesuit propaganda contained the story of an eighteenth century orphan whose father stipulated that she had to enter a convent in order to inherit his small fortune. The shocking descriptions of the sisterhood echoed the falsehoods found in Maria Monk's book about convent life. This tale used stories of immoral priests, sexual license, illegitimate children and infanticide, a despotic and cruel superior, and the murder of rebellious nuns to discredit the

---

51. Wright, *Secrets of the Convent and Confessional*, 105.
52. Dammast, *St. Mary's Convent*, 91.
53. Massey, *Love's Strife with the Convent*, vol. 2, 144.

Catholic religion and convent life, and it did not ignore the evils of the confessional. One member of the convent, Sr. Agnes, suffered imprisonment, torture, and death because she resisted the advances of her confessor priest. When she complained to the Abbess of the convent, this superior told Sr. Agnes that she had to obey the dictates of the confessor. She still refused, and revealed, "I have been tortured in almost every conceivable shape to make me yield . . . [and] for this am I punished."[54] Because she would not give into the wishes of the superior and the priest, Sr. Agnes had to suffer the horrible consequences: "A large feather bed was now brought forward by the elderly sisters . . . and placing it over her they got on top of it, and stamped and jumped upon it until death released her from her sufferings."[55] This work of anti-Catholic fiction is an exception, but it illustrates that the hatred and bigotry of critics would go to any extent to create abuses associated with both sisterhoods and auricular confession.

But was the convent confessional a den of sin and a place where unscrupulous priests used their power and authority to corrupt the naive nun who looked to the confessor for comfort and absolution? The use of well-known anti-Catholic images and charges of scandalous actions to attack and discredit Anglican conventual life for women would certainly give their detractors a great opportunity to carry on their attack against the perceived threats from Roman Catholicism. Opponents, therefore, could create pictures of evil confessors in an attempt both to smear Roman Catholic convents and to warn Anglicans about the dangers that would exist within their sisterhoods.

Works of nineteenth-century fiction could be harsh in their condemnation of convent life, but in general the critiques of the confessional seemed mild in comparison with the license some authors took in their descriptions of alleged cruel punishments, murder, and infanticide within the cloister. In the case of Roman Catholic convents, however, little evidence supports the charge of an abusive confessional. The testimony of several ex-nuns and examples of literature critical of sisterhoods do not support the claim that Roman Catholic priests misused the confessional to corrupt and ruin members of sisterhoods who sought their spiritual advice and comfort. Consequently, this allegation did not figure greatly in the rhetoric against Anglican sisterhoods. Like the

54. Viner, comp., *Priests and Their Victims*, 8.
55. Ibid., 9.

Victorian era, when Roman Catholicism and sisterhoods stood in stark opposition to the increasing secularization of the country and offered alternatives that challenged a society which appeared to abandon religious principles, the current opposition in America to Catholic values and its institutions, such as the sanctity of the family, the religious life for men and women, and its educational system, is motivated by anti-Catholic prejudices, exaggerations, and personal agendas.

Bibliography

Anonymous. *Awful Disclosures of Miss Julia Gordon, The White Nun or Female Spy! Her Vile Jesuit Plots; Scenes of Infamy, Torture and Murder in Convents! And the Strangling & Burning of New-Born Infants, in Lime Pit, To Conceal the Crimes of the Priests with the Nuns*. London: Abington, 1858.

Anonymous. *The Confessional: An Exposure of Its Mysteries and Iniquities As Practiced in Foreign and English Convents by Priests and Their Victims*. London: Elliot, 1873.

Anonymous. *The Marvelous Escape of "Sister Lucy" and Her Awful Disclosures*. London: Protestant Electoral Union, 1866.

Allchin, A. M. *The Silent Rebellion: Anglican Religious Communities 1845-1900*. London: SCM, 1958.

Anson, Peter F. *The Call of the Cloister: Religious Communities and Kindred Bodies in the Anglican Communion*. London: SPCK, 1954.

Bailly, Louis. *Theologia Dogmatica et Moralis, ad Usum Seminariorum*. Lyon: Rusand, 1804.

Miss A. F. B. (Adela F. Barlow). *Convent Experiences*. London: Scott, 1875.

Bentley, James. *Ritualism and Politics in Victorian Britain: The Attempt to Legislate for Belief*. Oxford: Oxford University Press, 1987.

Bourne, G. *Lorette: History of Louise, Daughter of a Canadian Nun*. New York: Small, 1834.

C. B. (David Bryce), translator. *The Confessional Unmasked: Showing the Depravity of the Priesthood and Immorality of the Confessional, Being the Questions Put to Females in Confession*. London: Johnston, 1851.

Caracciolo, Henrietta. *Memoirs of Henrietta Caracciolo, of the Princes of Forino, Ex-Benedictine Nun*. London: Bentley, 1864.

Colley, Linda. *Britons: Forging the Nation 1707-1837*. New Haven: Yale University Press, 1992.

Cusack, Mary Frances. *Five Years in a Protestant Sisterhood and Ten Years in a Catholic Convent: An Autobiography*. London: Longman, Green, 1869.

Dammast, Jeanie Selina. *St. Mary's Convent; or, Chapters in the Life of a Nun*. London: Partridge, 1899.

Dens, P. *Tractatus Theologicus de Sacramento Poenitentiae*. Dublin: Barlow, 1812.

Dill, Augusta. *The Anglican Sister of Mercy*. London: Stock, 1895.

Goodman, Margaret. *Experiences of an English Sister of Mercy*. London: Smith, Elder, 1862.

———. *Sisterhoods in the Church of England; With Notices of Some Charitable Sisterhoods in the Romish Church*. London: Smith, Elder, 1863.

Hastings, Adrian. *History of English Catholicism 1920-1985*. London: Fount Paperbacks, 1987.

Hogan, William. *Popery! As It Was and As It Is. Also Auricular Confession; and Popish Nunneries*. Hartford, CT: Andrus, 1854.

Kollar, Rene. "Foreign and Catholic: A Plea to Protestant Parents on the Dangers of Convent Education in Victorian England." *History of Education* 31 (2002) 335-50.

———. "The Oxford Movement and the Heritage of Benedictine Monasticism." *The Downside Review* 101 (1983) 281-90.

Lea, Henry Charles. *A History of Auricular Confession and Indulgences in the Latin Church*. Vol. 1. New York: Greenwood, 1968.

Liguori, St. Alphonsus de. *The True Spouse of Jesus Christ*. Edited by Eugene Grimm. Brooklyn: Redemptorist Fathers, 1929.
Massey, Edward. *Love's Strife with the Convent*. Vol. 2. London: Ward & Lock, 1864.
Monk, Maria. *Awful Disclosures of the Hotel Dieu of Montreal*. Salem, NH: Ayer, 1977.
Myhill, Charlotte. *Three Years as a Nun*. London: Protestant Truth Society, n.d.
New Catholic Encyclopedia.
Newman, John Henry. *Historical Sketches*. Vol. 2. Westminster, MD: Christian Classics, 1970.
Norman, Edward. *The English Catholic Church in the Nineteenth Century*. Oxford: Oxford University Press, 1984.
O'Brien, Susan. "Religious Life for Women." In *From Without the Flaminian Gate. 150 Years of Roman Catholicism in England and Wales 1850–2000*, edited by V. Alan McClelland and Michael Hodgetts, 108–41. London: Darton, Longman & Todd, 1999.
Paz, D. G. *Popular Anti-Catholicism in Mid-Victorian England*. Stanford: Stanford University Press, 1992.
Pusey, E. B. *A Letter to the Right Reverend Richard*. New York: Charles Henry, 1839.
Reed, John Shelton. *Glorious Battle. The Cultural Politics of Victorian Anglo-Catholicism*. Nashville: Vanderbilt University Press, 1996.
Richardson, E. *Personal Experience of Roman Catholicism: With Incidents of Life*. London: Morgan & Chase, 1864.
Roscoe, T., editor. *Female Convents: Secrets of Nunneries Disclosed. Compiled from the Autograph Manuscripts of Scipio de Ricci, Roman Catholic Bishop of Pistoia and Prato. By Mr. De Potter.* New York: Appleton, 1834.
Seymour, M. Hobart. *The Confessional: An Appeal to the Primitive and Catholic Forms of Absolution in the East and in the West*. London: Seeley, Jackson & Halliday, 1870.
Sister Mary Agnes. *Nunnery Life in the Church of England; Or Seventeen Years with Father Ignatius*. London: Hodder & Stoughton, 1890.
Slattery, Mrs. Joseph (Sister Mary Elizabeth). *Convent Life Exposed*. Cliftondale, MA: Mrs. Slattery, 1892.
Sparry, C. translator. *Translations (with the Original Latin) from Dens' System of Moral Theology on the Nature of Confession, and the Obligation of the Seal*. New York: privately printed, 1848.
Tonna, Lewis H. J. *Nuns and Nunneries: Sketches Compiled Entirely from Romish Authorities*. London: Seeleys, 1852.
Viner, G. M., compiler. *Priests and Their Victims; or, Scenes in a Convent*. London: Elliot, 1850.
Wolffe, John. *The Protestant Crusade in Great Britain 1829–1860*. Oxford: Oxford University Press, 1991.
Wright, Julia McNair. *Priest and Nun*. Philadelphia: Crittenden & McKinney, 1869.
———. *Secrets of the Convent and Confessional: An Exhibition of the Influence and Workings of Papacy upon Society and Republican Institutions*. Cincinnati: National, 1874.

12

Power and Control over Women in Victorian England

Male Opposition to Sacramental Confession in the Anglican Church

VICTORIAN ENGLAND CLEARLY EMBRACED a patriarchy, and women, consequently, occupied certain clearly defined subordinate roles. Psychologically, this society argued, females were naive, fragile and emotionally weak creatures who could not exist independently of a husband or a father's wise guidance. Until 1882, for example, the property of a woman passed to the control of her husband upon marriage.[1] Law excluded women from the political life of the country, and although the Matrimonial Causes Act (1857) brought some equality in the area of marriage and divorce, the legislation was hardly satisfactory in the eyes of women. Although the industrialized society sent many into a cruel workforce, the idealized place for a female still remained the domestic realm. Here she could fulfill her proper vocation as mother and wife, and the male could likewise exercise his rightful control and authority over the women of the household. With the exception of raising children and overseeing the daily running of the household, men exercised power within the family. Religion, however, offered women some avenue of escape and empowerment, and the increasing popular-

---

1. Price, *English Society*, 219.

ity of Anglican sisterhoods offered some opportunities. According to Susan Mumm, "Religion could be, and sometimes was, an avenue for successful revolt against male authority and conventional morality."[2]

Although this opened the door to independence, only a few women felt called to live the life of a nun. Auricular confession, that is, revealing one's sins to a priest in private, had also received some support by some Anglicans, and this became a way of breaking away from masculine authority and asserting power over one's life, at least in matters of religion. Anglo-Catholics, that is, those Anglicans who recognized much worth and value in some Roman Catholic practices and devotions unfortunately abolished at the Reformation, saw the importance in auricular confession. The confessional especially attracted wives and daughters, and this threatened the domination of men. "A woman who made her confession could be seen—and could see herself—as engaged in an act of considerable daring," John Shelton Reed argues, and "to do this without the approval of one's husband or father was an act of rebellion."[3] Opposition to auricular confession based on Reformation theology, in particular the primacy of Scripture, had been the traditional approach to discredit this Roman Catholic practice, but during the nineteenth century critics began to emphasize another threat to society associated with the confessional, namely, the perceived assault on the male-dominated culture of Victorian England.

Women confessing their transgressions to a celibate priest not only challenged the Protestant teachings on salvation, but also weakened the authority of men and their position within the family structure. The practice of auricular confession encouraged a rival patriarchal system by encouraging women to seek advice from a cleric instead of a husband or father. Issues of power, therefore, troubled Victorian men more than theology. Michel Foucault's study of sexuality recognizes the important role which control played in the ritual of making a confession. Foucault points out that Western civilization has become a confessing civilization, and "sex was a privileged theme of confession."[4] This subject, not surprisingly, offended the sensitivity of Victorian men. Moreover, "The confession is a ritual of discourse in which the speaking subject is also the subject of the statement; it is also a ritual that unfolds within a power

2. Mumm, *Stolen Daughters*, x.
3. Reed, *Glorious Battle*, 200.
4. Foucault, *History of Sexuality*, 61.

relationship, for one does not confess without the presence (or virtual presence) of a partner who is not simply the interlocutor but the authority who requires the confession, prescribes and appreciates it, and intervenes in order to judge, punish, forgive, console, and reconcile . . ."[5] The confessor usurped this intimacy from the husband or father. The one who heard the secrets of the heart exercised power. Foucault believes that the priest "was not simply the forgiving master, the judge who condemned or acquitted; he was the master of truth."[6] The confessor, either Catholic or Anglican, thus became an intruder who could easily destroy the male-dominated family and who could quietly gain control over the conscience of a daughter or wife. The Council of Trent (1545–63) reaffirmed that confession was necessary for salvation in response to the Reformers who had disavowed this sacramental practice. In the nineteenth century, however, the Anglo-Catholics had reintroduced and encouraged auricular confession, and the confessional attracted pious women. Males must be warned of the dangers that this posed to their power and authority within the family.

Anglican priests, especially those who claimed to possess the sacramental authority "to loosen or to bind" sins, posed a challenge to the country's masculine ethos. Many "Victorian men treated their wives in a fashion they preferred to keep to themselves rather than have revealed to a clergyman,"[7] and the confessors who heard the secrets of married or domestic life became a powerful rival to the traditional head of the household. "In other words, confession never occurs outside of particular relationships marked by privilege and dependence, authority and vulnerability."[8] In her study of confession in Victorian culture, Susan David Bernstein clearly recognizes the importance of power and how men feared the encroachments of the confessional: "the father confessor is repeatedly construed as the interloper in would-be domestic affairs, the enemy of the father and the state who violates their precious possession of women."[9] The confessor, consequently, became "a counterforce to the power of the husbands and fathers in the home."[10] Because the

5. Ibid., 61–62.
6. Ibid., 67.
7. Bentley, *Ritualism and Politics*, 34.
8. Bernstein, *Confessional Subjects*, xi.
9. Ibid., 43.
10. Ibid., 47.

female told the priest things of a personal nature, some intimate, which she would not dare to share with her husband, the confessor became a powerful influence in her life and threatened the integrity of the family.[11] John Shelton Reed also describes women frequenting auricular confession in terms of an affront to patriarchal privilege. Reed believes that the confessional represented "an attempt to undermine the authority of husbands and fathers and to destroy the patriarchal structure of the Victorian family."[12] Many feared that the power within the domestic setting, and society in general, was shifting from the male family member to the priest in the confessional. And many took pen to paper to warn the men of this danger and urged them to protect their women from the snares of auricular confession.

Anthony Gavin, a former Roman Catholic priest, wrote an eighteenth-century critique of the church in Spain, and his book appeared in several editions during the nineteenth century. Gavin gave examples of the dialogue that took place between a priest and a woman and mentioned the case of a confessor who had used his position to seduce several female penitents. According to the former priest, confessors "are the occasion of the ruin of many families, of many thefts, debaucheries, murders, and divisions among several families."[13] Instead of the father of the household directing the future of his daughters, the confessor might usurp this prerogative. They might, for example, convince a young girl to enter a convent, and "therefore are the cause of many families being extinguished."[14] Gavin concluded his warnings about the schemes of the confessor by pointing out that "the confessors, priests, and friars are the fundamental original cause of almost all the misdoings and mischief that happen in families."[15] Since the 1830s auricular confession had become a popular option for women who found value and worth in Anglo-Catholicism, and no shortage of English prophets warned unsuspecting husbands and fathers of the dangers the confession.

The Rev. R. P. Blakeney, a Canon of York and a critic of Roman Catholicism, wrote two books about the dangers of Rome, and he warned

11. Yates, "Jesuits in Disguise," 209.

12. Reed, *Glorious Battle*, 12.

13. Gavin, *Great Red Dragon*, 70. Gavin's book was published in Dublin in 1724, and during the next year an English edition appeared.

14. Ibid., 72.

15. Ibid., 76.

Anglican men about the abuses associated with confession, a practice encouraged by the Anglo-Catholics. After a general condemnation of auricular confession—it had no basis in Sacred Scripture and it gave to the priest a prerogative reserved to God alone—Blakeney discussed how it undercut the male-dominated family. "We are opposed to the confessional," he argued in *Manual of Romish Controversy*, "on account of the power which it gives to the priesthood. They acquire a knowledge of all secrets and affairs, and exercise both an indirect and direct control," thus weakening the role of husband or father over the family.[16] Moreover, the intimate nature of a woman's confession might cause a problem for a celibate priest, and the author pointed out that "what an immense power such a system affords to a wicked man of carrying out his designs, without danger of detection."[17] In the following year, Blakeney wrote *Popery in Its Social Aspect*, and again condemned auricular confession in a section titled, "The Influence and Power of the Confessional." After repeating scriptural and theological objections, he addressed the unhealthy influence of the confessor, especially when women confided to him: "He listens to subjects which the wife would not mention to her husband—which the daughter would blush to repeat even to her mother."[18] When a female revealed her innermost secrets, especially those dealing with sexuality, she suffered psychologically, and the priest became more powerful because of this knowledge. Blakeney emphasized this aspect of domestic control. The priest became "as God in the confessional . . . [and] he is venerated as God's vicegerent, vested with powers of a superhuman kind."[19] The confessor, according to Blakeney, "pries into the marriage bed," regulates relations between spouses, controls the conduct between parents and children, and even influences the making of wills and the distribution of property.[20] Walter Walsh's scathing critique of ritualism within Anglicanism echoed the same fear. Walsh maintained that the secrecy of auricular confession bestowed upon the priest power over

---

16. Blakeney, *Manual of Romish Controversy*, 85. This book was first published in 1851. References taken from this later edition with no date of publication.

17. Ibid., 87.

18. Blakeney, *Popery in Its Social Aspect*, 170. This book was published in 1852 as a supplement to *Manual of Romish Controversy*. References are taken from this later edition with no date of publication.

19. Blakeney, *Popery in Its Social Aspect*, 174–75.

20. Ibid., 176.

the penitent, especially women: "The Confessional frequently interferes with the confidence which should exist between husband and wife."[21] Any confessor, therefore, could manipulate the confessional and challenge the authority of the husband or father.

Real life situations, however, also revealed the dangers of an authoritative and powerful confessor and the damage he could inflict on the family. At Leeds in 1850, a married woman and a candidate for confirmation complained that the curate at St Saviour's had questioned her about "any indecent connection" with her husband or other men before her marriage.[22] In 1858, another female made similar charges against a curate at Boyne Hill, and in the same year *Astounding Revelations of Puseyism in Belgravia* attacked the Anglo-Catholic practice of auricular confessional at St. Barnabas in Pimlico.[23] This pamphlet recounted the events of a public meeting, restricted only to men, where the audience heard the stories of four women and their experiences in the confessional, in particular the questioning of the women by the priest and his control over their spiritual lives. When the assembly heard these remarks, expressions of indignation, horror and shame could be heard. The last page of this short publication described the scene of an anti-confession meeting outside another London church which was punctuated with cries of "the dirty confessional," "taking poor women into dark rooms," and "aren't you ashamed to take your wives and daughters to such a place?"[24]

Left Home; or, Convent Life told a horrible tale about the dangers of the confessional. This account took place before a woman eventually entered a Roman Catholic convent. Referring to the priest confessor as a "rattlesnake" and the female penitent as a bird or weak animal, the author announced that "there are human reptiles in this world who possess the powers of fascination to such a degree, that they put into the shade the fabled properties of the serpents."[25] This person believed that the priest "held her soul and mind in bondage." The description of this

21. Walsh, *Secret History*, 81.

22. Yates, "Jesuits in Disguise," 211.

23. Baring, *Astounding Revelations of Puseyism*. Because of this meeting and pressure put on the Bishop of London, Archibald Campbell Tait, by the author, the license of the Rev. Poole was suspended.

24. Ibid., 16.

25. Anonymous, *Left Home*, 10

control over women in the confessional probably shocked those men ignorant of the dangers of auricular confession.

> The power of the priest over his female victims is of a most despotic kind. He can tutor them to either good or evil, just as he wills it. It is in vain for them to struggle to release themselves from the net that encompasses them. A master mind holds them in the worst of bondage . . . A blow was dealt to them [priests] in the Reformation, but of late years the advance of priesthood has been rapidly progressing, and there is no telling where it will stop, unless some more active measures are used to crush the hydraheaded monster.[26]

But this sort of domination and control over girls and women also existed in the Anglican Church. Men should take notice and protect their wives and daughters.

One of the most influential exposés of the confessional's threat to family ties and the authority of men came from a French historian, Jules Michelet (1798–1874). Michelet published his anti-clerical book, *Priests, Women, and Families* (*Du Pretre, de la Femme, et de la Famille*), in 1845, and in the same year it appeared in an English translation. In addition to attacks against the Jesuits, convents, and Catholic education, he described for his readers the evils of confession, especially its alleged antipathy towards the patriarchal family structure. "Anti-Catholic propaganda warns against father confessors who threaten to overthrow the rule of domestic fathers," Susan David Bernstein argues, and "this discourse also worries about how priestly power shores up female resistance within the family."[27] And Michelet believed that the confessional encouraged rebellion against the male-dominated family structure. In *Roads to Rome: The Antebellum Protestant Encounter with Catholicism*, Jenny Franchot offers a succinct interpretation on Michelet's critique of confession: "In the suffering and envy of his own perverse celibacy, the priest intrigues to rob the husband of control over his wife by gaining complete spiritual dominion over her."[28] Michelet wanted to warn male Britons, Catholic and Anglican, of the clerical plot to subvert their power and authority.

26. Ibid., 12.
27. Bernstein, *Confessional Subjects*, 54.
28. Franchot, *Roads to Rome*, 123.

"When I reflect on all that is contained in the words confession and direction, those simple words, that immense power, the most complete in the world," Michelet wrote, "and endeavour to analyse their whole meaning, I tremble with fear."[29] The priest gained power over a wife by knowledge of her secret and intimate thoughts that she could not even reveal to her husband. The confessor, therefore, effectively snatched authority from the male head of the household: "The priest has the soul fast, as soon as he has received the dangerous pledge of the first secrets, and he will hold it faster and faster. The two husbands now share, for there are two —one has the soul, the other the body."[30] Eventually the skillful confessor could gain total control of the wife. The priest confessor has one goal, according to Michelet, namely, "to sever this woman from her family, to weaken her kindred ties, and, particularly, to undermine the rival authority—I mean, the husband's."[31] Anglican men should be on guard to protect their women: "*The Confessor of a young woman may boldly be termed the jealous secret enemy of the husband*" (Michelet's emphasis). Moreover, the man who recognized this danger and fought against the evils of the confessional, in Michelet's opinion, was a "saint, a martyr, a man more than man." Auricular confession, he argued, destroyed family life and encouraged rebellion and disobedience to the husband or father. The author of *From the Curate to the Convent*, for example, gave an example of priestly control which sounded similar to Michelet's fear of mutiny within the family: on occasions a confessor was known to use his powerful influence to direct young girls away from marriage, the proper vocation for a woman, to life in a convent.[32] Jules Michelet's book found an eager audience in anti-Catholic circles in England and touched a sensitive nerve among Anglicans who saw their women beginning to frequent the confessional in Anglo-Catholic churches.[33] The current view of weak, impressionable, and vulnerable women certainly contributed to this fear of domination by a confessor.

29. Michelet, *Priests, Women, and Families*, 115.

30. Ibid., 116.

31. Ibid., 117.

32. A Churchman, *From the Curate to the Convent*, 408.

33. By 1861, eight editions of Michelet's book had appeared, with several in English. Anti-Catholic works also printed extracts of his book. For example, see Murphy, *Popery in Ireland*.

"Certain aspects of Anglo-Catholicism had a special appeal for women,"[34] John Shelton Reed points out, and some critics saw this as a result of their weak and sentimental nature. Unlike men, the romantic liturgy and medieval practices of Anglo-Catholic churches could easily mesmerize females and draw them away from the stark worship of some Anglican churches. Moreover, a number of critics argued that the Anglo-Catholic priest filled the role of a caring and nurturing father figure and offered an alternative to the bored, alienated, or misunderstood wife or daughter. *Philip Paternoster: A Tractarian Love Story* (1858), a critique of Anglo-Catholicism and auricular confession, recognized the power which Tractarian priests exerted over women, whom the author described as "so soft, so pliable, so easily influenced for good, so unsuspecting of evil."[35] "It will be a fatal day for England," the author stated, "if ever England's wives and daughters were led to deem the confessional a more sacred place than home, the approval or the objection of the priest more eligible or more formidable than those of husband or father."

H. J. Brockman took a different approach in *Letter to the Women of England*. He challenged the women, and reminded them of their fragile and frail character. The "person who first confessed was a woman—Eve! That the being to whom she confessed, was that old serpent, the devil."[36] Both the Catholic and Anglican confessors, he pointed out, continue to follow the example of the seducing devil "to bring the female mind more particularly beneath their deadly and mysterious control."[37] Speaking directly to his women readers, Brockman reminded them that "Had your mother Eve been content to maintain that sweet communion with her Maker and her husband which alone was legitimate and safe, and rebuked in befitting terms the wily tempter who usurped their place, she had not fallen nor her posterity." Others used this association with sinful Eve to attack confession. *Women and Priests*, for example, pointed out that she "brought moral and physical ruin into the world by her weak concession to the enemy of God and man," and by giving into the "devices of the priest," such as confession, this "silly" female "darkens

---

34. Reed, *Glorious Battle*, 187.
35. Davis, *Philip Paternoster*, 2:65.
36. Brockman, *Letter to the Women of England*, 1.
37. Ibid., 2.

and degrades her own soul, and . . . shuts out Christ and heaven from her family circle."[38]

Women, moreover, did not possess the moral or mental wiles to resist the temptations of a father confessor, and this emerged as a theme in a series of cautions to the men of nineteenth-century England. The cunning of a confessor of questionable character might be too much for a female penitent to resist.[39] The "sensitive delicacy of her nature . . . and [the] feminine modesty and womanly reserve are annihilated in the presence of a priest,"[40] and some types of women, known as *femme dévote*, did not have the strength of character to resist the emotional attractions of religion and go to confession on a monthly basis.[41] Speaking directly to Anglicans and alerting them to the dangers of the confessional, another concerned male, Arthur Dadson, reminded husbands and fathers of the weak and gullible nature of women: "there is a great and irresistible fascination in the dim religious light which casts its soft mellow rays upon the rich decorations of the altar and the symbols of worship, which everywhere meet the eye, in these sensual image houses of Rome."[42] He described these females attracted to the confessional as "vain and silly" and argued that their veneration of auricular confession was "surely undermining the morals and breaking down the healthy tone of mind of future mothers of England."

An anonymous pamphlet with a catchy title, *Scandalous Revelations. The Confessional: An Exposure of its Mysteries and Iniquities as Practised in Foreign and English Convents by Priests and their Victims*, also mocked the Catholic doctrine of confession and disclosed some examples of seduction at the hands of the confessor, and it also pointed out the harmful authority the confessor exercised over women who sought priestly absolution. "In making the priesthood acquainted with the secrets of the people," the author maintained, "it has magnified their power, it has made them strong and the people weak, it has made the priesthood threatening and tyrannical lords, and the people fearful and trembling

---

38. Anonymous, *Women and Priests*, 3. Unlike other critiques of auricular confession, this short pamphlet also noted that the young, unmarried confessor might yield to the temptations of a woman.

39. Armstrong, *Confessional*, 7.

40. Seymour, *Confessional*, 182.

41. "*La Femme Dévote*," reprinted from *Church Review*, 26 August 1876.

42. Dadson, *High-Church Confessional*, 10.

slaves."[43] If these words did not offend, the picture on the cover of this publication certainly shocked people: it depicted a semi-nude woman being tortured in a dungeon while hooded monks looked on in approval. It was an American author and a convert from Catholicism, however, who in 1890 captured the fear and apprehension that many felt toward auricular confession and its disruptiveness of family life and the authority of the husband. The confessor "stands between him and his wife in their most sacred relations," and moreover the confessional is an "insult to pure wifehood and motherhood."[44]

How did this father confessor come to manipulate the female in the confessional and by what means did he exercise such a powerful influence that frightened many Victorian males? An exalted view of his priesthood and sacramental powers and a fascination on the part of women with a religious figure who would freely listen to her problems and then offer consolation certainly appealed to some women, but also offended many who feared that the confessor had become a rival to the authority of men and a threat to the family life. But the real source of power and control was the nature of the sensitive and probing questions that the woman had to answer to receive priestly absolution. For some time, Roman Catholic priests had been provided with manuals of moral theology to aid them in the confessional, and some sections contained questions dealing with sexuality and the intimate relations between the husband and wife. When English translations of these passages appeared in the early nineteenth century, anti-Catholic writers quickly responded. The interrogations carried on by the priest in the secrecy of the confessional indicated the danger of another papal plot to undermine the Protestant character of England. Moreover, the confessional symbolized "a gross intrusion of privacy," and some forcefully argued "that the authority of husbands and fathers should not be intruded upon by priests."[45] With the rise of Anglo-Catholicism and the popularity of auricular confession, some Anglican priests began to adopt these Catholic texts, but the outrage grew louder when it was discovered that some Anglicans began to produce their own guidelines for confession.

Manuals of moral theology attempted to educate Roman Catholic priests in the techniques of the confessional. Books by St. Alphonsus

---

43. Anonymous, *Scandalous Revelations*, 4.
44. Shepherd, *Confessional Unveiled*, 22.
45. Wolffe, *Protestant Crusade in Great Britain*, 123.

de Liguori, Pierre Dens, Louis Bailly, Jean Pierre Gury, Johann Reuter, and Jean Joseph Gaume were some of the numerous aids which sought to help the confessor in his questioning of penitents to ensure that they made a full and complete confession. When extracts from Dens and Bailly appeared in English translations, those queries dealing with nocturnal emissions, birth control, sexual temptations, and the intimate relations between spouses shocked many: Catholic women had to suffer such embarrassment and shame in order to have their sins forgiven. But when a number of Anglican clergy began to produce their own books, although fashioned largely on Catholic works, the threat to church and family became real. Edward Pusey (1800–82), a leading theologian of the Oxford Movement, acknowledged the reality of sin and recognized the power of the church to absolve.[46] Pusey preached on the importance of auricular confession, gave advice on the proper preparation needed, and published his own manual based on Gaume for Anglican priests, *Advice for Those Who Exercise the Ministry of Reconciliation through Confession and Absolution*.[47] His influence was great among ritualist priests, but another book for Anglican confessors, *The Priest in Absolution*, brought the dangers of confession and its challenge to family life to the public forum.

The Society of the Holy Cross, originally a secret society that wanted to encourage a sense of friendship between ritualist clergy, produced and circulated *The Priest in Absolution* as a guide for use in confession.[48] The publication of this book grew out of an apparent need for assistance. In "1862 a number of well-known confessors, including Pusey, were consulted about drawing up such a manual, and a special committee was set up to oversee this,"[49] and the Rev. J. C. Chambers set about to compile this manual for the Society of the Holy Cross. Two Catholic works of moral theology written by Reuter and Gaume provided the basis for Chambers's manual for Anglican confessors. The completed work appeared in two sections, the first in 1866 and the second in 1870,

---

46. See Liddon, *Life of Edward Bouverie Pusey*, III.

47. See Buckland, *Confessional in the English Church*, 5–13. Gaume's book was published in 1837. It contained extracts from Roman Catholic theologians such as Francis de Sales, Charles Borromeo, and Philip Neri. Reynolds, *Martyr of Ritualism*, 215.

48. Yates, *Anglical Ritualism*, 71. For a history of the Society of the Holy Cross, see Embry, *Catholic Movement and the Society of the Holy Cross*. Pages 97–127 discuss the question of auricular confession and the support this practice received by members of the society.

49. Yates, "Jesuits in Disguise," 211.

and this privately printed book was intended only for the eyes of Anglo-Catholic priests. When Chambers died in 1874, the Society of the Holy Cross purchased the copyright and the remaining copies of the work. Throughout its early history this book belonged to the secret world of the Society of the Holy Cross, which guarded its contents. In fact, Walter Walsh noted in *The Secret History of the Oxford Movement*, "The publication of the first half of the *Priest in Absolution* [sic] did not create any public excitement. Its unhappy birth appears to have been unnoticed by Protestant Churchmen."[50] On 14 June 1877, however, Lord Redesdale in the House of Lords quoted lengthy sections from the book, which had come into his possession.[51] Not only did the nature of questions that the priest put to females in the secrecy of the confessional shock the members of parliament, but they also stunned the sensitivities of Victorian society. Here was concrete proof that auricular confession might destroy the family bond and transfer masculine authority and power away from husband and father to a celibate cleric. But on the other hand, this book also emphasized a familiar nineteenth-century theme: the vocation of a submissive and obedient wife.

There was no reason why the first part of *The Priest in Absolution* should attract much public attention except for the fact that it supported the practice of auricular confession.[52] In the section titled "Hints for the Priest in Hearing Confession," the priest was characterized as a spiritual father, a spiritual physician, a theologian, a judge, and it emphasized the importance of questions. In the first place, the neophyte confessor should consult with an experienced priest about the techniques of questioning the individual about sins. "When the Priest has learnt how to put questions discreetly, how to absolve without error, and how to retain sins without loss to the penitent, provided he has the charity of a father, he need not think of relinquishing this ministry."[53] Another topic, "Hints for the Priest while a Confession Is Being Made," offered some practical but general suggestions, for example, the priest should encourage the

50. Walsh, *Secret History*, 94.

51. According to Reynolds, a Protestant layman, Robert Fleming, had received a copy of *The Priest in Absolution* from a prominent clergyman in the Anglican Church on the condition that he would not misuse it. Probably after consultation with members of the Church Association, he gave the book to the Earl of Redesdale in the summer of 1877. Reynolds, *Martyr of Ritualism*, 215.

52. Chambers, comp., *Priest in Absolution*.

53. Ibid., 14.

person making the confession "not to be ashamed to speak the truth for his soul's sake, and permit him first to set forth the result of his self examination."[54] The priest should take into consideration the age, sex, and occupation of the person making the confession, and should approach issues dealing with chastity with caution. This directive told the confessor not to question "married persons about conjugal duty, unless he has reason to think that they have sinned in excess: and in this case he may inquire whether they be unanimous, whether the husband is faithful to the wife, the wife obedient to her husband."[55] The remaining pages of this volume gave advice on admonishing the penitent, recognizing the contrition of the person, the kinds of penance which the priest should impose, the form of absolution, and ways to encourage the individual to avoid sin. With the exception of the section on sex, which was general and not too offensive since it noted the necessity of a wife's obedience to the husband, this book did not cause much of a stir. Part II, however, created a fire storm.

This book, printed four years after the first, explained the questions which the scrupulous Anglican confessor should ask the person seeking absolution for sins.[56] It discussed the so-called seven deadly sins (pride, covetousness, lust, envy, gluttony and drunkenness, anger, and sloth), general guidelines for the confessor to observe, and suggestions the priest should follow when healing the confession of different types of people, including family members, different professions, and individuals with certain physical or mental disabilities or personality problems. This section addressed the failings of men in particular. Transgressions against chastity were presented as psychological problems: "Impurity is what may be termed disorder and irregular pleasures of the senses, such as produces vehement perturbation of bodily functions."[57] A footnote, however, warned the confessor and urged caution when "entering into this subject of spiritual pathology." Yet it pointed out that "persons should be warned that it is highly dangerous to indulge in such delectations [embraces, physical contact, kissing], since in corrupt human nature there is always reason to fear consent to impure feelings."[58] Concerning impure

54. Ibid., 20.
55. Ibid., 24.
56. Chambers, comp., *Priest in Absolution*, Part II.
57. Ibid., 21.
58. Ibid., 23.

or indecent thoughts, this manual suggested that the penitent explain this subject and its nature, and if one confesses "sins of look" the priest should further explore the reasons behind the roving eyes. If the person admitted "impure sensations or pollution," the confessor was urged to probe the causes. In the case of "nocturnal pollutions," the priest should ask if the man did anything "to excite or cause them proximately or remotely, and whether on waking he wholly consented to them."[59] Prayer and mortification were the recommended remedies for these spiritual illnesses.

Issues surrounding female sexuality, however, angered critics who feared for the well-being of women because of the confessional. *The Priest in Absolution* clearly recognized the dangers of a vulnerable woman confessing to an Anglican cleric and warned the priest not to become too familiar with these penitents. Tactility, small talk, the receiving of small gifts were inappropriate. The advice that the book gave to the priest when questioning the "ill-instructed," that is, a man or woman who had little or no knowledge of the Christian faith could, and did, catch the attention of people. This chapter discussed each commandment in detail, and for the seventh (the sixth in the Roman Catholic tradition) it directed the confessor to ask the person about thoughts, words and deeds associated with purity. Questions dealing with one's deeds or actions probably shocked the Anglican reader who had no knowledge or experience of auricular confession: who was involved, was the act consummated or not, and the circumstances surrounding masturbation or "immodest touch." But the priest was told to be especially sensitive questioning wives when asking in particular "if they have rendered due benevolence [conjugal rights], and that only in the most modest way he can, and not to inquire further, unless he be asked questions himself."[60] This portion of *The Priest in Absolution* concluded with a litany of sins "contrary to purity" such as looking at naughty pictures, unnecessary familiarity with members of the opposite sex, indecent dress, keeping dangerous company, adultery, incest and birth control. This book stressed the apparent weak and inferior nature of women, a stereotype encouraged by Victorian men, but it was the asking of questions by the priest and the nature of these queries that outraged the opponents of the confessional.

Advice for women seeking absolution came under the heading, "How to Deal with Different Classes." The confessor again must be very

59. Ibid., 29.
60. Ibid., 115–16.

cautious: "He must avoid steadfast gaze, soft words and tones. He must not trust too much in their tears and complaints, but bid them pray for patience."[61] If the critic of auricular confession expected some manipulation on the part of the confessor, he was probably surprised by the rhetoric that mirrored the patriarchal atmosphere of nineteenth-century England which saw women as immature creatures. Suggestions included paying special attention to: "the special faults of women—such as fed vanity and pride by spending too much time at their toilette, making themselves conspicuous, aiming at being admired, and showing jealousy when others are admired; dressing to excess and exhibiting more of their person than is decent, wasting time in visits and gossip, neglecting Divine Service and preferring late Celebrations to early Communions." Women, moreover, should dress according to their age or position in society, and not "out of vanity or desire to assume the appearance of beauty . . . [and] it should not cause family difficulties through its expensiveness, nor sin in others by its immodesty." After the betrothal has been announced, "great care is demanded of the parties to avoid everything contrary to modesty and unbecoming. They should not be too familiar with each other . . .[and] everything should be avoided which tends to disturb the passions, and excite bodily emotions."[62] And future husbands would be glad to hear a final admonition: "The wife should obey in all things lawful . . . yield to her husband when angry, counsel him gently when doing wrong." The man, however, must treat his wife as a partner.

The duties of married people probably appeared straightforward and balanced to a Victorian husband. "The wife sins by arrogating too much authority—and the husband by treating her as a slave and not as a partner."[63] The wife was not required "to render due benevolence" at all times, for example, "if her husband be afflicted with [a] contagious disease . . . nor if she herself were ill in such a way as to be likely to suffer . . . nor if she cannot have any but stillborn children . . . nor if her husband be mad or drunk or brutal."[64] Any form of birth control was sinful, and moderation should govern sexual activity. *The Priest in Absolution*, regardless of the concerns of fathers and husbands that auricular confession might rob them of their power and authority over

---

61. Ibid., 152–53.
62. Ibid., 154.
63. Ibid., 159.
64. Ibid., 159–60.

their daughters and wives, also stressed a patriarchal relationship. "When a wife complains," for example, "the Priest should be willing to believe that she has not much reason on her side . . . [since] a woman's tongue is often the cause of domestic strife and unhappiness, and should therefore be restrained."[65] A wife should at all costs practice patience. "When her husband is in a passion, or overcome by drink, she should be silent, or at least give a soft answer, and behave as if she had been in the wrong . . ." This book or manual gave some practical suggestions to those Anglican clerics who heard confessions, and it offered some guidelines when the person entering the confessional was a woman. Some Anglicans believed that auricular confession represented a sad betrayal of the Reformation, but what did the Earl of Redesdale find so reprehensible in *The Priest in Absolution* that he attacked it in the House of Lords?

On 14 June 1877, the Earl of Redesdale, described in the biography of Archbishop Archibald Campbell Tait as "a sober and trusted High Church man of the earlier sort, and a prominent figure for more than 30 years as Chairman of Committees in the House of Lords,"[66] spoke in the House of Lords. A man known for his "shrewd insight and vigorous common sense," Redesdale questioned the propriety of *The Priest in Absolution*, especially Part II, which dealt with the sensitive questions a priest might ask during confession, and this became the important element of his critique. He began by informing the members of the House that the Society of the Holy Cross had produced this book "for private and limited circulation among the clergy."[67] Anyone interested in the welfare of the Church of England, he observed, should know about the contents of this book. After pointing out that many outstanding clerics were members of the Society of the Holy Cross, Redesdale maintained that one should view this book with suspicious eyes because the compiler (Chambers) clearly noted in the preface that it should be restricted only to those clergy who needed a manual to aid them in the confessional. He cited an example of a cleric who requested a copy, but was refused until he could provide the names of some priests who could vouch for his character and theological views. Redesdale then made several references to *The Priest in Absolution*. The first effectively captured the spirit and purpose of the book: only auricular confession and absolution

65. Ibid., 164.
66. Davidson and Benham, *Life of Archibald Campbell Tait*, vol. 2, 171.
67. *Hansard Parliamentary Debates*, 3rd series, vol. 234 (1877) cols. 1741–45.

could heal spiritual sicknesses, and this could be accomplished only by a trained confessor examining the penitent.

After drawing attention to the book's remarks on the necessity of questions, the examination of children ("Children may be asked with whom they sleep; if they have played with their bed fellows; touched each other designedly or unbecomingly"), the importance of the Blessed Virgin Mary as a mediator, and another dubious book, the *Priest's Prayer Book*, the Earl of Redesdale described the dangers of auricular confession in respect to family life, and suggested that the questions of the confessor might "bring about [rather] than avoid the evils to which they relate." The most shocking example from *The Priest in Absolution* concerned the questions dealing with "due benevolence" owed by the wife to the husband. According to this book, Redesdale told his audience, "Wives often by refusing [conjugal duties] . . . are damned, and cause the damnation of their husbands by driving them to thousands of iniquities." Even though this book reinforced the ideal of a submissive woman, Redesdale argued that questions of this type were not only insensitive, but also might lead to inappropriate actions on the part of the confessor. Consequently, he pointed out, *The Priest in Absolution* advised that the confessor should avoid words which sprung "from tenderness." Redesdale did not omit the veiled threats to the authority of the husband or father. The confessor assumed the role of a judge who represented God on earth, and he noted the consequence: the priest "assumes to himself perfect infallibility of decision in respect of persons who come to him to receive absolution." The Earl of Redesdale ended his speech by stating that "the time has arrived when there should be a decided condemnation of practices such as those indicated in the volumes from which I have quoted these extracts." These words, naturally, brought an immediate response from the Archbishop of Canterbury, Archibald Campbell Tait.

Tait, who became the Archbishop of Canterbury in 1868, thanked Redesdale for undertaking "a most disagreeable and painful task" in bringing "this very serious and important matter" to the attention of the House of Lords,[68] and he expressed a sense of pain and concern with the purpose and the tenor of *The Priest in Absolution*. It offended modesty and it was "a disgrace to the community that such a book should be circulated under the authority of clergymen [Society of the Holy Cross] of the Established Church." The Archbishop then reminded the House

68. Ibid., cols. 1745–48.

that in 1873 the Bishops of Convocation, the Upper House, drew up a statement in response to a petition that sought a change in the Book of Common Prayer, namely, the licensing of properly trained clerics to become confessors. The Archbishop described what the Convocation stated: penance was not a sacrament of the Anglican Church; forgiveness of sin comes through Jesus alone; and although the church made provisions in two cases—for those with troubled consciences who wanted to receive Holy Communion and for the Visitation of the Sick—the Bishops firmly rejected the concept of confession favored by Anglo-Catholic priests. And the Archbishop of Canterbury quoted this denunciation for the House of Lords:

> This special provision [Visitation of the Sick], however, does not authorize the ministers of the Church to require, from any who may resort to them to open their grief, a particular or detailed enumeration of all their sins, or to require private confession previous to receiving Holy Communion, or to enjoin or even encourage any practice of habitual confession to a priest, or to teach that such practice of habitual confession, or the being subject to what has been termed the direction of a priest, is a condition of attaining to the highest spiritual life.

Tait, however, had additional concerns about the current practice of auricular confession within the Anglican Church.

Tait viewed confession as "prying into the secret thoughts or hearts of those" people who sought absolution, and recognized the probing and the questioning on the part of the priest as a dangerous practice. The confessor could become a powerful and controlling figure, and auricular confession could produce "evil results" for families. Here Archbishop Tait reflected the male-dominated view of nineteenth century domestic life, and he ended his remarks on this point. "I cannot imagine that any right-minded man could wish to have such questions addressed to any member of his family," he argued, "and if he had any reason to suppose that any member of his family had been exposed to such an examination, I am sure it would be the duty of any father to remonstrate with the clergyman who had put the questions, and warn him never to approach his house again." The Archbishop of Canterbury's words carried much weight in the House of Lords, and others, such as the Bishop of Gloucester and Bristol (Charles John Ellicott), Lord Oranmore and Browne, and the Earl of Harrowby also expressed shock and disgust at the practice of auricular confession and the manner of questioning penitents as championed by *The Priest in Absolution*. The last words belonged to the Earl of Harrowby, and he spoke to the concerns of numerous husbands and fathers: "no steps could be too strong for stopping this pestilence which threatened to invade the sanctity of our homes and to destroy the character of our people." No member of the House of Lords attempted to defend this book or the Society of the Holy Cross.

The Earl of Redesdale's speech generated great public interest in the shortcomings and dangers of auricular confession and the questionable role of the confessor as a spiritual inquisitor. A number of publications printed sections of his speech and the extracts from *The Priest in Absolution* that dealt with issues of sex and impurity.[69] *The Times* informed the public about the sensitive and shocking nature of the questions contained in this book by printing the proceedings which took place in the House of Lords.[70] Commenting on Redesdale's exposure of the contents of *The Priest in Absolution*, the same edition of the newspaper called some of its passages "prurient," and demanded that the ecclesiastical authorities should take notice of the offending nature of the book and take the appropriate action.[71] And articles dealing with confession, some favorable, appeared throughout the summer in *The Times*.[72] On 30 June, *Punch* printed an illustration, titled "A Wolf in Sheep's Clothing," which showed John Bull protecting a woman (represented by Britannia) from a sinister looking cleric armed with a copy of *The Priest in Absolution* in his hands and identified as a member of the Society of the Holy Cross. John Bull addressed England's female population: "Whenever you see any of these sneaking scoundrels about, ma'am, just send for me. I'll deal with 'em, never fear!!"[73]

The official Anglican response to the revelations contained in *The Priest in Absolution* and the hostile reaction to auricular confession came from Convocation, which was scheduled to meet on 3 July. The Upper House of Bishops had already adopted a negative report on auricular confession in 1873, and sent this document to the Lower House

---

69. Ellsworth, *Charles Lowder*, 139.

70. *The Times*, 15 June 1877.

71. Ibid.

72. See, for example, *The Times*, 16 August 1877; 29 August 1877; and 31 August 1877.

73. Printed in Bentley, *Ritualism and Politics*, 32.

of Clergy, which accepted this declaration with only a minor change, before the episcopal speeches started. On 6 July, Tait critiqued confession, which he argued represented "a system altogether alien from the Church of England . . . [and] entirely alien from the spirit and teaching of the whole body of the divines of the Church of England from first to last."[74] *The Priest in Absolution* should not be viewed out of context; it was part of a dangerous movement within the Anglican Church to promote the apparent benefits of the confessional. Archbishop Tait then used evocative and emotional words to condemn auricular confession. He recognized the goodness in many of the priests who encouraged auricular confession, "but no admiration of any points in their character ought, I think, to make us hesitate as to whatever may appear to be our duty in the endeavour to counteract what I feel obliged to call a conspiracy within our own body, against the discipline, and the practice of our Reformed Church."[75] Other Bishops spoke out against confession, and the Upper House voted almost unanimously to adopt a resolution that held the Society of the Holy Cross responsible for the production and distribution of *The Priest in Absolution* and another which expressed a "strong condemnation of any doctrine or practice of Confession which can be thought to render such a book necessary or expedient."[76] This theological repudiation of auricular confession strengthened the earlier criticisms that this practice helped to weaken and fragment the family by replacing the father or husband with a confessor who might ask the penitent sensitive or uncomfortable questions. Auricular confession, therefore, posed a distinct threat to both the spiritual fabric and the domestic life of the English nation, even though it reinforced the popular deferential and submissive view of Victorian women.

The outrage caused by the Earl of Redesdale's revelations in the House of Lords marked a high point in the outcry against alleged abuses associated with auricular confession, especially the perceived threat to Victorian patriarchy. Theology and the fears of men combined to attack this harmful practice. The aftermath of Redesdale's speech, however, also had consequences for the history of the confessional in Victorian England. A number of priests began to shy away from becoming confessors, and those Anglican priests who continued to encourage this

---

74. Quoted in Davidson and Benham, *Life of Archibald Campbell Tait*, 176.
75. Quoted in ibid., 178.
76. Quoted in ibid., 178.

practice became more skilled in the techniques of asking the necessary questions, especially those dealing with sexuality and family life, and thus they tried to avoid the earlier mistakes of the inexperienced and enthusiastic colleagues. The Society of the Holy Cross suffered; about a third of its members resigned.[77] But, according to Nigel Yates, the membership of this fellowship slowly began to grow and "the number of regular penitents continued to grow, though slowly."[78] The suspicions of concerned men about the destructive nature of the confessional and the harm it might do to the Victorian family and the patriarchal nature of society also died down. Perhaps the public protests, the embarrassment caused by the types of questions asked by the priests, and the strong voice of the Bishops weakened the alleged spiritual benefits associated with auricular confession, and this probably assuaged the masculine fear that the confessional posed a real and substantial threat to their power and authority over women in matters of religion and family.

77. Yates, "Jesuits in Disguise," 203.
78. Ibid., 215.

Bibliography

Anonymous. *Left Home, or, Convent Life*. London: Farrah, 1865.
Anonymous. *Scandalous Revelations. The Confession: An Exposure of Its Mysteries and Iniquities as Practised in Foreign and English Convents by Priests and Their Victims.* London: Elliot, 1873.
Anonymous. *Women and Priests*. London: Haughton, 1878.
Armstrong, John. *The Confessional: Its Wickedness. A Lecture*. Brighton: Verrall, 1856.
Baring, F. *Astounding Revelations of Puseyism in Belgravia, Containing the Most Frightful Disclosures of Diabolical Plots against Female Chastity by the Rev. Mr. Poole and Miss Joy, at the Fashionable Church of St. Barnabas, Pimlico*. London: Hatswell, 1858.
Bentley, James. *Ritualism and Politics in Victorian Britain: The Attempt to Legislate for Belief*. Oxford: Oxford University Press, 1978.
Bernstein, Susan David. *Confessional Subjects: Revelations of Gender and Power in Victorian Literature and Culture*. Chapel Hill: University of North Carolina Press, 1997.
Blakeney, R. P. *Manual of Romish Controversy: Being a Complete Refutation of the Creed of Pope Pius IV*. Edinburgh: The Hope Trust, n.d. (orig. ed., 1851).
———. *Popery in Its Social Aspect: Being a Complete Exposure of the Immorality and Intolerance of Romanism*. Toronto: Gospel Witness, n.d.
Brockman, H. J. *Letter to the Women of England, on the Confessional*. London: Protestant Electoral Union, 1867.
Buckland, A. R. *The Confessional in the English Church*. London: Nisbet, 1901.
Chambers, J. C., compiler. *The Priest in Absolution: A Manual for Such as Are Called into the Higher Ministries in the English Church*. 2nd ed. London: Masters, 1869.
———, compiler. *The Priest in Absolution: A Manual for Such as Are Called into the Higher Ministries in the English Church*. Part 2. Privately printed for the use of the clergy, 1870.
A Churchman. *From the Curate to the Convent: A Narrative Belonging to the Latter Half of the Nineteenth Century*. London: Haughton, 1877.
Dadson, A. *The High-Church Confessional: An Exposé*. London: Wilkes, 1880.
Davidson, Randall Thomas, and William Benham. *Life of Archibald Campbell Tait Archbishop of Canterbury*. Vol. 2. London: Macmillan, 1891.
Davis, Charles Maurice. *Philip Paternoster: A Tractarian Love Story*. 2 vols. London: Richard Bentley, 1858.
Ellsworth, L. E. *Charles Lowder and the Ritualist Movement*. London: Darton, Longman and Todd, 1982.
Embrey, J. *The Catholic Movement and the Society of the Holy Cross*. London: Faith Press, 1931.
Foucault, Michel. *The History of Sexuality*. Vol. 1, *An Introduction*. Translated by Robert Hurley. New York: Vintage, 1990.
Franchot, Jenny. *Roads to Rome: The Antebellum Protestant Encounter with Catholicism*. Berkeley: University of California Press, 1994.
Gavin, Anthony. *The Great Red Dragon; or the Master-Key to Popery*. New York: Jones, 1854.
Liddon, H. P. *Life of Edward Bouverie Pusey*. 4 vols. London: Longmans, 1894.
Michelet, J. *Priests, Women, and Families*. London: Protestant Evangelical Mission, 1874.
Mumm, Susan. *Stolen Daughters, Virgin Mothers: Anglican Sisterhoods in Victorian England*. Leicester: Leicester University Press, 1999.

Murphy, Patrick. *Popery in Ireland; or Confessionals, Abductions, Nunneries, Fenians, and Orangemen*. London: Jarrold, 1866.
Price, Richard. *English Society 1680–1880*. Cambridge: Cambridge University Press, 1999.
Reed, John Shelton. *Glorious Battle: The Cultural Politics of Victorian Anglo-Catholicism*. Nashville: Vanderbilt University Press, 1996.
Reynolds, Michael. *Martyr of Ritualism: Father Mackonochie of St. Alban's, Holborn*. London: Faber & Faber, 1965.
Seymour, M. Hobart. *The Confessional: An Appeal to the Primitive and Catholic Forms of Absolution, in the East and in the West*. London: Seeley, Jackson & Halliday, 1870.
Shepherd, Margaret. *The Confessional Unveiled*. Boston: British-American Citizen, 1890.
Walsh, Walter. *The Secret History of the Oxford Movement*. London: Thynne, 1898.
Wolffe, John. *The Protestant Crusade in Great Britain 1829–1860*. Oxford: Oxford University Press, 1991.
Yates, Nigel. *Anglican Ritualism in Victorian Britain 1830–1910*. Oxford: Oxford University Press, 1999.
———. "'Jesuits in Disguise'? Ritualist Confessors and Their Critics in the 1870s." *Journal of Ecclesiastical History* 39 (1988) 202–16.

13

An Anglican Sisterhood and Auricular Confession

A Popish Practice in a Devonport Sisterhood

ON JUNE 30, 2002, *The New York Times* printed a shocking story introduced by the headline, "Woman Secretly Taped While Confiding in Her Priest Sues Him Alleging Malpractice."[1] According to the newspaper, the former governor of Mississippi discovered that his wife was having an affair, and he convinced their priest to tape record a meeting between himself and the adulterous woman. After the divorce, the husband used her admission of guilt in a custody dispute. The wife eventually sued the priest for this breach of confidentiality and brought charges of clergy malpractice against him. According to the article, "Legal experts said that claims of clergy malpractice had uniformly failed, though more general claims against members of the clergy and their churches for breaches of special relationships of trust occasionally succeeded." Charges of impropriety associated with the confessional occur frequently, but in the anti-Roman Catholic climate of Victorian England the alleged abuse of auricular confession supplied the fuel for opponents of both Roman Catholicism and the form of Anglicanism that adopted this practice.

The veil of secrecy and the intimate conversations between priest and penitent, it was claimed, contradicted the work of the reformers, who had declared that a sinful person should approach God alone.

1. *The New York Times*, June 30, 2002, sec I, 14.

Just as in the disgraceful incident reported in *The New York Times*, the purported harm against women and the abuse of power at the hands of a confessor caught the indignation of the English public and occasioned attacks against what was seen as an insidious popish practice. For nineteenth-century male culture in England, fragile and naive women must be protected from celibate clergymen who heard their most secret thoughts and desires and who might exercise control over their marriage and household.

Another Victorian institution that some believed corrupted females was Anglican sisterhoods. Tyrannical superiors, Romish practices and devotions, and loss of liberty, which robbed women of their rights and corrupted their Protestantism, ensured that religious zealots would campaign against sisterhoods. Whenever an Anglican convent encouraged confession for its members, the outcry was deafening. In 1848 Priscilla Lydia Sellon (1821–1876) responded to a request from the bishop of Exeter, Henry Phillpotts, to work among the poor and outcasts of Devonport, near Plymouth. A small sisterhood soon developed, and critics complained that this group of women had strayed from the wide guidelines of The Book of Common Prayer. Sellon's encouragement of auricular confession, moreover, especially rankled loyal Protestants who had grown up in an environment of hostility to individual, private confession.

Prior to the sixteenth century, confession to a priest was an accepted practice, but the reformers, including the English, abolished it on the grounds that it had no basis in scripture. A sinful and sorrowful individual should approach God directly to seek forgiveness instead of approaching a man who might be spiritually immature, lacking in common sense, or uneducated. The Council of Trent (1545–1563) condemned the theology of the Reformation and restated orthodox Roman Catholic theology in strong terms. On March 3, 1547, for example, the council reaffirmed that Jesus Christ instituted the seven sacraments, including confession, that were necessary for salvation. In England the Anglicans continued to avoid confessing sins to a clergyman to receive absolution, but this practice began to gain some acceptance in the early years of the nineteenth century. The theology of the Oxford Movement and the support of E. B. Pusey, who played an influential role in the controversy over Sellon's sisterhood, gave the institution of confession new life in some sections of the Anglican Church.

Why did confession receive this new emphasis? John Shelton Reed offers several explanations: pardon for sins committed after baptism; a desire to emulate Roman Catholicism or the pre-Reformation church; and, finally, a sign of defiance against the established church.[2] Critics responded with tracts and books, but the theological principles of the sixteenth century could not offset this Roman Catholic invention. Opponents, consequently, pointed out the inherent evils of confession during which women revealed their shortcomings. Arcane aspects of theology took second place to fears about manipulation by priests. Cunning clerics could easily exploit weak women.

The Anglo-Catholic movement greatly appealed to women. John Shelton Reed recognizes other aspects of its popularity in addition to the aesthetic elements or emotional pulls that nineteenth-century men emphasized. According to Reed, "The view that some women were attracted to Anglo-Catholicism because it offered authoritative dicta from clerical 'fathers' was not one that Anglo-Catholics often expressed, but it can sometimes be read between the lines of their writings."[3] In this interpretation an Anglican priest, who spoke the words of comfort and advice, could also act as a substitute for a husband whose patriarchal values might fail to appreciate the needs of a wife, and the males saw this as an affront to their status and power. "Nowhere was the conflict between Anglo-Catholic practice and Victorian family ideology clearer than in the matter of confession."[4] Reed points out that many of the attacks against confession were directed against the spiritual relationship between the female sinner and the confessor that might include sharing of the most intimate details of domestic life and sex. John Wolffe, moreover, argues that "fear for sexual purity blended with concern that the authority of husbands and fathers should not be intruded upon by priests."[5] Auricular confession, therefore, amounted to an attack against domestic masculine control and damaged the sanctity of the Victorian family.

This surrender of domestic power to a cleric, who in effect displaced the husband, dominated the debate. Questions surrounding the propriety of confession usually emphasized gender and the issue of male authority instead of theology. In *Confessional Subjects: Revelations of Gender*

2. Reed, *Glorious Battle*, 47–48.
3. Ibid., 190.
4. Ibid., 195.
5. Wolffe, *Protestant Crusade*, 123.

and Power in Victorian Literature and Culture, Susan David Bernstein shows how anti-Roman Catholic literature used the idea of power in its condemnation of auricular confession. Opponents of confession, both the Roman Catholic and Anglo-Catholic varieties, believed that "the father confessor is repeatedly construed as the interloper in would-be domestic affairs, the enemy of the father and the state who violates their precious possession of women."[6] Michel Foucault also describes confession in terms of power. Believing that this ecclesiastical institution greatly influenced Western society insofar as individuals have become "confessing" people, he recognizes the importance of power or control. "The confession is a ritual of discourse in which the speaking subject is also the subject of the statement; it is also a ritual that unfolds within a power relationship, for one does not confess without the presence (or virtual presence) of a partner who is not simply the interlocutor but the authority who requires the confession, prescribes and appreciates it, and intervenes in order to judge, punish, forgive, console, and reconcile."[7] Topics dealing with sex, according to Foucault, became a dominant subject between a female penitent and priest, and even if the subject matter did not bother the Victorian male, the dynamics of revealing one's sexual thoughts or deeds which involved vivid descriptions, images, and pleasures one enjoyed surely repulsed husbands and fathers.

During the early nineteenth century, critics of confession stressed the hazards and temptations that another type of woman might encounter in the confessional, namely, the Anglican nun. If scandalous activities took place between nuns and priests under the guise of this Roman Catholic sacrament, and if clerics used their position to control or dominate the sister in their role of confessor, then parents might rightly fear for their daughters' virtue in Anglican convents that encouraged confession, such as Priscilla Lydia Sellon's sisterhood.

Hatred of Roman Catholicism can be seen in some early eighteenth-century pornographic writings dealing with convents. When Matthew Lewis wrote *The Monk* in 1796,[8] he shocked the English reading public with horrific descriptions about the lives of monks and nuns in Spain. This work of fiction told graphic stories about murder, convent dungeons, pregnant nuns, torture, and the flagrant disregard of religious

6. Bernstein, *Confessional Subjects*, 43.
7. Foucault, *The History of Sexuality*, vol. 1, 61–62.
8. Lewis, *The Monk: A Romance*.

vows. It also painted a picture of scandalous sexual impropriety between monks and nuns. Other authors, however, had sounded the same alarm before the nineteen-year-old Lewis published his tale about unholy lust. A former priest, Anthony Gavin, wrote *A Master Key to Popery, Giving a Full Account of the Customs of the Priests and Friars and Rites and Ceremonies of the Popish Religion* in 1724. He tried to expose clerical wickedness, including rape, seduction, and sex with nuns. Confessors, moreover, "are the occasion of the ruin of many families, of many thefts, debaucheries, murders, and divisions among several families."[9] In 1732 *A Compleat History of the Intrigues of Priests and Nuns* also talked about confession.[10] Some of the material was a reprint of Gavin's earlier work, and although the book did not describe any sexual activity between a nun and her confessor, the engraving opposite the title page showed a "lascivious" priest absolving a kneeling penitent nun. His countenance appeared fox-like; the nun's expression was attentive and submissive. On the floor lay a discarded book and a cross, and, more suggestive, this print showed the friar's cincture or belt loosened from the fold of his religious garb, which suggested imminent sexual activity. The traditional screen or grate that usually separated the priest and the penitent was missing in this illustration, also implying the possibility of physical contact. In 1750 sections of this book were reprinted,[11] but both editions probably reached only a small, educated audience. The nineteenth century, however, saw an increase in allegations of sexual activities between nuns and priests, and the confines of the confessional provided the venue.

The upsurge in anti-Roman Catholic writings, including attacks against auricular confession, can be attributed to the perceived growth in political power of Roman Catholicism following the Catholic Emancipation Act of 1829. Roman Catholics could now sit in Parliament after years of exclusion based on their religion. Instead of heralding a new era of toleration and liberalism, however, "its effect was, if anything, to strengthen active anti- Catholicism."[12] Immediately following the pas-

9. Gavin, *The Great Red Dragon, or, The Master-Key to Popery* (1854), 70. Reprinted several times in England and the United States during the nineteenth century, the quotation in the text is taken from the 1854 American edition. This title is different from the aforementioned first edition (1724) published in England.

10. ["G.B."], *A Compleat History of the Intrigues of Priests and Nuns*.

11. *Cloisters Laid Open*.

12. Wolffe, *Protestant Crusade*, 1. See also Paz, *Popular Anti-Catholicism in Mid-Victorian England*.

sage of the act, John Wolffe points out, a sudden outburst of religious prejudice appeared, followed by a period of quiet, but prejudice "reached a peak in the summer of 1835, and continued at a high level until 1841." This period of agitation corresponded to the early, intense years of the Oxford Movement, which some believed wanted to introduce Roman Catholic devotions and practices into the Anglican Church. The generous financial grant to Maynooth College in Ireland by the government occasioned new outbursts in 1845; the restoration of the Roman Catholic hierarchy in England in 1850 marked the beginning of another round of protests against Roman Catholicism, which now appeared strong, confident, and gaining in numbers, especially converts from Anglicanism. Two popish institutions, auricular confession and sisterhoods, had traditionally been objects of derision, and in the 1830s both came under attack. When some leaders of the Oxford Movement encouraged the practice of confession in convents, loyal Protestants could easily draw upon an abundance of vitriolic writings to connect and condemn it. Indeed, to detail the wickedness of confession in sisterhoods would certainly strengthen the case against both.

Two North American books of fiction, which soon crossed the Atlantic, gave vivid expression to the evils of auricular confession in the Roman church and the dangers that the innocent and pure nun might encounter at the hands of an unscrupulous priest. In 1833 the Reverend George Bourne wrote *Lorette: The History of Louise, Daughter of a Canadian Nun, Exhibiting the Interior of Female Convents*. Within four years the book was published in England. Maria Monk's *Awful Disclosures of the Hotel Dieu Nunnery of Montreal* was published in January 1836, and this account of scandalous happenings at a Canadian convent appeared in London the next year. Both works of fiction fit into the category of what Jenny Franchot calls "convent captivity narratives."[13] Based on the fear of captivity, especially at the hands of the Indians, early nineteenth-century Americans developed a genre of captivity literature that stressed loss of freedom and imprisonment by a foreign, alien people. The pope eventually replaced the Native Americans in the minds of the freedom-loving Yankee, and women who entered the confines of a

---

13. Franchot, *Roads to Rome*, 118. Franchot also characterizes Rebecca Reed's *Six Months in a Convent* (1835) as a "convent captivity narrative," but Reed's story of her life in and escape from a Massachusetts Roman Catholic convent does not describe the confessional in the same graphic or sensational manner as Bourne or Monk.

convent were imagined to suffer the same sentences of cruelty, mental and sexual abuse, and loss of liberty. Like the poor women imprisoned by the Indians, nuns could only gain their integrity and freedom by fleeing or escaping from the convent. This is the story that George Bourne and Maria Monk told.

Bourne wanted to warn his fellow Americans about the plot of Rome to enslave the new republic. He hoped that "the perusal of this narrative may enhance the love of freedom, intelligence, purity and truth."[14] This story contained the usual anti-Roman Catholic stereotypes set against the background of a sisterhood: deceptive Jesuits, arrogant and seducing priests, sexual encounters with clerics, pregnant nuns, descriptions of the convent as a tomb and prison, and the eventual escape. The evils of the confession also surfaced. Asked if she would consider making a confession to a priest, Louise, the daughter of the Canadian nun, retorted, "I will never go to confession unless I am dragged there. The ceremony is a farce and delusion, and it is connected with great wickedness."[15] Louise later gave her own experiences of confession at the convent. She described all priests as infidels who preyed upon the nuns, and stated, "By their artifices at confession, they unravel every character, and transform each individual into an instrument to subserve their unholy designs."[16] These clerics marked the young girls as their victims and, using their wicked skills and "with the aid of their female seducing adepts, find the deluded silly creatures an easy and willing victim."[17] These nuns existed only "to administer to their [the priests'] enjoyment." The confession became the scene for an orchestrated act of clerical seduction.

The Awful Disclosures of Maria Monk, which appeared in 1836, appealed both to the dark side of human nature and to anti-Roman Catholicism. The book told the story of Maria Monk and her horrific life in a convent, where she witnessed murder, inhuman punishments, infanticide, and secret entrances for the local priests who used the nuns as prostitutes. To save her own life and her unborn child, Maria Monk eventually escaped to safety. This book, consequently, clearly fits into the model of captivity stories, and like the other works of fiction, *The Awful Disclosures* was a fabrication. A group of anti-Roman Catholic

14. Bourne, *Lorette*, v.
15. Ibid., 25.
16. Ibid., 110.
17. Ibid., 111.

writers, including George Bourne, relied on the concocted stories of the real Maria Monk, who was probably delusional and suffering from mental problems, to compose this false description of convent life.[18] The book enjoyed phenomenal success. By the 1860s it is estimated that this diatribe against convent life had sold approximately 300,000 copies; only Harriet Beecher Stowe's *Uncle Tom's Cabin* topped this figure. Part of the degradation of these poor women living in a convent revolved around the practice of confessing their sins to priests intent on seducing them.

Monk described the clerics who heard and absolved sins as hypocrites. Before Maria entered the convent, a young girl told her about some "criminal and shameful" activities of a priest whom she encountered in confession. "She was partly persuaded by the priest to believe he could not sin, because he was a priest, and that anything he did to her would sanctify her; and yet she seemed somewhat doubtful how she should act."[19] After suggesting that a priest had murdered a young penitent because he feared that she might expose his shameful behavior, Maria complained about the indecent and sensitive questions the priest had asked her and his "improper conduct" as she revealed her shortcomings. Her disgust at the improper actions of confessing did not change after she entered the convent. Here, the priests demanded absolute obedience from the nuns, and since the priests could not sin, Maria was told that "to refuse to do anything they asked would be sinful."[20] Priests frequently visited the convent and took advantage of these nuns, often impregnating them. The American public believed her stories and viewed convents as harems for the celibate clergy, the practice of confession playing an important part in this drama of seduction.

Ex-Roman Catholic priests could be counted upon to smear their former church, and the American William Hogan succeeded in conveying his disdain. He published *Auricular Confession and Popish Nunneries* for the benefit of his countrymen in 1846, and in that same year the book was printed in England. For Hogan, confession was an act of abomination: "I now declare, most solemnly and sincerely, that after twenty-five years in full communion with the Roman Catholic church, and officiating as

---

18. Material on the background of Maria Monk's book and the question of its authorship is plentiful. See, for example, Franchot's *Roads to Rome* and Schultz's introduction in *Veil of Fear*.

19. Monk, *Awful Disclosures*, 19.

20. Ibid., 75.

a Romish priest, hearing confessions, and confessing myself, I know not another reptile in all animal nature so filthy, so much to be shunned, and loathed, and dreaded by females, both married and single, as a Roman Catholic priest, or bishop who practices the degrading and demoralizing office of auricular confession."[21] Convents proved especially good hunting grounds for these predator priests, and Hogan gave numerous examples of the confessors seducing penitents. Relating some information that he learned as a priest, Hogan declared, "There is scarcely one of [the nuns] who has not been herself debauched by her confessor."[22]

According to Hogan, however, another shameful activity took place within the cloister. Numerous illegitimate children were born in the convent, and the scandal had to be avoided. According to this former priest, mother superiors prescribed medicines to produce abortions, but sometimes the expectant nun gave birth anyway. Hogan told stunned readers how this problem was solved. "It is not generally known to Americans, that the crime of procuring abortion,—a crime which our laws pronounce to be a felony,—is a common every-day crime in Popish nunneries. It is not known to Americans,—but let it henceforth be known to them,—that strangling and putting to death infants, is common in nunneries throughout this country. It is not known that this is done systematically and methodically, according to Popish instructions."[23] Hogan also included a woodcut of an abbess strangling an infant in the presence of a priest, who baptized the child so that the soul could immediately go to heaven after the murder. For the readers of this account, nunneries appeared as places of sin and debauchery. And the confession provided the optimum place for seduction and sex.

The English critics of the conventual life adopted the same tactics as their American counterparts: sisterhoods emulated Roman Catholic practices, infected the integrity of Anglicanism, and encouraged conversions to Rome. In 1841 Miss Marion Hughes took religious vows in the presence of E. B. Pusey, and this is usually seen as the beginning of the revival of sisterhoods in the Anglican Church.[24] Historians have identified several reasons for the growth of conventual life for women in the

21. Hogan, *Auricular Confession and Popish Nunneries*, 252.
22. Ibid., 247.
23. Ibid., 283.
24. For histories of Anglican sisterhoods, see Allchin, *Silent Rebellion*; Anson, *Call of the Cloister*; and Mumm, *Stolen Daughters, Virgin Mothers*.

Church of England: the influence of the Oxford Movement that stressed a continuity with ancient Christian practices and thus saw benefit in religious life for both men and women; an opportunity for women who wanted to participate in their church without masculine supervision; and the possibility of ministry to the spiritual and physical well-being of the country's poor and outcasts within a communal framework. Convents did attract vocations. By 1849, when Priscilla Lydia Sellon began her work in the diocese of Exeter, five sisterhoods existed. Beginning around 1850, their popularity grew, and by the end of the century approximately fifty-five had been founded; however, some were short-lived. Sellon belonged to one of the early communities, and her support of confession attracted fierce criticism.

Priscilla Lydia Sellon arrived at Devonport in response to the invitation of Bishop Henry Phillpotts to work among the destitute of the area.[25] With the help of E. B. Pusey, she began a sisterhood, the Devonport Sisters of Mercy, to work in the local slums. Sellon's community soon established an orphanage and a school, and nursed the sick during a cholera epidemic. Her community, however, became a target for some hostility because of the Roman Catholic atmosphere of its spiritual life: the importance of the Virgin Mary, the presence of crucifixes in the convent, veneration of the cross, and prayers that were Roman Catholic in spirit. Some critics also questioned the propriety of auricular confession within the sisterhood, and pointed out the dangers of this practice. The opposition to confession and the dangers it posed to the nuns had reached England from America, and other pamphlets and books gave the defenders of the Protestant tradition more ammunition.

One short pamphlet, *The Romish Fox Unearthed: A Few Words on Popish Nunneries and Confessions*, painted strong images of the convent as a prison and a place of slavery, and it called for Parliament to legislate the inspection of sisterhoods to protect the liberty of the nuns. Although written against two Roman Catholic convents in the north of England, the critique of auricular confession alerted the English public to its hidden traps or snares. "Will you permit popish priests," the author asked, "to beguile into their seraglios, under false pretences, young females and to pollute them by their obscenity and filth?"[26] The author drew attention to Maria Monk and argued that priests acted the same everywhere. The

25. Williams, *Priscilla Lydia Sellon*.
26. A True Catholic, *Romish Fox Unearthed*, 2.

questions that the cleric asked the women in the confessional about her sins, printed in Roman Catholic manuals of moral theology, tended to be suggestive, personal, inappropriate, and dealt with a woman's sexual relationship with her husband.[27]

The French historian, Jules Michelet, published *Le Pretre, La Femme, La Famille* in 1845, and a translation appeared in England the same year. Michelet emphasized the power of the confessor over women and the ability of the priest to destroy the sacred bond of the family by usurping the authority of husband or father, but he also recognized the dangers that existed within convents. The confessor exerted questionable influences over the nun under his spiritual care. Temptations of a sexual nature were never absent. Michelet described the experience of a woman who testified that "she felt herself fascinated, like the bird by the serpent."[28] An English review of Michelet's book also emphasized the vulnerability of women. The confessor could easily exert his influence and displace the authority of the husband, but other perils existed. The atmosphere of the confessional proved conducive to trysts or seduction where the confessor could easily defile women. "We say that celibacy, confession, and [spiritual] direction," the review noted, "have an almost inevitable tendency to convert the priest into a lover."[29]

Another anti-convent work that pointed out the dangers of the confessional, published first in France, appeared in English during the same year that Sellon began her work in Devonport. According to the author, Count C. P. De Lasteyrie, the Roman authorities invented confession "for the purpose of subjecting Christians to a shameful and intolerable bondage."[30] This author became more candid: "The numerous instances of seduction that had occurred in the confessional, especially

27. Opponents of Roman Catholicism and its practice of confession focused on the questions that the priest would ask the female penitent with regard to sex, her desires, or the relationship with her husband. These were formulated in manuals dealing with moral theology, the most important being Pierre Dens's eighteenth-century work, *Theologia Moralis et Dogmatica*, which was published frequently during the nineteenth century. When non-Catholics read some of these extracts contained in anti-Catholic writings, they naturally were appalled by the intimate nature of the questions. "The passage most strongly objected to was more analogous to a biology textbook than to a pornographic magazine. It was a discussion of sexual sins which could be committed within marriage, particularly *coitus interruptus*." Wolffe, *Protestant Crusade*, 123.

28. Michelet, *Priests, Women, and Families*, 116.

29. "Michelet on Auricular Confession and Direction," 196.

30. De Lasteyrie, *History of Auricular Confession*, vol. 1, viii.

in Italy and Spain, had long been known to the court of Rome."[31] He also used examples of seduction, rape, and infanticide from Juan Antonio Llorente's *A Critical History of the Inquisition of Spain* to demonstrate the evils of the confession.[32] Nuns became the victims of these clerics who used the confessional to pursue their unholy conquests. According to Llorente, "It is easy for monks and depraved priests to seduce, by means of confession, especially among the lower orders, females who live in the world; the thing becomes more so relatively to the nuns or pensionnaires confined in convents."[33] He quoted extensively from the published papers of Scipio De Ricci, the former Roman Catholic bishop of Pistoia and Prato, which contained the testimonies of several defiled nuns to show the extent of sexual abuses that took place in Italy.[34] These lusty priests used the sacrament of confession for a vile purpose, namely, the seduction of nuns. Toward the end of his book, Llorente paraphrased Erasmus and pointed out "that confession tends to deprave the morals of young priests by the detailed accounts of obscenities which excite their curiosity and inflame their passions." Who could trust wife, daughter, or nun with these creatures? Because Sellon encouraged confession within her community, people would attack her for supporting this popish and demeaning practice.

E. B. Pusey not only played an instrumental part in the establishment of the sisterhood at Devonport, but he also greatly influenced the spiritual and devotional life of the convent. Pusey's promotion of confession eventually provoked the anger of some who saw it as an evil Roman institution. "Occasional confession was not unknown among old-fashioned High Churchmen," John Shelton Reed points out, "but it was the Tractarians and their successors who used the license the Prayer Book allowed to develop a high doctrine of the Sacrament of Penance."[35] Both Pusey, who began hearing confessions in 1833, and John Keble, who eventually became Pusey's personal confessor in 1846, believed that confession did not depart from the guidelines of The Book of Common Prayer. "The Prayer Book clearly implied in its forms of absolution and in the ordination service that Anglican clergymen were empowered to grant absolution to

31. Ibid., 1.234.
32. Llorente, *Critical History of the Inquisition of Spain*.
33. De Lasteyrie, *History of Auricular Confession*, 2.2.
34. See de Potter, *Female Convents*.
35. Reed, *Glorious Battle*, 47.

the penitent; and in the Order for the Visitation of the Sick, ministers were instructed to move the sick to confess their sins, if their consciences were troubled. This was one of the 'fossils' that Evangelicals regretted or ignored and that Anglo-Catholics began early on to revitalize."[36] Pusey's biographer, H. P. Liddon, suggested that a strong personal sense of sinfulness contributed to his subject's appreciation of confession, and he did not shrink from publicizing its benefits.[37] In 1846 Pusey delivered a sermon at Christ Church Cathedral, Oxford, entitled *Entire Absolution of the Penitent*,[38] which argued that confession and absolution did not deviate from The Book of Common Prayer, and in 1851 he published *Hints for a First Confession*.[39] This gave advice and suggestions to a person preparing for confession and offered ways to examine one's conscience. E. B. Pusey's close association with Sellon's sisterhood and her support of auricular confession attracted hostile attention.

In April of 1852 the Reverend H. Hobart Seymour gave a lecture at the Assembly Rooms, Bath, which attacked all nunneries, both Roman Catholic and Anglican. An inveterate opponent of conventual life for women, Seymour had traveled to Italy to explore sisterhoods in that country. At one convent, for example, he learned about four nuns who became pregnant; the sisters and the father confessor were stationed elsewhere to avoid scandal.[40] And at Bath he castigated nunnery life in England.[41]

---

36. Ibid. Also important in this debate was, of course, the final paragraph in the Pre-Exhortation in "The Order for Administration of the Lord's Supper or Holy Communion" in the 1662 BCP: "And because it is requisite, that no man should come to the holy Communion, but with a full trust in God's mercy, and with a quiet conscience; therefore if there be any of you, who by [self-examination and prayer] cannot quiet his conscience herein, but requireth further comfort or counsel, let him come to me, or to some other discreet and learned minister of God's Word, and open his grief; that by the ministry of God's holy Word he may receive the benefit of absolution, together with ghostly counsel and advice, to the quieting of his conscience, and avoiding of all scruple and doubtfulness." The editor of STR remembers Anglo-Catholic churches in London as late as the 1950s and 1960s with these words displayed prominently on their noticeboards, generally next to a list of times when clergy were available to hear confessions: the obvious implication was that this quotation from the BCP gave Anglican authority for the practice.

37. Liddon, *Life of Edward Bouverie Pusey*, 4 vols.

38. Pusey, *Entire Absolution of the Penitent*.

39. Pusey, *Hints for a First Confession*.

40. Seymour, *A Pilgrimage to Rome*, 180.

41. See Kollar, "Two Lectures at Bath," chapter 3 above. The text of the speech also appeared in *The Bath and Cheltenham Gazette* on April 28, 1852.

All nuns forfeited personal freedom and liberty, suffered cruel treatment at the hands of tyrannical superiors, faced "kidnapping" from England to foreign convents, and might experience sexual abuses. Parliamentary inspection, he argued, would cleanse sisterhoods of these crimes. Sellon's espousal of confession, however, drew special attention. According to Seymour, all the nuns had to reveal their failings and shortcomings to their mother superior, Sellon. This was not sacramental confession, although it probably offended a number of people in the audience.

Some, however, supported Sellon. A supporter of the Devonport convent, author Agnes Stewart defended her friend and stated that Seymour's characterization of convent life at Devonport was false and based on rumor. Stewart quickly dismissed his accusations about confession as bunk. "As a female writer, we would not stain our pages with the remarks [of Seymour] concerning the confessional." She also noted, "The multitudes who daily join the Church well know its efficacy, and none value it more than do the most pure-minded and innocent of her children."[42] Still, Sellon's appreciation and encouragement of auricular confession seemed dangerous to others.

The encouragement of other priests, in addition to Pusey, drew unfriendly attention to the sisterhood. Perhaps the frequent visits of the Reverend George Rundle Prynne, whom Seymour described as Sellon's personal confessor, might negatively influence other sisters.[43] One cleric, W. G. Cookesley, recognized the possible dangers. "The Rev. Mr. Prynne is one of the Confessors of the Establishment," Cookesley pointed out. "The 'Sisters' are expected to make regular confessions of their sins to him."[44] The author contended that the strict vow of obedience to Sellon necessarily meant that the nuns "are of course compelled" to seek out Prynne. Cookesley gingerly discussed the sensitive nature of the questions this confessor might ask, and he questioned "whether such a mode of confession is consistent with purity of mind on the part either of the confessor or the penitent." Moreover, Prynne had the authority and might even "at his pleasure" withhold absolution. His role as confessor in the sisterhood also made some question Sellon's work among orphans. In 1852 "Prynne was brought before Bishop Henry Phillpotts on charges

---

42. Stewart, *World and the Cloister*, xviii.

43. Prynne defended the integrity of Sellon's sisterhood and his role as her confessor. *An Address Delivered to the Members of the Congregation of S. Peter's Church*.

44. Cooklesley, *A Letter to His Grace The Archbishop of Dublin*, 15.

that he had compelled orphans in the sisters' care to confess and had asked them 'corrupting questions.'"[45] The bishop, who defended confession, eventually cleared Prynne of all charges when it became apparent that witnesses had lied.

Other critics of Sellon's sisterhood pointed out that her encouragement of confession (not just among the other nuns but beyond, as the allegation against Prynne showed) might harm the orphans under her charge. In 1852 a former member of the sisterhood who left in 1851, Sister Winifride, told a family friend, the Reverend James Spurrell, of her experiences at Devonport.[46] Spurrell began a pamphlet war by acquainting the public with the rules, devotions, and Roman Catholic atmosphere of the convent. The "sacramental efficacy of Confession" was one of the questionable practices advanced by Sellon.[47] "Confession," according to the ex-nun who informed Spurrell, "was practised by her children who were under spiritual guides." Sellon, she continued, lectured each sister on the importance of confession, and each community member could select her own spiritual father. Spurrell's pamphlet described the rubrics of the confessional—confessing sins, asking for absolution, and a penance—and he probably shocked the public by revealing that at times "this penance was varied into the making of the sign of the cross with the tongue on the floor of the Oratory!"[48] *The Bulwark*, the publication of the Scottish Reformation Society, soon printed extracts from Spurrell's pamphlet, including his remarks about confession, so that the readers north of the border could be alerted to the new dangers posed by popery.[49]

Sellon quickly replied to Spurrell's attack against her sisterhood and its religious practices. She began by stating that Bishop Phillpotts had requested her to answer the charges made about her and the community. Sellon strongly disavowed that she merely copied the rules and constitutions of Roman Catholic religious communities. She defended several religious practices that Spurrell had criticized and asserted that some of the "information" that he had printed was simply false. She also took the opportunity to explain her views on confession. Sellon claimed that she did not force any of her sisters to confess to a priest, but left the matter

45. Reed, *Glorious Battle*, 48.
46. Williams, *Priscilla Lydia Sellon*, 107–12.
47. Spurrell, *Miss Sellon*, 12.
48. Ibid., 24.
49. "Miss Sellon and Her Nuns," *The Bulwark* (Edinburgh), April 1852.

entirely up to one's conscience. She abhorred forced or required confession. Contrary to Spurrell's contention, only a few of the orphans went to confession. The church, she argued, did not prohibit confession: "The Church of England advises confession to burdened consciences before Communion."[50] Finally, Sellon argued that the ex-nun who mentioned her inhumane penance, namely, licking the floor with her tongue, probably exaggerated, "but if given at all, it must have been recommended to her to practise as an act of self-abasement when she found herself alone 'in the oratory.'" This explanation, however, probably still offended some who saw the penance as cruel and degrading.

The bishop of Exeter, Henry Phillpotts, now entered the controversy. Phillpotts was no enemy of auricular confession and even tolerated some devotional practices that other Anglicans hated. Spurrell's pamphlet, however, did affect the bishop, and it caused him to seek an explanation from Sellon, which had resulted in the reply to her detractor. Bishop Phillpotts served as the "episcopal visitor" of the community, but this, he acknowledged, was little more than an honorific or symbolic office. (Anglican bishops enjoyed no real authority over religious communities of men and women until the Lambeth Conference discussed the issue in 1897.[51])

On March 20, 1852, the bishop wrote to Sellon. He expressed his support of the good work of the sisterhood, but then, surprisingly, relinquished his office of visitor. Phillpotts could not continue as the ecclesiastical sponsor of the sisterhood: "There are particulars in your case, as stated by yourself, which make it my duty to withdraw from that connection with your institution which is indicated by the title of Visitor, but which has been, as might be expected, little more than a mere title."[52] Phillpotts pointed out two facts that appeared to contradict the community's rule, which he had previously sanctioned. Members of the sisterhood, he believed, should be free to depart at any time, but it appeared that Sellon tried to use moral pressures, such as telling the sisters that leaving would be sinful, to force dissatisfied women to stay. Secondly, Sellon's reply to Spurrell indicated that, if a sister did depart from the community, she forfeited any property invested in the community's hands, whereas the bishop believed that personal property should

50. Sellon, *Reply to a Tract by the Rev. J. Spurrell*, 4.
51. See Kollar, "1897 Lambeth Conference."
52. Henry, *Letter to Miss Sellon*, 2.

follow the sister out of the community. Consequently, "I only say that the two principal rules which I deemed it necessary to require, as conditions of my being officially connected with your society, have been violated; and the conclusion to which I am unwillingly brought, is, that my official connection with you must cease."[53] He also cautioned Sellon on the exaggerated sense of obedience that she demanded as the religious superior.

The allegation that Sellon forced the orphans to confess their sins to a priest also caused Phillpotts some concern, and the bishop wrote to the local pastor asking for clarification. This cleric replied and assured him that the children in the orphanage were instructed in the beliefs of the Church of England. Moreover, he did not find any Roman Catholic practices, especially devotions to the Virgin Mary, present in the sisterhood. Spurrell had also overstated the prevalence of confession. It was not mandatory for the orphans or the nuns. At the orphanage, "A few of the elder orphans have been to me for confession, but it was at their own desire, and they have found in it, I believe, great comfort and help. It met their need, poor children, before going to holy communion, considering what had been the scenes and temptations of their early life."[54] This report probably disappointed those who hoped for descriptions of coercion, intimidations, or threats. "Confession is not part of the regular discipline of the house," this priest reported to Bishop Phillpotts, and "Those who desire confession are free to use it, but none are required to confess, or considered in any way to break rule by not doing so." He emphasized again that "it is purely a voluntary matter," and that a number of women "who have been with the Sisters a considerable time do not use confession." It appears that this explanation satisfied Bishop Phillpotts about the orthodoxy of Sellon and her sisters, but he still felt that he could not continue as the official visitor.

Questions about alleged Romanism at Devonport, however, continued. The Reverend James Spurrell kept up his attack and wrote another pamphlet in response to Sellon's defense of her sisterhood. He claimed that her explanations represented a shallow attempt "to fritter away, evade, or slur over some of my assertions."[55] Spurrell, moreover, claimed that Sellon had misinterpreted his remarks on confession. He had never stated that she forced the nuns to go to confession. Even the ex-nun who

---

53. Ibid., 6.
54. Ibid., 10.
55. Spurrell, *Rejoinder*, 1.

had provided Spurrell with the information about life at the convent admitted that she freely approached the confessor, the Reverend G. R. Prynne. This woman, nonetheless, still maintained that he forced her to lick the floor as part of her penance. In the same year, *The Christian Examiner and Church of Ireland Magazine* (November 1852) published an article discussing the Sellon-Spurrell feud. This account attacked Sellon's purported Roman Catholic tendencies and mentioned the practice of confession at the sisterhood without commentary. Finally, in 1853 *Protestant Nunneries; or, "The Mystery of Iniquity" Working in the Church of England* referred to confession as "one of the worst features of Tractarianism," but did not make any direct reference to Sellon's community.[56] In it the author announced, "The evil still continues, and nothing has been effectively done to uproot it."

The last critiques of the Devonport sisterhood came from former members of the sisterhood. In 1862 Margaret Goodman wrote *Experiences of an English Sister of Mercy*.[57] She described her life at Devonport from 1852 to 1854, when she left to accompany Florence Nightingale to nurse the wounded in the Crimea. This account criticized Sellon's iron rule, the harshness of convent life, and the Tractarian devotions in the sisterhood. It did not, however, mention confession. One year later, Goodman published Sisterhoods *in the Church of England: With Notices of Some Charitable* Sisterhoods *in the Romish Church*.[58] Again, she critiqued the strict leadership of Sellon, drew attention to the harmful influence of Pusey, emphasized the Roman Catholic devotions of the convent, and pointed out the self-indulgent and luxurious lifestyle that Sellon lavished on herself, but she did not touch upon confession at the sisterhood. Mary Frances Cusack, another former member of the sisterhood, likewise described the strict life and the obedience demanded by Sellon. Episcopal supervision might correct these shortcomings. Cusack mentioned that the nuns had the opportunity for confession, and she made some interesting observations. Sellon might keep a sister from seeing a priest as a penance for one of her shortcomings; no one was allowed to confess to Pusey unless she was present in the convent; and Pusey might even have informed Sellon of unfriendly remarks made about her in confidence. Many of the sisters, however, never understood

56. Gladstone, *Protestant Nunneries*, 5.
57. Goodman, *Experiences of an English Sister of Mercy*.
58. Goodman, *Sisterhoods in the Church of England*.

the practice of confession in the sense of Roman Catholic theology: "Happy for our peace of mind, none of us realized in any way that confession was a sacrament in which we obtained absolution for our sins. It was to us merely a 'comfort.'"[59] The last critique of Sellon's sisterhood singled out confession for attack.

Published first in 1869, *Maude; or, the Anglican Sister of Mercy* discussed the subject of confession in terms of Protestant theology. Based on the accusations of Spurrell and information from Margaret Goodman's books, Maude appeared as a work of fiction. The author, Elizabeth Jane Whately, was the daughter of Richard Whately, former archbishop of Dublin, and she used fictitious names for real characters in the Sellon story. Maude told the reader that all the members of the sisterhood regularly went to confession, but she at first had refused because she doubted its efficacy. She saw no value it in and resisted even when another nun tried to pressure her. Eventually, Maude gave in and approached a priest who visited the convent and made an appointment for confession. This proved to be painless: she told him the sins, and the priest absolved her. After this first encounter, however, Maude began to have doubts. "To begin with, she could not confess to a man as she did to God; and with regard to spiritual guidance, in her short conversations with Mr. Leigh [the priest confessor] after confession, she felt he was incapable of satisfying her mind even on points of doctrine."[60] She eventually came to the realization that confession had no real spiritual benefit, and when she told this to Sellon, the superior accused her of "pride, deep, intense, spiritual and intellectual pride and presumption."[61] Maude ended her discourse on confession with a cry to defend Protestant principles against the dangers of Roman Catholicism: "Confession must be either a mere form, or be carried on in a way to involve evils of the most serious nature. The confessional and priestcraft have always proven themselves to be inseparable. Are we prepared to welcome them back after three centuries of Reformation, light, and apostolic truth?"[62]

---

59. Cusack, *Five Years in a Protestant Sisterhood*, 98.

60. This book first appeared under the title, *Maude; or, the Anglican Sister of Mercy*. Quotations are from a later edition with a different title: Whately, *The Anglican Sister of Mercy*, 54.

61. Whateley, *The Anglican Sister of Mercy*, 55.

62. Ibid., 56.

Critiques of Sellon and her sisterhood declined after the publication of *Maude*, and she continued to build up the conventual life for women in the Anglican Church until her death in 1876. She successfully joined her Devonport community with a London sisterhood, the Sisters of the Holy Cross, in 1856. Sellon took the title of abbess, and the new group became known as the Society of the Most Holy Trinity. This community still exists. Critiques of Anglican sisterhoods, however, did not disappear. For some, religious life for women threatened the liberty of the country's vulnerable women, and Parliament made several unsuccessful attempts to bring convents, both Roman Catholic and Anglican, under a system of state inspection that would ensure the freedom of these women.[63]

Attacks against auricular confession continued throughout the century. Critics relied on the theological arguments of the Reformation, re-enforced by the Protestant element of the Anglican Church, to demonstrate that confession was a mere human invention and had no basis in scripture. Moreover, opponents continued to portray women as victims of alleged abuses by the father confessor. They continued to emphasize the sensitive nature of the questions asked by the priest and could point to recent books to "prove" their point. In 1865 *The Confessional Unmasked* (published first in 1836 and then again in 1852) contained a list of delicate questions taken from Roman Catholic moral theological books, and it was sent to each member of Parliament. The intimate nature of the queries shocked these legislators.[64] In 1866 and 1872, the Society of the Holy Cross (an Anglo-Catholic organization) published *The Priest in Absolution* in two parts for Anglican confessors, and this manual also caused an uproar when passages were read in the House of Lords in 1877. "On that occasion, the bishops unanimously condemned any doctrine of confession that could be thought to make such a book necessary, and set up a committee to investigate the secret society that had produced it."[65]

Throughout the nineteenth century, the growth of sisterhoods and the popularity of auricular confession among Anglo-Catholics caused concern among those who thought that the Protestant faith was being corrupted by these popish innovations. A shocking stereotype of

63. See Arnstein, *Protestant versus Catholic*.
64. Ibid., 89–90.
65. Reed, *Glorious Battle*, 87.

convent life developed in the early decades of the nineteenth century: the confessional box was a place of sin and seduction. By mid-century, however, a change occurred in the tactics of the opponents of nunneries and confession, as seen in the case of Priscilla Lydia Sellon's sisterhood, and confession became associated with the loss of freedom and one's integrity. The blatant pornography of Maria Monk gave way to fears of the misuse of the authority and power exercised by the convent's confessor. The threats to a nun's personal liberty in a convent became more important than painting scenes of lecherous priests preying on vulnerable nuns. Parliamentary inspection, and not the rhetoric of Maria Monk, *Lorette*, or the books of William Hogan or M. Hobart Seymour, became the accepted method to protect Anglican nuns from the snares of confession. The case of Sellon's sisterhood is an early example of this shift away from the sensational and prurient to the more "rational" brand of religious prejudice.

Bibliography

Allchin, A. M. *The Silent Rebellion: Anglican Religious Communities, 1845–1900*. London: SCM, 1958.
Anson, Peter. *The Call of the Cloister: Religious Communities and Kindred Bodies in the Anglican Communion*. Revised and edited by A. W. Campbell. London: SPCK, 1964.
Arnstein, Walter L. *Protestant versus Catholic in Mid-Victorian England: Mr. Newdegate and the Nuns*. Columbia: University of Missouri Press, 1982.
Bernstein, Susan David. *Confessional Subjects: Revelations of Gender and Power in Victorian Literature and Culture*. Chapel Hill: University of North Carolina Press, 1997.
Bourne, George. *Lorette: History of Louise, Daughter of a Canadian Nun, Exhibiting the Interior of Female Convents*. New York: Small, 1834.
The Cloisters Laid Open, or, Adventures of the Priests and Nuns. London: Meanwell, n.d.
Cooklesley, W. G. *A Letter to His Grace The Archbishop of Dublin, on the Nature, Government, and Tendency of Miss Sellon's Establishment at Devonport Called the "Sisters of Mercy."* London: Ridgway, 1853.
Cusack, Mary Frances. *Five Years in a Protestant Sisterhood and Ten Years in a Catholic Convent: An Autobiography*. London: Longmans, Green, 1869.
De Lasteyrie, C. P. *The History of Auricular Confession, Religiously, Morally, and Politically Considered, among Ancient and Modern Nations*. Translated by Charles Cocks. 2 vols. London: Bentley, 1848.
Dens, Pierre. *Theologia Moralis et Dogmatica*. 8 vols. Dublin: Coyne, 1832.
de Potter, Louis Joseph Antoine. *Female Convents: Secrets of Nunneries Disclosed: Compiled from the Autograph Manuscripts of Scipio De Ricci, Roman Catholic Bishop of Pistoia and Prato*. Edited by Thomas Roscoe. 1829. U.S. edition, New York: Appleton, 1834.
Foucault, Michel. *The History of Sexuality*. Vol. 1, *An Introduction*. Translated by Robert Hurley. New York: Vintage, 1990.
Franchot, Jenny. *Roads to Rome: The Antebellum Protestant Encounter with Catholicism*. Berkeley: University of California Press, 1994.
Gavin, Anthony. *The Great Red Dragon, or, The Master-Key to Popery*. Boston: Jones, 1854.
"G.B." *A Compleat History of the Intrigues of Priests and Nuns: Consisting of authentick Relations of Confessions, and the lewd use made of them; including the Case of Miss Cadiere, with the Tryal of Father John-Baptist Girard her confessor, before the Great Chamber of Parliament at Aix in France. To which is added, A Signal Cheat transacted by the Dominican Fryars, as related by Dr. Burnet late Bishop of Sarum. Also The Case of Abbee des Rues, now under Confinement at Paris, for committing Rapes upon 133 Virgins. With the Case of Seduction stated at large in the Proceedings at Paris, from the several Depositions exhibited against him; with his Defence*. 4th ed. London: Marshall, 1732.
Gladstone, John E. *Protestant Nunneries; or, "The Mystery of Iniquity" Working in the Church of England. A Letter to Sir Culling E. Eardley, Bart. Concerning Ann Maria Lane, Now a Sister of Mercy, against Her Father's Wish, in Miss Sellon's Institution at Eldad, Plymouth; with an Introductory Letter, and Sir Culling E. Eardley's Reply*. London: Hall, 1853.
Goodman, Margaret. *Experiences of an English Sister of Mercy*. London: Smith, Elder, 1862.

———. *Sisterhoods in the Church of England: With Notices of Some Charitable Sisterhoods in the Romish Church*. London: Smith, Elder, 1863.
Henry, Lord Bishop of Exeter. *A Letter to Miss Sellon, Superior of the Society of Sisters of Mercy, at Plymouth*. London: Murray, 1852.
Hogan, William. *Auricular Confession and Popish Nunneries*. Hartford: Andrus, 1854.
Kollar, Rene. "The 1897 Lambeth Conference and the Question of Religious Life in the Anglican Communion." *Cistercian Studies Quarterly* 26 (1991) 319–29.
———. "Two Lectures at Bath: The Rev. H. Hobart Seymour and Cardinal Nicholas Wiseman and the Nunnery Question." *Revue d'Histoire Ecclesiastique* 96 (2001) 372–90.
Lewis, M. G. *The Monk: A Romance*. London: Bell, 1796.
Liddon, Henry Parry. *Life of Edward Bouverie Pusey*. 4 vols. London: Longmans, 1894–1898. Online: http://justus.anglican.org/resources/pc/pusey/liddon.
Llorente, Juan Antonio. *A Critical History of the Inquisition of Spain*. 1823. Reprinted, Williamstown, MA: Lilburne, 1967.
Michelet, Jules. *Priests, Women, and Families*. London: Protestant Evangelical Mission, 1874.
Monk, Maria. *Awful Disclosures, by Maria Monk, of the Hotel Dieu Nunnery of Montreal*. New York: Maria Monk, 1836.
"Michelet on Auricular Confession and Direction." *Foreign Quarterly Review* 35 (April and June 1845) 196.
Mumm, Susan. *Stolen Daughters, Virgin Mothers: Anglican* Sisterhoods *in Victorian Britain*. London: Leicester University Press, 1999.
Paz, D. G. *Popular Anti-Catholicism in Mid-Victorian England*. Stanford: Stanford University Press, 1992.
Prynne, George Rundle. *An Address Delivered to the Members of the Congregation of S. Peter's Church, Plymouth, March 15, 1852 in Consequence of Some Statements Contained in a Pamphlet Written by the Rev. James Spurrell, A.M., Vicar of Great Shelford, Cambridge*. London: Masters, 1845.
Pusey, E. B. *Entire Absolution of the Penitent: A Sermon Preached before the University, in the Cathedral Church of Christ, in Oxford, on the First Sunday in Advent, 1846*. Oxford: Parker, 1846. Online: http://justus.anglican.org/-resources/pc/pusey/pusey6.html.
———. *Hints for a First Confession*. London: Smith, 1884. Online: http://justus.anglican.org/resources/pc/pusey/puseyl.html.
Reed, John Shelton. *Glorious Battle: The Cultural Politics of Victorian Anglo-Catholicism*. Nashville: Vanderbilt University Press, 1996.
Schultz, Nancy Lusignan, editor. *Veil of Fear: Nineteenth-Century Convent Tales by Rebecca Reed and Maria Monk*. West Lafayette: Purdue University Press, 1999.
Sellon, Priscilla Lydia. *Reply to a Tract by the Rev. J. Spurrell, Vicar of Great Shelford, Containing Certain Charges concerning the Society of the Sisters of Mercy of Devonport and Plymouth*. London: Masters, 1852.
Seymour, M. Hobart. *A Pilgrimage to Rome*. London: Seeleys, 1849.
Spurrell, James. *Miss Sellon and the "Sisters of Mercy": An Exposure of the Constitution, Rules, Religious Views, and Practical Workings of Their Society; Obtained through a "Sister," Who Has Recently Seceded*. London: Hatchard, 1852.

———. *A Rejoinder to the Reply of the Superior of the Society of the Sisters of Mercy of Devonport and Plymouth, to a Pamphlet Entitled Miss Sellon and the "Sisters of Mercy" by the Rev. James Spurrell, A. M., Vicar of Great Shelford, Cambridgeshire*. London: Hatchard, 1852.

Stewart, Agnes M. *The World and the Cloister; To Which Is Added, Prefatory Remarks on a Lecture on Nunneries, Lately Delivered at Bath, by the Rev. Hobart Seymour, M.A.* London: Richardson, 1852.

A True Catholic. *The Romish Fox Unearthed: A Few Words on Popish Nunneries and Confessions*. Darlington: Wilson, 1837.

Whately, Elizabeth Jane. *The Anglican Sister of Mercy*. London: Stock, 1895.

Williams, Thomas Jay. *Priscilla Lydia Sellon: The Restorer after Three Centuries of the Religious Life in the English Church*. London: SPCK, 1950.

Wolffe, John. *The Protestant Crusade in Great Britain, 1829–1860*. Oxford: Clarendon, 1991.

"Woman Secretly Taped While Confiding in Her Priest Sues Him Alleging Malpractice." *The New York Times*, June 30, 2002, sec. 1, 14.

Giacinto Achilli versus the Roman Catholic Church

Morality, Religion and the Court of Public Opinion in Victorian England

LITIGATION HAS BECOME ALMOST a national pastime in America. Libel cases have become frequent occurrences, and it appears that juries compete to award large cash settlements to the aggrieved or wronged party. Recently clergy, including prominent church leaders, and churches have become the object of civil and criminal suits. In 1852, a famous (or infamous) libel case took place in London which exhibited several elements which the American public might read about in today's newspapers or hear on the evening news. Giacinto Achilli, an ex-priest, a convert to Protestantism with a dubious moral character, and a popular lecturer against Roman Catholicism, brought charges against John Henry Newman. Achilli sued Newman, a former Anglican luminary who had become a vocal champion of Roman Catholicism, for libel because of remarks he had made against Achilli in a lecture and which later appeared in print. According to Owen Chadwick, "The accounts of the trial made nauseating reading; witnesses coming forward to testify to rape in Italian sacristies [by Achilli], Maria Monk stories brought to reality in the cold decorum of an English law court."[1] And both the secular and religious press provided commentaries on the sensational proceedings. In the anti-Catholic atmosphere of mid-nineteenth-century England, the jury,

1. Chadwick, *Victorian Church*, Part I, 307.

not surprisingly, found Newman guilty following a slanted summation by the judge, who also refused a petition for a new trial. Newman had to pay a fine of £100 and court costs of £12,000.[2] *The Times*, however, rushed to Newman's defense and described the verdict as a miscarriage of justice and a slight on the character of the English people.[3] Before these two antagonists faced each other in court, the debate over Achillo's character had been fought out between his supporters in the Evangelical or Protestant party in the Anglican Church and Roman Catholics who sought to defend the integrity of their religion by calling into question the moral character of Achilli.[4]

By the 1850s, those English interested in matters of religion were acquainted with the outlines of John Henry Newman's life and his accomplishments in both the Anglican Church and his new church. Achilli was a newcomer on the religious scene, but because of his public controversies with Catholicism, aspects of his life would be repeated, and his supporters and his opponents would give different interpretations to key events that would later become important elements in the 1852 libel case against Newman. Some parts of his life, however, could not be disputed. Giacinto Achilli was born in Viterbo, Italy, in 1803, and received his early education from the Jesuits. He joined the Dominicans in 1819, and was ordained a priest in 1825. Achilli taught Philosophy at the seminary in Viterbo, but left this position under a cloud. from there, he went to Capua, where he lived from 1834–35. Fr. Achilli then made his home in Naples until 1841 when he moved to Rome, where the Inquisition arrested him in June 1841 on charges of alleged heresy and immorality. As penance and punishment, church officials sent him away to a Dominican house, but he fled to Corfu. In the same year, he also left the priesthood. Achilli found his way to Malta, and in 1847 he took up a teaching post at the Protestant College there. While a member of

---

2. Ibid., 309.

3. *The Times*, 26 June 1852.

4. Reports of the trial and the publicity leading up to the court case contain biographical sketches of Achilli, some favorable and others critical of his life and behavior. A good objective outline of his life appears in the Index of Persons and Places in Dessain and Blehl, eds., *Letters and Diaries of John Henry Newman*, vol. xiv, 539. This book also traces the life of Achilli after the trial. In spite of his legal victory over Newman, his popularity soon fell, and he went to America, where he became a Swedenborgian. According to this sketch, he sent his wife back to Italy in 1859 and was later charged with adultery. He deserted this woman in 1860, and probably died during that year.

the staff, he visited England in 1847 and in 1848. Achilli left Malta permanently and returned to Rome in 1849. He was arrested immediately by the authorities, but escaped and traveled to England in 1850, where he began his career as an ex-priest denouncing the Roman Catholic Church. Both the supporters and enemies of Giacinto Achilli would fill in the blanks or gaps in his life with incidents or allegations in an attempt either to canonize or discredit him.

In the autumn of 1849, before his arrival in England, the public became acquainted with the ordeals and sufferings of Giacinto Achilli, in particular his arrest and imprisonment in Rome. On November 15, *The Times* published a lengthy account of his trials. The correspondent from the newspaper noted that the Achilli case was acquiring notoriety in Protestant England where some saw him as a victim of religious persecution at the hands of an intolerant papal government.[5] This article in *The Times* promised to review the facts of the case in an objective and unprejudiced manner, and argued that in England one was presumed innocent until guilt was proved. In the first place, it pointed out, Achilli, who argued that he was a British subject because of his sojourn in Malta, could not offer any evidence of this assertion. Even if Achilli could establish the validity of his adopted citizenship and thus claim the protection of the English government, he had still violated the laws of Rome by writing, speaking, and acting against the Catholic Church. The writer for *The Times* then answered some questions. The civil authorities arrested Achilli at the request of the papal authorities, and the reason that prompted this religiously motivated action appeared to be his earlier escape from the clutches of the Inquisition. He had been sent to a Dominican house because of a number of crimes against the Catholic Church, including alleged immoral dealings with a nun, his anti-Catholic activities, and his status as an apostate priest, still, according to this report, considered a crime in the Papal States.

Could the politicians work on Achilli's behalf to secure his freedom? This correspondent did not believe that diplomacy on the part of France or England could solve the impasse and free him, even though it was rumored that Lord Palmerston, the English Foreign Secretary, had intervened on his behalf. Achilli claimed to be a British citizen, and Palmerston had earlier championed the cause of Don Pacifico, who claimed English citizenship because of his birth in Gibraltar. Palmerston

5. *The Times*, 15 November 1849.

supported Don Pacifico's demand for financial restitution after a mob in Athens destroyed his home in 1847, and the Foreign Secretary even threatened the use of force.[6] But the situation was different in Rome. France had only recently re-established the civil authority of Pope Pius IX in 1849 after a revolution had proclaimed a Roman Republic in 1848 and forced Pius IX into a brief exile at Gaeta. A French army became the protector of the Pope's conservative government, and it would be difficult for the English government to demand that the Holy See should free Achilli, a citizen of Rome and under its jurisdiction. Nonetheless, the English friends of Giacinto Achilli probably hoped that the bluster of Palmerston might succeed as it did with Don Pacifico, though this never materialized.

Giacinto Achilli had become a newsworthy person, and readers continued to follow the story of imprisonment from a number of documents that Sir Culling Eardley sent to *The Times* in December 1849. Eardley, chairman of the Evangelical Alliance, an anti-Catholic organization established in the 1840s, and a number of his friends composed a "memorial" addressed to the French Minister of Foreign Affairs on behalf of Achilli. Writing from Paris, Eardley pointed out that the Evangelical Alliance had voted to appoint "a delegation to wait upon the French Government on behalf of Dr. Giacinto Achilli, a member of the Evangelical Alliance, who has been cast into the prison of the Holy office [sic] in Rome, in the name of the French police."[7] He suggested that a deputation of English and French members of this organization should go to Rome "to secure the liberation of a brother whom they believe to be innocent." Achilli's claims of religious persecution at the hands of Roman Catholics, which appeared in print below this letter, could thus be verified. Eardley doubted the prisoner's claims that he was a British subject, but believed the charges of criminal acts "to be manifestly and on the surface false." He begged the French government to use its influence to work for the release of Achilli immediately because he was "made a prisoner under the French authority." Eardley also feared for the well-being of the prisoner. The papal powers planned to transfer him from the Castle of St. Angelo to the prison of the Inquisition where he would await trial, and "his doom may be regarded as certain."

---

6. Ridley, *Lord Palmerston*, 374–76. Palmerston eventually threatened military action against Greece in January 1850, which resulted in restitution to Don Pacifico.

7. *The Times*, 1 December 1849.

The French, therefore, should attempt to rescue this innocent person. Eardley and three other members of the Evangelical Alliance signed this letter on October 22.

Following this plea to the French authorities appeared a brief description of Achilli's life and the protest against the arrest, both written by Achilli who wanted to portray himself as a victim of the intolerant Roman Catholic Church. This statement, written on October 1, 1849, described his clerical career in the Roman Catholic Church, which ended in 1841 when he renounced his priesthood. Achilli then stated that he left Italy in 1842 for "the English dominions," namely Malta, where he taught at a local college until 1849 when he returned to Italy. He believed that his sojourn on the island entitled him to British citizenship. Any questions of improper "moral conduct" or involvement in questionable political activities, he argued, lacked any substance or proof because these accusations had never surfaced prior to 1849. Then, on the night of July 29, French officials arrested and imprisoned him because his anti-Catholicism jeopardized the peace. Achilli lashed out against this illegal act of ecclesiastical vigilante justice. He believed that he had been arrested for so-called heretical statements made against the Catholic Church. Moreover, no legal action had been taken against him during his two months as a prisoner. Arguing that he enjoyed English citizenship, Achilli appealed to that government for justice. He concluded his statement with a demand that a French tribunal, and not a papal court, hear his case. He was no longer a Catholic priest; he was an English citizen; and no one had yet accused him of committing crimes against the Roman state. Achilli did enjoy some support. His English friends, led by Eardley, sent the French government a formal protest through the English ambassador on October 23, the day following the memorandum that they had personally submitted to the French Minister of Foreign Affairs.[8]

On December 4, *The Times*'s correspondent in Rome sent a lengthy story to the London newspaper, and the Achilli saga again became reading material for the British public. Some friends of the imprisoned man had recently appeared in Rome to take up his defense. Although they

---

8. This protest, which passed through the English embassy to the French government, also appeared in *The Times* along with the letter signed by Eardley and other members of the Evangelical Alliance and Giacinto Achilli's protest and short autobiography. This third document, the protest, did not differ in substance from the one sent by Eardley and his friends.

had some association with the Evangelical Alliance, the article made it clear that the men acted out of a personal desire to see justice done. These individuals did not represent the interests of this anti-Catholic organization, but they only wanted to visit Achilli in prison and to review the evidence against him. The French officials whom they visited, however, told these supporters of Achilli that the papal authorities had jurisdiction in the case. Private individuals had no right to interfere in official government business. This correspondent pointed out the problems which Achilli faced, and they dealt with issues of religion and nationality: "I am told that the doctor [Achilli] finds much difficulty in showing that he abjured the Roman Catholic religion, or was formally nationalized as a British subject."[9] Achilli had little defense, the article argued, because he could not produce substantial proof that he had formally abandoned the Catholic religion or that he possessed an English passport. Moreover, the author of the story correctly prophesied how a solution would be reached: "I have a shrewd suspicion that the escape of the prisoner will be connived at, as the only means of avoiding a conflict with the French Government."

The imprisonment of Giacinto Achilli, consequently, became a crusade for the Evangelical party in England against the intolerance of the papal government in Rome. And rumors of his possible release signaled a victory. On December 20, 1849, the French authorities announced that they would work for Achilli's freedom provided that he leave Italy immediately, but Pope Pius IX would not agree to this deal. Because of this intransigence on the part of the Holy See, Achilli took another approach: he successfully escaped from the Roman prison in disguise on January 19, 1850. England would welcome him, but this did not end the adventures of Achilli. Innuendo, rumors, and accusations of a criminal and sexual nature continued to color his career in his adopted country. If he were to become a martyr to Protestantism and a potential spokesperson in England against the Roman system, these charges had to be addressed. C. E. Eardley, the most vocal champion of Achilli's cause, wrote *The Imprisonment and Deliverance of Dr. Giacinto Achilli, with Some Account of His Previous History and Labours* in February 1850. This collection of documents and testimonies not only tried to explain some of the more questionable charges against Achilli, but it also served as a harsh indictment against Roman Catholicism. The Achilli drama

9. *The Times*, 4 December 1849.

quickly moved from the world of Roman politics to books and articles which would champion his crusade in England. Eardley's book provided the necessary information and background to the Achilli story that had not appeared in earlier press stories, and it encouraged his supporters to welcome this victim of Catholicism on English soil. After praising the French government for its role in the release of Achilli, which was ambiguous at best, the author told his readers that "dr. [sic] Achilli's imprisonment will open the eyes of thousands to the unchanged and unchangeable intolerance of the Court of Rome."[10] Eardley emphasized some facts that the Roman Catholics disputed. Achilli renounced the priesthood in 1841. He was legally married, and did not, as the Roman authorities would claim, live an "immoral" life. The author also pointed out that during the short-lived Roman Republic, Achilli had received letters of encouragement and some financial assistance from Evangelical friends in England, including Eardley, to support his efforts to popularize the study of the Bible and to reveal the persecution that critics of Roman Catholicism had suffered. In one letter back to England, for example, Achilli described in vivid details the scene when the prisons of the Inquisition were opened for public view: "the ragged remains of the dresses, nor only of men, but of women and children . . . But a subterranean cave occasioned especial horror, covered with remains of bones and earth mixed, including human skulls and skeletons of different forms and sexes, indicating persons of different ages and sexes."[11]

But this Protestant experiment in Italy, Eardley lamented, was doomed to failure. Achilli sent sad letters to England, which were circulated among the members of the Evangelical party, describing the capture of Rome by the French, the entry of their army into the city, and its re-establishment of the papal government. Yet he continued to promote Protestant principles and the importance of Sacred Scripture. Achilli expected persecution, which began with his arrest on July 29, 1849, and Eardley devoted the remainder of his book to the events surrounding the legality of the arrest and the imprisonment of his colleague. What prompted the papal authorities to arrest this courageous Protestant? According to Eardley, "his sole offence was preaching the Gospel and spreading the Scriptures under the *de facto* Roman Government, which

10. Eardley, *Imprisonment and Deliverance*, 5.
11. Ibid., 22.

had made these acts perfectly legal."[12] He also identified some other specific reasons that prompted Rome to take action against Achilli.

For the first time, Eardley revealed the extent and the enormity of the accusations against the ex-Roman Catholic priest. The Roman authorities charged that Achilli, while still a cleric, had a sexual relationship with a woman. Eardley denied the validity of this "bare-faced fabrication," and demanded that the church authorities produce concrete evidence to substantiate this wild claim. Rome, moreover, had not forgotten the charges of heresy against Achilli. The author then described the journey to Rome by the English supporters to take up Achilli's cause. It was during this visit that the church authorities accused Achilli of another unsubstantiated and heinous crime: he had poisoned a nun! The delegation, however, did procure enough evidence to prove that Achilli had legally contracted a marriage, and Eardley could not avoid some patriotic rhetoric. "We shall see how far, in the present case, that thoroughgoing love of liberty, which, thank God! characterises England, has or has not been represented at Rome."[13]

Eardley's book also shed light on the events that surrounded Achilli's flight from his imprisonment while negotiations for his release with a British diplomat, Mr. Petre, were taking place in Rome. The possibility of Achilli's freedom seemed within reach, and the accusations of a political nature were dropped. He stood accused of heresy, but the charge of killing a nun had been a mistake, and this information was quickly circulated throughout England. Finally, as reported previously in *The Times*, a compromise had been reached to release Achilli, but at the last moment Pius IX refused to approve this plan. Achilli, therefore, took matters into his own hands. Eardley published Achilli's February 3, 1850, letter, which described his heroic escape disguised as a French soldier and his journey to Paris. He ended his book by publishing two letters from Achilli to Pope Gregory XVI (1842 and 1844) and one to Pope Pius IX in 1846 urging the pontiffs to reform the church. According to Eardley, Giacinto Achilli planned to live in England, where he would continue to preach the Bible and condemn the intolerance and wickedness of the Roman Catholic Church. Controversy, however, followed Achilli into England.

12. Ibid., 36.
13. Ibid., 99.

Achilli's struggles with Rome certainly presented the anti-Catholic forces in England with great propaganda material. Here was an ex-priest who had suffered greatly because of his religious convictions. Consequently, Achilli could expose Roman Catholicism as dangerous to English life. Catholics had made notable gains in the political and social life of the country. Catholic Emancipation in 1829, which gave Roman Catholics the right to sit in Parliament, generous financial assistance to Maynooth College in Ireland, and rumors that the Pope planned to re-establish the Roman Catholic hierarchy—an event that took place in September 1850—gave force to a wave of anti-Catholic activities which ranged from riots to attempts by zealots in Parliament to inspect the growing number of sisterhoods, both Anglican and Roman Catholic, in the country.[14] In addition to sectarian violence, usually directed against the Irish, attacks against Catholicism in both the secular and religious papers and eager itinerant preachers, financed by anti-Catholic individuals and groups, could be counted on to spread the seeds of hatred. During the nineteenth century, two non-English lecturers, Alessandro Gavazzi, a former monk, and William Murphy, an Irishman who had converted from Catholicism, achieved fame and notoriety for their religious prejudice. Giacinto Achilli shared similar characteristics with these individuals: he was a foreigner; he was an ex-cleric; and he was a convert to Protestantism. After fleeing Rome, Achilli found backing for his campaign in England, where rumors about the imminent re-establishment of the Roman Catholic hierarchy shocked many non-Catholics.

The anti-Catholic forces welcomed Achilli in England. One pamphlet, which contained lengthy quotations and extracts from Eardley's passionate defense of the ex-priest, noted that "With no small degree of excitement, Dr. Achilli has been introduced to the Christian public in London and the English Provinces, as a man that has been called to endure a great fight of affliction, and of persecution for righteousness' sake."[15] On February 16, Giacinto Achilli arrived in London and a public thanksgiving service took place at St. Giles's chapel in gratitude for his safe deliverance from the clutches of Rome. A week later Achilli wrote a

14. See Wolffe, *Protestant Crusade*, for a discussion of anti-Catholicism in nineteenth-century England.

15. *Who and What Is Dr. Achilli?*, 3. This book served as a defense of Achilli. Drawing almost exclusively on Eardley's *Imprisonment and Deliverance*, it offered no new information on his life. It did, however, contain one of the few speeches that survives in print that Achilli delivered in England.

letter of appreciation to his English supporters. He described his struggles with the papacy as "the battle between light and darkness—between the power of Christ and the opposition of the Pope—between the belief of the gospel and the superstition of the canons."[16] After thanking his Protestant friends who supported him during his trials, Achilli emphasized the sufferings of people in Italy who were committed to the Scriptures. He hoped that his life would serve as "evidence that the Church of Rome becomes every day more unworthy of the name Christian because she persecutes the believers in the gospel of Jesus Christ."[17] Achilli also received other expressions of encouragement: Lord Palmerston received him at a gathering; a crowd welcomed him to Exeter Hall in the Strand, the center of Evangelical activities in London, with a hymn, "Hail Roman Prisoner, Hail"; and his supporters, especially the Evangelical Alliance even supplied him with a chapel in London and encouraged his public appearances.[18] The harangues of Achilli against Roman Catholicism, his friends believed, would certainly draw large crowds.

Achilli had already delivered some anti-Catholic talks in the country. While still on the staff of the Protestant College in Malta, Achilli gave an address at Cheltenham on September 2, 1847, during his first trip to England. He began by describing his conversion from Roman Catholicism, when he "was immersed in darkness, and blinded in mind," to the true religion of Protestantism.[19] After ridiculing Transubstantiation, Masses for the dead, auricular confession, the papal claim to speak infallibly, and the worship of the statues and images of saints, Achilli prophetically announced that he expected harassment and imprisonment. He emphasized the importance of Sacred Scripture and his vocation to evangelize the Christians of his native land to set them free from the evils of Catholicism. Malta, he noted, would become the center for this sacred mission. But he also pointed out some dangers to English Protestantism. The Oxford Movement and in particular the teachings of Edward Bouvene Pusey threatened the integrity of the Anglican religion. Moreover, the growing strength of Roman Catholicism and the presence of the Jesuits could not be taken lightly. These forces wanted to destroy the Protestant character of the country. Achilli ended this

16. Quoted in Eardley, *Brief Sketch*, 48.
17. Ibid., 49.
18. Nash, "Introduction," xxii.
19. Achilli, *Address*, 1.

short talk by again referring to the idolatry of Roman Catholicism and repeating his desire that his fellow Italians would eventually embrace the Scriptures and denounce their spiritual and political allegiance to the papacy. These themes would again surface when Achilli undertook a lecture tour in England after his arrival in 1850.

Soon after he began his permanent exile from Italy, Giacinto Achilli gave a series of talks, and Exeter Hall in London provided the venue. On March 7, Achilli addressed a meeting in Italian, and his friend and supporter, L. H. J. Tonna, served as the translator. Achilli began by reminding the listeners of his previous short visits to England in 1847 and 1848, and then immediately launched into one of his favorite projects, namely, the importance of the Scriptures and his efforts to provide his countrymen with the Bible translated into Italian by Giovanni Diodati (1576–1649). His support for this version, which had become the accepted translation for the Protestants in Italy, had been the cause for his sufferings and eventual imprisonment in Rome. "This book, so well translated by a man of God," he pointed out, "had been persecuted by the Popes, and only persecuted on this account, that it was a faithful translation."[20] This Italian Bible had become a living witness of the Christian faith unlike the fables of Roman Catholicism. Like the Apostles, Achilli expected to be hounded by the Roman authorities, and he described the details of his arrest and sojourn in a papal prison. It was the Bible and the support from England, specifically the encouragement of several members of the Evangelical Alliance, which gave him the strength to persevere. He made a short reference to his conversion to Protestantism, where he had found the true visible church: "the Church of all Christians scattered throughout the world."[21] Achilli ended his brief talk by thanking his English backers for their kind words and actions and by telling them that he wanted to return to Italy some day to continue his work. Achilli's growing popularity, consequently, gave the Roman Catholic authorities a cause for concern.

Nicholas Wiseman (1802–65),[22] who would become the Cardinal Archbishop of Westminster when Pope Pius IX re-established the hierarchy in September 1850, had acquired ecclesiastical fame by his staunch

20. Printed in *Who and What Is Dr. Achilli?*, 21.

21. Ibid., 23.

22. For biographies of Wiseman, see Schiefen, *Nicholas Wiseman*; and Ward, *Life and Times of Cardinal Wiseman*.

defense of his church, his efforts to Romanize English Catholicism, and his attempts to draw converts away from the Anglican Church. Less than two months before the Pope appointed him as Archbishop of Westminster, Wiseman wrote an anonymous review in the July edition of *The Dublin Review*,[23] which savaged two books supportive of Giacinto Achilli: C. E. Eardley's book and another, *Brief Sketch of the Life of Dr. Giacinto Achilli*. The latter contained the correspondence between Achilli and the members of the Evangelical Alliance that had appeared in Eardley's book, the newspaper reports dealing with his imprisonment and escape, and the letters sent to the two popes.[24] The anonymous author or editor of this book, however, included an interesting addition in an attempt to embarrass Roman Catholic authorities—a handsome print of Giacinto Achilli, bedecked in his Dominican habit, when he was prior of the order's establishment in Naples.

Wiseman believed that he had a sacred obligation to expose this ex-priest as a rogue and sexual predator. Achilli had attracted some attention and popularity. Wiseman, to challenge this perceived threat to Catholicism, had collected "evidence of a career of extraordinary licentiousness"[25] and would reveal his true character in the pages of *The Dublin Review*. Wiseman feared that Achilli might become a hero in the eyes of some and that his story might be interpreted as a romantic struggle of truth and righteousness against the alleged deceptive nature of Catholicism. And it was the task of this Irish journal to inform people about the scandalous past of this former Catholic priest. "It has then been ever the particular function of this *Review* to meet such calumnies of the day, and especially such as require a more troublesome research," Nicholas Wiseman wrote, and "We will therefore fearlessly undertake our present task, and see what pretensions Achilli has to the character, we will not say of a martyr, but of a decent member of civilized, or moral society."[26]

Wiseman cast serious doubts on the positive descriptions of Achilli that had appeared in Eardley's book and in other favorable portrayals of his life. He characterized these accounts as exaggerations, falsehoods, misinterpretation of facts, and riddled with inconsistencies. Wiseman

---

23. [Wiseman], "Dr. Achilli," This review article also appeared as a short pamphlet: *Dr. Achilli*.

24. See note 16 above.

25. Ward, *Life and Times*, 2.39.

26. Wiseman, "Dr. Achilli," 477.

gave an outline of Achilli's life and emphasized several disputed points: he was not an English citizen; he was not legally married; he did preach heresy; he was dismissed from several posts because of inappropriate actions of a sexual nature; his description of the public opening of the Inquisition, which allegedly exposed the wicked nature of the institution, could not be trusted; and he did take an active part in politics during the short-lived Roman Republic. In fact, Wiseman argued, the Achilli legend was a fabrication based on a series of well-calculated lies that sought to damage the character of the Roman Church. Wiseman introduced a new element that had remained in the shadows, namely, details of Achilli's numerous sexual transgressions while he was a Catholic priest, misdeeds which continued after he converted to Protestantism.

Seductions and cases of adultery could and did ruin people in Victorian England. In addition to the issues of morality, the deception and dishonesty involved necessarily meant that the individual could not be trusted. Clearly, Giacinto Achilli, Wiseman believed, fit this category. If one could blemish the integrity of his personal life, could anyone confidently believe the explanations of the difficulties and persecutions he experienced at the hands of the Roman Catholic Church? Wiseman, therefore, attempted to demonstrate that Achilli and his supporters had strayed far from the truth. The Diocese of Viterbo, where Achilli ministered as a priest, was the scene of his first crimes. According to Wiseman's evidence, "In February, 1831, he was proved to have caused the ruin of a girl of eighteen. The same crime was a second time committed [in 1833] with a person of twenty-eight; and a third [in 1834] with one of twenty-four years."[27] The litany of alleged transgressions continued. In Capua, where he resided from 1834–35, Fr. Achilli "committed the same crime of seduction."[28] In 1841 while in Naples and still a priest, "Achilli, known for habitual incontinency," seduced a girl of fifteen.[29] He renounced his priesthood in that year, but, according to Wiseman, his sexual conquests did not stop. While at Corfu, where Achilli arrived in 1841, his cohabitation with a local woman became public knowledge, and in 1843 a man caught Achilli with his wife. His indiscretions continued at Malta, prior to his visit to England in 1848 to attend the annual conference of the Evangelical Alliance. Achilli arrived back in Rome in

27. Ibid., 482–83.
28. Ibid., 485.
29. Ibid., 487.

1849, where he was eventually arrested and imprisoned soon after he married a Miss Hely on June 24 of the same year. Nicholas Wiseman tried to paint Giacinto Achilli as a profligate and a liar in strong and uncompromising terms. Wiseman, moreover, claimed that he had the necessary documents to prove his charges. Achilli's supporters had to answer these damning accusations of immorality and attempt to rescue their hero from Wiseman's condemnation.

One of the first to rush to Achilli's defense was Lewis H. J. Tonna, an ultra-Evangelical churchman who had befriended the ex-priest and who had carried on a lengthy correspondence with him after his return to Rome in 1849. Tonna answered Wiseman's accusations in a short pamphlet.[30] He dismissed the unfavorable comments about Achilli's life as lies and falsehoods concocted by the Catholic Church to smear his character. Tonna sneered at the charges of immorality, which he characterized as malicious fabrications. If Achilli did violate these women, Tonna queried, why did not the Dominican order or the church fail to discipline him immediately? If Achilli had acquired the reputation as a seducer of females, then surely the Roman Church would have censured him. But the failure on the part of his ecclesiastical superiors and other church officials to act, he argued, demonstrated that enemies made up these accusations.

A group associated with Tonna, the London Committee for the Religious Improvement of Italy and the Italians, printed a short pamphlet that attempted to clear Achilli of any charges of impropriety connected with his dismissal from the Malta Protestant College. This defense argued that the officials at this institution had wrongly dismissed Achilli, and it claimed that he possessed real "moral worth."[31] The unfortunate and irresponsible action against Achilli was driven by the "insinuations, innuendoes, and suspicions" of his enemies. What offended this committee the most, however, was that fellow Protestants released Achilli and then justified their actions by uncomplimentary remarks about his character. This unfortunately provided the real enemy, Roman Catholicism, with additional ammunition, including his involvement in a cover-up of a colleague allegedly involved in a sexual scandal and some uncomplimentary comments he made about the Malta college. These words of support presented a weak defense; one had to confront Wiseman's dam-

30. Tonna, *The Real Dr. Achilli*.

31. London Committee for the Religious Improvement of Italy and the Italians, *Dr. Achilli*, 17.

aging accusations. In 1851, therefore, Giacinto Achilli broke his silence and published *Dealings with the Inquisition; or, Papal Rome, Her Priests, and Her Jesuits*.[32]

This book represented a sweeping refutation of all negative statements concerning Achilli's religious beliefs and his relationship with the Roman Catholic Church. Wiseman's merciless attack forced Achilli to defend his character. "And here observe how far malice will lead men astray. *The Dublin Review*, in July, 1850, stigmatizes me to the religious world as a mere political adventurer, while to the political world it represents me as a religious enthusiast, changeable, inconsiderate, and inexperienced, and an immoral person, and a hypocrite to boot."[33] This was the only direct reference to Wiseman's review, but Achilli's book did provide a lengthy and detailed defense of his life and an equally strong condemnation of Roman Catholicism. In fact, his hatred and disgust of the Catholic faith eclipsed the attacks against his character. Achilli portrayed himself as a martyr persecuted by the evil Roman Catholic religious system, and he described his imprisonment as an action of a satanic institution directed against a true Christian believer. Achilli asserted that the Catholic Church had consciously maligned him. He maintained that Catholicism had mistakenly judged some of his theological beliefs, which were based on Sacred Scripture, as heresy, but he did not mention the purported sexual adventures enumerated in the pages of *The Dublin Review*. Instead of a defense of his character and private life, Achilli used this book to attack the Inquisition, the Dominicans and the Jesuits, auricular confession, "the worship of saints," and a number of other Roman Catholic devotional practices. Instead of trying to discredit or disprove the unsavory accusations against him, Achilli cast himself as a modern prophet who vowed to travel and speak out against the wickedness of Roman Catholicism.

Achilli's attacks against Roman Catholicism brought a quick response. *The Rambler*, which represented the views of liberal Catholicism, printed an unfavorable review of Achilli's book in its September 1851 edition.[34] The article, probably written by its founder, J. M. Capes, ridi-

---

32. Achilli, *Dealings with the Inquisition*. Achilli's book first appeared in London during the same year (1851). Quotations and references are taken from this American edition.

33. Ibid., 266.

34. "Dr. Achilli and the Inquisition." In addition to a harsh critique of Achilli's

culed Achilli. "We do not know which most to admire in the book, he asked the readers, "its folly or its effrontery; its folly considered only with references to its own manifest absurdities, self-contradictions, falsehoods, and impossibilities; or its effrontery, considered with reference to the circumstances under which it makes its appearance before the tribunal of public opinion in this country."[35] The chief weakness of Achilli's defense, however, centered around his failure to answer the derogatory comments in *The Dublin Review*: "yet that no attempt is made to refute them, we are certainly lost in astonishment; we can only conclude that the author [Achilli] feels the task of vindication to be either impossible or unnecessary." This book, consequently, did not live up to its expectations as a solid defense of Achilli. Achilli seemed eager to refute Wiseman's charges against him, especially those of a sexual nature, but the ex-priest had so far failed. However, hostile comments by the influential convert, John Henry Newman, provided an occasion for Achilli not only to defend himself on the national stage, but also gave the anti-Catholic forces an opportunity to embarrass Newman.

When Newman left the Anglican Church and embraced Roman Catholicism in 1845, he entered a church under siege by enemies who believed that Catholicism had grown in strength and influence, and Newman began to confront this anti-Catholic prejudice through his lectures and writings. The foes of Catholicism had the support of several religious organizations and used the press to expose the alleged dangers that this foreign religion posed to the English character. Rallies or gatherings where speakers could vilify Roman Catholicism, its priests, customs and devotions had also found a place in the Victorian culture. "One of the features of anti-Catholic campaigns was the holding of public meetings addressed by ex-Catholics, sometimes priests, who denounced their former popish errors and gave lurid accounts of the horrors of Catholic life."[36] Such a celebrity was Giacinto Achilli. The Evangelicals financed the publication of Achilli's *Dealings with the Inquisition*, and this itinerant speaker also received monetary support as he traveled throughout the country castigating the wicked Catholic Church and revealing its

---

book, the article gave a good review to one written in Italian by an Oratorian priest, Fr. Augustine Theiner, which questioned some of Achilli's statements and pointed out the weaknesses of Protestantism.

35. Ibid., 235.

36. Nash, "Introduction," xxi–xxii.

hidden scandals. One engagement had taken Achilli to Birmingham, where Newman had established the Oratorians in 1849. John Henry Newman would also take the platform in that city to defend his religion against Achilli.

Newman gave a series of lectures at the Corn Exchange in Birmingham in the summer and early autumn of 1851. They were published soon afterwards, and the collection of these talks eventually appeared as *Lectures on the Present Position of Catholics in England.*[37] Owen Chadwick describes Newman's motive behind these lectures as "intended to expose the more ludicrous and revolting forms of antipopish prejudice."[38] On July 28, John Henry Newman delivered his fifth lecture, "Logical Inconsistency of the Protestant View," to the Birmingham audience. In the previous talk (Lecture Four) Newman poked fun at the mythical exploits of Maria Monk, the Protestant heroine who escaped from a Montreal convent, and stories of infanticide, broken religious vows, and the cruel treatment the nuns endured at the convent. It had become apparent, Newman pointed out, that some American anti-Catholics had fabricated the story of her life in the Montreal convent. The book, *Awful Disclosures of the Hotel Dieu Nunnery of Montreal*, was published in 1836, and immediately became a bestseller on both sides of the Atlantic. But Maria Monk was the creation of bigoted minds and her exploits took place in distant Canada. For Newman, a real life villain, Giacinto Achilli, was attacking Roman Catholicism with lies throughout England, and he attempted to expose his wicked past and evil intent in Lecture Five.

After criticizing "This narrow and one-sided condition of the Protestant intellect,"[39] Newman turned his attention to Achilli. He admitted that this Protestant speaker had attracted large crowds, even at Birmingham, and that he had become the darling of the anti-Catholics in England. Newman then spoke through the voice of Achilli in a sarcastic and condemning voice: "I have been a Catholic and an infidel; I have been a Roman priest and a hypocrite; I have been a profligate under a cowl, I am that Father Achilli."[40] John Henry Newman's impersonation

---

37. Gilley, *Newman and His Age*, 268. For another recent biography of Newman and a discussion of the Achilli trial, see Ker, *John Henry Newman*.

38. Chadwick, *Victorian Church*, Part I, 306.

39. Newman, *Lectures* (1851 ed.), 170.

40. Ibid., 197. This section dealing with Achilli's sexual crimes later became the

of Giacinto Achilli then told the listeners about the numerous sexual crimes he had committed, repeating the dates, places, and young ages of some of the women—pointing out that one violation took place in a sacristy of a church and another on Good Friday—which Wiseman had already revealed. Commenting on his stay at Malta, Newman's mockery of Achilli reported that he "was dismissed from my post [as professor at the Protestant College] for offenses which the authorities cannot get themselves to describe." How then could one possibly believe anything that came from the mouth of this wretch, Newman queried, and he emphasized this point: "With you the argument begins; with you too it ends: the beginning and the ending you are both. When you have shown yourself, you have done your worst and your all; you are your best argument and your sole. Your witness against others is utterly invalidated by your witness against yourself. You leave your sting in the wound: you cannot lay the golden eggs, for you are already dead."[41] The Roman Catholic Church recognized his evil nature, and forbade him to teach, to preach, or to hear confession. The church in no manner ignored his wicked exploits. John Henry Newman ended his diatribe against Achilli by arguing that this profligate could not be trusted to tell the truth. Accusations against the Catholic Church and Achilli's explanations of his past contradicted established evidence, but the conflict between these two men soon moved from Birmingham to the courts of London.

The possibility of libel arising out of his attacks against Achilli had worried Newman since he planned to quote the damning evidence that Wiseman used in *The Dublin Review*. Might not the Evangelical Alliance use the courts to embarrass Newman when he published his lecture? To protect himself and the Roman Catholic Church, John Henry Newman approached a friend, James Hope, for legal advice, and he told Newman not to worry about a charge of libel. "Hope advised him that there was no great danger of prosecution if the charges were true and had not been answered when they appeared in print before."[42] In August, however, Newman was informed that Achilli did intend to take him to court.

---

crucial part of the case of libel which Achilli brought against Newman. Because Achilli won the case, these examples of his sexual transgressions did not appear in the later editions of Newman's lectures.

41. Ibid., 199.

42. Gilley, *Newman and His Age*, 269–70. For the legal advice given to Newman, see Dessain and Blehl, eds., *Letters and Diaries of John Henry Newman*, vol. xiv, 338–39.

Ian Ker, one of Newman's biographers, believes that several factors accounted for this decision.[43] In the first place, Newman's lectures had angered the anti-Catholic element in England and Achilli could count on support if he brought charges of libel against this noteworthy Catholic priest. Secondly, Wiseman's name had not appeared as the author of *The Dublin Review* article, but Newman's lecture had been a public event and it appeared in print with Newman's name. Finally, the repetition of the charges of immorality by Newman probably pushed Achilli into action. Andrew Nash offers another explanation why Achilli failed to sue *The Dublin Review*: "the case would be heard in Ireland where the jury would be likely to be largely made up of Catholics," and thus less likely to convict Wiseman than a jury in England would Newman.[44] Nicholas Wiseman, however, must take some responsibility for the trial that led to the libel conviction. Newman believed that Cardinal Wiseman could easily produce the incriminating evidence that he had used in his article against Achilli, "but Wiseman did nothing to find the papers proving Achilli's immoralities which might have stopped the case going to trial."[45] When Wiseman eventually produced the documentation, it was too late to stop the legal proceedings against Newman.

The Times and a number of short booklets reported the events leading up to the court case, the graphic and sordid testimony of witnesses who supported the accusations of both Wiseman and Newman, and the unfair decision of the jury against John Henry Newman. This publicity ensured that the trial, cast as a struggle between Catholicism and Protestantism, would attract attention.[46] Owen Chadwick points out that the outcome of the court case would damage the Roman Catholic Church regardless of the verdict. Achilli's victory would mean that "Newman was liar and knave who hired Italian harlots to commit perjury. If the charges [of libel] were true, they disclosed a sordid pit of priestly depravity."[47] The trial, however, represented the final scene of

43. Ker, *John Henry Newman*, 373.
44. Nash, "Introduction," xxiii.
45. Gilley, *Newman and His Age*, 270.
46. See, for example, *Achilli v. Newman*; *Achilli vs. Newman*; Finlason, *Report of the Trial*; and *The Trial of Giovanni Giacinto Achilli v. John Henry Newman*. Both *The Times* and the Roman Catholic publication, *The Tablet*, also published accounts and commentaries on the trial. Biographies of John Henry Newman and histories of English Roman Catholicism also contain descriptions of the trial.
47. Chadwick, *Victorian Church*, Part I, 307.

this example of anti-Catholicism that took place in an era of increasing prejudice occasioned by the Restoration of the Hierarchy in 1850. Yet English sensitivities to religious issues had to contend with the sensationalism generated by charges of gross immorality against Giacinto Achilli. Accusations of sexual impropriety alone would have attracted interest and would have harmed the reputation and integrity of Roman Catholicism even if Achilli and his followers would not have brought accusations of libel against Newman. The damage to Catholicism and the reputation of John Henry Newman already occurred before the trial opened. The court of public opinion had already reached its verdict before the two contestants faced each other in the court of law.

Bibliography

Achilli, Giacinti. *The Address of the Rev. Dr. Achilli, Formerly a Romish Priest, Superior of a Monastery of Dominicans, and Professor of Theology for Many Years in the Celebrated College of the Minerva, at Rome, Delivered at Cheltenham, on Thursday, September 2, 1847*. Glasgow: Dunn, 1847.

———. *Dealings with the Inquisition; or Papal Rome, Her Priests, and Her Jesuits. With Important Disclosures*. New York: Harper, 1851.

Achilli v. Newman: A Full and Authentic Report of the Above Prosecution for Libel, Tried before Lord Campbell and a Special Jury, in the Court of the Queen's Bench, Westminster, June, 1852. London: W. Strange, 1852.

Achilli vs. Newman: A Full Report of the Most Extraordinary Trial for the Seduction and Adultery Charged against Dr. Achilli, the Apostate Catholic Priest, by the Celebrated Dr. Newman, the Oxford Puseyite, Both of Whom are Seceders from Their Former Creeds. New York: Dewitt & Davenport, 1852.

Brief Sketch of the Life of Dr. Giancinto Achilli, Including a Narrative of His Proceedings during the Inquisition When It Was Broken Open, An Account of His Imprisonment, and Full Particulars Relative to His Escape from Rome. Also Two Letters to His Holiness Pope Gregory XVI, in 1843, and One to Pio Nono in 1846. Dublin: Hardy, 1850.

Chadwick, Owen. *The Victorian Church*. Part I. London: A. & C. Black, 1971.

Dessain, Charles Stephen, and Vincent Ferrer Blehl, editors. *The Letters and Diaries of John Henry Newman*. London: Nelson, 1963.

"Dr. Achilli and the Inquisition." *The Rambler* 8 (1851) 235–52.

Eardley, C. E. *The Imprisonment and Deliverance of Dr. Giacinto Achilli, with Some Account of His Previous History and Labours*. London: Partridge & Oakley, 1850.

Finlason, W. F. *Report of the Trial and Preliminary Proceedings in the Case of the Queen on the Prosecution of G. Achilli v. Dr. Newman*. London: Dolman, 1852.

Gilley, Sheridan. *Newman and His Age*. London: Darton, Longman & Todd, 1990.

Ker, Ian. *John Henry Newman: A Biography*. Oxford: Oxford University Press, 1988.

London Committee for the Religious Improvement of Italy and the Italians. *Dr. Achilli and the Malta Protestant College*. London: Partridge & Oakley, 1851.

Nash, Andrew. "Introduction." In *Lectures on the Present Position of Catholics in England*. Notre Dame: University of Notre Dame Press, 2000.

Newman, John Henry. *Lectures on the Present Position of Catholics in England*. London: Burns & Lambert, 1851.

Ridley, Jasper. *Lord Palmerston*. New York: Dutton, 1971.

Schiefen, Richard J. *Nicholas Wiseman and the Transformation of English Catholicism*. Shepherdstown, WV: Patmos, 1984.

Tonna, Lewis H. J. *The Real Dr. Achilli: A Letter to Dr. Wiseman, In Reply to an Article in a Recent Number of the "Dublin Review."* London: Pattidge & Oakley, 1850.

The Trial of Giovanni Giacinto Achilli v. John Henry Newman. London: Lloyds Weekly, 1852.

Ward, Wilfrid. *The Life and Times of Cardinal Wiseman*. 2 vols. London: Longmans, Green, 1897.

[Wiseman, Nicholas]. "Dr. Achilli." *Dublin Review* 28 (1850) 469–511.

———. *Dr. Achilli: Authentic "Brief Sketch of the Life of Dr. Giacinto Achilli" Containing a Confutation of the Mis-statements of Former Narratives*. London: Richardson, 1850.

Who and What Is Dr. Achilli? His Origin, Imprisonment and Escape. Also, His Speech at Exeter Hall. London: Houlston & Stoneman 1850.

Wolffe, John. *The Protestant Crusade in Great Britain 1829–1860.* Oxford: Oxford University Press, 1991.